LORDS
OF THE
LEFT-HAND PATH

"*Lords of the Left-Hand Path* is an important contribution to the literature of the contemporary magical revival. Stephen E. Flowers celebrates the 'way of the hero' and champions the courage of the individual who dares boldly to 'breach the gates of eternity.' This book will surely be hailed as a classic in its field."

Nevill Drury, Ph.D., author of *Stealing Fire from Heaven: The Rise of Modern Western Magic*

"*Lords of the Left-Hand Path,* by Stephen E. Flowers, is perhaps the most influential work in the construct of the 'left-hand path' as a particular current of contemporary esotericism. Flowers draws on a wide range of sources, many of which are exceedingly difficult to find elsewhere, and argues convincingly for his conclusions. This book is essential for anyone who wants to understand 'the left-hand-path.'"

Henrik Bogdan, author of *Western Esotericism and Rituals of Initiation* and coeditor of *Aleister Crowley and Western Esotericism*

Thus, then now as ever, I enter the Path of Darkness, if haply so I may attain the Light.
(Aleister Crowley, *The Supreme Ritual*)

"Anyone who is aware of the 1980s and its dastardly slanders of Satanic ritual child abuse—incited by a collusion between faux law enforcement, bogus psychology, and a hysterical media—will especially welcome this book. It presents a sober, scholarly, and revealing explication of the true nature of the left-hand path and its most prominent adepts through recorded history. Stephen Flowers makes an essential contribution to rational philosophic discourse while exploring the hidden byways of the Promethean archetype."

JAMES WASSERMAN,
AUTHOR OF *THE TEMPLE OF SOLOMON: FROM ANCIENT ISRAEL TO MODERN SECRET SOCIETIES*

"*Lords of the Left-Hand Path* examines the principle of isolate intelligence and the subjective universe throughout history from ancient India and Iran to Lucifer and the Faustian Age and beyond. It devotes much attention to the revival of the occult, cosmology and Satanic beliefs and practices, being very informative on these issues."

THE LATE EDGAR C. POLOMÉ,
PROFESSOR OF COMPARATIVE RELIGION AND LANGUAGES
AT THE UNIVERSITY OF TEXAS AT AUSTIN
AND DISTINGUISHED LINGUIST AND INDO-EUROPEANIST

LORDS *of the* LEFT-HAND PATH

FORBIDDEN PRACTICES & SPIRITUAL HERESIES

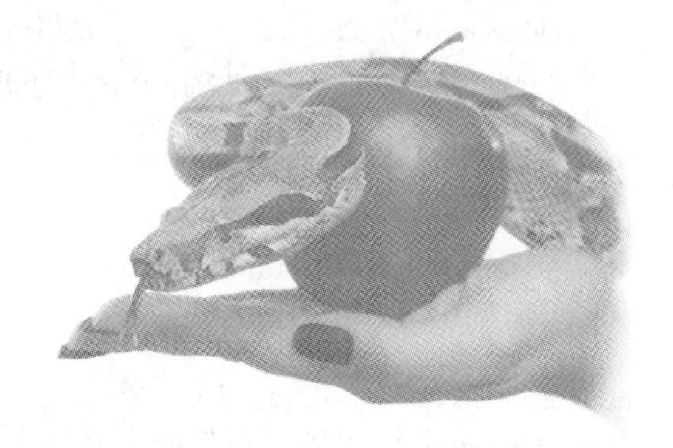

Stephen E. Flowers, Ph.D.

Inner Traditions
Rochester, Vermont • Toronto, Canada

Inner Traditions
One Park Street
Rochester, Vermont 05767
www.InnerTraditions.com

Originally published in 1997 by Rûna-Raven Press under the title *Lords of the Left-Hand Path: A History of Spiritual Dissent*

Library of Congress Cataloging-in-Publication Data
Flowers, Stephen E., 1953–
Lords of the left-hand path : forbidden practices and spiritual heresies from the cult of Set to the Church of Satan / Stephen E. Flowers.
p. cm.
Includes bibliographical references (p.) and index.
ISBN 978-1-59477-467-6 (pbk.) — ISBN 978-1-59477-692-2 (e-book)
1. Satanism. 2. Church of Satan. 3. Seth (Egyptian deity) I. Title.
BF1548.F56 2012
133.409—dc23
2012001840

Printed and bound in the United States by Versa Press, Inc.

10 9 8 7

Text design by Jack Nichols
Text layout by Virginia Scott Bowman
This book was typeset in Garamond Premier Pro and Gill Sans with Bernhard Modern, Ampere, and Agenda used as display typefaces.

To send correspondence to the author of this book, mail a first-class letter to the author c/o Inner Traditions • Bear & Company, One Park Street, Rochester, VT 05767, and we will forward the communication, or visit the author's website at **www.runaraven.com**.

Pro Omnis Dominis Viae Sinistrae

contra stupidos

Contents

Acknowledgments

I would like to express my appreciation to the many who helped in the shaping and reshaping of the work: Michael A. Aquino, Don Webb, Lilith Aquino, R. L. Barrett, Nikolas Schreck, Zeena, J. Chisholm, Seth Tyrsen, Dianne Ross, Sir Ormsond, Michael Moynihan, Diana DeMagis, Robert Lang, Lothar Tuppan, and my beloved wife, Crystal Dawn.

Additionally, thanks are due to Jon Graham and Inner Traditions for their courage in bringing out the present edition.

PREFACE

Under the Lens of Reason

The left-hand path and those who practice it attract the historical aura of dark romance and sensationalism. This path, viewed from the outside, is fraught with obscurity and misinformation. The purpose of this book is to elucidate the darkness and inform the reader from the inner perspective of the path itself.

The present volume was born of the circumstances of a specific period in Western cultural history, a time when the Eastern Bloc was withering away and the "other," the enemy, was ill-defined. Given this age of angst, our culture once more—albeit in a short-lived fashion—turned to face its inner demons. In so doing, it manifested its age-old fear of the darkness. This spawned an atavistic rebirth of medievalism splashed across tabloids and tabloid television. The true evil is that this distant aftershock of the witch hunts and the Inquisition ruined many people's lives. Although born from this womb of history, *Lords of the Left-Hand Path* does not, in retrospect, belong to it.

The contents of this book present the ideas of practitioners of the left-hand path—or those who have been considered such—under the lens of reason. By entering into the minds of the masters of the left-hand-path philosophies, the darkness is illuminated and deeper truths are revealed. No one who reads and understands the contents of this book will ever be subject to the tyranny of superstition perpetrated by the tabloid mentality as it regards the actual practitioners of the left-hand path—whether they are called Satanists, Setians, or devil worshippers.

The common trait of all left-hand-path practitioners is that they focus on their own selves as their first source of power and they seek to cultivate, develop, and enhance that separate and unique source as the surest path to their happiness. This turning inward to the dark depths of one's own self to find the light is as old as mankind. It is a path fraught with peril. This book is a chronicle of those who have dared to master it.

INTRODUCTION

An Untimely Meditation

Is there a sinister conspiracy of Satanic forces loose in the world causing mayhem, abducting, abusing, and even sacrificing children and others to His Satanic Majesty? The media have asked these and other equally sensational questions in the recent past, and offered the most dramatic and entertaining answers possible for consumption by a bored and dull public.

If the question arises as to whether there is a coherent Satanic or left-hand-path philosophy or theology, the answer has to be that there is, and that there has been for centuries. However, the philosophers of this "sinister" path have rarely been directly heard from until this century. The present age offers us the unique opportunity to hear directly from the lords and ladies of the left-hand path in a way unknown since the days of ancient philosophers.

We live in an age that enables us to become better informed of a wide variety of viewpoints and approaches to the spiritual problems of human beings; at the same time, however, it is an age that encourages a monotonous sameness in the answers to fundamental questions acceptable in a mass culture. The philosophers of the left-hand path have always challenged the all-pervasive common ways of doing things—whatever those ways might have been—and thus have always been agents for change. The left-hand path, as expressed in the world today, is an open challenge to certain individuals who are ready to take it. It is also now for the first time in ages being expressed openly in the hope that by knowing what its true character is, those who choose not to follow it will at least be informed as to what it is all about and, in this knowledge, be able to shed at least some of their age-old fear of it.

This is a forbidden book. The point of view championed in it is decidedly that of the left-hand path itself. I have years of training as a scholar, and have put these and other skills I have acquired to use in shaping a sympathetic, yet objective, analysis of the major historical and contemporary manifestations of this fascinating ultimate adventure of the human spirit in the cosmos. This will be a refreshing departure. There have been dozens of recent books, and hundreds of books throughout history, that have purported to study the devil and all his works from a decidedly antagonistic viewpoint. There have also been a very few studies for public consumption written by modern philosophical Satanists from a highly polemic angle. In the case of *Lords of the Left-Hand Path,* I, the author, am not a Satanist but may be characterized as a practitioner of the left-hand path based on purely indigenous Indo-European models. I trust that the objective reader will be no more put off by my viewpoint than he or she would be if a Catholic priest would write a book on the history of Christian theology.

There is a clear and present need for the present study as there has never been a work of its kind, and this vacuum is becoming dangerous to the philosophical fabric of the postmodern world. Again the cries of "Burn the witch!," "Kill the heretic!," and "Death to the Satanist!" are being heard. This time they come not so much from priests and evangelists—who have already largely been discredited in this day and age—but from therapists and law enforcement officers, bolstered by the medieval worldviews of extremist theologians. In the past it was impossible for the lords of the left-hand path to speak out; now the time has come when it is necessary that they must do so. This book indirectly gives a voice to all those who have tread the leftward spiritual road throughout history and who continue to explore it in the present world. If it brings just one ray of enlightenment on these matters, it will have done its work.

I began writing *Lords of the Left-Hand Path* at the beginning of

1989 and for all practical purposes it was completed by late 1992. It was written during a time of great dynamism in my own life, and although the contents of the book may appear to many outward observers to be staid and even static, this dynamism is present just below the surface. This book was composed in large measure as a response to the irrational "Satanic scare" of the late 1980s and early 1990s. It was written with the intention of reaching a wide readership of thinking individuals capable of understanding the historical and cultural scope of ideas underlying the images of the left-hand path.

The manuscript proved to be an untimely one in this regard. I attempted to interest literary agents and publishers of all kinds in the manuscript—it was universally rejected. Large publishers were evidently only interested in books that sent one of two messages: either "devil worshippers are dangerous and lurking in your schools and day-care centers and you should be very afraid," or "there are no such things as Satanists and those who call themselves that are buffoons." Of course, this book provided neither of these approved cultural messages. *Lords of the Left-Hand Path* is a sober, objectively sympathetic, and scholarly look at individuals and schools of thought that have been referred to as being left-hand path. This serious approach was thought to be "too disturbing"—as one agent put it to me—to be published for a broad readership.

Smaller publishers, too, found reasons to reject the manuscript. In these cases it was usually because the interpretations of their own sacred cows were seen as too controversial, or that certain individuals or schools of thought simply could not ever be mentioned in a book published by that company. Such are the forces at work in the media today.

The contents of this book come through my own lens of understanding, and I take full responsibility and credit for both its shortcomings and any glory attached to it. However, it must also be said that, because of my particular hermeneutic, each of the individuals and schools observed in this text also contributed to the shaping and refinement of that lens. Beyond these there are other such shapers, chief among them my experience in academia. The intellectual techniques learned in that environment, perhaps more than any other, are responsible for the form and nature of this text.

This is the first and last book I shall write on the subject of the left-hand path. What I have to say about the major schools discussed here will be found in this text. I have now returned to my own garden, there to tend the saplings of seeds long planted.

Abbreviations

AL	*Liber AL vel Legis* (*The Book of the Law*) by Aleister Crowley
Ar.	Arabic
BCE	Before Common Era (= B.C.)
CE	Common Era (= A.D.)
DMP	Demotic Magical Papyri
G.	German
Gen.	Genesis
Gk.	Greek
Heb.	Hebrew
Lat.	Latin
l(l).	line(s) of a poetic work
PGM	*Papyri Graecae Magicae* (= Preisendanz's edition of the Greek magical papyri)
pl.	plural
Rus.	Russian
sg.	singular
Skt.	Sanskrit
st.	stanza

1
The Left-Hand Path

We will begin with definitions. Philosophical inquiry calls for clarity, and we need clarity for this publicly unexplored realm. Without these precise definitions, anyone exploring this path on any level will be led into the sea of misunderstandings and confusion (evident in the section below on the historical portrayals of the left-hand path and "black magic"). Exact understanding of the nature of the left-hand path hinges on a precise theory of the universe in which it is perceived. This theory and the model it presents will prove useful in analyzing the left-hand-path traditions throughout history.[1]

The universe is the totality of existence both known and unknown. This is a complex model, divided into at least two components: the objective universe and the subjective universe. The objective universe is the natural cosmos or world order. This is essentially mechanical or organic, for example, it is ruled by certain predictable laws manifested in a time/space continuum. The objective universe, including the laws governing it, can be equated with "nature" as well as with "God" in the Judeo-Christian tradition. All of natural science as well as orthodox theology are predicated on the concept that these laws of the objective universe can be discovered and quantified or described in a purely rational manner in the first instance or by "divine revelation" in the other. When considered closely it is evident that what is usually referred to as "God" in orthodox religions is actually identical to that which he is said to create: the natural/mechanical/organic order or *cosmos.* It might also be pointed out that there has generally been a popular but sometimes misleading distinction between the concepts "mechanical" and "organic." On one level, they are the same in that both are governed by predictable laws. A clock-work or the human body are both ruled and maintained by certain mechanical structures, which allow them to function in their environments. At another level, there is a distinction between the mechanical and the organic in that the organic model has the ability to propagate and mutate its mechanical structures to ensure its survival. This is possible because there are coded mechanisms within the organism expressly for this purpose (DNA) and because the malleable molecular structure of the mechanism allows for these mutations.

The *subjective universe* is the "world" of any sentient entity within the universe. There are as many subjective universes as there are sentient beings. The subjective universe is the particularized manifestation of consciousness within the universe. Usually, experience of the *objective universe* is only indirect, as information concerning it must come through the subjective universe. Curiously enough, the subjective universe does not seem governed by the same natural/mechanical/organic laws as the objective universe. In fact, this is the main distinction between them. The subjective universe has the option of acting in a *nonnatural* way—free from the limitations of the world of five senses and three dimensions.

At this point it might be worth pointing out that the terms objective/subjective have nothing in common with the distinction between accurate/inaccurate, or exact/inexact, which popular usage might have projected onto the terms. The subjective universe is capable of far more accurate and exact manifold operations than the objective universe. A good example would be your reading and understanding of these words, which is based on the exercise of a faculty within your subjective universe. In simple grammatical terms, the subject is the reader (i.e., that which reads) and the object is that which is read. The subjective universe is capable of a full spectrum of possibilities, which range from virtually absolute precision to almost total delusion, because it is not bound by natural laws. The focus or epicenter of this nonnatural subjective universe is equated with human consciousness, or soul, or self.

The *nonnatural* aspect of this soul is clearly and basically indicated by humanity's drive to impose structures artificially created in that subjective universe upon the objective universe. All artificially created structures (i.e., those made by art/craft) are by definition something separate and apart from the natural cosmos—be those structures pyramids, poems, or political institutions. Animals, many of which may have complex social organizations, are bound by nature and by their organic programming. The wolf pack, no matter if in one part of the world or another, now or a million years ago, has the same social order. But you will look in vain to find *any two* human social institutions that are absolutely identical. Anything that is the product of the subjective universe—individual or collective—will bear the mark of variation.

Each particular instance of this soul—this phenomenon of the subjective universe—implies the existence of a first form or general principle from which all the particular manifestations are derived. In the most philosophically refined of the schools of the left-hand path, this first *principle of isolate intelligence* is identified as the "Prince of Darkness," or the ultimate deity of the left-hand path. (Note that words *prince* and *principle* both derive from Lat. *princeps,* "emperor, leader," with the literal sense "he who takes first place.") This is the archetype of the self from which all particular selves are derived. This is also an element of the nonnatural universe that objectively belongs to the universe itself. In this way, the Prince of Darkness can be seen as an independent sentient being in the objective universe because this is the very *principle* of that quality in the universe. Humanity is the only species we know of which shares that quality.

THE RIGHT-HAND PATH AND THE LEFT-HAND PATH

The central question now becomes: what is the way in which this conscious, free soul is going to relate to, or seek to interact with, the objective universe or the universe as a whole? The right-hand path answers this question simply by saying that the subjective universe must harmonize itself with the laws of the objective universe—be that envisioned as God or Nature. Humanity is to seek knowledge of the law, and then apply itself to submitting to that law in order to gain ultimate union with the objective universe, with God, or with Nature. The right-hand path is the path of union with universal reality (God or Nature). When this union is completed the individual self will be annihilated; the individual will become one with the divine or natural cosmic order. In this state the ego is destroyed as "heaven" is entered or a nirvana-like existence/nonexistence is "attained." This is clearly the goal of all orthodox Judaic, Christian, Islamic, or Buddhistic sects.

The left-hand path considers the position of humanity as it is; it takes into account the manifest and deep-seated desire of each human being to be a free, empowered, independent actor within his or her world. The pleasure and pain made possible by independent existence are seen as something to be embraced and as the most reasonable signs of the highest, most noble destiny possible for humans to attain—a kind of independent existence on a level usually thought of as *divine.*

Just as most humans go through their natural, everyday lives seeking that which will give them maximal amounts of such things as knowledge, power, freedom, independence, and distinction within their world, those who walk the left-hand path logically extend this to the nonnatural realm. They eschew right-hand-path admonitions that such spiritual behavior is "*evil*" and that they should basically "get with the program" (of God, of Nature, etc.) and become good "company men." The self-awareness of independence is seen by many as the fundamental reality of the human condition: one can accept it and *live,* or reject it and *die.* By accepting the internal, known reality of human consciousness, an eternally dynamic—ever moving, ever changing—existence is embraced; by rejecting it and embracing an external, unknown reality of God/Nature, an eternally static—ever still and permanent—existence is accepted. From a certain enlightened perspective, both paths are perfectly good, it is just a matter of the conscious exercise of the will to follow one of these paths in an aware state without self-delusion.

Essentially, the left-hand path is the path of nonunion with the objective universe. It is the way of isolating consciousness within the subjective universe and, in a state of self-imposed psychic solitude, refining the soul or psyche to ever more perfect levels. The objective universe is then made to harmonize itself with the will of the individual psyche instead of the other way around. Where the right-hand path is *theocentric* (or certainly alleocentric: "other-centered"), the left-hand path is *psychecentric,* or soul/self-centered. Those within the left-hand path may argue over the nature of this self/ego/soul, but the idea that the individual is the epicenter of the path itself seems undisputed. An eternal separation of the individual intelligence from the objective universe is sought in the left-hand path. This amounts to an immortality of the independent self-consciousness moving within the objective universe and interacting with it at will.

WHITE MAGIC/BLACK MAGIC

The terms "white magic" and "black magic" have been so bandied about in popular jargon that they might be said to have lost most of their meaningfulness. For my purposes, I will restore them to a meaningful philosophical context. Magic can be defined as a methodology by which the configuration of the subjective or objective universe is altered through an act of will originating within the psyche, or the core of the individual subjective universe. Perhaps the most famous definition was offered by the English magician, Aleister Crowley, who said: "Magic(k) is the Science and Art of causing Change to occur in conformity with Will."[2]

Actually, there is no one definition of magic universally accepted by academics and practicing magicians alike, nor is there common agreement on the distinctions between *religion* and *magic.* But taking most of the current theories into account, a more comprehensive definition might be proposed: magic is the willed application of symbolic methods to cause or prevent changes in the universe by means of symbolic acts of communication with paranormal factors. These factors could be inside or outside the subjective universe of the operator. Magic is a way to make things happen that ordinarily would not happen. Religion may be distinguished from magic only when the nature of the human will is taken into account. In magic, the individual will is primary and is considered to have a real and independent existence. The magician makes the universe do his bidding so as to harmonize itself with his will, whereas in religion the human community attempts to harmonize its behavior with a universal pattern that is perceived to derive from God or Nature.

In a precise sense, the distinction between white and black magic is simply that white magic is a psychological methodology for the promotion of *union* with the universe and pursuing aims in harmony with those of the universe, while black magic is such a methodology for the exercise of independence from the universe and pursuing self-oriented aims. Structurally, white magic has much in common with religion as defined above, while black magic is more purely magical in and of itself. This is why magic as a category of behavior is often condemned by orthodox religious systems.

The historical conceptualizations of white magic and black magic will be discussed below, but for the sake of precise understanding here, I will simply be using white magic as a designation for the spiritual methodology or technology of the right-hand path and black magic as a designation for that of the left-hand path.

LORDS OF THE LEFT-HAND PATH

In this book I examine the ideas and careers of many magicians and philosophers of the past and present. Some are figures widely thought to be "Satanic" or evil, while others may have gone through history without such an image. But images rarely correspond to reality, despite what Madison Avenue or Washington DC would have you believe. In the final analysis, some of these figures will be rejected as being something other than practitioners of the left-hand path. The criteria I use in determining the true left-hand-path character of those so deemed must be laid out clearly at this point. Some of those considered in the book will fulfill a number of the criteria, but not enough to be considered a "lord" or master of the path.

There are two major criteria for being considered a true lord (or lady) of the left-hand path: deification of the self and antinomianism. The first of these is complex: the system of thought proposed by the magician or philosopher must be one that promotes individual self-deification, preferably based on an initiatorily magical scheme. This first criterion will be seen to have four distinct elements:

1. Self-deification: the attainment of an enlightened (or awakened), independently existing intellect and its relative immortality.
2. Individualism: the enlightened intellect is that of a given individual, not a collective body.
3. Initiation: the enlightenment and strength of essence necessary for the desired state of evolution of self are attained by means of stages created by the will of the magician, not because he or she was "divine" to begin with.
4. Magic: the practitioners of the left-hand path see themselves as using their own wills in a rationally intuited system or spiritual technology designed to cause the universe around them to conform to their self-willed patterns.

The second criterion, antinomianism, states that practitioners think of themselves as "going against the grain" of their culturally conditioned and conventional norms of "good" and "evil." True lords and ladies of the left-hand path will have the spiritual courage to identify themselves with the cultural norms of "evil." There will be an embracing of the symbols of conventional "evil," or "impurity," or "rationality," or whatever quality the conventional culture fears and loathes. The lords and ladies of the left-hand path will set themselves apart from their fellow man; they will actually or figuratively become outsiders, in order to gain the kind of inner independence necessary for the other initiatory work present in the first criterion. The practice of this second criterion often manifests itself in "antinomianism," that is, the purposeful reversal of conventional normative categories: "evil" becomes "good," "impure" becomes "pure," "darkness" becomes "light."

Literally speaking, antinomianism implies something "against the law." But the practitioner of the left-hand path is not a criminal in the usual sense. He or she is bound to break the cosmic laws of nature and to break the conventional social laws imposed by ignorance and intolerance. But in so doing, the left-hand-path practitioner seeks a "higher law" of reality founded on knowledge and power. Although beyond good and evil, this path requires the most rigorous of ethical standards. These standards are based on understanding and not on blind obedience to external authorities.

This latter characteristic of the true left-hand path is the chief cause of its misunderstanding, not only for those on the outside, but for some who would follow this path as well. It takes an enormous amount of spiritual courage to persevere in the face of rejection by not only the world around them but by elements within their own subjective universes as well. Many break under the strain and fall away from the aim and sink back into the morass of cultural norms.

To be considered a true lord or lady of the left-hand path, then, someone must have rejected the forms of conventional "good" and embraced those of conventional "evil," and have practiced antinomianism, as part of the effort to gain a *permanent, independent, enlightened,* and *empowered* level of being. This self-deification does not seem sufficient without the "Satanic" component, which acts as a guide through the quagmire of popular sentiment and conventional beliefs.

In completing research for this book, I discovered that there are, in fact, two distinct *branches* of the left-hand path. Both of these branches fulfill the criteria outlined above, but approach the process from distinct points of view. One of these, which I will call the "immanent branch of the left-hand path," proceeds from an "objectivistic" and even *materialistic* outlook. Its magical methods are often steeped in *imagery,* and its orientation is almost exclusively toward the objective or mundane universe. In this branch, the antinomian aspect is especially pronounced. Among modern schools it is exemplified by LaVeyan Satanism (see chapter 9).

The second branch, which I will name the "transcendental branch of the left-hand path," is based upon a psychecentric (soul- or intellect-centered) model. It is highly idealistic and its magical methods are usually founded on *eternal forms* or *archetypes.* The ultimate separation of the human mind from the cosmic order around it is recognized and celebrated. In its highest forms, the transcendental branch is focused on the subjective universe—on the separation of the self from the cosmic order and the evolution of that self into a permanent and empowered form. In this branch, the self-divinizing aspect is especially pronounced. Among modern schools it is exemplified by the Setian magical philosophy of Michael Aquino (see chapter 10).

I will begin with the left-hand path as understood in "Eastern" religious systems, that is, systems that have their origins in the Indo-Iranian cultural sphere. I will discuss the concepts of the right-hand path *versus* the left-hand path in the context of Hinduism and Buddhism (in which the terms first originated). This section will place the whole discussion in a non-Judeo-Christian context, one in which the two paths coexist within the same cosmology. Also included here is a treatment of the Zoroastrian doctrines of dualism and how they affected the development of the left-hand path in the West.

The philosophical systems of certain great world cultures, such as those of the Far East (China and Japan), or the Meso-American world, will be noted for their absence. This is partially due to limitations in my own knowledge, but it also seems that the systems of Taoism and Shinto, for example, lack the strict dichotomies necessary to understanding the role of the individual in the universe in terms of the "two paths." The degree to which they are present in either system seems to have been the result of contact with Indo-Aryan thought in the form of Buddhism.

In the second part of the book, I will discuss the Western branches of the left-hand path. First we must understand clearly the true nature of the "Western" traditions. It is important to know the degree to which indigenous European systems share elements with the "Eastern" traditions, and the degree to which the "West" is really a product of southern influence—chiefly coming from the Middle East and Egypt. What we often call "Eastern" is in fact more truly Western (or northern), while what we call "Western" is really more truly "Middle Eastern" or southern.

In the discussion of the original European traditions, we will first explore the Greco-Roman world. The Promethean myth is seen as a paradigm of the relationship of the "creator god" and the "giver of the gift of the divine spark." In the North, we will see the Odinic myth as an original paradigm of the Prince of Darkness, which foreshadows the Faustian themes to come.

The West, of course, became greatly influenced by Middle Eastern traditions through the conversion to Christianity (a Judaic cult from the east), as well as Judaism itself and late Islam. Understanding of this tradition is essential to understanding the left-hand path in the West today. Interesting here are Sumerian as well as Semitic backgrounds on the role of "gods of evil" in non-Judaic Semitic religion.

The Egyptian tradition, especially as it regards the cult of the god Set, is important not only for the understanding of ancient left-hand-path traditions, but also for its possible significance for the contemporary Temple of Set.

In order to grasp the deepest significance of the left-hand path in the West from the time of the conversions to the dawn of our own postmodern age, we must discover the Judaic roots of Christianity in Christian ideas of "evil" and of the nature of Satan. In this regard, we cannot ignore the importance of the Gnostic (especially Ophite and Naassene: "serpentine") interpretations on the role of the Serpent/Lucifer and his Promethean relationship with humankind.

This can be starkly contrasted with the orthodox Christian doctrine concerning the same Edenic myth. It will be apparent that a close, rational, and objective reading of the "Myth of Eden" shows that the Serpent is indeed the "savior" of humanity and its "creator" in a spiritual sense.

We will also see the remarkable history of the left-hand path within the Islamic tradition where we will meet some of the most self-aware followers of this path before this century.

Many people, modern practicing Satanists among them, somehow believe that the Middle Ages were a great time for Satanic activity. Nothing could be further from the truth. The medieval period was almost devoid of true left-hand-path activity, although the church often liked to believe (and encourage others to believe) that Satanic cults were lurking under every rock. This ended in the "witch craze" of the sixteenth and seventeenth centuries as a predictable manifestation of right-hand-path ignorance and fear run amok.

One interesting outgrowth of the medieval tradition in Germany was the Faustian myth, which leads us into the modern age and beyond. This will depend greatly on the transition from the ideas surrounding the Faustian magicians of the late Middle Ages to those surrounding Goethe's *Faust*—the transition from the medieval mindset (seeking of knowledge and power is inherently "evil") to a modern mindset (seeking of knowledge and power is good). Here we really have a return to ancient precepts. Images of the devil in Classical and Romantic ideologies are certainly important to this transition in Western culture.

Along the way, we will touch upon the left-hand-path tendencies of the Renaissance and the Enlightenment, Milton's Satan, the Marquis De Sade, and the notorious Hell-Fire Club. The nineteenth-century "Satanists" of France cannot be ignored, even though they offer up a disappointing picture when viewed from a left-hand-path perspective. Most of them have little or no understanding of the positive traits of the left-hand path, but merely wallow in the darkness as an exercise in obscure aesthetics. We will also seek to discover what aspects of the left-hand path may have manifested in two opposing (but in many ways related) political ideologies of the late-nineteenth and early twentieth centuries, Marxism and National Socialism.

For the understanding of the rise of philosophical Satanism in the latter half of the twentieth century, no period of history is more important than the occult revival of the late nineteenth and early twentieth century. The original Luciferian/Ophite-Gnostic doctrines of the Theosophy of H. P. Blavatsky (especially as expressed in *The Secret Doctrine*) form one branch of this tradition, while the Thelemism of Aleister Crowley forms another. Crowley must be viewed here from a totally philosophical perspective. He is doubtless one of the most important theorists concerning the left-hand path in the modern Western world, yet he holds an extremely ambiguous relationship to it. In connection with Thelemism, we must also discuss the German school of Saturnians, originally led by Gregor A. Gregorius (Eugen Grosche). We will also examine the "Fourth Way" teachings of G. I. Gurdjieff. The final part of the book will deal in detail with the two most important contemporary exponents of left-hand-path philosophy: Anton LaVey's Church of Satan and Michael Aquino's Temple of Set.

Throughout this book I will try to cut through the confusion, misinformation, and even disinformation about the left-hand path and the practice of actual black magic based on the exact principles outlined in this chapter. I am well aware that throughout history certain of these terms have been used by followers of the right-hand path, or by those who have simply been misled by such sources for many years, in ways very different from the way I am using them. The distinction must simply be made that I am writing about the left-hand path from an internal perspective, while most other sources are written from an external one. Reading what someone from the right-hand path has to say about the left-hand path is rather like reading a book on Wall Street written by an economics professor schooled at the University of Moscow during the Soviet era. He may have interesting insights, but without the perspective of a Wall Street broker you will probably not get much closer to really understanding how the stock market works.

Historically, the left-hand path has sometimes been identified by the *methods* it is said to use, such as necromancy (raising the dead for divinatory purposes) and sexual magic (it seems the right-hand path has always had a problem with sexuality). In point of fact, there are no categorical methodological proscriptions on the left-hand path within its various traditions East or West. Methods are usually chosen for purely pragmatic reasons. If it works, it will usually be implemented. There is often a strong antinomian element in the magical methodology of the left-hand path. Going *against the grain* of social conventions or natural boundaries is often seen as a mode of consciously exercising the divine faculty inherent in humanity. This factor must be seen in the broadest perspective, however, as some behaviors, which may *seem* to be antinomian or against social conventions or propriety, such as ingesting massive doses of intoxicants, are actually roundly condemned by the most sophisticated practitioners of the left-hand path in the West. The philosophical basis for this is that such intoxicants impair the exercise of the individual will and of the self, which together comprise the supreme faculty viewed from the perspective of the left-hand path. Drugs would, from this point of view, be more effective at attaining the self-annihilation sought within the right-hand path.

Another way in which black magic has sometimes historically been differentiated from white magic is the classification of entities with which, or with whom, the magician is said to deal. White magicians would invoke only "angelic" beings, while black magicians would call on "demonic" entities. This is, of course, predicated on medieval Christian angelologies and demonologies, and one quite often finds in the old grimoires that demonic forces are coerced by the power of the names of God to do the magician's bidding, which could be virtually anything. Angels could be used to seduce or kill demons to gain wisdom and discover truth. From the point of view of the left-hand path itself, this distinction would be seen as hypocritical. Again the focus would not be on the "hows" but rather on the purpose, the "whys."

In this regard, the black/white distinction is sometimes historically made between maleficent and beneficent magic: magic designed to do harm is black; magic designed to heal or do good is white. This distinction at least has some valid aspects. The only problems from the left-hand-path viewpoint are that (1) it does not address any of the essential cosmological or theological questions regarding the two paths, and (2) it is generally unrealistic. "White magicians," when push comes to shove, usually have no problem in asking (or coercing) God or angels into giving them victory over their enemies and vanquishing their "diabolical foes" (i.e., anyone who dares cross them). The left-hand path views magic as a technique or methodology of human action; in and of itself, magic is devoid of moral value. In other words: magic doesn't kill people, magicians kill people. The use of black magic would be viewed as being governed by the same ethical standards as all other categories of human behavior. The black magician refuses to be limited in his use of magic just because this activity belongs to a class of behavior usually condemned by orthodox religion. If a goal is worth attaining by *any means,* it is perfectly acceptable to use magic if necessary to attain it. If a war is worth waging, or if a man has good reason to defend himself from attack, the black magician will have no problem with using magic to destroy his enemy. He also sees nothing but hypocrisy in the white magician who prays, or who uses physical means for the same ends while condemning the black magician as evil. The use of black magic is simply a logical extension of human motives into the realm of magic.

Finally, there is the fundamental distinction between the two paths, that of union *versus* nonunion, which has already been discussed. It is from this basic principle that even the other misguided distinctions can be best understood. From a position of magical independence, the black magician would be able to employ pragmatically any magical technology he willed, deal with any kind of entity (or most probably dispense with interaction with exterior entities altogether), and seek any end he desired—in each case being guided by an *internal* sense of purpose and responsibility. Ultimate spiritual independence is the essential quality of the left-hand path. With the freedom this quality provides comes the possibility for unethical behavior. This is, after all, the price of freedom.

The existence of the left-hand path is not easily discovered, but once its principles have been uncovered it slowly becomes apparent just how widespread the philosophy is. In this work I am concentrating on schools and individuals who either are self-avowedly followers of the left-hand path (such as in tantrism, or in the Church of Satan or the Temple of Set), or who have knowledge of it and perhaps though they try to differentiate themselves from it (at least publicly) seem to have actually been practitioners of the left-hand path when viewed from the perspective of the path itself (e.g., H. P. Blavatsky or Aleister Crowley). However, the basic precepts of the left-hand path have for centuries penetrated far beyond the sphere of magical and occult activity. Many ancient philosophies were based on principles held in common with the left-hand path, and it was only with the advent of Christianity that those philosophies were either first suppressed as evil, or "Christianized" so as to be made palatable (e.g., the cult of Odin or Pythagorean/Platonic philosophy, respectively). More recently, modern philosophies and political ideologies have fully embraced principles basic and fundamental to the left-hand path, almost all of which have become the accepted norm in the West. It is quite understandable why the forces of orthodox Christianity fought every advance in scientific, political, or religious philosophy, for each advance in spiritual freedom and enforcement of the interests of plurality over unity is indeed a victory for the Prince of Darkness—the principle of isolate intelligence—over the monolithic, singular force of the rule of God.

2
The Eastern Traditions

I contemplate in my heart the nonfearful divinity of shining darkness.

(*Shivatoshini* 1.1.14)

THE LEFT-HAND PATH IN THE EAST

For the Western reader, the examination of the left-hand path within the context of orthodox right-hand-path cults of the East will quickly demonstrate, in a uniquely objective fashion, the true structural meanings of what the left-hand path is really all about. It has the added advantage of showing this within cultures that have been *relatively* tolerant of the aims and motives of the left-hand path. By exploring the left-hand path from the perspective of Eastern traditions *first,* we can solve a few problems for ourselves later. An approach via the East will disentangle many of the arguments from the sometimes hopelessly confused jumble we find in the historical sources of the left-hand path in the West. It will eventually become apparent that the division into "Eastern" and "Western" branches has been done simply to present certain ideas in a clear and organized fashion. The left-hand path is an ever-recurring answer to humanity's questions beyond the restrictions of time and place.

Here I will consider as "Eastern" those traditions that have their distinctive origins in the Indo-Iranian cultural sphere of central and southern Asia: Hinduism, Buddhism, and Zoroastrianism.

The East/West division dissolves when an understanding is gained concerning the common traditional roots of both branches, which lie in the substrata of Indo-European philosophies. Furthermore, the entirely cross-cultural nature of the left-hand path will become more obvious. The principles that underpin the distinction between the right-hand path and left-hand path are found throughout the history of humankind and across a broad cultural spectrum. The true lords of the left-hand path have dwelled in the world at all times and in all places and cannot be limited to any single time or geographical area.

The ultimate roots of the Indo-Iranian (Aryan) religious and philosophical traditions are not to be found on the Indian subcontinent itself, but rather in the Caucasus region and on the planes of present-day southern Russia. It was most probably in this region that a multiphased migration of local populations began during the fourth millennium BCE.[1] This population is known by the cumbersome and unromantic name "Indo-European." This is because the final migratory destinations of this originally unified group were to stretch from western Europe all the way to India and to the border of China.

The original Indo-Europeans were a seminomadic people who domesticated the horse on the open steppes, invented the wheel (essential to their war-chariots and wagons), and learned to smelt metals as hard as copper. The combination of horse, wheel, and copper made them virtually invincible in battle, and in this way they spread themselves out over vast expanses of territory. They slowly conquered and subdued the local populations, largely imposing their culture, language, and religious system on the region by means of a combination of their military strength and their cultural prestige. Thus, roughly at the same time the cities of Mesopotamia were beginning to thrive and the pyramids were being built in Egypt, there was in fact another "high culture" that descended from the north and spread itself throughout most of the known world. But whereas the Mesopotamians and Egyptians built in stone, the Indo-Europeans built *intellectual* monuments. The most striking of these is perhaps the Rig-Veda, which has been orally transmitted from the time of its codification beginning at the end of the second millennium BCE *to the present day.* This invisible intellectual edifice has proved many times more durable than all the stones of other cultures, for it has remained *alive,* dynamic, and meaningful throughout this time.

Ancient Indo-European philosophy and religion were not based on a unified cult, but rather on a stratified structure of several levels. These levels, or *functions,* have been most elaborately commented on by the French Indo-Europeanist Georges Dumézil and his followers.[2] The first order belongs to the realm of the *intellect,* both rational and intuitive. In the most archaic Indian system, these aspects of the intellect are ruled by the gods Mitra and Varuna respectively; in the Germanic realm, these same functions are filled by Tyr and Odin. The second order belongs to the realm of physical force. This is ruled over by the god Indra in the Vedas and the god Thor in the Norse *Eddas.* The third order is that of natural procreation or vitality, which is governed by the Ashvinau in India and by the Vanic deities Frey and Freya—the Lord and the Lady—in Germania. These mythic orderings are reflected in the society as well, which is organized in an intelligentsia class of

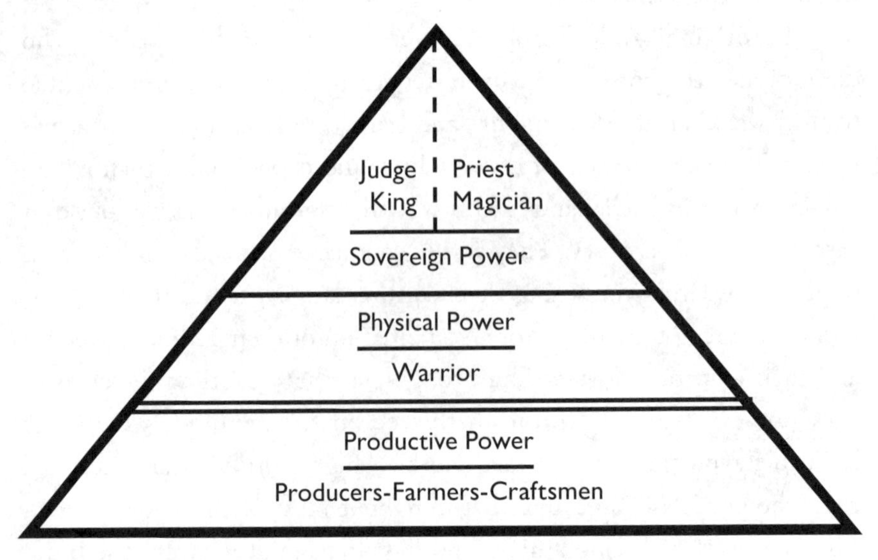

Figure 2.1. Indo-European Functions

kings, philosophers, judges, and magicians; a warrior class; and a provider class of farmers, craftsmen, entertainers, and so forth. This very ancient division is also reflected in Plato's *idealized* society discussed in *The Republic* (ca. 350 BCE),[3] where he outlines a state of tradesmen or craftsmen, auxiliaries or warriors, and guardians or philosophers, all with their specialized functions in the organized society.

What is essential to realize here is that the religions or philosophical attitudes of those of the first order are radically different from those of the second or third. Those of the first function focused their attention on the intellect, on the soul or psyche of man. This was the center of their attention from the beginning. Even in the earliest texts of the Rig-Veda the statement is made by the priests that "we created the gods," meaning that the gods and goddesses were really projections of the true divine paradigms concentrated in the intellectual or psychic faculty of human beings. The second function concerns physical force and its use, especially in the capacity of the warrior. The third function is centered in nature and in the cycles of nature and organic life: the powers of production and reproduction. This external reality is the focus of their religions and philosophical conceptions. Thus we can see that even at this most archaic stage there was a certain dichotomy between those who "worshipped" the self or intellect and those who worshipped "nature." But from the beginning in the Indo-European framework there was room and a place for both ends of the spectrum within a productive system. In this context it was not so much a matter of lateral division, right-hand path/left-hand path, but rather a vertical one, reflected in the "social structure" of divinities and humanity.

As mentioned above, there was also an original division within the first function. This is exemplified in the distinction between Mitra and Varuna or between Tyr and Odin. Mitra or Tyr represent the rational, ordered mind—the rationality of cosmic order. Varuna or Odin represent the mantic, dynamic mind—the freedom of chaotic flux. This same configuration will later be recognized by the German philosopher Friedrich Nietzsche as the Apollonian and Dionysian tendencies in humanity.[4] Both must work in an integrated fashion, much as the left and right hemispheres of the brain must work. But here, too, there may be a primal seed in the structures of the psyche, which will at times be expressed in terms of the right-hand and left-hand paths.

Because the ancient Indo-European peoples would migrate, conquering and subduing indigenous populations with forces largely made up of those of the first and second stratum, the third stratum was often subject to broad influences from the religious and philosophical concepts and practices of the indigenous populations. However, it would be a radical error to assume that the original system did not already contain structures capable of assimilating input from native religions. This is why, for example, although historians of Indian tantrism will point out that much of tantric practice originates in the lower castes, and is anti-Brahmanical, there is already precedent for it in the oldest evidence of the Rig-Veda itself.[5] The non-Aryan element did not create the system, but it radically affected its form as practiced in later Hindu times. It has also been noted that the later "Vedic Way" of Hinduism is not an embodiment of the actual attitudes present in the Vedas themselves, and that paradoxically the tantric systems exemplify the spiritual attitudes of the Vedas much more vibrantly than the modern "Vedic Way."[6]

RIGHT-HAND PATH/LEFT-HAND PATH

The actual origin of the terminology of right-hand path *versus* left-hand path is rooted in the vocabulary of Indian tantric sects. The two main divisions of these are the *dakshinachara,* "right-way," and the *vamachara,* "left-way." The variations in these sects will be discussed in the section on Hinduism below. The eventual elaboration of the distinction between right-hand path and left-hand path is quite complex, but its origins are most probably rooted in the widespread tantric doctrines of a natural flow of universal force through the human body along a left-to-right line that enters from the left and exits to the right. This is mirrored by a cosmic flow of force from the north to the south. When the human being is *oriented* toward the east, this flow pattern is said to be in harmony with the one natural to his body, as his left hand is to the north, his right hand to the south.[7] Here are the roots of the key to the common antinomianism and the reversal of normal patterns, which are found in left-hand-path tantrism. To reverse the left-to-right pattern, contrary to nature and cosmic law, requires an exercise of the faculty of will. This is an act of rebellion against nature and against divinely ordained cosmic order. In almost technical terms, the dakshinachara is going with the natural flow and the vamachara is going against the natural flow. In going against this flow, individuals more fully articulate—individuate—themselves within their environments. Independence and freedom are attained and maintained, and perhaps even personal immortality is to be gained.

It has been noted that the essence of what came to be called the vamachara is actually the true *tantric* one and that the term and practices of the dakshinachara were only introduced later as a reform movement within tantrism.[8] Julius Evola remarks on the distinction between the two paths.

> The creative and productive aspect of the cosmic process is signified by the right hand, by the color white, and by the two goddesses Uma and Gauri (in whom Shakti appears as Prakashatmika, "she who is light and manifestation"). The second aspect, that of conversion and return (*exitus, reditus*), is signified by the left hand, by the color black, and by the dark, destructive goddesses Durga and Kali. Thus, according to the Mahakala-Tantra, when the left and right hands are in equilibrium we experience samsara, but when the left hand prevails, we find liberation.[9]

Another fascinating delineation of the two paths of spiritual development in the Hindu context is the distinction found between the two pathways the soul may take upon death: the *devayana,* the way of the *devas* (gods), or the *pitriyana,* the way of the *pitris* (ancestors). The devayana is the polar path, marked by the summer half of the year, when the sun is moving toward the North Pole. Those who take the devayana upon death are enlightened and become like gods, and will only reincarnate according to their wills. Those who take the pitriyana, which is the equatorial path marked by the sun's motion toward the equator in the winter half of the year, will reincarnate according to a natural order and will thus eternally reincarnate their ancestors.[10]

Alain Daniélou remarks that the left-hand path corresponds to a "disintegrating-tendency" (*tamas*) that

> uses the power of Nature, the passions and instincts of man, to conquer, with their aid, the world of the senses . . .
>
> This way leads directly from the physical to the abstract because . . . the descending tendency is at both ends of the manifested. [Therefore the left-hand path] may utilize even eroticism and drunkenness as a means of spiritual achievement.[11]

Clearly the left-hand path in Hinduism is associated both with the idea of *dis-integration* (separation) and with the practice of antinomianism—of "going against the grain" of conventions in order to gain spiritual power.

Within the Sanskrit terminology of the Indian sects, the right-hand path is that which seeks a union or merger between the *jivatman,* the individual self or soul, and the *paramatman,* the supreme or universal soul. The left-hand path seeks only to differentiate the jivatman: to articulate, individuate, evolve, and immortalize it without ever consciously seeking to merge it permanently with anything else.[12]

One who has attained this union with the jivatman is said to be in a state of *jivanmukti:* an individually liberated state. The classic exposition of the concept of jivanmukti is found in a fourteenth-century text by Vidyaranya (died 1386), *Jivanmuktiviveka.*[13] The idea of "liberation in life" was perhaps formally introduced by Samkara (788–820 CE) and it remains an important component of the school of Advaita Vedanta, which is based on Samkara's reading and interpretations of the Upanishads. The *Trpti-dipika* by Vidyaranya contains discussions of lives of *jivanmuktas.*

THE LEFT-HAND PATH IN HINDUISM

In recent times the most insightful and important studies of left-hand-path spirituality in the Hindu religious context are the brilliant presentations of the teachings of the mysterious and shadowy Indian sage Vimalananda by the American Ayurvedic physician Robert Svoboda: *Aghora: At the Left Hand of God* (1986) and *Aghora II: Kundalini* (1993).

Generally speaking, "Hinduism" is the name for a spectrum of religious sects based on the ancient Aryan tradition ultimately rooted in the Vedas. There are hundreds of sects within Hinduism. Often they hold opposing views on what might seem to be fundamental questions. There are, however, things upon which most of these sects generally agree:

1. The Veda contains infallible wisdom.
2. The soul (*atman*) is immortal and real.
3. The soul undergoes continual rebirth (*samsara*).
4. This rebirth is tantamount to suffering.
5. The cause of rebirth and its suffering is action (*karman*).

The aim of orthodox Hinduism is a cessation of rebirth and/or fusion with the universal absolute.[14] This fusion with the Absolute is called liberation (*moksha* or *mukti*). Despite the agreement upon such general principles, the specific *methods* used to effect this end by the various Hindu sects are very diverse.

The major sects of Hinduism are Vaisnavite (derived from the worship of Vishnu) and Saivite (derived from the worship of Shiva). These major sects are further divided into hundreds of subdivisions. At one extreme end of the spectrum of Hindu "sects" are the philosophical schools chiefly found among the Brahmins. At the other extreme are found the tantric cults. These are rarely strictly Vedic and are often anti-Brahmanic. It is, however, a great mistake to think that all tantric sects are of the left-hand path.

Since the time of the rise of Buddhism (sixth to seventh century BCE) there can be said to have been truly heretical sects in Hinduism. Heresy as such would only tend to be a "problem" in a religion with an elaborate fixed dogma. Hinduism is remarkably free of these dogmas since its prehistoric transition from the Vedic religion. It is for this reason that sects and philosophies making up a wide spectrum of ideologies can be found within Hinduism, and why what is called the left-hand path can be tolerated within the fold of Hinduism without its being entirely "orthodox."

This toleration of the left-hand path does not stem from any enforced or legislated moral sense of "fair play," but rather from the fact that the original *multiplicity of paths* inherent in the archaic Indo-European system has been preserved in both Indian traditions, Hinduism and Buddhism. When the *ideal* is a many-hued spectrum of variation, from left to right and from bottom to top, the likelihood of developing dichotomized thinking in terms of black/white is lessened. Typically, they do not think in terms of "this or that," but rather "this *and* that." In this system, a sense of *layers* of meaning and reality is vigorously preserved. This underlying sense provides for a *systemic* tolerance more enduring than anything imposed dogmatically or legislatively. This does not mean, however, that orthodox followers of the right-hand path would typically think that the left-hand path is just as valid as their own path. It remains a trait of the right-hand path to think in terms of either/or, so most typically the orthodox will simply think of the practitioners of the left-hand path (or any path other than their own) as being "wrong" or to some degree in error. In the *Vaikhanasasmarta Sutra* (fourth century CE), this is explicitly outlined of the Visaragas, who are said to "walk the wrong path."[15]

Within Hinduism (as elsewhere), the left-hand path can be distinguished first in a description of its aims or goals, and then in terms of its techniques or methods. According to some self-proclaimed practitioners of the *vamamarga* (left-way), the final destination of the left-hand path is the same as the right-hand path. It is said that these are two paths to the same end. But it remains a matter of the perspective of the speaker as to what the exact character of this end is.

Strictly speaking, in Hinduism the aim of the practitioner of the left-hand path (vamamarga) is the individual's union with the individual soul (jivatman) and the continued independence of that realized jivatman from the universal or supreme soul (paramatman).[16] Another way of putting this might be that the follower of the vamamarga seeks to actualize his individual self (atman)—the personal divinity—and then maintain the ongoing independence and freedom of that individuated self.

Historically, this is not that much, if at all, different from archaic Indo-European beliefs, which held that men could become as gods if they lived heroic or magical lives. The "metaphysic" is the same as it always was, there has just been a revaluation, or new value judgment, placed on the life of struggle and victory or defeat. Where the ancients saw it as a glorious existence, which they wanted to perpetuate throughout eternity, the "reformers" of Hinduism and Buddhism both saw this same "cycle of becoming" (samsara) as "suffering."

Among others, Julius Evola recognizes that the Tantras actually carry on the oldest tradition of the Vedas, as *understood in the Vedic Age itself.*

> It is through this [operative] worldview that a part of the spirit of the early Vedic age, despite all, remains alive in the Tantras. In that age humans did not live as ascetics, struggling with the world and with *samsara,* but rather as free, uninhibited forces, in the company of various gods and supernatural energies, rapt in a state of cosmic and triumphant bliss.[17]

LEFT-HAND-PATH IN THE FRAMEWORK OF TANTRISM

Since the division into dakshinachara and vamachara is a relatively late one in the history of Hinduism—perhaps going back no more than a thousand to fifteen hundred years—the sects of Hinduism, which strictly can be said to belong to the vamamarga, do not formally belong to the most archaic levels of historic Vedic religion. As we have seen, the technical term "left-hand path" actually comes from Hindu tantrism. In the more global way that I am presenting the left-hand path, it does not, however, have to be limited to tantric sects alone. Nevertheless, discussions of the left-hand path fall most naturally within the framework of tantrism.[18]

Some tantric texts identify seven "paths" or "ways" (Skt. *acharas*). These are divided into the "right-path" (dakshinachara) and the "left-path" (vamachara), and certain other paths belong within these two.[19]

dakshinachara	*vamachara*
Vedachara	*Siddhantachara*
Vaisnavachara	*Kaulachara*
Saivachara	

Figure 2.2. Seven Tantric Paths

It is said that one is born into one of the dakshinacharas, but that one must be *initiated into* any of the vamacharas.[20] This is certainly in keeping with the typically nonnatural tendencies found within the left-hand path elsewhere. Merely to follow the path *dictated* by nature, by birth, is to conform to outer circumstances. But to rebel against one's lot—to determine consciously and willfully what one's path is to be—is an exercise of the faculty that sets the initiate apart from his environment.

The three levels of initiation in preparation for the vamachara are:

1. *pashu*
2. *vira*
3. *divya*

The pashu is the "fettered man." This is the noninitiated individual soul. The pashu transforms himself into a vira, "hero, warrior," through the efforts of his own will. A vira can be recognized by his politeness, courage, intelligence, and activity. Once the stage of vira has been established, one becomes eligible for initiation into either the dakshinachara or the vamachara. If he goes into the right-hand path, he will follow the ways of *bhakti* (devotion) and/or *jnana* (knowledge), but on the vamachara he will also learn *shakti-mantra* (mental power-patterns) and the *panchatattva* (five elements). Both of the latter are forms of theory and practice that include sexual rituals. The divya (divine) state is achieved when all of the qualities the initiate has gathered have "become part and parcel of himself, when they cannot be dissociated from his own entity."[21]

Another way of looking at the various "paths" is that the Vedic, *Vaishnava,* and *Shaiva* are meant for pashus, the dakshinachara and vamachara are for viras, and the *siddhanta* and *kaula* are only open to the divyas of the left-hand path, although the *kaulachara* can be practiced symbolically by right-hand-path initiates as well[22] (see figure 2.3).

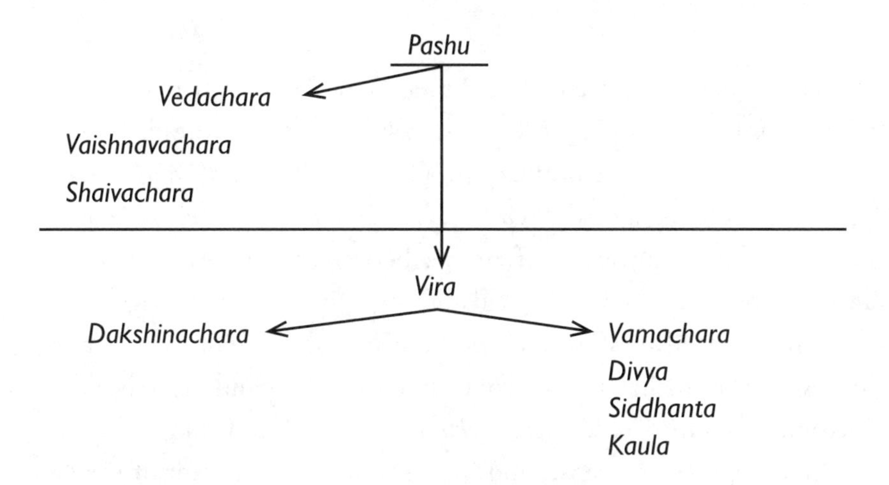

Figure 2.3. The Paths of the Hindu Sects

The *Kulavana-tantra* categorizes the viras of the vamachara into several categories or levels:[23]

1. *kshatriyas* (characterized by boldness and indifference to danger)
2. *siddhas* (who have reached a level of perfection, and who may be called "adept")
3. *kaulas* (whose "law" [*kaladharma*] obliterates all others).

Vimalananda uses the word *siddha* to mean "one who has achieved immortality and supernatural powers as a result of *sadhana* [spiritual practice]."[24]

Concerning the *kaulas,* Evola remarks:

> Nothing is forbidden to the *kaula* and to those who have achieved the condition of true *siddha-vira,* since they *are* and they *know.* They are lords of their passions, and they fully identify with Shakti [power]. As the supreme Shakti, or Parashakti, is over and beyond any pair of opposites, likewise the *kaula* is beyond good and evil, honor and dishonor, merit and sin, and any other value cherished by ordinary people, the so-called *pashus.*[25]

Shakti (power) is often referred to as being "absolutely free," and by the same token the kaula is called *svecchakari* ("one who can do as he or she pleases"). Pashus, or ordinary people, will often fear, shun, or condemn the kaulas because of their behavior, or simply for their presence.[26]

One of the significant differences between the two tantric paths, although both are under the aegis of Shiva, is that on the right-hand path the adept always experiences "someone above him," even at the highest level of realization. By contrast, on the left-hand path the adept "becomes the ultimate sovereign [*chakravartin* = world ruler]."[27]

In a more general sense, and in a structure reminiscent of the levels of man outlined by the Italian Renaissance Neoplatonic philosopher Pico della Mirandola (discussed in chapter 6 of this book), Vimalananda lays out three levels at which various types of humans can exist: as a *khara* ("donkey"), a *nara* ("man"), or as a *Narayana* ("God Himself"). The khara is said to believe "only in the three lowest chakras" (= eating, procreating, excreting); his realm is that of *abhibhautika* (the mundane). The nara, or true human, is said to live exclusively in the upper three chakras. It is further stated that only a few naras live in the world at any given time. Their realm is that of the *adhyatmika* (the spiritual). Only a nara can become a Narayana, and technically they are said to do this by gaining access to the secret chakras located within in the head. (These are discussed below.) The realm in which the Narayana lives is called the *adhidaivika* (or "astral").[28]

Vamacharins, or practitioners of the left-hand path, may be found most commonly among persons belonging to sects devoted to the gods Ganesha, Rudra, Vishnu, Shiva, Svayambhu, Veda, Bhairava, Ksetrapala, China, Kapalika, Pashupata, Bauddha, Kerala, Vira-Vaishnava, Sambhava, Chandra, and Aghora; or to the goddesses Kali, Tara, Sundari, Bharavi, Chinnamasta, Matangi, and Vagala. Here it is wise to keep in mind that the right-hand path and left-hand path are *methods* or approaches rather than sects in and of themselves.

METHODS OF THE HINDU LEFT-HAND PATH

Although vamacharins can be found in any of the various cults mentioned above, it is principally in the method of worshiping the *Goddess,* in the form of a human woman or symbols of her, that especially the male vamacharin will practice the left-hand path. Besides meaning "left," the Sanskrit word *vama* can also mean woman, or the Goddess.[29] The real meaning behind this is that the Goddess and woman are thought to be the embodiments of shakti (power).[30] Here it is quite clear, at least from the masculine perspective, that the essence of the vamachara is the total transformation of the human initiate into something superhuman or god(dess)-like. This lies at the root of why antinomianism (inversions of all kinds of normatives) is so important in the methodology of Eastern forms of the left-hand path.

An often overlooked aspect of both individualism and antinomianism in the Indian systems of the left-hand path is contained in the doctrines of *hatha yoga.* The Sanskrit word *hatha* literally means "violence" or "violent effort," though it has come to refer to yogic methods that primarily focus on the physical vehicle, the human body.[31] The practice of pure hatha yoga is said to be able to produce jivanmukti and to give immortality to the individualized existence by preserving "all psychophysical energies."[32] The Upanishads state "Every god is enclosed here, in the body," and the Tantras valorize the body and *individual existence:* "Jiva is Sadashiva [= Shiva in his pure aspect of 'being']."[33] In the Tantras, as in the Vedic Age, there is no contempt for the body—to the contrary, there is the enjoyment and exploration of it for the revelation of secrets it affords.[34]

Externally, one of the chief distinguishing features between the methods of the dakshinamarga and the vamamarga is that the dakshinacharin practices "worship through substitutes," while the vamacharin actualizes what is otherwise only symbolic. He may have to participate in exercises of cruelty and other aberrations of social and religious norms as a way of placing himself totally outside profane society. Thereby he is "unfettered" from the bonds and taboos of society as a way of unfettering himself from spiritual bonds.[35] (Remember the virtual identity between spiritual order and social order, as indicated in the Indian caste system.) The methodology of the left-hand path appears to be by far the more archaic of the two.[36]

One of the chief principles of left-hand-path tantric practice is to attain liberation (here called yoga) while still being able to have enjoyment (*bhoga*). The method that makes this possible involves the identification (*smadhi*) of the individual self with a higher self *while* in a state of enjoyment (bhoga).[37] The *Kularnava Samhita* (5.219) states: "Through enjoyment one gains liberation; for enjoyment is the means of reaching the Supreme Abode. Hence the wise who wish to conquer [the spirit] should experience all pleasures."[38]

Vimalananda alludes to a reason why a left-hand-path practitioner does not unify with the divinity outside himself. It is simply because they enjoy loving the divine object so much, and being in Her company, that they control their thoughts and emotions to be able to better enjoy the reality of the "company of the Beloved."[39]

Those on the vamamarga eventually reject totally the methods and rituals of the dakshinamarga as being inefficient or of no real help in their progress. They may, however, continue to worship their deity during the day in a traditional way while they perform rites of the vamachara at night. Night worship is often a feature of antinomian schools.

Vimalananda distinguishes between two "ways": the way of jnana (knowledge) and the way of bhakti (devotion). In following the way of jnana, the disciple is said to split from his normal body and to self-identify with his "causal body," and from that point on, one follows the *adesha* (commands) of an internal guru. In following the way of bhakti, on the other hand, the disciple maintains continuous devotion to an entity conceived of as being outside the self. In discussing the question of unity with a divinity (in this case, Krishna), Vimalananda says: "But most devotees of Krishna never want to unite with Him; they always want to maintain their own identities so that they taste His sweetness over and over again, forever and ever."[40]

Regarding the left-hand-path perspective, Svoboda further adds that "on the path of jnana you actually become Shiva, while on the path of bhakti you worship but remain separate from Krishna."[41] The distinction is an important one that should be well understood. It seems universal in the practice of the left-hand path. On the path of jnana, the practitioner is himself transformed into a being of the divine *typos* without sacrificing his individuated existence, whereas on the left-hand path of bhakti, the practitioner seeks the company of the divine counterpart and exists in the presence of this divinity without *unifying with it.*[42]

Antinomianism is an element found in many schools of the left-hand path throughout the world. In each school the practice or philosophy has its own raison d'etre, but underlying them all is the left-hand-path imperative to *transform* both one's self and one's world. In order to transform something, it must first be de-formed before it can be re-formed into the willed transformed object. In order to re-construct something, that thing must be de-constructed. This postmodern idea is very ancient indeed.

When discussing antinomian, left-hand-path tantrism, the French Indologist Louis Renou states: "we observe the inversion of normal worship and common ethical principles. The fact that those objects are 'worshipped' is evidence that the stage has been passed at which they would be considered sinful."[43] Thus, objects or practices that would normally inspire shame, hate, or fear in the orthodox (dakshinachara) Hindu will be willfully worshipped and engaged in with a sublimated attitude of sacrality, in order to cut the so-called three knots of shame-hate-fear. "The fundamental principle of the left-hand path is that spiritual progress cannot be achieved by falsely shunning our desires and passions, but by sublimating those very aspects which make one fall, as a means of liberation."[44]

According to Daniélou, the *Kularnava Tantra* informs us that "the lord-of tears (Rudra) has shown in the left-hand doctrine that spiritual advancement is best achieved by means of those very things which are the causes of man's downfalls."[45]

In discussing the *Kulavana-tantra,* Evola further relates that the work of the vira on the path to becoming a divya consists of *icchashuddhi* (purification of the will). This pure will is characterized as being *naked, transcendent, capable of self-determination, beyond all antithetical values and all pairs of opposites.* In the practice of icchashuddhi, the following eight bonds or fetters must be broken systematically: *daya* (sympathy), *moha* (delusion), *lajja* (shame or the idea of sin), *bhaya* (fear), *ghrina* (disgust), *kula* (family, kinship, clan), *varna* (caste), and *sila* (customary rites and precepts).[46] As each of these bonds or fetters is broken, the vira becomes progressively more liberated.

As we will see later in chapter 9, this technique of icchashuddhi is in many ways reminiscent of Anton LaVey's injunction that his followers should *indulge* in the "seven deadly sins" of Christianity—greed, pride, envy, anger, gluttony, lust, and sloth—in order to liberate themselves similarly from the conditionings of modern Western civilization.[47]

Part of the reason why such techniques are considered effective in Hindu practice is that we are now living in what is called a *Kali Yuga:* a phase of history characterized by materialism and a lack of interest in spiritual matters. In this kind of age, "passion alone, when astutely directed, can overcome egoism and pride and sordid calculation. Alone it has the momentum to draw man away from the bonds that chain him to his interests, his beliefs."[48]

The real importance of antinomianism lies in how it relates to the individual soul (jivatman) and how it is to be transformed into a divine being. This is affected by the union of the personality with its personal divinity, the jivatman itself. The limitations, or bonds, placed on the jiva (self) both internally and externally. Merger of the self with the jivatman is impossible so long as the eight bonds constrict the will of the vira.

Although in the tantric context none of this can be equated with crude "egotism," an element of a "divine egoism" can be discerned in the teaching that the western face of Shiva, which is red and is called *Vamadeva* ("Left-handed Deity"), is equated with "I-ness," the *ahamkara*, which is associated with fire, sight, and action.[49]

Such radical *individualism* is essential to the character of the left-hand path. Svoboda relates that seekers should "try to redirect their urge to individuation from Maya [unconsciousness/objectivity] to Chit [consciousness/subjectivity]" and should not allow themselves "to be carried along by the current of their lives and of their neighbors' lives."[50] He further states: "Aghoris [practitioners of the Aghora left-hand-path tradition] never permit themselves to be passively defined by the external environment; they define themselves and by so doing define their surroundings."[51] In a way reminiscent of the cosmo-psychological system of laws taught by G. I. Gurdjieff (which we will examine in chapter 8), Svoboda also relates:

> all of us are part of the manifested universe, subject to its laws until we develop the power to redefine ourselves in other terms. A Tantric aims to become *sva-tantra* ("self-functioning"), to be free of

all limitations, including especially the limitations of his or her own personality.[52]

The theme of the *creative* aspect of the practice of the left-hand path will be noticeable in many schools around the world and throughout history. The practice of the left-hand path is not simply a matter of finding a "program" and working with it. On the leftward way one does not worship a god but rather one *enacts divinity from a subjective perspective.* When describing the development of doctrines within Aghora, Svoboda says: "precepts [are] engraved not on tablets of stone but on the heart of the individual practitioner who must use them to create an individual system, thereby carving his or her own spiritual niche."[53]

Especially for men, antinomianism includes the notion of Goddess "worship." The vamacharin does not merely worship the Goddess in the form of a woman, but he himself seeks to *become a woman.* This *may* have its roots in a historical development in which men took over the priesthood function from women, and thus to practice that function with its timeless authority the men had to "become women." Evidence in support of this idea might be seen in such practices where priests wear feminine robes to certain rites, or in the myths and legends that show men transforming themselves into women.[54] This may be true on a historical level. However, there is a more profound and eternal, ahistorical principle of which these practices and beliefs may also be reflections. In Indian (and perhaps Indo-European) lore, the structure or essence of a subtle or spiritual body attached to, or contained within, the physical body is thought to be feminine (at least in the case of men). In other words, there is a spiritual entity of the opposite sex within each person. (This is echoed in the lore of Iran, with its *fravashis,* and in Scandinavia, with its *fylgjur, hamingjur,* and so forth, not to mention the concept of the anima in the highly sympathetic modern psychology of C. G. Jung.) In the Indian system we also discover many technical details demonstrating why and how this is so. The seven major *padmas* (lotuses) or *chakras* (wheels) are said to be the seven seats of femininity inherent in every human being: each of these is the seat of a shakti (power) that is, of course, also feminine in nature.[55] By awakening these shaktis and activating the padmas or chakras (through the force of *kundalini* [serpent force], also feminine), the vamacharin slowly (or quickly) transforms himself into the Goddess within and thus "becomes a woman." He has undergone a transformation into his "opposite."

In a left-hand-path context, the aghori sage Vimalananda relates that the aim of kundalini yoga is to reunite Shiva and Shakti, in order to re-create Shiva in his eternal form (as Sadashiva): "Sadashiva's left side is female and right side is male; the two principles have united but have not merged. If they were to merge that would be the end of the play [*lila*], and that would be no fun at all."[56] Here it should be carefully noted that Vimalananda subtly distinguishes between *union* and *merger.* His ultimate reason for wanting to avoid a merger of the two principles hinges on the *pleasure* he would lose if this were to occur.

The essential principle behind how the kundalini shakti (serpent power) is caused to rise in the body depends on the ability to *reverse* the ordinary or usual (i.e., *natural*) flow-patterns of force in the body. The *prana* energy, which naturally flows *upward* and *inward* in the body is made to flow downward and outward, and the *apana* energy, which ordinarily flows *downward* and/or *outward* is caused to flow upward or outward. When these two meet, contrary to their normal paradigm of motion, it is said that they "kiss," and it is then that kundalini shakti begins to rise. Here it is clear that "antinomianism" in the tantric system has extended itself even into the realm of esoteric physiology.

In the usual (right-hand-path) practice of kundalini yoga, the purpose is to reach the *sahasrara chakra* above the head. But it seems that from a left-hand-path perspective the point is only to raise the serpent power to the sixth chakra, or *ajna chakra* ("command center"), and from there to enter into the three hidden chakras. These are the secret chakras of *golata, lalata,* and *lalana* located on the uvula at the back of the throat, above the ajna chakra, and within the soft palate, respectively. The *aghori,* or left-hand-path tantric, will not merge with the sahasrara wherein all discrimination between *this* and *that,* between "I" and "not-I," or "I" and "Thou" would disappear—for, as Vimalananda would say, that would be no fun.

Vamacharins are actually known to engage in various practices considered nefarious by more orthodox dakshinacharins. Among the aghora sects, for example, acts of necrophilia and cannibalism are known. These and other practices are not engaged in for perverse pleasure, but rather they are dependent on the fact that they represent deep-seated cultural and religious taboos. It is by breaking these taboos and going beyond the barriers of good and evil that the aghori attains new levels of power and "liberation" (from his human limitations).

The word *aghora* literally means "the Non-Fearful," and this quality is equated with the southern face of the five-faced Shiva. This face is blue-black in color, and embodies the principle of intellect (*buddhi tattva*) or eternal law (*dharma*).[57]

More usual than engaging in these extreme forms, however, are the milder practices of sexual mysticism. Many of these are meant to break down social, sexual, as well as dietary taboos. "Tantrism" has been used as a synonym for "sexual magic" in the West since the appearance of popular treatments of the subject in the 1960s and 1970s. There is much more to the tantric tradition than sexual mysticism, but the left-hand tantrics in particular do make actual sexual rituals a part of their practices.[58]

The most essential form of sexual mysticism is contained in the rite called *panchamakara* (five-Ms). This is described in the *Kalivilasa Tantra* (X–XI), but the warning is also given that it must be practiced only with initiated women. The "five-Ms" refer to five elements used in the ritual, the Sanskrit names for which all begin with the letter "M": *matsya* (fish), *mamsa* (meat), *madya* (intoxicating drink), *mudra* (cereal), and *maithuna* (coitus).

On the right-hand path, substitute substances are traditionally used: incense, food, sandalwood, a lamp, and flowers. In either case, however, there is a regular correspondence to the five traditional Hindu elements, or *tattvas:* aether, water, earth, fire, and air, respectively.

In a typical performance of the panchamakara on the left-hand path, the two celebrants partake of the four food items before entering into an act of sexual yoga. These elements have been described as aphrodisiacs, and they are also usually considered taboo substances (generally thought to be profane by the orthodox Hindus), which have been sacralized through mental discipline and tantric practice. In other words, the substances and acts involved in the panchamakara are usually thought to be instruments of *bondage,* and therefore to be counterproductive to liberation, but the left-hand-path practitioner uses these substances and experiences for the purpose of raising kundalini and is not used by them.

Another important variation of the sexual ritual is the rite known as *chakra puja* (circle worship). Here a whole group of tantrics engage in a sexual ritual in which men and women are paired by chance. One way of doing this is by the women throwing their bodices (*choli*) into a basket and having each of the men take a bodice from the receptacle. The woman to whom that bodice belongs will be his ritual partner for the night—be that woman his wife, sister, mother, or whatever. The participants will all sit in a circle, alternating male/female, with the man's partner always sitting on his *left.* This is the probable origin of the term "left-*hand* path," and also shows the ritual correlation between *woman* and *left.* In the middle of the circle, a single girl—usually very young—is worshipped by the chief officiating priest. The rite, which lasts for several hours, ends in a collective panchamakara.[59]

These and similar tantric rites are not as straightforward to interpret as they might seem at first. An important element in their functioning clearly seems to be the idea of antinomianism: the sanctification of the profane. But the attitude of erotic enjoyment evident in advanced practices seems to indicate that this is not a continuing factor. The original magical or psychologically transformative aspect might have been the overcoming of inhibition and the breaking of conventional taboos, but once this stage is past, the activities continue in a new and resacralized sense. The fact that the relatively mild sexual and dietary taboos have been broken may contribute to the practices of more extreme sects, which seek to push back even stronger taboos. Some sects reinterpret the five-Ms to mean: *meha* (urine), *mamsa* (human flesh), *mala* (excrement), *medha* (juice, i.e., blood), and *mehana* (penis, i.e., semen). Perhaps in keeping with the two poles or schools within the left-hand path, however, there are also those at the other extreme who interpret these "five essentials" (*panchatattvas*) not as carnal realities, but as spiritual symbols. Always the overriding factor seems to be the idea of a Nietzschean *Umwertung aller Werte,* a "re-valuation of all values." Barriers are broken, social and psychological chaos are created, out of which a new, revivified, renewed, and transformed order can emerge according to the will of the tantric.

Commonly, the left-hand-path tantric is said to be able to ingest poisons—perhaps symbolic of substances that hinder liberation—with nothing but beneficial results. This is made possible once the tantric has become [a] Shiva, that is, he has *real*ized his real self or soul and now possesses the power of Shiva to convert everything that he ingests into *amrita* (the divine nectar of immortality, or nondeath).[60] The magical principle transforming or "purifying" any substance or experience to serve the purposes of the pure will of the magician is typical at all levels of the left-hand path.

Another important vamachara technique, which involves the reversal of norms or natural tendencies, is the control of the flow of semen. On the surface, this appears to be one of many magico-technical practices that is only tangential to the purpose of this study. But the *rationale* behind it—if not the philosophical sophistication or actual objective effectiveness—is an important left-hand-path statement.

Among tantrics, semen is thought of as the essence of Shiva,[61] and as long as they are able to retain it or reabsorb it they will have immortality. In esoteric tantric physiology, it is conceptualized that the semen, or the spiritual component of it (Skt. *bindu*), has its origin in the crown chakra sahasrara and is normally and naturally transmitted downward through a subtle artery (*nadi*) and ejaculated and lost. This is viewed as a loss of power, selfhood, and life.[62]

It then becomes the task of the tantric adept to reverse the natural process in some way in order to retain and reabsorb this spiritual substance. Thus, the tantric may arrest the ejaculation, causing the bindu to rise again in reverse direction back to the crown of the head, nourishing and empowering self-hood and immortality. Alternatively, a similar effect may be gained by ejaculating into the *yoni* (vulva) and then drawing it back up through the penis and up the subtle nadi to the crown chakra. It is also possible to ingest orally the "fallen" bindu.[63] Similar beliefs were perhaps held by certain Gnostic sects (see chapter 4) in which there was often talk of the "power to reverse the river Jordan."[64]

The importance of actual *worship* of Shakti in the form of womankind and the physical vulva in Hindu tantrism would explain why practices involving the emission of semen, and its mixture with female emissions before reabsorption takes place, are more common than in Buddhistic tantrism.[65]

What is important here is the left-hand-path technique or philosophical model of inverting or reversing *natural* processes through the power of will and consciousness. By being able to reverse natural "flow patterns"—be they subjective (in the body) or objective (in the world)—practitioners of the left-hand path demonstrate or exercise their independence from the natural universe. In doing so, they establish what is divine in their individualities (jivatman). This would seem to be the central philosophical and magical statement underlying the machinations of the tantric semen cult.

The concept of the sovereign power of a "lord" is highly consistent with the Hindu terminology surrounding those called *mahapurushas* or "great-souled" ones. These exist in four ascending grades or levels of power: *siddha* ("an immortal one of special ability"), *nath* (master), *muni* or *mauni* (silent one), and *rishi* (seer).[66]

The vamamarga appears to be a path consistent with Hinduism's most archaic roots and to be a logical flowering of certain aspects of Indo-European thought. The development of the individual self (jivatman) to the level of a divinity—and the maintenance of that level of being for eternity, never seeking the final liberation or total annihilation of the individual self in the universal self (paramatman or *brahman*)—is the clear goal of the original vitality of Indo-European thought.

THE LEFT-HAND PATH IN BUDDHISM

In Buddhism, the position of the left-hand path is more philosophically paradoxical, yet in fact and in practice it is perhaps as prevalent as in Hinduism. The reason the Buddhist left-hand path is paradoxical is that the very foundation of Buddhism lies on the basis that *there is no individual self,* as the concept of the self is only an illusion created by the mind. The Hindu holds that the self does exist, as do the gods and goddesses. The Buddhists' original denial of these assertions, as well as their rejection of the ultimate validity of the Vedas, are the main reasons they were themselves rejected as heretics in India. Originally, Buddhism was not so much a *religion* as it was a *technique* or *method* of "enlightenment" for the realization of the state of nirvana. Historically, many elements have accrued to the Buddhist method as it adapted itself to local cults and social conditions throughout Asia.

The historical Siddhartha Gautama, called the Buddha ("Awakened One"), died in 544 BCE. He was an Indian (Aryan) prince of a *kshatriya* (warrior) tribe paradoxically using a Brahmanic clan name: Gautama, "descendant of the sage Gotama." Siddhartha established a radical teaching for gaining enlightenment. This teaching is based on the so-called Four Noble Truths:

1. Life is inherently full of suffering (Pali *dukka*).
2. That suffering is due to craving (Pali *tanha*).
3. Suffering can be stopped by "eradication of craving" (Pali *nibbana,* Skt. *nirvana*).
4. "Eradication of craving" can be achieved by following the Noble Eightfold Path (Pali *ariya*).

The Noble Eightfold Path consists of: right understanding, right thinking, right speech, right action, right livelihood, right effort, right mindfulness (contemplation), and right meditation (one-pointedness of mind). By following the Eightfold Path, the practitioner will gain the awakened state of Buddha-hood.

Buddhism at this level is a highly developed and sophisticated doctrine that epitomizes the right-hand path. The root of this can be easily understood by analyzing the first of the Four Noble Truths. In a chain of causation, sorrow is equated with ignorance, ignorance causes imagination, imagination causes consciousness of self, which causes embodied existence, which gives rise to the senses, which cause perception. Perceptions cause emotion, emotion causes craving (tanha), craving causes attachment (to the things craved), attachment leads to becoming, which leads to rebirth—the principal phenomenon equated with "suffering" in both Hindu and Buddhist traditions. The ignorance, which started the whole chain in motion, is equated with an ignorance of the nature of the universe, that it is full of sorrow (dukka), instability or becoming (*anicca*), and "lack of self" (*anatta*). If Buddhists had remained true to those fundamental philosophical stances and practices, there could be no talk of a Buddhist left-hand path.

The most "orthodox"—or simplest—school of Buddhism has come to be referred to as Theravada ("teaching of the elders"), and is strongest in southern Buddhism in Sri Lanka and southeastern Asia. But beginning around the first and second centuries CE, learned monks began to develop a more esoteric tradition that came to be known as the Mahayana ("greater vehicle"). In this context, Theravada is often referred to as the Hinayana ("lesser vehicle"). Mahayana Buddhism eventually came to dominate in the north: in Tibet, China, and Japan. The orthodox view is that each person is fully responsible for his own enlightenment and that the realm of bliss, or nirvana, is fully separate from the realm of illusion or *maya* (the phenomenal world).

There was a tendency in mahayana to bridge the gap of absolute separateness between nirvana and maya. One way was found in the doctrine of the *boddhisattva* ("one bound for awakening"). A boddhisattva was a near-perfected being who could effect the enlightenment or development of less awakened people through a kind of magical intervention from his ascended state. (This doctrine, as found in Tibetan Buddhism, is apparently the main source for later ideas of "unknown superiors," "secret chiefs," and mahatmas found in certain

Masonic, quasi-Masonic and Theosophical schools in the West.)

A certain school within the Mahayana tradition called Madhyamika asserted philosophically that in fact there was no difference between maya and nirvana: both were equally void (*sunyata*) or, alternately, the phenomenal world (maya) exists only in the mind of the perceiver.

These ideas might remind the reader of the "sense-data" theories of the British philosophers George Berkeley (1685–1753) and David Hume (1711–1776), whose application of empiricism led them to conclude that we can only know the subjective contents of our minds as fed by impressions made upon them by the senses. The "reality" of the world outside our minds is uncertain. Already in ancient times the epistemologies of Hinduism and Buddhism had passed through the radical stages of subjective observation that would only be possible in the West after the demise of the intellectual hegemony of Christianity (see chapter 6).

The most striking development within Mahayana Buddhism is the emergence of the Vajrayana ("thunderbolt or diamond vehicle"), especially prevalent in Tibet. Philosophically, the Vajrayana is virtually synonymous with Tibetan Buddhist tantrism. Thus, if maya = nirvana, then indulgence in the phenomenal world can lead to the world of bliss. Maya is used to attain nirvana. In practical terms, this opens the way to antinomianism. "Profane" things are made "pure" as an exercise of the mind. Vajrayana is heavily influenced on a philosophical and practical level by Indian (Hindu) tantrism, indigenous Tibetan religion (Bon), and Central Asian shamanism. Again, in an antinomian spirit, the "over culture" absorbs techniques from the "under culture."

In Buddhism, as in Hinduism, the left-hand path ends not in the absorption or annihilation of individuality in *moksha* or nirvana, but in a perpetuation of that individuality on a more permanent plane of existence. Within Buddhist terminology, the practitioner of the left-hand path aims to attain only to the boddhisattvic state—and to remain there as a deity—"angelic" or "demonic." The final annihilation is resisted.

Of course, when we look at the original Buddhist teachings, such aims are theoretically antithetical to the very premise of Buddhism. But in the history of religious ideas such contradictions often arise.

Who would think, for example, that the teachings of the Nazarene, as reported in the Gospels, could be used to support such institutions as the Crusades and the Inquisition? So it is not surprising that Buddhism would develop within itself patterns out of synch with the founder's original intentions. Over the fifteen hundred years following Gautama's death, Buddhism spread from India in a largely peaceful way throughout the cultures of southeastern Asia, China, Tibet, Mongolia, and Japan. With this kind of cultural diversity as its matrix, it is certainly no wonder that teachings at odds with those of the founder took root in the religious soil called Buddhism.

Left-hand-path tantrism seems to have had various epicenters of development in the Buddhist world. Principal among these were Tibet and Bengal (present-day Bangladesh). In the latter region, Buddhism was eventually driven out by Muslim conquest starting about 1200 CE, and from there it spread to Java and up to Nepal.

METHODS OF LEFT-HAND-PATH BUDDHISM

One of the chief aspects of left-hand-path Buddhism is its positive attitude toward sexuality. The left-hand-path Buddhist accepts certain Shakta ideas that the creative energy or "potency" of a deity, angel, demon, or boddhisattva is personified as his wife or consort. In the left-hand-path Buddhist tantra, the *shaktis,* or female aspects of supermundane entities, are worshipped as lovers. The Buddhist tantric practitioner seeks sexual union with these shaktis in order to draw on their power and to use the power gained from such unions for further spiritual development. Another chief feature of left-hand-path tantric Buddhism is the utilization not only of "deities" or "angels" (i.e., entities considered generally beneficent), but also of "demons" and their consorts. The god Bhairava ("the Terrible") is worshipped, and elaborate rites are performed in burial grounds. Sexual intercourse and other activities considered immoral by the general population are also utilized as practices that lead to spiritual development or salvation.[67]

Buddhist left-hand-path tantrism holds that the passions and desires, which the right-hand path seeks either to annihilate or sublimate, can be utilized in their direct, unsublimated forms as vehicles for "awakening."

Walter Evans-Wentz cites the following technical instructions from the Tibetan Buddhist text called the "Epitome of the Great Symbol" (87–88):

> 87. Whatever thoughts, or concepts, or obscuring [or disturbing] passions arise are neither to be abandoned nor allowed to control one; they are to be allowed to arise without one's trying to direct [or shape] them. If one do no more than merely to recognize them as soon as they arise, and persist in so doing, they will come to be realized [or to dawn] in their true [or void] form through not being abandoned.
>
> 88. By that method, all things, which may seem to be obstacles to spiritual growth, can be made use of as aids on the Path. And therefore, the method is called "The utilizing of obstacles as aids on the Path."[68]

Left-hand-path Buddhism, like so many other expressions of the left-hand path in the world, eschews institutional forms and socially acceptable norms. It tends more in the direction of individualized expression and socially unacceptable behaviors.

In actual sexual practice, the male Buddhist left-hand-path tantric practitioner is more likely to retain his seminal fluid totally, or, having ejaculated it, to reingest it in its entirety orally. The retention of seed (Skt. *bija*) is tantamount to retaining power and vitality, both physical and mental. Also, it seems that although there might be a generally more spiritually positive attitude toward sexuality and womankind in Buddhist left-hand-path tantrism, there is still the fear that women, and especially female demonic entities, can vampirize men of their vital spiritual powers.[69]

In philosophical terms, the Buddhist left-hand path concentrates more on a subjective—intrapsychic—process. The Buddhist view would be that such polarities as implied by the male/female dichotomy (or that of the right-hand/left-hand path) are illusory creations of the mind of the individual. Practices are engaged in to demonstrate this illusory aspect. The Buddhist left-hand-path practitioner will tend to create his own subjective internally complete and closed system, whereas the Hindu left-hand-path practitioner will tend to acknowledge as real the objective existence of the Goddess (Shakti).

Practitioners who hold that the realm of the five senses is purely a construct of the mind and in reality the product of illusion (maya) may often rely on what appears to noninitiates to be chicanery and tricks involving slight of hand. If the world we see before us is an illusion, then the magician is pointing this out to us not by means of philosophical discourse, but by means of a direct attack on those senses and the ways they (mis-)inform the mind. Thus, what may at first glance appear to be an attempt at deception or trickery is in fact conceived of as the most direct method of teaching about the central fact (from a Buddhist perspective) that the world is a creation of the mind. This is a much more entertaining approach to the problems addressed by Plato's "Myth of the Cave."[70]

Because of the long-standing and continuing proliferation of doctrines and sects within both Hindu and Buddhist tantra/shakta, no unifying or definitive summary of either what they believe or practice, or final conclusion on what distinguishes them, can be reached with certainty. It only seems certain that the desire for continued—if continually transformed—individuality, and lack-of-annihilation, are universal (even if often obscured in actual texts of the left-hand-path Tantras).

The influence of the left-hand path as practiced by philosophies based on Indian-derived systems (both Hindu and Buddhist) on the modern Western forms of the left-hand path has been enormous. Historically, it seems that this influence came in at least two great waves. The first came perhaps with the opening of cultural channels between "East" and "West" occasioned by the conquests of Alexander (d. 323 BCE). Following this time there was a flood of ideas from the

"East" (India and Iran), which both formed and reformed sects in the Mediterranean region. These sects in turn exercised a secondary influence on India with Christian missions (often Gnostic in character) beginning in the first century CE.[71] The second wave of influence from the Eastern left-hand path is better documented. In essence, it came originally as a result of another "conquest" from the West: the extension of the British Empire into India (beginning in the eighteenth century). As the West was again increasingly exposed to ideas stemming from India and Tibet, this eventually filtered down to a more popular level of culture where it emerged in forms such as the Theosophical Society (founded 1875) and the Ordo Templi Orientis (founded 1896 or 1904). As we will see in chapter 7, doctrines of left-hand-path Hinduism and Buddhism played significant roles in both cases. The forms of sexual magic taught by Aleister Crowley and his followers, as well as the antinomian chicanery practiced by Anton LaVey (see chapter 9), similarly have analogs in the left-hand-path practices of India.

ZOROASTRIANISM AND THE LEFT-HAND PATH

No system of thought shaped the classical form of Western left-hand-path mythology more than Zoroastrianism. The idea that there is a whole hierarchy of the forces of good arrayed as if in a battle against a hierarchy of the forces of evil came to the West from Iranian religion (in one form or another) through Judaism or Gnosticism in some cases—or perhaps directly into the heathen north in other cases (see chapter 3). Originally the Iranian religious system differed little from the Vedic system of India. This is because the Aryans and Iranians constitute two limbs of the same branch of the Indo-European tree of cultures and religions.

The Iranian systems have contributed considerably to Western left-hand-path mythology, and are themselves often very dualistic and concerned with matters of good *versus* evil. When one analyzes these systems, then, it is all the more surprising to find they exhibit very little underlying tension over the essential philosophical questions that differentiate the left-hand path from the right-hand path, both East and West. The Iranian systems seem to have characteristics that in some way or another belong to the left-hand path!

The study of Iranian religion is complex and obscured by the fact that its cultural basis and epicenter was destroyed in the Muslim conquest of Iran over a thousand years ago. Many Zoroastrians (now known as the Parsis) escaped to India, however, where they continue the religion, and some non-Islamic practitioners of various forms of Iranian religion (including Zoroastrianism) have survived in Iran to this day. But their schools of sophisticated thought have long since been shattered.

Zoroaster (or Zarathustra), who probably lived around the eleventh or tenth century BCE, was essentially a reformer of the Iranian religion as practiced by various tribal groups. He was himself trained as a priest or *zaotar* of this sacrificial religion. Even before Zoroaster's time, the Iranian system had developed highly dualistic tendencies,[72] which would continually find expression in Iranian religions, both within Zoroastrianism and outside it. Zoroaster's reforms seem to have been aimed at creating a *moralistic* dualism within a theoretically "monotheistic" system. Zoroaster's chief opponents in his efforts were the ultraconservative representatives of the old Indo-Iranian order: the *mairyas,* who were organized in *haenas* or "men's societies." This appears to be a logical opposition, as monotheism would tend to divest the ruling *class* of its power and invest that power in a single ruler or *Shah.*

The haenas were the repositories of archaic religious practice and culture. They practiced animal sacrifice (especially of horses and cattle) and drank a holy intoxicating liquid (*haoma,* which corresponds linguistically to Skt. *soma*). They were a society of horse-riding warriors who were accompanied on their ways by a troop of women called *jahikas* or *jahis.* These women sometimes fought alongside the warriors, but were certainly the concubines of the men. On the spiritual level, these jahis were reflected by the fravashis (supernatural female entities who were the protective and empowering souls of the warriors; see page 38). The word *jahi* later came to refer to the chief demoness of the Zoroastrians, Jahi or Jeh ("the Whore").

The religion of the mairyas was certainly one based on life, the preservation and continuation of life, and the glories of the individual soul. As the prophet Zoroaster saw them, these bands must have seemed the very incarnations of the evil minions of Ahriman. They wore black leather (although they fought naked from the waist up), bore black weapons, and flew a black flag emblazoned with silver dragons. Their hair was long and they wore it in braids. In their initiation rites they were known, like members of other Indo-European warrior bands, to don the skins of wolves—thereby transforming themselves into the likeness of wolves. In addition, they made use of a magical fury called *aeshma.*[73]

This aeshma is doubly interesting to us for the following reasons. On the one hand, it is a close parallel to the magical fury or inspiration attained by the Germanic warrior/magicians under the leadership of their god Woden/Wotan/Odin (see page 76). But the word aeshma itself also found its way into the Judeo-Christian demonic lore in the form of Aeshma-daeva (the god/demon of fury)—the Iranian term *Aeshmadaeva* eventually became *Asmodeus,* who is variously referred to (depending on the source) as a demon of lust, a king of demons, and a prince of hell.

Zoroaster vilified the religious culture of the warrior societies, and many of his reforms seem aimed at correcting what he saw as excesses in their practices and in their violent natures. Essentially his reforms consisted of a replacement of most (if not all) of the gods (*daevas*) of the traditional Iranian pantheon with hierarchies of personifications of largely abstract entities or principles (*yazatas*).

In Zoroaster's theology, there is one god who is absolutely wise and purely good, but not all-powerful. He is called Ahura Mazda (Wise Lord). Through Thought, he created a hierarchy of all-seeing spirits. In fact he created a whole good universe, called *menok.* It is said that Ahura Mazda chose the Good of his own free will.[74] This clearly implies that somehow beyond the gods there is a system of morality to which they themselves are subject. Among the creatures Ahura Mazda engenders are the twins Spenta Mainyu (Beneficent Mind) and Angra Mainyu (Destroying Mind). Angra Mainyu, exercising his own free will, for the first time chose evil instead of good. The very existence of Angra Mainyu in effect limited the good of Ahura Mazda. Angra Mainyu then began to plan an attack on the good creation of Ahura Mazda (who in some accounts is virtually identified with Spenta Mainyu). But Ahura Mazda, with his all-seeing wisdom, sees Angra Mainyu's plan and in defense of his preexisting spiritual universe (menok) he creates a material universe (*getik*) from its pattern. This material universe is created by Ahura Mazda as a weapon or shield against Angra Mainyu. (The later systems of Gnosis that contrived to make the material universe the creation of the "evil god" would have been highly heretical to Zoroaster himself.)

Some accounts relate that Angra Mainyu began a "counter-creation" in which he made monsters (such as wolves and spiders) for each beautiful creature Ahura Mazda had fashioned (such as dogs and eagles). Other accounts have it that Angra Mainyu began to possess or indwell in the good creations of Ahura Mazda, thus corrupting them.

But what has Angra Mainyu—known as Ahriman in later sources—really done but give Ahura Mazda the license he needs to extend his power limitlessly while only acting morally in defense of his good creation? Here it becomes evident that Angra Mainyu actually—though unconsciously and involuntarily—collaborates in Ahura Mazda's plans of perfection. So Angra Mainyu can be seen as an example of "evil" that promotes the cause of good. A parallel can be drawn in this respect to J. W. von Goethe's devil, Mephistopheles, who says of himself:

> *[Ich bin] ein Teil von jener Kraft,*
> *Die stets das Böse will und stets das Gute schafft.* (*Faust* I, ll. 1136–37)
> [I am] a part of that force / that always desires what's evil, yet always works for the good.

In the orthodox Zoroastrian system, mankind is exhorted—in imitation of Ahura Mazda—to choose the good always as a matter of free will. In so doing, the evil machinations of Ahriman will be thwarted. Mankind is seen as the chief battleground between good and evil, and mankind is seen as the fulcrum on which the fate of the world is balanced.

The Zoroastrians were by no means immediately successful in their efforts to reform the Iranian religion and their system does not appear to become the official religion of the court of the Shah, Darius, until around 522 BCE.[75]

Although Zoroaster lived in eastern Iran (on the eastern side of the Zagros mountains) and his system flourished there to the greatest degree, the various Iranian Empires (from around 800 BCE) and the realm of Iranian cultural influence spread through Mesopotamia into Asia Minor (present-day Turkey). In the western part of the Persian Empire, the cult of the *magus* (sing. *magu,* "priest") remained strong and resisted Zoroastrian influence. Magu is the ultimate source of the term "magician." It was also Latinized as the singular *magus* (pl. *magi*) and used to designate highly initiated (and ostensibly wise) practitioners of sorcery. As time went on, however, the cult of the magus became progressively more influenced by Zoroastrian ideas until they eventually came to be *identified* (by outsiders) as Zoroastrian priests.

In fact, pre-Zoroastrian religious systems continued to flourish throughout this time both inside and outside the Persian Empire, and some say they still persist to the present day. In any event, the native Iranian beliefs (i.e., forms of daeva worship) are certainly known to have still existed in the mountainous region of Sogdia at the time of the Islamic conquest, which took from 636 to 800 CE to complete.

The principal pre-Zoroastrian systems, which nevertheless began to include Zoroastrian elements over time (just as Zoroastrianism incorporated pre-Zoroastrian elements), were Zurvanism and Mithraism.

Zurvan is an Iranian deity embodying infinite time and destiny. According to the Zurvanites, Zurvan is the "father" of both Ahura Mazda (Ohrmazd) and Angra Mainyu (Ahriman). This conception is apparently extremely ancient, perhaps even predating Zoroaster's system.[76] It is probably in the system of Zurvanism that the idea of the *moral dualism* preached in Zoroaster's theology finds expression in a dualism expressed between spirit (as a manifestation of good) and matter (as a manifestation of evil). It cannot be overemphasized that the ideology in which spirit = good / matter = evil is *not* Zoroastrian. It is an extreme heresy in orthodox Zoroastrianism to believe such a thing, although it does seem to be an Iranian idea. In Zurvanism, Ahura Mazda (Ohrmazd) is reduced to a creature of Zurvan. This is also a heretical notion for orthodox Zoroastrians.

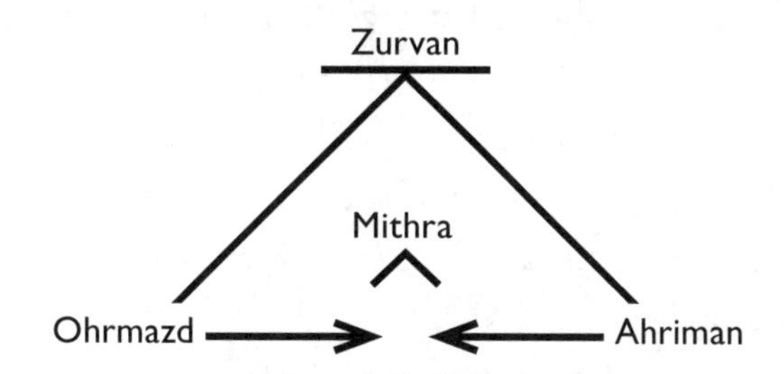

Figure 2.4. The Zurvanite System

In the Zurvanite system, the god Mithra (Vedic Mitra) is seen as a mediator between Ohrmazd and Ahriman. In Mithra we see another persistent manifestation of the pre-Zoroastrian religion; such manifestations appear throughout the history of Iranian religion as well as in religious systems derived from Iranian thought. The Mithraic cult was strong for a long time among the magus of the western Persian Empire, especially around the Black Sea. It is clearly a non-Zoroastrian, warrior-oriented mystery cult.[77] A close study of Mithraism reveals that it is a sophisticated system developed from the religion of the warrior bands (haenas) of early Iranian culture. This is often eclectically mixed with elements from religions and mystery cults with which the Mithraists came into contact. When the Romans came into contact with this cult (after the middle of the first century CE), it spread among soldiers throughout the Roman Empire. In contrast to other common forms of Iranian religion, Mithraism is remarkably free of dualistic thinking. Mithras, who in some respects resembled another "culture hero" also born on December 25, achieved salvation through the sacrifice of a bull.

Eventually, this bull-sacrifice cult lost out to the human-sacrifice cult of Christianity.

From the standpoint of orthodox Zoroastrian religion, both Zurvanism and Mithraism represent heretical, "evil" paths of darkness: Zurvanism because it sees Ohrmazd as a subordinate to Zurvan and Ahriman as the complete equal of Ohrmazd, and because it reduces the material universe to a creation of the evil god; Mithraism because it revolves around the worship of one of the old gods (daevas), Mithras. What is more, he is worshipped at *night* (which in itself constitutes an evil act of "devil worship" among orthodox Zoroastrians) and he is a warrior god who sacrifices a cosmic bull to create the world, which is reminiscent of the sacrificial cult of the old Iranian warrior cults (haenas). The followers of Mithras take part in that sacrifice, thus becoming creators themselves.

Zoroastrianism and the Iranian religious systems in general have exerted tremendous and sometimes formative influences on the religious and magical traditions that existed around them. These systems originated such important historical religious ideas as the strict dualism between the forces of good and the forces of evil, the idea of the coming of a world savior (Saoshyant) at the end of a linear stretch of time, the notion of all souls being judged (with the good going to Paradise* and the wicked to a realm of punishment), and the idea of the resurrection (or reconstruction and reanimation) of the physical bodies of the dead in a renewed world. In fact, some of the most important Judeo-Christian myths are Iranian in origin: certain aspects of Eden (Genesis 1–2), the Nativity of Jesus (Matthew 2:1–12), and various details of the Apocalypse.

The symbolic complex in Judaism (and hence Christianity) of the first man and woman (together with a malevolent female figure), and the tree of Paradise in conjunction with a serpent, definitely seems to originate from Iranian sources.[78] While these symbols have been present in the Near East for millennia, it is most likely that they entered into

*The word derives from the Iranian term *pairi-daeza,* "an enclosed garden or park."

Hebrew mythology following the time of the Jewish liberation from Babylon in 539 BCE. After that time, until the conquest of Alexander in 332 BCE, Israel was part of the Persian Empire.

More obviously of Iranian (specifically "magian" or Mithraic) origin is the myth of the Nativity of Jesus Christ. In the Iranian (Mithraic) lore, it was believed that the future Redeemer-King of the world would be born in a cave and that this would be signaled by a "star or column of light" shining above the cave. This explains why the three *magoi* (magus) are said to have visited the Christ child in the accounts given in the Gospel of Matthew.[79]

Scholars have also noted the striking resemblance between details given in the biblical depictions of the Apocalypse and other eschatological scenarios from the Indo-Iranian world (and, indeed, the entire Indo-European tradition). These include a clear series of parallels featuring monstrous creatures, a violent final battle, and an ultimate renewal.[80]

Often the Yezidis, an ethnic group living in Iraq, Turkey, and Syria, are thought to have a connection to left-hand-path ideas. It is just as likely as not that the original impetus and essence of that sect is Iranian (the Yezidis are Kurds, an Iranian people). Also, the apparent fact that they give some sort of honor to the god normally associated with evil, and that he has already been, or will be, forgiven by god, is consistent with heterodox Iranian beliefs.[81] I treat the Yezidis in more detail in chapter 4.

In the final analysis, it seems virtually impossible to classify any of the systems of Iranian thought as either right-hand path or left-hand path according to the criteria set out in this study. Although there is usually a strong polarity between good and evil in these systems, the good is not a matter of following the "Law of God," or in seeking self-annihilation either literally or as a by-product of "doing God's will," but rather it is doing or choosing the Good, which the god himself must also seek to choose. The Good seems to be an objective construct comparable to the Platonic *agathôn*. The individualities of the good ones are not annihilated but instead preserved and even resurrected in physical reality. At one point in Zoroastrianism it was determined that all human beings are destined for salvation, because their presence in the world is a sign of the choice made by their fravashis, or souls, in heaven to go to earth and fight for the Good.

Because the "East" has historically been able to preserve more or less intact the full range of religious "paths" envisioned and practiced by humanity, and because sages and magicians have consciously worked these methods out in an atmosphere of relative philosophical toleration, the methods and vocabulary of *both* paths seem more precise there. Much of the dichotomy between the methods and aims we have identified as right-hand path and left-hand path for this study was originally developed in an Eastern (Indo-Iranian) context. In chapter 3, when we look to the oldest foundations of European culture in the West, we will find a striking contrast with the existence of the range of paths relatively free of the dichotomizing tendencies that lead to the left-hand-path/right-hand-path labels.

3
The Roots of the Western Tradition

ROOTS OF THE WESTERN LEFT-HAND PATH

With varying degrees of appropriateness, the phrase "left-hand path" has come to mean Satanism in European culture. This is both accurate and inaccurate. It is accurate insofar as the Judeo-Christian religious system—which coined the name "Satan" (from Hebrew *śāṭān,* "opponent, adversary")—saw in its conception of evil many traits and characteristics of left-hand-path philosophy and religion. As a result, when left-hand-path practitioners look at the orthodox Judeo-Christian systems, they might feel a high degree of sympathy with and for the devil. This seems to have happened with many Gnostic sects.

The equation of the Western left-hand path with Satanism is inaccurate insofar as the practice of the left-hand path predates the imposition of the Judeo-Christian ideology in Europe. There was—*and still is*—the practice of the left-hand philosophy in a purely pagan or heathen (i.e., pre-Christian) religious context, which does not *need* to refer to Satan or Lucifer to be intelligible. The left-hand path would have existed in Europe without the advent of Christianity (as was, and still is, the case in India). But when Christianity did arrive, it labeled not only the indigenous left-hand-path practices of the heathens as diabolical, but the right-hand-path ones as well. It was, however, only the left-hand-path practitioners who were insightful enough (and perhaps courageous enough) to identify in some degree their ways with those of the adversary of the right-hand-path Christians.

THE PAGAN ROOTS IN EUROPE

The great Indo-European cultural and linguistic migrations beginning around 4000 BCE graphically reveal the true root of "Western" culture. The cultural roots of the peoples now speaking Celtic, Italic, Germanic, Slavic, or Hellenic (Greek) languages is probably to be found somewhere to the northeast of the Black Sea.[1] The national mythologies and religio-philosophical systems of these groups are closely related due to their common ultimate origin. What these migration routes also show, however, is the equally common origin shared between this western branch of the family and an eastern branch, which is the Indo-Iranian tradition discussed in chapter 2.

Just as the left-hand-path philosophy developed in the East, we could equally expect to find one developed in the West. In fact, the basics of the left-hand-path philosophy in the West seem to have had virtual equal footing with right-hand-path philosophies. In the northern parts of Europe, they even seem to have dominated.

An important thing to remember about the Indo-European cosmology is that it postulates a divine order, which partakes of a higher or more permanent level of reality, and the human order is then a reflection of the divine one. The human soul, the *psyche,* is a gift of the gods and the human social order is a reflection of the ordering of the various pantheons of gods. This primal understanding was developed into an articulated *philosophy* by Plato in the "West"—just as it had been by the school of Indian sages responsible for the Brahmanas and Upanishads in the "East."

History is full of tragedies and apparent tragedies. At least on a certain level, one of these tragedies was the slow erosion and ultimate destruction of the *established* forms of European religious systems through the incursion of an "exotic Eastern religion" that we now call Christianity. Over a period of nearly thirteen hundred years, the ecclesiastical institutions, or churches, supposedly based on the teachings of an executed holy man named Jesus, slowly disestablished the indigenous religious and philosophical traditions of the European nations and replaced them with the establishment of an international institution. This institution was characterized by an obsession for dogmatic unanimity when it came to matters of "spiritual" doctrine.

A map of the ideological campaigns of the church would show a spread of Christianity from cities in the Mediterranean region northward and outward into the countryside. Of course, the church was nowhere able to impose itself absolutely. To be successful it had to compromise at every step along the way. But it was willing to do so in exchange for its ultimate prize: *universal establishment.*

Everywhere the church advanced, one of its standard practices was to turn the native gods into devils and to destroy the old temples and sacred groves and in their places build churches. We will return to the Christianization process in chapter 4, but for right now it is important to realize that:

1. The oldest roots of European and Indo-Iranian culture are identical (Indo-European).
2. The present established religious culture in Europe has its roots on foreign soil (the Middle East).
3. The exotic Christian tree was only able to disestablish the native tree in a partial, external way.

In very many ways, what we call the "Western tradition" is therefore largely *southern* and non-Indo-European in origin, while what is often referred to as the "Eastern tradition" really has roots in common with actual European culture.

However, as the "Western tradition" stands now, it is indeed a synthesis (albeit an awkward and uncomfortable one) of actual European and southern traditions derived from the Nilo-Mesopotamian (Egyptian and Mesopotamian) magical cultures. Therefore, we must also examine the presence of the left-hand-path philosophy in those regions as one of the possible roots of the modern left-hand path.

THE HELLENIC LEFT-HAND PATH

In the history of the world perhaps no other single culture has exerted a greater influence over a wider expanse of time and space than the Hellenic. Moving down from the north, Hellenic, or Greek, tribes invaded and established themselves throughout the southern Balkan and Italic peninsulas and throughout the islands of the eastern Mediterranean Sea from about 1600 to 1100 BCE. The indigenous (non-Indo-European) culture that they overcame was an unusually vibrant and powerful one. Its apparent epicenter was on the island of Crete. The Greek culture of the Homeric Age (850–750 BCE) is largely a true synthesis of Hellenic (Indo-European) and Minoan (Old European) cultures. The major Hellenic cultural traits are *synthesis,* together with a sense of *harmony* and *moderation.*

Because the Hellenic culture was so much a sea-going and mercantile one, it made deep-level contacts with Egypt and with other cultures of the eastern Mediterranean, for example, that of the Phoenicians. But whatever cultural elements the Greeks might have adopted or borrowed from other cultures—such as writing (from the Phoenicians) or building in stone (from the Minoans)—the one aspect that remained thoroughly Greek and Indo-European was their *idealism.* Whether we see it in India or Ireland, in Rome or Greece, the Indo-European cosmology—its understanding of the world-order—hinges on the theory that this world is a material reflection of another, more real one (for example, the realm of the gods and goddesses), beyond which looms a yet more real world of abstract principles. In Ancient Greek terms, this is expressed in the intrinsic dichotomy between *physis* (nature) and *psychê* (soul).

This idealism (which was ultimately codified by the philosopher Plato) coupled with the Greek language and writing system (one so simple and convenient that even sailors and merchants could master it) allowed Hellenic culture to transform most cultures with which it had any long-standing contact. At the same time, this idealism was also first criticized by another school of Greek philosophy, that of the Epicureans.

PROMETHEUS AND PANDORA

The Origins of Evil and Its Transformative Effects on Humanity

The exact age of the myth of Prometheus (whose name means "the one with foreknowledge") is unknown. However, the idea of a transpersonal—or semi-divine—figure who is responsible for providing humanity with the spiritual faculty by which humans may *know* things seems to be a common Indo-European one. Such a figure would normally be considered a benefactor of humanity or, in fact, its true *creator* (in a spiritual sense). One fourth-century source (Pausanias 10.4.4) even says Prometheus fashioned men from clay.[2] This would seem to be a borrowed myth from the Middle East identifying Prometheus with Jehovah. Also, perhaps under the influence of the Middle Eastern notions concerning the "evil" of knowledge, the Greeks at one point turned this figure into a paradigm of the origin of human misery.

Hesiod's *Theogony* (ca. 700 BCE) is the oldest written reference to the myth of Prometheus. Hesiod portrays Prometheus as a titanic (pre-Olympian) entity who engenders a division between the gods and humanity, who had until that time lived in harmony together. Gods and men wished to part on good terms, so Prometheus institutes the first sacrifice of an ox to seal their pact of separation and independence. This rite is said to have occurred at a place called Mekone. After the slaying of the ox, Prometheus divides it into two portions: one of bone, and one of flesh and entrails. The bones he covers with fat so that the smoke rising from them attracts the attention of Zeus, supreme deity of the Olympians. The meat is disguised by the fat of the ox. A choice is offered to the Olympian, and he chooses the fat-covered bones. When Zeus discovers the truth, he becomes angry at Prometheus and mankind and withdraws the divine fire, which had presumably been one of those things previously shared by gods and humans.

This division of the sacrificial animal between edible parts, which are consumed by humans, and generally inedible parts, which are presumed to be the gods' share, is common Indo-European practice and the myth is on one level a later attempt to "explain" this practice.

Again according to Hesiod, Prometheus responded to this by stealing the divine fire from Olympus. He carries it back to the world of men in a hollow fennel stalk. And once more Zeus is moved to punish mankind and Prometheus. This time Prometheus is pinned to a great rock where an eagle comes daily to eat of his liver. To punish humanity, Zeus sends them a woman—Pandora ("All-Suffering")—out of whose box all the woes of mankind spring.

Hesiod's portrayal of Prometheus is avowedly negative, although the primitive, pre-Hesiodic roots of the myth may have not been so. After all, it is a myth of the self-determined and independent actions of our species, a myth of its "coming of age." Such transformative myths always seem to involve rebellion against authority. Zeus himself had not merely disobeyed his father (Kronos)—he killed him and created a new divine order through his rebellion. By taking a negative attitude toward Prometheus' actions, Hesiod shows himself to be one who longed for the "good old days" before humanity had individuated or differentiated itself from its divine ancestry. Belief in a divine ancestry is also a common Indo-European tradition.

The negative attitude toward Prometheus was not universal, however. This is evident from a later version of the myth presented by the Attic tragedian Aeschylus (525–456 BCE). Aeschylus portrays Prometheus as a tragic hero and savior of mankind.

Aeschylus apparently originally wrote a Promethean trilogy consisting of three tragedies, but only the first of these, *Prometheus Bound,* survives. In this version of the myth, Zeus simply refuses to give humanity the divine fire, while at the same time complaining that humanity is wretched and deficient. Zeus plans to destroy humanity and create a new race. Prometheus protests man's destruction, and tells Zeus that what humanity needs to fulfill its potential is the divine fire. Zeus refuses to relinquish it, so Prometheus steals the fire from Olympus and is punished for it in the same way as described by Hesiod. Where Hesiod had emphasized the fall of humanity from a "Golden Age" in which it was undifferentiated from the family of the gods, Aeschylus stresses a "myth of progress" in which the species begins to evolve faculties of consciousness after its contact with the gift of the divine fire.

Although the text of Aeschylus' final tragedy is lost, we know from accounts that in it Zeus releases and forgives Prometheus. He does this basically because the prediction of "the One with Foreknowledge" concerning the potential of humanity in possession of the gift of the divine flame turned out to be right—although the fact that Themis, the mother of Prometheus, has given him the secret of the future fall of Zeus also plays a role.

Historically, this reconciliation of Zeus and Prometheus may have been spurred by the fact that in the time of Aeschylus—at the end of the Hellenic Age—there was an annual festival in Athens dedicated to Prometheus. Although this began as a festival mainly patronized by craftsmen, by the time of Aeschylus it was also popular with intellectuals. The cult of this "god of evil" had become a widespread phenomenon.[3] It may well be that the story of the forgiveness of Zeus was created more to promote Zeus as a god of forgiveness and wisdom than to rehabilitate the reputation of Prometheus. Zeus is even said to have forgiven his father, Kronos, and made him king of Elysium.

THE MYTH OF PROMETHEUS AND THE LEFT-HAND PATH

In the history of the kind of thought we are calling left-hand path in the West, it is difficult to overestimate the importance of the myth of Prometheus. In it, we have perhaps the oldest Western representation of the myth of the Bringer of the Gift of Divine Light or Fire *portrayed as a villain* in the history of humanity. The fact that he is eventually revaluated as a hero is also a significant Western phenomenon we will encounter repeatedly. In this regard, it is curious to note that the American pioneer of modern Satanism, Anton LaVey, much admires the work of the sociologist Orrin Klapp and his book *Heroes, Villains and Fools,* which analyzes the ways in which modern figures are transformed from among those categories in the public perception.

In the Indo-European metalanguage of myth, the patterns of the right-hand-path and left-hand-path ideologies—although they openly vie with one another and compete for validation—are somehow reconciled and learn to co-exist. This is in marked contrast with the fanatical approaches of right-hand-path systems of Middle Eastern (or southern) origin in which their "Satans" are never forgiven or reevaluated.

The myth of Prometheus is one that shows the spiritual or intellectual tutelage of a figure who provides humanity with its divine aspect—its intellect—and who is therefore the true father of its spirit. Prometheus promotes the individuation of mankind from the gods and sets it as a species on its heroic quest to develop its own sense of divine power. As long as humanity was closely linked to the gods, it could not evolve in accordance with its own mysterious quest. Prometheus forced humanity out of its Olympian nest and made it so that the species would have to fly or destroy itself. However, he also saw to it that the species was provided with the *one thing* that was absolutely necessary to flight: the divine fire of the gods. The myth clearly places the unbound exercise of the intellect—the divine faculty of consciousness—in the cultural mainstream of an aristocracy of intellectual merit.

Promethean mythology has been tremendously influential over the course of European cultural history. Since the time of Aeschylus, the figure of the light-bearer was seen, at least to some extent, as a tragic hero. The myth itself probably did much to shape the lives of martyred philosophers such as Socrates and perhaps Jesus of Nazareth, or at least the literary representations of them. Beyond this it is interesting to note that Mary Shelley gave her Gothic novel *Frankenstein,* which is also a Romantic manifesto of sorts, the subtitle "the modern Prometheus," which implies a complex metaphor (and even the genesis of a neo-mythology) worthy of study in its own right.

THE GREEK MYSTERIES AND THE LEFT-HAND PATH

The whole subject of the various mystery systems—their origins, interrelationships, and especially the exact nature of what they taught and how they taught it—remains, as one might expect, *mysterious*.[4] The initiatory function of the concept "mystery" (Gk. *mysterion*) is powerful and pervasive in many systems of religion, magic, and initiation, but its full significance is yet to be discovered.[5] It also remains obscure just what aspects of the mysteries can be designated as right-hand path or left-hand path, but I hope to be able to shed some light on this question here.

As Nietzsche was to emphasize centuries later, there are essentially two philosophical approaches present in Hellenic (and, by inference, Indo-European) culture: the Dionysian and Apollonian. Of course, there tends to be the human, all-too-human urge to equate one with good and the other with evil, but this is always counterproductive. In fact, either philosophical approach to enlightenment can be used for the spiritual aims of the right-hand path or left-hand path—and a synthesis of both is perhaps the ideal.

The Dionysian approach is that of the *orgia* (orgy), by which human consciousness is united with that of the divine by means of a lowering of peripheral consciousness to a level where the divine—or "the other"—subsumes it. Dionysian spiritual technology makes use of rhythms (drumming, dancing, etc.), drugs (e.g., wine), and perhaps sex to lower the normal threshold of consciousness by overloading the physical senses, which allows a union with the divine to occur.

The Apollonian approach is that of *katharsis* (purification), by which the consciousness cleanses and distances itself (through intellectual discipline and physical austerities) of impurities to such extent that consciousness is eventually raised to the level of divinity. Apollonian spiritual technology makes use of reason and physical austerities (such as dietary restrictions, vegetarianism, and so forth) to raise the threshold of consciousness by suppressing the physical senses, which allows the psyche to gain union with the divine.

Orphism or the Orphic mysteries (so-called after the myth of Orpheus) make use of both technologies, though the Apollonian seems to predominate. Both the Orphic and Pythagorean mystery schools—which may share a common origin—practiced vegetarianism. Whatever the historical origins of this practice, it is mythically traced back to that first animal sacrifice held by Prometheus at Mekone. Social participation was virtually mandatory in such sacrifices. In Indo-European practice, such sacrifices were a matter of ritually slaughtering an animal and sharing the parts of the animal with the gods—the hard or inedible parts going to the god(s) and the edible portions being consumed by the faithful as an act of communion with the god(s). Animals were ceremonially slaughtered with a minimum of pain and fear to the animal, as the latter was thought to embody a divine essence. The Orphics and Pythagoreans saw the institution of the eating of flesh as a sign of the presence of the "Titanic" (i.e., base or subdivine) element in humanity and carnivorous practice as a perpetuation of that Titanic element. Their rejection of meat-eating also had the socio-religious effect of separating them from the mainstream of Hellenic society. They rejected the established practices of religion and society of their day.[6]

The overall process of initiation in these mysteries—which presupposed that humans were now a mixture of a Titanic nature and a divine nature—involved purifications (*katharmoi*), followed by initiation rites (*teletai*), and the constant leading of an "Orphic life." Through these methods one could eliminate the Titanic element and become *bakkhos:* "separated out" and in a "divine, Dionysiac condition."[7]

This theme of "separation" from the conventional social and natural order of the cosmos is one common to the left-hand path. Eliade concludes that the Orphic is "able to free himself from the 'demonic' element manifest in all profane existence (ignorance, flesh, diet, etc.)" and that the final goal is "the separation of the 'Orphic' from his fellow men and in the last analysis, the final separation of the soul from the cosmos."[8] This same theme will also be emphasized in the Setian philosophy of Michael Aquino in the Temple of Set (see chapter 10).

In the Orphic or mystery traditions of the Greeks there are also some original contributions to the mythology of the right-hand *versus* the left-hand *paths*. Apparently drawing on mystery traditions, Plato states in his *Republic* that the dead follow two paths to judgment: the just "to the right upwards through the sky . . . the unjust were condemned to the downward road to the left . . ."[9] This is no literary or heuristic invention by the philosopher, for there is archaeological evidence in the form of tomb complexes in southern Italy and Crete that have plaques with inscriptions indicating those who take the "right hand road" go "toward the sacred fields and grove of Persephone."[10]

In this Orphic eschatology, it seems that the good and just take the right-hand road and are not reincarnated. They drink of the spring waters of *Mnemosyne* (Memory) and "reign with the other heroes." But the wicked must drink from the spring called *Lethe* (Forgetfulness) and so lose all memory of the otherworld, before being reincarnated in this world as "punishment."[11]

In other words, the point of Orphic initiation was for the initiate to become a god—or godlike. In the underworld the Orphic initiate is told: "O fortunate, o happy one! Thou hast become a god, having been a man."[12]

The attitudes toward what a desirable postmortem existence consists of have shifted over time. In the early historical phase, it seems that the virtuous and good were rewarded with rebirth after rebirth in the world, which was seen as a highly desirable place to be. This amounted to an earthly immortality in ever-rejuvenated bodies. Eventually, these virtuous humans would be called by duty to the level of the immortal gods. By contrast, the wicked in this early stage of such beliefs were "punished" with a permanent death, or nonexistence. Later, there seems to have been a shift in the attitudes of some cultures (for example those of Greece and India) toward life in this world. In this later phase, it is believed that the wicked are *punished* with cycles of rebirth in this world and the virtuous are rewarded with a permanent existence among the gods and heroes.

PYTHAGORAS AND THE LEFT-HAND PATH

The doctrines of the Greek philosopher Pythagoras (ca. 582–507 BCE) are said to be drawn from a wide variety of sources—Egypt, Chaldea (Babylon), as well as Hyperborea (the extreme north).[13] However, virtually all of the major doctrines ascribed to Pythagoras can be derived from native Hellenic or Indo-European analogs. Although Pythagoras may have indeed traveled and learned in the far-flung centers of esoteric knowledge, it seems most likely that he synthesized what he learned according to a uniquely Hellenic methodology. Most of the basic Pythagorean assumptions about the origin and destiny of the human soul are derived from the Orphic mysteries. Pythagoras and his followers transformed the methodology of the process of initiation from an external or experiential one to an internal or *philosophical* one. Plato would further refine this Hellenic philosophical tradition.

Pythagoras made philosophy into a "whole science," a holistic understanding of existence. He postulated that number is the "root" or principle (Gk. *archê*) of all things. But in his philosophy, numbers were more *qualities* than quantities,[14] and therefore his apparently quantitative science was understood as a qualitative one. Mathematics revealed a hidden reality lying beyond the veil of appearances. To Pythagoras, understanding the relationships and harmonies among numbers is tantamount to understanding the harmonies among things themselves.

The left-hand-path characteristics of Pythagoreanism are more implicit than explicit. Pythagoras was primarily interested in discovering the bases of universal harmonies, the ways all things fit together so beautifully, and the "music of the spheres."

PLATO AND THE LEFT-HAND PATH

Although even Plato himself would never have claimed to have invented his system of philosophy, as he understood all true knowledge to be a matter of "recollection" (Gk. *anamnesis*) of the soul's inherent contents, he can be called the single greatest codifier and synthesizer of idealistic philosophy. Plato drew openly from a wide variety of philosophical sources, especially the Hellenic mysteries and Pythagoreanism, but he brought to those sources a clarity of objective purpose hitherto unseen.

The idealism of Plato should not be seen as the *beginning* of philosophy. It is a product of a millennia-long process of traditional speculation and intellectual inquiry begun at the dawn of Indo-European culture. Among all the languages of the world, only the Indo-European and its derivatives has a true verb meaning "to be" in the sense of "*to exist.*" There were originally at least two Indo-European verbs to describe "being": one of these meant "to be" in the sense of equivalence, such as in a descriptive statement like "the chair is red," and one meant "to be" in the sense of existence, such as in the famous line "To be or not to be, *that* is the question." In the ancient Indo-European tongue these two verbs were **bheu-* (to be equivalent) and **wes-* (to exist).* This distinction came down to us in Old English in the verbs *beon* and *wesan,* respectively. With the demise of the innate Indo-European system of thought—precipitated by the influx of Middle Eastern thought-forms promoted by the church—the two verbs collapsed together into one verbal paradigm. This linguistic process is called suppletion, and it is the reason why the verb "to be" in modern English is so highly irregular: it is derived from a mixture of different verbal stems.

What does all this have to do with Plato or the left-hand path? This is not hard to realize: Plato's philosophy is an attempt to define being (in the sense of existing) and develop a system of training so that others may *know what exists*—what is real—about themselves and the cosmos.

Although *all* of Plato's works are essentially focused on the development of the soul, many have practical applications as well. As viewed from the modern perspective, the chief practical benefit of Plato's philosophy would be *political,* not religious, since the philosopher-kings produced by the system would characteristically first exercise their knowledge in practical, socio-political ways. In this aspect of

*The asterisks preceding these verbal roots are included to show that they are reconstructed forms that have been deduced according to the science of comparative historical linguistics.

his philosophy, Plato harkens back to some very basic Indo-European assumptions and structures. As in the ancient roots of his culture, the terrestrial socio-political arrangements were seen as reflections of such structures existing in the world of the gods. In the *Republic,* Plato lays out his wish to (re-)institute a political structure based on Indo-European principles:

Function	Platonic Terminology
Rulers/Priests	Guardians (Philosopher-Kings)
Warriors	Auxiliaries
Craftsmen/Farmers	Artisans/Tradesmen

Figure 3.1. Platonic System of Social Functions

But in Plato's case it was not a wish merely to return to archaic models for their own sake, but rather to realize and newly *understand,* on a philosophical basis, the principles and forms on which these structures stood. As T. S. Eliot expressed it in part V of his poem "Little Gidding":

We shall not cease from exploration
And the end of all our exploring
Will be to arrive where we started
And know the place for the first time.[15]

The Academy, Plato's school near Athens, was to be a place where elite students could be trained as far as possible to hold right beliefs, think rationally, and ultimately to be able to intuit *rationally* and thus *understand* the very forms (Gk. *eide*) or principles that are the ultimate source of all things or phenomena in this world. To do this Plato devised a system of education based on a specific understanding of the soul (psychology) and theory of *how* that soul (or souls) can know its objects of knowledge. In many ways, Plato's system is a philosophical refinement (and in some cases a simplification) of the traditional psychologies of the Indo-European peoples.[16] Figure 3.2 shows

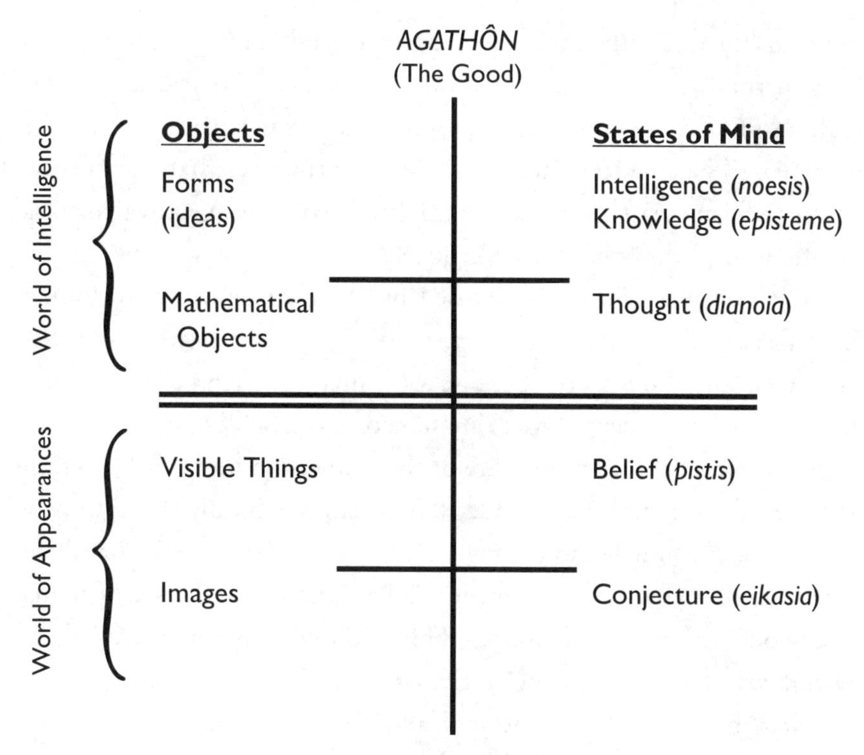

Figure 3.2. The Platonic Scale of Knowledge

the Platonic scale of knowledge. In this scheme, the student, or initiate, can be moved out of the realm of totally subjective *conjectures*—the objects of which are not real things but only shadows—into the realm of right *beliefs* based on established traditions and "common sense." This is the highest level of knowledge possible for the mass of humanity and it is itself a great achievement. Beyond this, however, is a rational form of thought (*dianoia*) or logical thought based on mathematics. It is here that the influence of the Pythagorean school on the Platonic synthesis is most profound. Both the quantitative and qualitative aspects of number could be approached here. But this "dianetic" thinking is not the apex of knowledge. Perhaps the modern establishment "academics" (an unfortunate etymological development, which Plato would have certainly not approved of!) consider the quantification of knowledge most desirable—to "know" something becomes tantamount to "get the numbers on it." This is *an* aspect of *dianoia,* but it is only a means to a greater end. This greater end has been virtually forgotten today in our "academies." Logical training is really a preparation for *noesis* (perception, cognition), in which the initiate will be able to understand the *real* principles that exist in the realm of forms. At this point the initiate becomes the equivalent of a guardian or philosopher-king (or queen!).

The system of Plato, as codified by the Neoplatonists (including Kabbalists, Sufis, etc.), underlies most current Western systems of initiation and occult training, but because the source has often been intentionally obscured, the essential roots are sometimes difficult to discover. One might still inquire into the nature of the connection between Platonism and the left-hand path as we understand it philosophically. The ultimate root of this teaching lies in the mysteries. The simple answer is that Plato taught a rationally based system for the attainment of a state of living "godhood": the philosopher-king. This is the virtual equivalent of the jivanmukti state of attainment in the system of Indian philosophy.

Plato has arrived at a rational and *noetic* method of attainment of godhood formerly attained in the mysteries by means of initiatory experiences and dramatic ordeals as well as purifications and physical austerities. The idealistic philosophy and noetic methods of Platonism would, in the history of Western systems of initiation, be used as the underlying structure augmented and complemented by every sort of initiatory, philosophical, and magical technology in the ancient world. This synthesis would emerge in Neoplatonism (from the second century CE onward) from which it would spread into many varied speculative initiatory schools, such as Kabbalism,[17] Sufism,[18] as well as Christian mysticism.[19]

Most, if not all, of these schools developed Platonic idealism in the direction of right-hand-path mysticism. They aim not for the elevation of the individual intellect to the equivalence of divinity, or the Good (agathôn), but rather for the reabsorption or total regimentation of the individual in the substance of the One.

The pure Platonic aims have perhaps been revived—and placed in the context of a magical technology—most eloquently by Michael

Aquino of the Temple of Set (see chapter 10), who openly avows his initiatory debt to pure Platonism.

THE EPICUREAN AND STOIC SCHOOLS

Two philosophical streams of thought with their origins in ancient Greece of the fourth century BCE, but which are expressions of universal categories and ones that continue to influence life today, are Stoicism and Epicureanism.

Epicureus (341–270 BCE) founded a school of thought largely based on the atomic physics of Democritos of a century earlier. Greek atomism declared that *everything*—including that which is called soul or spirit—is made up of *atoms:* particles so small they can be divided no further. The Epicurean holds that upon death the human soul, as well as the body, simply dissipates back into undifferentiated nature. Everything is material. However, the more rarified substance of the soul or intellect can help lead a person to the most perfect and happy state of being known as *ataraxia:* "unperturbableness" or "serenity." As the senses are the only access points through which pleasure or pain enter the mind or soul, in order to attain the state of ataraxia an Epicurean must control the quality of sensual experience. He or she avoids pain and maximizes pleasure. The *outer* life must be harmonized with the ideal quality of experience.[20]

The Stoic aims for ataraxia as well, but does so in a very different way.

Stoicism is named for a school of philosophers who used to meet in the fourth century BCE at the *stoa* (portico) of the market at Athens. The Stoic claims a separate, nonnatural existence for the soul. The soul or psyche may then control the quality and/or quantity of sensual stimulus and thus attain ataraxia not by controlling the outer stimuli but rather by how the mind responds to such stimuli. The Stoic conditions his or her *inner* life to harmonize with an ideal state of being. Outer events become—or can be made to become—inconsequential. The Stoics hold that the soul existed before the body and that it will continue to exist after the body dies in a future state of "rewards and punishments." In this and other respects, Stoicism was very much in harmony with other schools of the mystery traditions as well as Platonic philosophies. The Stoic typically needs a transpersonal ideal or principle to which loyalty and duty can be devoted in order for the philosophy to work.

Both of these philosophies were popular in Hellenistic Greece as well as in Republican and Imperial Rome. Stoicism virtually became the "official philosophy" of Rome in the days of the Empire. The republican Cicero (106–43 BCE) and the Emperor Marcus Aurelius (121–180 CE) are two of its most well-known exponents.[21]

From our perspective, both of these ancient schools supply critical ideas for understanding the philosophy of the left-hand path. The Epicureans provide a materialistic, carnal cosmology essential to the ideology of the "immanent branch" of the Left-hand Path, while Stoicism further develops Platonic and Neo-Platonic idealism, even providing for the divinizing of the dead.

THE LEFT-HAND PATH IN THE NORTH

The Germanic Left-Hand Path

While important roots of the left-hand path in the West were being developed in the Mediterranean region on a philosophical and anti-establishment basis, in the northern climes the roots of the left-hand path are found in the established cultural soil. Whereas the Indo-European god of law and order—Zeus-Jupiter—ruled in the South, in the North the god of magic and death—Odin/Woden—had come to hold sway. This same original Indo-European divinity is called Lugh (pronounced "loo") among the Irish and Lleu (pronounced "hligh") among the Welsh. Lugh/Lleu literally means "light"—and the common Welsh name Llewellyn means "light-bringer" (cf. Roman "Lucifer")!

The figure of Odin and his myths hold our attention when we seek to find the dark side of the northern world. The name Odin means "the master of inspiration."[22] The Old Norse form is Óðinn. The key to the name can be found in the Old Norse word *óðr,* which means "poetic inspiration" and is derived from the earlier Proto-Germanic root *wōð-,* meaning "rage" and "inspiration." The Old Norse name Óðinn is identical to Old English Woden. (It is a regular linguistic rule in Old Norse to drop the initial /w-/ before certain vowels.) This is a decidedly "psychic" god in the sense that his name and function refer to essentially *soul*-related or psychological powers and faculties. He is often depicted as a dark god of intrigue and mysterious motivations.

Odin's essential importance in the shaping of the world and humanity is clear in Norse mythology. Together with his two brothers (actually hypostases of himself), Vili (Will) and Ve (Sacred One), Odin performs the first sacrifice by killing their ancestral father, the giant Ymir. From the parts of his body, they shape the material cosmos. To gain universal wisdom, Odin gives (sacrifices) "himself to himself" that he might take up the runes: symbols of articulated universal knowledge.[23] These runes he shares with certain humans. Odin further pledges one of his eyes, which is then sunk into Mimir's Well (the Well of Memory), so that he may gain the special sight that drinking from the well gives.[24] He (along with his two other aspects) endows humankind with threefold spiritual qualities shared with the gods.[25] In sharing divine consciousness and the runes of wisdom with humankind, Odin is very much like the figure of Prometheus in Hellenic mythology. The major difference is that in doing so he is not transgressing against authoritarian rule of law.

Odin, in the guise of Rig ("Ruler") also sires the three classes of human beings—farmers, warriors, and rulers—by three different human women.[26] Thus, he is responsible for not only the psychological structure of humanity but for its social structure as well—both of which are reflections of the divine order. For these reasons he is called the Alfaðir or Alföðr (All-Father). Odin, in his guise as Bölverkr (Worker of Evil), obtains for the gods and humans the poetic mead of inspiration through an act of oath-breaking deceit.

Even in ancient, pre-Christian times, Odin had a somewhat "sinister" or dangerous reputation. This is due to a whole complex of issues, but the most essential principle underlying this reputation appears to be that he is immersed in things—universal order, mysteries, inspiration, death—that humans rarely understand and hence often fear and dread. Nevertheless, Odin is acknowledged as the highest of the gods throughout the Germanic world, from Anglo-Saxon England to Germany and from Iceland to Sweden. Further adding to his sinister reputation is the fact that he committed the two greatest ethical crimes in pursuing his quest for power and knowledge: to create the world order, he killed a kinsman (a crime Odin shares with the Greco-Roman Zeus-Jupiter); and to rewin the poetic mead, he breaks an oath. These and other acts render Odin unreliable to the mass of humanity.

In the ancient Germanic tradition, Odin is *both* the lord of light and the prince of darkness. He is the god of the elite nobles, and thus the god of royalty and rulership. He is the father of magic and the *power* to create and destroy. He is the god of poetry: the god of the art of effective linguistic formulations and codifications of *knowledge*. Both his magical power and his "gnostic" formulas are embodied in the runes ("mysteries"). Finally, he is the lord of the dead, and rules over the phenomenon of death, thus showing his mastery over all transformational processes. It might also be noted that the Celtic Lugh/Lleu shares almost all of these essential characteristics with his Germanic counterpart.[27]

The story of the conversion of the Germanic tribes to Christianity is pertinent to understanding subsequent left-hand-path developments in the Germanic world and among the descendants of those tribes.

The earliest converts to Christianity among the Germanic peoples were some Gothic tribes who were part of the Arian school of theology. Arianism is named after a fourth-century priest, Arius of Alexandria, who held that the Son was created by the Father and hence was not coeternal with the Father. It is most likely, however, that the Goths developed their own form of uniquely Germanic Christianity, for all Germanic tribes that converted to the new faith did so with this "Gothic Church." The Goths kept their religion and their people separate from the Roman Church and the citizens of Rome. This type of national self-determination is, however, an anathema to the universalistic and imperialistic Roman (Catholic) mind. The Gothic form of Christianity is marked by a willingness to make biblical texts available in the common language (the Gothic bishop Ulfilas translated the Bible around 350 CE), involvement of the people in the liturgy (the Roman Christians disdained the Gothic practice of rewriting traditional folk songs with religious lyrics), and a general belief that humans are born free of original sin, that they win salvation by their own virtuous efforts, and that Jesus was a man who had attained to a godlike status, thus showing the way for others to follow. When these doctrines are compared to the orthodox Roman system outlined below, the differences are obvious. In a free world—as the Germanic peoples had been used to—these cultural/religious differences would have been a normal and expected state of affairs, but the divine plan adhered to by the Roman Catholic (= universal) Church called for "one God, one Church, one Pope!"

The historical break came for universalism when the Frankish ("French") king Chlodwig or Clovis (Ludwig/Louis) converted to Roman Christianity in 496 CE. He did so in order to get foreign military aid from Rome in his attempt to conquer southern France, then dominated by the Arian Visigoths. From that time onward, the Frankish king was the chief military agent for the Pope. Eventually, the Goths were eradicated and apparently their faith along with them, although some secret assemblies still claim to carry on their traditions. I have chronicled the esoteric aspects of the older Gothic tradition in my book *The Mysteries of the Goths* (2007).

The story of the conversion of Germany is generally a bloody one. Most of the conversions were carried out upon threat of death after military conquest by Frankish kings working as agents for the Roman Pope.

Around 597 CE, an early Roman mission was sent to England, which at the time was made up of a confederation of seven independent kingdoms. The king of Kent, Æthelbert, under the influence of his wife, converted to Roman Christianity and began a long program of military and ideological warfare (although oftentimes conducted half-heartedly) against the other kingdoms. Finally, by the middle of the eighth century, England was at least nominally Christian.

In Scandinavia, we find a variety of scenarios for the conversion to Christianity. Denmark was converted in an effort by monarchal forces to consolidate their total control of the land. Norway, which had been a loose confederation of free landholders, was the object of attempts to conquer the country by men such as Olaf Tryggvason, who then imposed monarchal control over the whole land. It was during these attempts that freemen left the region and settled on the previously uninhabited island called Iceland. Iceland peacefully converted to Christianity in the year 1000 by a vote of its parliament. The last region to be conquered by Christian kings was Uppland, in Sweden, where the last great heathen temple of Uppsala was burned in the year 1100.

The pre-Christian traditions nevertheless continued long after official conversions had taken place. For hundreds of years there existed in Europe the same type of religious creolism or syncretism one now finds in the Caribbean basin. For the history of left-hand-path ideas, the all-important figure of Odin underwent a radical, yet predictable, splitting of image. He was—like all the other gods—portrayed as the epitome of evil. In parts of Germany, the speaking of his name was forbidden. It is for this reason that the modern German name for the day of the week usually called after him was renamed *Mittwoch,* "Mid-Week," while Thor (German Donar) keeps his weekday name, *Donnerstag.* The original name survives in some German dialects as *Wodenestag* or *Godensdach.*[28] However, even after Christian conversion he still retained his patronage over the ruling elite. All the Anglo-Saxon kings continued to claim descent from Woden,[29] and in the English language he retains his weekday name, Wednesday (Woden's day).

In the spiritual technology or magic of the ancient Germanic peoples, the Odinic magician would, by using runic formulas, actually transform himself into a godlike being analogous to the general characteristics of the god Odin. In this transformed state he would then work his will directly upon the fabric of the world—again usually by using the sacred runes first won by his patron god, Odin. In the most ancient period these magicians called themselves Erulians. This was a tribal designation that seems to have become synonymous with those prestigious runemasters who had, through their skills, "risen up" into a godlike state.[30]

The model of behavior provided by Odin—a brooding and relentless seeker of knowledge and power—can be seen as an archetypal foreshadowing of the early modern myth of Dr. Johann Faustus, who broke all barriers in his search for these qualities.

What is essential to realize about the left-hand-path aspects of ancient Odinism is that it provided a traditional, established method of self-transformation along a divine model without an intended melding with that god. Ancient Odinism, which derived from the same ultimate religious stream of thought that we find in eastern Indo-European forms of the left-hand path, was a path of making the self godlike according to the mythic and heroic patterns exalted in the Germanic national traditions. It is into this general religious matrix that Christian ideas were inserted, and therefore left-hand-path ideas rising up in the cultural context should not be unexpected. Note also that the form of Christianity first accepted by the Goths was one not lacking itself in left-hand-path qualities!

THE SLAVIC LEFT-HAND PATH

The Slavic mind has always been one more "at home" with the devil than perhaps any other European culture. This may stem from the fact that even into recent times the Slavs have conservatively maintained a cult of household spirits whose nature was quite ambiguous in terms of "good" and "evil."

In his introduction to Ouspensky's *Talks with a Devil,* J. G. Bennett remarks:

> The devils are not hostile to man except insofar as man is a friend of God. It is they who have been responsible for every kind of technical

> progress: from them mankind learned the arts of iron working, brewing and distilling; the devil himself discovered fire, built the first mill, and constructed the first wagon. The art of reading and writing was one of his gifts to mankind. All these were bestowed to make man independent of God and so break the link whereby man was able to help God in governing the world.[31]

Two kinds of devils can be identified in Slavic lore: one is called Lukhavi, which means "crafty one," and the other is Chort, which simply means "the black one."[32] The "crafty" devil seems the more archaic and most truly Slavic. The appellation *Chort,* on the other hand, seems clearly to be an influence from the dualistic cults, which became extremely popular in Slavic regions in the Middle Ages and after.

In Russian lore, the devil is often seen as a personification of the material world. This is a point of view informed by both the ancient Slavic idea of the Lukhavi (providing skills and knowledge on how to manage the material universe) and by the idea of Chort (embodying the material world in opposition to the spiritual world).

This later dualistic aspect is clarified by M. Dragomanov, who shows how Satanail, a medieval Slavic form of the name of Satan, plays a central role in the creation of the world and man. God tells Satanail to dive into the primeval sea to retrieve earth and flint. Satanail gives God the material, which God keeps in his right hand and uses to create dry land on the sea. Out of his left hand he gives flint to Satanail, who creates his angels by "[hewing] a numberless raging rout of carnal gods."[33] Some traditions hold that Satanail created the visible world, god the invisible, while others hold that Satanail creates man's body and God gives the soul. These ideas are clearly either influenced by Bogomil teachings (see pages 135–37) or related to them in some way.

Indeed, a Bulgarian tradition holds that the devil—called Zerzevul—created a counter-paradise to oppose the one created by God. In triumph, Zerzevul says to his band of devils:

> Ho, my band, have you seen that we too can make a paradise like what God can make? Come, go in, eat, drink, of everything that is inside; I don't forbid you anything the way the Lord forbade something to the men he put inside to live with his wife; I give you freedom to do whatever you want to do. Say this to the people: "Whatever any one wants to do let him command. In my paradise there is food, drink, pleasure-seeking, as much as they ask of me."[34]

It might be noted that among twentieth-century writers in the Russian cultural field, Ouspensky saw the devil as an obsession with the material world, while Gurdjieff saw him as an extraterrestrial being.

The Slavic devil is an important, if usually obscure, prototype for the archetype of the materialistic libertinism of late-nineteenth-century and twentieth-century Satanism, as expressed, for example, by Anton LaVey (see chapter 9).

Although there are significant differences between the root of pre-Christian western Indo-European ideology in Europe and the root of that same tree among the eastern Indo-Europeans, there are profound similarities as well. In addition, through the nomadic northern Iranian tribes, such as the Scythians and Sarmatians, Eastern ideas probably influenced the Hellenic, Slavic, and Germanic worlds. This contact was maintained from as early as 700 BCE to as late as the sixth century CE. Indo-Iranian influence also streamed into the West—into the European as well as Middle Eastern regions for several centuries of the Hellenistic period—from about 300 BCE to 200 CE.

The similarities between the original Western and Eastern roots of the Indo-European worlds make it clear that had the Western root continued its evolution along its own lines of development, there would indeed be an establishment oriented left-hand-path tradition in the West today. Or if it were not a part of the establishment itself, it would certainly be tolerated—and perhaps even encouraged—by the mainstream culture.

However, the historical development of the Western world reflects a split heritage. The ideologies of the Middle East—or the true *southern* tradition—invaded the north in the form of Christianity and eventually forged an uncomfortable symbiosis with the original European culture. Virtually all of the manifestations of "heretical," "deviant," or "diabolical" religious behavior in Europe from the time of the arrival of Christianity to the present day can be traced to native impulses present in the manifold pre-Christian culture of Europe.

It almost goes without saying that in order to understand fully the left-hand path as it developed in the West, one must grasp the essence of the Middle Eastern or southern tradition—both in its right-hand-path and left-hand-path manifestations. It is in these cultures that the popular modern attitudes and imageries of the left-hand path, often embodied in the word "Satanism," developed and were spread.

THE LEFT-HAND PATH AMONG THE SEMITES

For a complete understanding of the history of what would be thought of as "Satanism" in Western Europe, no culture of antiquity is more important—with the possible exception of the Iranian/Zoroastrian—than that of the Semites in general and the Hebrews specifically. A complete survey of this field is not possible here,[35] and furthermore such an investigation would only show that from the *philosophical* perspective the Hebrew tradition has very little to offer of an original character. Its chief importance is historical. The Hebrews forged a synthesis of several theological and mythic streams—from Mesopotamia, Egypt, Canaan, and Iran—along with their own primitive Semitic religion.[36] But since the Hebraic religion, as we have records of it, is relatively monolithic, it gives us little evidence of the development or existence of anything autochthonous that is akin to the left-hand path. However, the synthetic Hebraic and later Judaic (after 586 BCE) religion bequeathed a definite morphology and terminology for a whole "symbology of evil" to the later Christian and Islamic worlds, and also to the Gnostics who made widespread use of Judaic mythology to illustrate their (often left-hand-path) ideas.

It will be seen that the Semitic view of the world, although not originally strictly dualistic, contained a hyperintensive feeling for the notions of sin and redemption, and of defilement and purification. This made for a kind of de facto dualism that proved to be even more durable than that of Zoroaster, although the Semitic religion was certainly influenced by the mythology and theology of Iranian Mazdaism at a secondary level.

In order to be able to understand fully the Semitic mindset, we must start historically with a non-Semitic people, the Sumerians. The already heterogeneous Sumerians had their origins either in the north or east of Mesopotamia (present-day Iraq)[37] and by 4500 BCE they had established themselves in the region around the mouths of the Tigris and Euphrates rivers. Their magnificent civilization would last in its authentic Sumerian form until around 1750 BCE, but it would continue in a "Semiticized" form until after the conquest of Babylon by Cyrus II of Persia in 539 BCE. The springtime of Sumerian civilization was between 3200 and 2360 BCE. It would be an oversimplification to try to lump the Sumerians together with their successor Semitic systems.[38] The Sumerians appear to have been constantly fearful of sudden and catastrophic upheavals, whether natural or socioeconomic in origin. This has been contrasted with the Egyptian idea of ordered processes within secure surroundings, and has been traced to the contrast in the agricultural cycles of their respective river systems: the Nile region, which is dependent on the regular rising of the waters to flood the river valley, and the Mesopotamian region, which is dependent on rain and storms to bring waters to the valleys of the Tigres and Euphrates. Be all that as it may, the original Sumerians seemed to have no real concept of immanent divinity throughout the cosmos. Instead, everything is ruled by the divine force of *me* (divine order).

"Evil" as such was understood as a disruption of the divine order in the forms of death and disease. The introduction of death is not the responsibility of an evil figure, but rather of the Earth-God himself, En-ki, who, instead of "determining the destiny" of certain herbs, *eats* them. In doing so, En-ki committed a "cosmic crime," for he "did not behave in accordance with the principle that he incarnated."[39]

In the Sumerian religion, the gods were forms or principles that worked together in the divine order. Man's role was to "serve the gods," or in other words, to serve the divine order. It is, however, also recognized that it is the gods themselves—not man—who introduce the original disruptions in the divine order. Thus, when Gilgamesh (who is perhaps the oldest epic hero in the history of literature) struggles against death to attempt to gain immortality, he is not seen by the Sumerians as one who strives against the gods, and who is thus "evil," but rather as one who is attempting to restore the original divine order of things. Gilgamesh is seen essentially as a *divine hero*, not as an evil transgressor. When looking at the originally Sumerian material in Mesopotamian religion, one is struck by an ambivalence reminiscent of the Hindu tradition.[40]

The Sumerian culture underwent a curious metamorphosis. From as early as 2800 BCE, Semitic peoples (later identified with the Akkadians) began to infiltrate Sumer from the north and west and began to "Semiticize" the culture, the language, and the religion from the lower echelons of the society.[41] From 2350 to 2150 BCE, Akkadian kings ruled in Mesopotamia, a rulership destroyed by invasions of the Gutians from Iran who dominated Akkadia until the Sumerians underwent a renaissance and restored themselves to power in 2050 BCE. But by 1950 BCE, another Semitic group, the Assyrians, gained control. Semitic culture and language would dominate Mesopotamia until the Persian conquest in 539 BCE.

To a great extent, the Mesopotamian Semites—the Akkadians, Assyrians, and Babylonians—were "Sumerianized" in their religious and cultural forms. They adopted Sumerian writing (cuneiform), and outer cultic forms and mythology. The old Sumerian myths were virtually Semiticized. But the Semites were an essentially different people who brought their own connotations to these Sumerian forms.

The optimistic Sumerian anthropogenesis—in which man is created by the gods—is reinterpreted so that humanity is created from the blood of an evil entity: Kingu. Thus, in the Semitic version, man is "condemned by his own origin."[42] Here we have a basic idea very close to "original sin." This rather pessimistic anthropogenesis then virtually necessitates a new cult form of personal prayers and penitential psalms. Here we hear the penitent praying for the forgiveness of sins and the removal of transgressions.[43] But it would also be a mistake to see the Mesopotamian Semites as mere forerunners to the Hebraic attitudes. The Babylonian view of human existence was far more optimistic than that of the Hebrews.

The so-called Canaanites were another important Near Eastern Semitic people. They occupied the region of the coast of the eastern Mediterranean Sea from as early as 3000 BCE. Really there were a series of apparently Semitic city-based civilizations in this region, each of which was in turn conquered by seminomadic "barbarians." The Hebrews, or Israelites, who invaded the territory around 1250 BCE, were just another ethnic group in this series. We know most about this civilization, which is identified in the Old Testament as Canaan, from texts found at Ras Shamra (Ugarit) on the Syrian coast. From this material it seems that the Canaanites had an ambivalent attitude toward what might be termed "evil." Ultimately, they saw the world locked in a struggle between the forces of life (represented by Ba'al and his sister Anath) and death (represented by Mot). There seems to be a recognition of this fact and an acceptance of its reality.[44]

From this brief survey of some non-Hebraic religious attitudes, it is clear that the polytheistic systems of Semitic religion were not particularly obsessed with the evil nature of the world or of humanity. However, the Mesopotamian Semitic evidence does show an early predisposition toward a notion of "original sin." At the same time, it is very difficult to talk in terms of a left-hand-path/right-hand-path dichotomy in early Sumerian or Semitic forms. This is probably due to the fact that we do not possess enough knowledge about these people's philosophical understandings of the relevant issues. Gilgamesh stands out as a heroic individuated being, possessed of self-consciousness, who desires immortality. This would qualify him at least in part as a paradigmatic figure on the left-hand path. It is most likely that the manifold and ambivalent traditions of early Mesopotamian and Near Eastern religion, like the old Indo-European or Egyptian traditions, contain the seeds of what will develop into a right-hand-path/left-hand-path dichotomy. In the view of the orthodox philosophies of Judaism, Christianity, and Islam, the religious systems of Canaan and Babylon (as well as that of Egypt) were fundamentally "wicked" (that is to say, while they may not have been essentially left-hand path, they were at least open to the values of the left-hand path, among others). This allowance for such multifaceted religious freedoms would in and of itself be theological grounds for condemnation from an orthodox monotheistic perspective. But no such dichotomy was really possible until after the Hebraic synthesis.

THE ORTHODOX HEBREW SYNTHESIS OF THE RIGHT-HAND PATH

The Hebrew or Israelite synthesis of their own primitive nomadic Semitic beliefs together with elements from the traditions of the Egyptians and Canaanites, as well as the Babylonians and Iranians, took place over a long period of time between about 1750 and 500 BCE. Hebraic nomads had become somewhat settled in the region around Hebron in the earliest phase, while somewhat later the Israelites (or more accurately the Arameans) settled down in the region of Shechem. These tribes lived on the fringes of the urbanized and apparently indigenous Canaanite society. The Arameans probably began to assimilate certain features of the Canaanite religion during the time between 1750 and 1250 BCE. Into this region came a third wave of Hebraic settlers after about 1250 BCE. These were probably a mixture of Hebrew tribes that had been settled in Egypt for several centuries and perhaps some Egyptian and other non-Hebraic peoples who had been outwardly Hebraicized during the exodus from Egypt under the leadership of a (former) Egyptian priest whom tradition names Moses. An important synthesis of ancient Hebraic, Canaanite, and Egyptian philosophies took place in this cultural context during the centuries between 1200 and 600 BCE. The

Israelite kingdom was utterly conquered by the Babylonians in 587, and from that time until 538 the Israelites lived in exile within Babylonia. This is the so-called Babylonian Captivity. There they further assimilated Babylonian—but especially also Iranian lore—which is the most important catalytic element in the development of a Hebraic or Judaic "philosophy of evil."

When looking at the Hebrew-Judaic material (i.e., the canonical and apocryphal biblical literature of that tradition), it must be remembered that these myths do not constitute a continuous and coherent narrative. They are made up of fragments of myths and legends often pieced together with little or no effort being made in the text to make the narrative consistent. The first example of this occurs in Genesis 1:2–4, where one complete and coherent version of the creation myth is offered and then later another quite different yet equally complete and coherent version is given (Genesis 2:4–25). The former is certainly an older version, the other being added later (probably after the Babylonian Captivity). This is typical of Hebraic mythology, but is an aspect of it that is usually obscured by popular assumptions of a consistent and unified "revealed" text, rather than a product of centuries of reediting by historically and cross-culturally influenced writers.[45]

The only original and unique ideas the ancient Hebrews might have had on the subject of this aspect of "evil" are submerged under layers of assimilations from other cultures. It seems likely that the Hebraic immigrants from Egypt brought with them a theological and ritual structure that had been heavily influenced by Egyptian thinking. It has been speculated that Moses was influenced by the ideas of the monotheistic reforms of the pharaoh Akhnaten, and it is further possible that the Hebraic ideas of who or what might oppose the divine plan was influenced by the shape of the established cult of Set during the nineteenth dynasty (1300–1200 BCE). The "exodus" of the Semitic tribes from Egypt most likely occurred sometime toward the end of this dynasty. The monotheistic reform of Hebrew religion undertaken by Moses naturally led to a model of belief in which the "One God," called "Yahweh" by Moses, *could* be opposed in his plans by another force in the cosmos. Before these reforms, Hebraic polytheism would have accounted for "evil" (i.e., death and disease) as a part of a whole patchwork of cosmic reality, just as the Canaanites had. In Mosaic monotheism (perhaps coupled with knowledge of the principle represented by Set) the *potential* groundwork was thus laid for this cosmic opposition. In reality, however, awareness of the full implications of this potential took centuries to develop.

As the third wave of Hebraic migrations came into the Levant, archaeological evidence strongly indicates that—far from destroying everyone and everything in the "Promised Land," to make it pure for "God's Chosen" (Joshua 1–18)—the Canaanite "Land of Milk and Honey" almost completely seduced the Hebrews, as did the Moabite god, Ba'al-Peor (Numbers 25). The Hebraic religion from the time of the exodus to the Babylonian Captivity indicates a continuous assimilation of Canaanite myths and cult forms, along with periodic opposition to this ongoing tendency by the so-called prophets.

The Canaanite influence on the Hebraic concepts of "evil" comes in one form through the idea of a cosmic *conflict* between the forces of life (Ba'al) and death (Mot). The Hebrew word for death is *mot*. The notion of a cosmic rebellion on the part of younger gods to overthrow older gods is also very strong in Canaanite mythology,[46] where we see that Ba'al is not only locked in combat with Death (Mot), but he is also trying to overthrow the older god, El. El is a "Name of God" also taken over into Hebrew (see *El Shaddai*), and in the plural form *Elohim*. The plural can be used in Hebrew to indicate the magnitude of something without necessarily implying that there is actually more than one in quantity.

As far as the Babylonian influence is concerned, it probably came more indirectly through the agency of Canaanite theology than directly from the Babylonian into the Hebrew. This was true until the time of the Babylonian Captivity, at which time the Hebraic, now Judaic, theology was opened to two great direct influences: Babylonian learning, and Iranian cosmology and doctrine.

During the period of the Babylonian Captivity, a learned priestly tradition developed within Judaism. The attitude of this priestly tradition toward "evil" was twofold. First it is the result of the *lust* of the "Sons of God" (Heb. *bene elohim*) for the daughters of men (Genesis 5:1–7). The resulting mixture of divine and human natures ends in the revelation of forbidden divine *knowledge* to humanity by the "Sons of God." In the "Enochian" literature there are lists of the (demonic) angels and the categories of "forbidden knowledge" they reveal to mankind (I Enoch 8). As Neil Forsyth observes: "Thus the myth links the origin of culture and the origins of evil in the world. . . . Lust causes the transgression of the boundary between divine and human; this results in humans learning forbidden mysteries, and this in turn leads to the corruption of the earth."[47] This myth of the origin of forbidden knowledge, which results in the influx of "evil," is a parallel alternative (or allomorph) of the better-known Edenic myth.

Evil is therefore associated both with *knowledge* and *carnal existence:* one is an evil of the *psyche,* the other an evil of the *flesh.* These two poles will prove to be ongoing features of schools of the left-hand path in the Western world.

Although both the Hebrew myth of the Garden of Eden and the whole cosmology found in Genesis 1–2 are ultimately of Semito-Sumerian origin, the paradigmatic correspondences with Iranian mythology seem too close to ignore totally.[48] It is most likely that the basic *structures* of the Edenic myth were taken into Judaic lore from the body of Canaanite-Babylonian traditions and that only later were some of the interpretations of the myths "enlightened" by more abstract Iranian thought, which, along with Hellenic ideas, would form the basis of the secret traditions in Judaism (Kabbalah, etc.). These aspects will be discussed in more detail in chapter 4 in the context of *gnosis.* In any event, we again have an alternate way in which "evil," in the form of *divine knowledge,* is introduced to humanity. This myth can be said to be a part of the lore of the left-hand path only in the traditions of non-Zoroastrian Iranian systems (such as Mithraism) or in some of the myriad of Gnostic sects (e.g., the Ophites).

THE HAMITIC LEFT-HAND PATH

The Cult of Set

Set is an Egyptian god-form that became a model of the paragon of evil in the latter days of the civilization. But that was not always the case with Set. Although Set was not always considered "evil," the characteristics that he displayed remained more or less consistent. It is the culture and its values that changed. We are, of course, especially interested in understanding this ancient god-form as much as possible due to the present-day importance and influence of the Temple of Set on the contemporary left-hand path.

The culture of the Nile civilization had developed to a level of unique and independent existence before any significant contact was made with the Sumerian civilization around 3000 BCE.[49] The influence from Sumeria seemed only to provide impetus to an already ancient culture. Egypt began to take cultural shape around 5000 BCE, and to have become a distinct civilization in the prehistoric period between 3800 and 3200 BCE. From these foundations, Egyptian civilization would continue in its singular and culturally independent form until its loss of political independence to Rome in 42 BCE with the death of Cleopatra. But the fact that knowledge of hieroglyphics continued to be preserved by Egyptian priests and scribes until the fifth century CE[50] indicates that we are dealing with an intellectual culture with a continuous living legacy of at least four thousand years. Thus, the Egyptian civilization is the oldest, most continuous culture known to us. The only possible rival to this claim would be the Chinese civilization, which has much more recent roots (about 1500 BCE), but which actually continues to the present day.

It is probable that in most of its fundamental aspects Egyptian religion had reached a refined and highly articulated stage of development by the beginning of the Dynastic Period around 3100 to 2750 BCE.[51] Although at this time a fairly unified material culture existed along the Nile between the Mediterranean and present-day Aswan, politically—and perhaps religiously, as the "politics" of the region was heavily influenced by cultic institutions—the land was divided into the northern delta region (Lower Egypt) and the rest of the Nile valley to the south (Upper Egypt). From the most archaic period it seems that a hawk-god (Heru/Horus) dominated in the north and a god symbolized by an unidentified beast (Suta/Set) ruled in the south.

According to traditional Egyptian history, the north effectively conquered the south and unified the country in 3100 BCE under the first pharaoh, Menes, with his capital in the delta city of Memphis. Although the symbol of the unified country and unified cosmic principles represented by the dominant gods in each region is one depicting Horus and Set as a bipolar but single entity (see figure 3.3), there seems to have been the tendency to consider Set as the inferior, enemy aspect from this earliest beginning. However, it cannot be overemphasized that the essence and power of Set was highly valued and honored by Egyptians until the close of the twentieth dynasty (around 1170 BCE).

The continuity of the value of Setian ritual and magical symbolism can be seen clearly in the double crown of the pharaoh, which is made up of the red crown of northern Egypt and the white crown of southern Egypt, and the scepters of *was* and *tcham*, which are clear symbolic representations of the Set-animal. These scepters were signs of the divine power that could be wielded by the gods and their incarnate agents, the pharaohs.

"Orthodox" Egyptian religion seems to have been dominated by two concepts or principles: the regulation of the cosmic/agricultural cycle embodied in the annual rising of the waters of the Nile, which ensured material prosperity, and the continuance of the life of the individual in a transcendental realm beyond this world. There does not seem to be a shred of evidence beyond the statements of Herodotus (II, 123) that the Egyptians believed in any sort of earthly reincarnation or metempsychosis.[52]

It could easily lead to misunderstandings if the right-hand-path/left-hand-path distinction were made too early or too deeply when trying to comprehend the historical development of Egyptian religion. In many ways, early Egyptian religion was much like the Sumerian religion or ancient Indo-European religion in that the strict moral dichotomy

Figure 3.3. Union of Set and Horus

of "good" *versus* "evil" was lacking. However, as time went on, the Egyptians pioneered this dichotomization in a way very similar to that of the Zoroastrians in Persia.

The roots of one prototype of the right-hand path in the West are to be found in the Egyptian cosmic/agricultural cult built around the regular cycles of the rising of the Nile, perhaps coupled with the extreme isolation and xenophobia of the Egyptian land and culture. This religious and mythical tradition eventually became embodied in the cult of Osiris. This cult promoted and developed the idea of regular and *internally ordered cycles* of existence and the resurrection of the body in a transcendent realm, which was perhaps understood in some way parallel to the cycles of nature experienced in the Nile valley. By the time of the ultimate development of the Osirian cult in the time of the New Kingdom (and Ptolemaic Period) it constituted an exclusionist right-hand-path cult predicated on the harmonizing of human activity with the cycles of nature. These cycles were in turn symbolized by the community of Egyptian gods and goddesses.

The Egyptian word for "a god" was *neter* (pl. *neteru*). Erik Hornung devoted a whole study to this and other terms for "god" in Egyptian. The etymology of the word is unclear.[53] But his conclusion on its meaning states, in part:

> In their constantly changing nature and manifestations, the Egyptian gods resemble the country's temples, which were never finished and complete, but always "under construction."
>
> The gods of Egypt . . . are formulas rather than forms, and in their world one is sometimes as if displaced into a world of elementary particles. . . . A god is combined with another and becomes a new being with new characteristics, and then in the next moment separates into a number of entities. What he is remains hidden, but his luminous trail can be seen, his reaction with others is clear, and his actions can be felt. He is material and spiritual, a force and a figure, he is manifest in changing forms that should be exclusive, but we know that within all this something exists and exercises power.[54]

But there was one who stood against the other *neteru* by virtue of his very character, and this was Set. As we have already seen, the cult of Set stretches well back to the very beginning of Egyptian culture, especially in Upper Egypt. From the very beginning and throughout his history, Set seems to have stood for:

1. *opposition* to certain natural processes
2. the *out*side (desert, foreign lands, etc.)
3. *power* or force (physical or magical)
4. *disturbance* of the natural order caused by the activity of these factors.

These characteristics were at first seen as a necessary balance within the whole of the cosmos, but in time these very factors would become the programmatic paradigm for *evil* as seen from the Osirian Egyptian viewpoint.

Originally, however, Set was not thought of as evil so much as he was considered *overwhelmingly powerful.* Hornung writes concerning the Egyptian gods and evil:

> The gods of Egypt can be terrifying, dangerous, and unpredictable, but they cannot be evil. Originally this was true even of Seth, the murderer of Osiris. Battle, constant confrontation, confusion, questioning of the established order, in all of which Seth engages as a sort of "trickster," are all necessary features of the existent world and of the limited disorder that is essential to living order.[55]

A worldly aspect has perhaps been overemphasized in many discussions of how and why Set became a paragon of evil in the Egyptian system, for the conflict between the Osirian priesthood and those of Amen and Set was heavily overlaid with what we might call "political factors" from a modern viewpoint. It is true, for example, that he was the major god of the earlier subjugated Upper Egypt and that he was identified as the god of foreign forces of the Semitic Hyksos people who invaded and dominated Egypt from about 1700 to 1550 BCE.

But the following is also true and of greater importance to our study. In his very essence, Set represents something almost always treated with suspicion: the human psyche in *opposition* to the natural vehicle of the body, expressed as a force from the *outside,* giving humanity a *power* to *disturb* the natural cosmos around it. Set was the god of the outsider and foreigner and represents that quality in the Egyptian pantheon and society. Of all the gods, only Set was possibly truly immortal.[56] Set has the power and will "to act against law and order" in the universe.[57] Here is the essence of why the cult of Set is seen as a prototype of the left-hand path in the Western tradition.

Despite the great number of ancient documents available, the Egyptian tradition unfortunately remains one of the most difficult to understand on a consistent philosophical basis today. This is due in part to the concrete mode of expression of (pre-Hellenic) Egyptian philosophy, and in part due to their latter-day attempts to vilify and darken the function of Set. However, it also largely due to certain idiosyncrasies of Egyptian ritual worship. As opposed to the Sumerian and Indo-European tendency to identify certain principles or functions with specific god-forms, the Egyptians would identify virtually any and all functions with practically any god-form or name. This made it very easy for them to retain all of the important functions and symbols of Set by later transferring them to gods such as Amen-Ra, Thoth, and Anubis. In these later times, it seemed of the utmost importance to avoid the use of the actual *name* of Set or the depiction of the "Set-animal."

Already by the time of the fourteenth dynasty, the epithet "follower of Set" was being used pejoratively. A scribe named Kenhirkhopeshef (who died around 1191 BCE) wrote a papyrus in which he described the "Marks of the Followers of Set." The papyrus is in poor condition, hence the gaps in the text, but the description is clear enough:

> The god in him is Set . . . he is a man of the people. He dies by a death of fallings . . . sinews . . . He is one dissolute of heart on the day of judgment . . . discontent in his heart. If he drinks beer he

> drinks it to engender strife and turmoil. The redness of the white of his eye is this god. He is one who drinks what he detests. He is beloved of women through his greatness—the greatness of his loving them. Though he is a royal kinsman he has the personality of a man of the people . . . He will not descend into the west, but is placed on the desert as a prey to rapacious birds . . . He drinks beer so as to engender turmoil and disputes . . . He will take up weapons of warfare—He will not distinguish the married woman from . . . As to any man who opposes him he pushes . . . Massacre arises in him and he is placed in the Netherworld . . .[58]

From this description, we can infer various clues as to the antinomian nature of some of the ancient Setian practices. When actual human beings are referred to as "followers of Set" in the ancient literature, it is usually their disruptive behavior to the order around them that is cited as the chief characteristic they demonstrate.[59]

By the twilight of the Egyptian culture, from the twenty-second dynasty and into the Ptolemaic and Roman periods, the Osirian cult carried out a virtual "inquisition" against the Setian cult, eradicating the images and temples of the god and celebrating festivals by torturing crocodiles, which they thought embodied the god Set. The only philosophical haven for Setian principles was in the Hellenized Gnostic sects in Egypt.

It is perhaps in this magical context of Hellenized Egyptian culture that Set reaches his greatest state of philosophical development. In the Great Magical Papyrus in Paris (PGM IV), Set is called the "Ruler over the Gods," and even the "Creator of the Gods." To a certain extent this may be explained by the old Egyptian magical tradition of identifying god-forms with various attributes, but there seems to be more at work here. It appears that during the first few centuries of this era (about 100 to 400 CE) within a sect of Gnostics known as the "Sethians" there occurred a great synthesis of Greek philosophy, Egyptian religion and magic, Judaic mythology and theology, as well as other elements from Iranian and other magico-religious systems in the eastern Mediterranean region.[60] The ancient Egyptian god Set (Gk. Σηθ = *Seth*) became identified with—or passed into Hebrew mythology as—Seth (Heb. *Šet*), especially in Gnostic sects. But we do not have to go into Hebrew lore here. It is clear that the Gnostic interpretation of the "classical" myth of the conflict between Osiris and Set was interpreted as an analog to the dichotomy between the evil demiurge Ildabaoth (Yahweh Elohim of Genesis) = Osiris and the good (serpentine) god of light = *Seth-Typhon*. Thus, the Gnostic Sethian sect could indeed be interpreted as a sort of Hellenized philosophical revival of the ancient Egyptian cult of Set. In fact, the remnants of "orthodox" Egyptian religion referred to the Gnostics as a whole as "the sons of Typhon (= Set)." In this Gnostic epilog to the history of the cult of Set, it can be seen clearly that the ancient philosophical meaning of Set as a god of opposition to natural static cycles of existence, who enters nature from a position outside it to exercise his transformative power to disturb the natural order, was either continued or revived by the Hellenized Gnostic Egyptians of the early centuries of this era.

It has been theorized that the cult and figure of Set had some influence on the formation of the name and character of the Hebrew and eventually Christian *Satan*. This would be possible chiefly due to the influences that might have passed into Hebrew lore during the period in which the Hebrews were in Egypt and due to the fact that they seem to have been led from Egypt, probably around 1250 BCE, by an Egyptian priest named *Mesy,* Moses. The Egyptian word *msy,* which means "son," also is found, for example, in the name *Re-msy* or Rameses, "son of Re."[61]

While the name Set probably has no etymological connection to the Semitic *śṭn* (Heb. *śāṭān,* Arab. *šayṭān*), the names were doubtlessly associated with one another at an early time among the Hebrews. In the syncretic, Hellenized world reflected in the Greco-Egyptian magical papyri, it seems that Seth-Typhon may not only be linked with Satanic aspects, but with the One God of the Hebrews, Yahweh, as well. This is because the writers of the papyri were interested in Yahweh (transcribed into Roman letters as YHVH; Gk. Iao) as an expression of raw cosmic power on a physical level, not in his supposed theological role in orthodox Hebrew lore. Iao was "creator of this world"—and so his name could cause further magical transformations in it. A tendency of human groups to "diabolize" the gods of their neighbors seems to be a constant theme throughout history and a cause for continuing difficulties to historians of religious ideas.

It is, of course, difficult tell much about the ways in which the ancient Setians approached the essential questions of the left-hand path. In recent years we have seen great inroads made by scholars in this regard, along with the work of modern Setians such as Don Webb and his students. Given the general characteristics of the god himself, it seems likely that the Setians of old practiced something very much akin to what we are calling the left-hand path. Perhaps one of the reasons why the sect was so persecuted is that it offered a path of deification for more than just the pharaohs.

4
The First Millennium

At the dawn of the time that we have come to call the "Common Era," the religious and philosophical cultures of the Mediterranean and Near Eastern regions were in a high state of flux and dynamism. Politically and militarily, the Romans had become the dominant force in that part of the world, but in the realm of philosophy it was Hellenic thought that remained the most prestigious. Nevertheless, religious systems of all sorts (dualistic and nondualistic) from the East—and especially from the Iranian cultural sphere—also exerted a continual influence on the development and reformation of sects in the West.

In philosophy the most important school of thought was that of Neo-Platonism, which can be dated from about 244 CE, when its chief proponent, Plotinus, became influential in Rome. This philosophy, essentially based on a system of Platonic idealism, was to be a decisive influence on all schools of "mysticism": the Judaic Kabbalah, Islamic Sufism, as well as various Christian traditions. Hellenic thought also became the matrix for the reception of Iranian systems, and from this synthesis of East and West many sects were formed, which included Mithraism, "Hermeticism," and various Gnostic systems.

At this time certain sects and cults (e.g., Mithraism or various Egyptian cults) found great favor among contemporary sophisticated and philosophically trained Roman politicians, while others (especially those directly connected with Judaism) were reviled as being "paradoxical and degraded."[1] This is mentioned here only as a way of giving, in some small measure, a more balanced view to the popular image (essentially fostered by Hollywood) of the sophisticated and morally superior Jews and Christians being surrounded by barbaric and cruel Romans.

It is within this cultural milieu that Christianity—which, in its earliest phase, was essentially a Judaic heresy—had its origins. Early Christian doctrine can be shown to be a system developed over the years between the first and fourth centuries from a complex synthesis of Judaic, Hellenic (Neoplatonic), and Iranian thought. From its very beginnings, Christianity adopted and adapted elements from the various systems, theological as well as socio-political, that it sought to supersede.

This is obviously not the place to go into all the details of this process, so I limit myself to one of the most essential aspects of this development: the place and nature of "evil." There have been many attempts to create a "Christian philosophy." This is perhaps a contradiction in terms as a *philosophy* implies a system of open-ended inquiry, while "Christian" implies that the final conclusion is already fixed—with the philosophical jargon only being used to sound more convincing to those impressed by such rhetoric. These attempts were utterly thwarted by the fact that there seemed to be an ongoing effort to fuse two quite distinct philosophical cosmologies and concepts of "evil" into the Christian, and essentially Judaic, worldview.

The first of these two philosophical stances is that of Neo-Platonism, where we find the following model:

In Christian parlance, the triad of creative principles would be renamed "the Father, Son (Logos), and Holy Spirit." Here we see a *gradual* or *hierarchical* model, namely one that posits a gradual decline or descent of *Being* (= the Good/the One) until it utterly ceases to "*be*." At the point where there is a *lack of Being,* one finds the origin of evil. The Good is unity and Being; evil, by contrast, is a negative state, a lack of Being. Each stage along the way down the

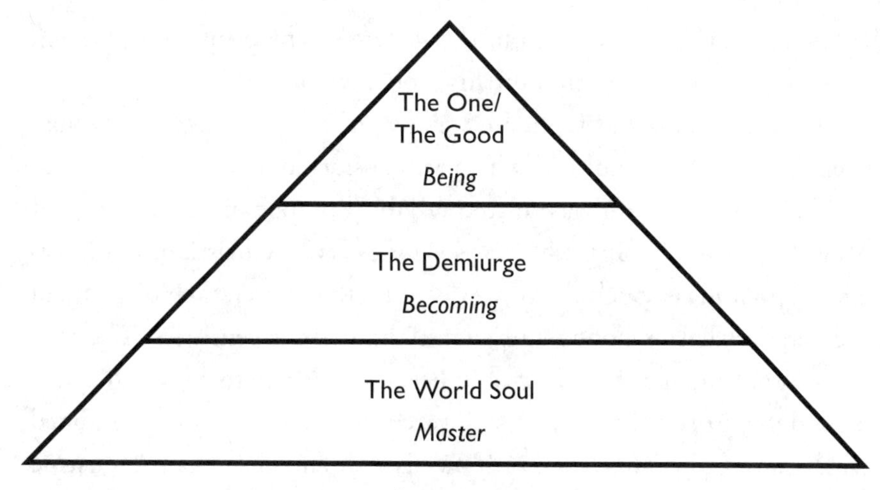

Figure 4.1. The Neoplatonic System

gradual scale of Being is a descent into "relative evil." One way to visualize this is to imagine a flashlight shining into the night sky, as its beam grows less dense and more diffuse, the darkness, which is considered "evil," becomes more dense until there is no more light. In this model, evil does not exist in any real way—it is, by definition, a lack of reality.

This negative conception of evil (that is, evil as a lack of Being) was the one eventually adopted and promoted by orthodox Christianity, but another conception existed alongside it (within orthodox thought as well as in numerous Christian heresies). This was the idea of *positive evil:* it assumes the *real existence* of a force of darkness identified as "evil." Historically, this model was pioneered and perfected in

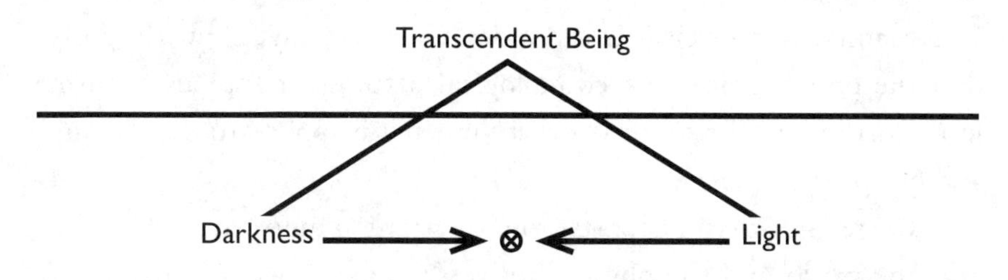

Figure 4.2. The Dualistic System

Iranian traditions derived from the system of the prophet Zoroaster. The simplest representation of this model would be:

Here Darkness and Light are equally real and are locked in combat over the world and mankind, which are considered mixtures of darkness and light. This system was to find a radical proponent in the prophet Mani (ca. 216–276 CE), who was a synthesizer of Christian, Buddhist, and Iranian ideas. Such dualism was to be the cornerstone of many of the heresies that orthodox Christianity battled for centuries. The root of the problem, or at least part of it, lies in the degree to which so-called orthodox Christianity and its scriptures have themselves been imbued with Iranian dualism. One only needs to remember that Augustine of Hippo was at one time a Manichean, or that the Hebraic myth of Paradise was perhaps heavily influenced by Persian (Iranian) thought, to realize why it seems so natural to ascribe *reality* to evil. Although from a "philosophical" perspective the theologian might say that evil is a lack of Being, on most other levels belief in a devil with positive powers of evil becomes too attractive to resist.

GNOSTICISM AND THE LEFT-HAND PATH

Although the ideology that is commonly known as "Gnosticism" has its ultimate roots in Iranian dualism, its exact shape was determined by a confluence of philosophical, theological, and mythological streams from Zoroastrianism, Judaism, Platonism, Greco-Roman mystery religions, Egyptian magic and philosophy, and the nascent form of Christianity. In fact, Gnosticism is a development parallel to "orthodox Augustinian Christianity." Gnosticism is the Judeo-Christian myth superimposed over the philosophical and cosmological patterns of Iranian dualism, just as orthodox Christianity is that same myth applied to the Platonic and Neoplatonic scheme.

Where Gnosticism departs from the Iranian model is in the belief that the world and the physical universe are actually the *creation* of the evil, dark spirit, and not just the zone between the spirits of light and darkness. For the Gnostic, material creation is a priori evil and must therefore be the result of a creative act on the part of an "evil god."

In the time between the first and second century, the period of Gnostic foundations, there were actually dozens of major schools of Gnosticism (such as those of Simon Magus, Basilides, Marcion, Valentinus, and others) and sects (such as the Cainites, Barbelites, Sethians, Ophites, and Borborians).[2] One of the major reasons for this tremendous plurality of systems is the fact that Gnostics did not attempt to unify their doctrines into an "orthodox" system, but rather encouraged the creation of diverse schools of thought. This put them at a distinct social and political disadvantage vis à vis the "orthodox" Christians who strove to create a monolithic body of catholic (i.e., universal) doctrine whereby "heretics" (such as the Gnostics) and pagans could be identified and subsequently eradicated.

This process of attempted elimination of heretical and pagan schools of thought—which has ultimately failed—went on for centuries into the modern age. Some vestiges of it may still be seen in fringe groups in society today in the form of freelance hate groups using Christian dogmas to attempt to suppress religious freedom. There are many St. Cyrils waiting to martyr today's Hypatias and bring about a new dark age. "They got the library at Alexandria—they're not getting mine!" as the button reads.

One of the most important of the early Gnostics, and perhaps a true lord of the left-hand path from antiquity, is Simon Magus. We mainly know about his philosophy from treatises written against it by early "church fathers." Their recounting of his philosophy seems rather accurate, as it can be corroborated with other actual Gnostic texts, but the apocryphal tales about his magical duels with the apostles, and so forth, seem like typical sectarian propaganda.[3] The figure of Simon Magus is perhaps best known from the account given of him in Acts 8, although the Simon mentioned there may in fact be another one and not the Gnostic "Magus" vilified by the church fathers.

Simon was born around 15 CE in Samaria, a region known for its irregular culture from a Jewish point of view. He was the son of an ostensibly Jewish sorcerer, but was educated in Alexandria in Egypt. Simon became the disciple of an "Arab" named Dositheos, who may have been a follower of John the Baptist. This Dositheos may or may not have been the author of a text found in the Nag Hammadi Library called the *Three Steles of Seth* (or *The Revelation of Dositheos*).[4] Simon is said to have traveled widely, to Persia and Arabia, as well as in Egypt and elsewhere, always in search of magical lore. In any event, when Dositheos died (ca. 29 CE), Simon took over his school. What were the Dositheans now became the Simonians. Dositheos had had a female disciple named Helene, and Simon later traveled with his main disciple, a former slave and prostitute from Tyre, also known by the name Helene. However, the Helene of Simon and the one attached to Dositheos were probably not the same person. But it is certain that Simon did have a female companion with whom he practiced erotic magic, some of which made use of semen and menstrual blood. (Such practices are shared by tantrism and later sexual magic practiced by Aleister Crowley.) In light of this and other features of Simon's practices that link up with certain Eastern ideas, it is most likely that the accounts were not merely propaganda by his enemies. Simon is said to have died in Rome where he was engaged in a magical contest with the apostles Peter and Paul. One account has it that he died while trying to fly to heaven (while Peter prayed for his fall).[5] Another report has it that he was buried alive, but failed to resurrect himself.[6]

It is quite possible that Simon was an initiate of the occidental branch of the "Iranian mysteries," hence the appropriateness of his cognomen "Magus." This priesthood was quite strong in Mesopotamia and Asia Minor at this time. But Simon's true importance is his role as a nexus for certain preexisting ideas, a possible originator of new realizations, and a teacher of future Gnostic leaders. He was the teacher of Menander, who practiced a "bath of immortality" in which a visible fire descended into the water to bestow miraculous power on the initiate. Menander was in turn the teacher of Saturninus and Basilides, both important Gnostic teachers.[7]

Simon taught a cosmology that was an ingenious synthesis of Iranian dualism and Platonic idealism. He held that the One, the undivided and eternal Divine Mind (Gk. *Nous*), *reflected* upon and within itself, thus giving rise to the First Thought (Gk. *Epinoia*) and thus the first aeon (Gk. *Aion*), which is also called *Ennoia* (power of thought) or *Sophia* (wisdom). Unity is broken, Duality is begun, and the Fall into manifestation has been set into motion. Hans Jonas summarizes that "through the act of reflection the indeterminate and only negatively describable power of the [One] turns into a positive principle committed to the object of its thinking, even though that object is itself."[8] This process of reflection is continued as successive emanations, each of which had less of the original Unity of divine Nous.

Simon taught that the One Mind, the True God of Light, had nothing to do with the creation of the material universe; in fact, the One Mind was not even aware of its existence. This world, he taught, was the creation of a wicked demiurge, whom Simon identified with the Creator of Jewish tradition. It is because Simon had determined Yahweh Elohim to be evil that he concluded that his Laws were also actually wicked and led men to evil, not to good. This, then, is the root of Simon's libertinism and antinomianism: the practice of willfully breaking normative codes to attain higher spiritual truths.

In Simon's system, the First Thought, the aeon Epinoia, fell through all of the successive aeons and was eventually incarnated as a human woman. She had transmigrated from female body to female body throughout history as the Rulers (Gk. *Archons*) fought to possess her. She had been Helen of Troy, for example. Simon believed that he had found the current incarnation of Epinoia in the persona of his consort, Helene, the whore of Tyre. He also held himself to be the incarnation of the Divine Mind itself. So in the terrestrial act of saving and redeeming Helene, Simon saw a reflection of the Ultimate Subject, the Nous, redeeming its First Object, Epinoia.

Many of the doctrines taught by Simon, whether he originated them or not, became mainstays of Gnostic thought throughout the centuries. Hans Jonas epitomizes his novel teaching as "the revolt against the world and its god in the name of absolute spiritual freedom."[9] In this bold doctrine Simon Magus shows himself to be a true heir to and prophet of the left-hand path.

Gnostic sects are especially difficult to study because the creation of differing systems was part of the initiation into them at the highest levels. Leaders were encouraged to innovate and generate more sects. But there are certain common characteristics among most of them which make them *Gnostic.* The major Gnostic tenets adhered to by most sects are:

1. *Dualism,* namely a strict dichotomy between *spirit* (that which is good and created by God) and *matter* (that which is evil and created and ruled by the Archons).
2. *Absolute transcendence of God;* in other words, God, as the "Father of the Spirit," is in no way mixed up with the matter of this world.
3. *Gnosis:* human "salvation" is to be gained by *gnosis,* "knowledge," of a suprarational, experiential kind. This is not intellectual knowledge as we usually think of it, but a direct comprehension of the transcendent absolute: God.
4. *Election:* the individual Gnostic is "called" or "elected" to his status from the transcendent source of light beyond the cosmos (natural order).
5. *Aions* or cycles of existence act as gradual barriers between this world and the realm of transcendent light.

Some of these tenets are shared in some form by other schools of thought, such as Neoplatonism or Hermeticism, but it is this combination of tenets that sets Gnostic sects apart from all others.

Gnostic sects hold that the material world is ruled by an evil force, and most say that the material world is actually the creation of the evil demiurge. What might be surprising is that when Gnostic thinking is applied to the Judeo-Semitic myth of Genesis, a picture that is the absolute reversal of the conventional understanding emerges. In the Gnostic mind, the (Yahweh) Elohim of Genesis is identified as the demiurge, the creator-god of this world, who is therefore the Evil One.

Yahweh, called Ildabaoth by many Gnostic sects, created the world and the natural parts of humanity, but tried to keep mankind in slavery and darkness, separate from the transcendent light. The savior of humanity is the Serpent (Heb. *nachash*), who is the bringer of light from beyond the cosmos. Those schools in particular that extolled the virtues of the Serpent, such as the Ophites (from Gk. *ophis,* meaning "serpent") and the Naasenes (from a Greek rendering of Hebrew nachash), could easily be identified on a superficial level as practitioners of the left-hand path. Their spiritual aim is to become god-men in life and to maintain their identities—as spiritual entities—as they pass through the aeons to reach the ultimate source of light. Some see this as a true *imitatio Christi.*

To Ophite Gnostics, the figure of Christ, as the Son of the Good God, is identified with the Serpent. Christ came as a manifestation of the light-bearing Serpent. The identification between the Serpent and the Messiah can be made on the basis of the Greek and Kabbalistic occult science of *gematria* as well. In Kabbalistic gematria, in which every Hebrew letter has a numerical equivalent, the value of the word for the Serpent of Eden, nachash (= N.Ch.Sh. = 50 + 8 + 300 = 358), and the word Messiah, "Anointed One, King" (= M.Sh.Y.Ch. = 40 + 300 + 10 + 8 = 358), work out to be the same. In gematria, two words that have the same numerical value are seen as identical in essence on a higher level of being. The Serpent brought humanity *knowledge* (gnosis) of good and evil (Genesis 3:1–7) and can further aid man in gaining the fruit of eternal life, thus making man like God, or like Christ.

Of the five major traits of Gnostic thinking mentioned above, all but the radical dualism is in some way shared by the contemporary intellectual left-hand-path philosophy of the Temple of Set. This rejection of radical dualism is also the principal distinction between what can properly be called Gnosticism and what can be called Hermeticism. Gnostics have inherited the basic positive dualism of the Zoroastrians, while the more precise Hermeticists have maintained the Platonic (and hence Neoplatonic) model. This model was perhaps in some sense shared by certain Egyptian priesthoods, and it is noteworthy that the cradle of this Greco-Egyptian philosophy is to be found along the Nile.

It is, of course, this heterodox synthesis of Hellenic, Semitic, Egyptian, and Iranian ideas, which is the oriental matrix of the so-called Western magical tradition. Those ideas were resynthesized in late medieval and Renaissance Western Europe, and then again renewed during the "occult revival" of the late nineteenth and early twentieth century. But before we can fully appreciate the heterodox value of these ideas, we must understand what is meant by "orthodoxy."

Christian orthodoxy is really founded on Augustine of Hippo's synthesis of Neoplatonic philosophy and Judeo-Christian mythology.[10] Although he wrote extensively against all of the numerous "heresies" of his day, he himself had at one time been an adherent of Manicheanism. The four pillars of doctrine upon which Augustine's system of orthodoxy rests are:

1. God is a *Trinity* (Father, Son, and Holy Spirit)—three and one at the same time.
2. *Free will* is enjoyed by God absolutely, and at one time man possessed this.
3. Man however transgressed against God's commandments and committed *original sin,* which separates man from God. All men are born in with original sin.
4. Only the *grace* (free-will gift) of God can save a man. What is specifically orthodox Christian about this is the idea that Jesus (the Son) was a unique historical phenomenon of God's grace and is the way by which all men are to be saved.

There is a certain genius of sorts in Augustine's system in that it is founded on an irrational basic theological premise (the Trinity), which is derived from the Neoplatonic doctrine of *emanations:* the Logos emanates from the One and the World Soul is created by the Logos. Man is put in the position of having transgressed against God's law as a matter of his own fault; the fault for this cannot be laid at God's doorstep for, after all, he gave man free will. Man chose to rebel against God (perhaps in league with Satan) and is thus eternally separated from God. In this position, man can only be "saved" by God's gift to him. In the orthodox view, however, if a man turns to God, this does not actually come about though self-will or effort, but rather it is a *sign* of God's grace that a man does so. Thus, in this system of doctrine, man's *will* is utterly devalued—really made unreal. True free will was only exercised by Adam and the punishment for his transgression is now visited on every offspring of the human species. This is by far the most complex and convoluted explanation of a right-hand-path philosophy known. One of the main reasons for its convolution is the historical fact that it represents an attempt to create a dogmatic, *inflexible,* pseudo-rational hybrid between Judaic (Semitic) theology and Hellenic (Indo-European) ideology. This hybrid seemed workable with Gnostic flexibility; however, when submitted to councils of church fathers who approved or disapproved dogmas, the cracks in the system would always be obvious. If we are to understand the historical development of the left-hand path in the West, a firm idea of the essence of the right-hand path is extremely helpful.

It is often tempting to be drawn into discussions of the Judeo-Christian models of *evil* when exploring the left-hand-path philosophy in the West. It must be continually remembered, however, that in the "West," as in the "East," the right-hand path and the left-hand path are models of spiritual working or action, not models of "good" *versus* "evil." The great problem in this is that from the right-hand-path viewpoint, it is usually understood as precisely that: a battle between *good* (= the right-hand path) and *evil* (= the left-hand path). This is most likely to be explained in terms of the psychology of adherents of the right-hand path. The essence of "knowledge" for followers of the right-hand path (especially in the West) tends to be *faith* or belief (Gk. *pistis*). Those who have pistis as the object of their knowledge—those who are true believers—tend to think always in "binaric" terms of yes/no, right/wrong, good/evil, *ad nauseam.*[11] In actuality, however, there is nothing evil about the left-hand path. In fact, most of what contemporary Western man likes to point to as examples of evil are the results of the philosophies of blind *faith:* the Inquisition, concentration camps, gulags, and so on.

WAS JESUS A LORD OF THE LEFT-HAND PATH?

This may seem a ludicrous question to ask, but the perfection of the left-hand path comes about from asking questions. Is it possible that the teacher called Jesus was in fact a virtual Satanist in his own day—someone whose teachings were so corrupted by unscrupulous followers that what he taught is for all intents and purposes buried in a morass of conflicting dogmas and doctrines? I cannot hope to answer this question fully here, but I think I can present some provocative evidence suggesting that Jesus was not what the institution founded in his name later made him out to be. To begin to answer this question, I will use evidence both from within and outside Christian literature.

The criteria for being named a lord of the left-hand path, it will be remembered, are that the person either developed for himself or taught a magical (willed) system of evolutionary self-deification with an antinomian embracing of elements within the culture of the individual considered to be forbidden or taboo (hence "Satanic"). Perhaps shockingly, Jesus fulfills most of these criteria if the evidence is viewed objectively.

Morton Smith's study, *Jesus the Magician,* is perhaps the greatest single trove of information concerning the probable true nature of the "Naasarene." Smith reports what the *non*-Christian contemporaries said of Jesus.[12] For us, the important elements of this report are that he was said to be the illegitimate son of a Roman soldier (named Panthera) and a prostitute, that he became expert in magic and became "a son of a god" by these practices, and that he taught his followers to despise

Jewish Law and to practice a sexually libertine doctrine of love. Of course, I am well aware that ideological enemies can, and do, simply make up the wildest and most unsubstantiated stories for propagandistic reasons. Surprisingly, however, there is ample evidence for this interpretation within the very Gospel accounts themselves.

One interesting bit of evidence for the idea that Jesus was thought to be a Satanic or "evil" god or "son of a god" (at least by outsiders) is graphically portrayed in a well-known piece of graffito in the imperial palace on the Palatine hill in Rome (ca. 200 CE):

The drawing, which is scratched in the plaster of a schoolroom wall, depicts a donkey-headed figure being crucified with a man raising his hand below the figure. An inscription (in bad Greek) reads: "Alexamenos worships god." The donkey-headed figure is, in this cultural context, to be identified with Set-Typhon, who was by this time

Figure 4.3. Graffito from the Palatine Hill

a god of evil in the Helleno-Egyptian mythology. At least for some, then, Jesus may have been identified with Set-Typhon. Perhaps he was seen as the "son" of this god? This too is possible, since the Jewish god Yah(weh), in Hellenic manuscripts represented as Iao (pronounced "ee-ah-oh"), was unequivocally identified with Set-Typhon by the Egyptians themselves. This is fitting since Set was the "god of foreigners" among the highly xenophobic Egyptians, and the Jews were the largest foreign population in Egypt at the time. Furthermore, the Egyptian (Coptic) word for donkey just happens to be *io* or *eio*—which sounded very much like the Hellenic representation of Yah![13] Internal evidence in the Gospels that points to this symbolic complex includes Jesus's riding into Jerusalem on an ass that he told his disciples to steal from the town (Matthew 21:1–7).

Evidence in the Gospels also shows the antinomian nature of Jesus's work and teachings, at least from the viewpoint of the established Jewish culture and religion of his day. Jesus rejected the practice of the Law. In words reported to be his own, he says: "Think not that I am come to send peace upon the earth: I came not to send peace but a sword. For I am come to set a man at variance against his father" (Matthew 10:34–35). Jesus was a social revolutionary bent upon the annihilation of the family and tribes as the Jews had known them. In contradistinction to the orthodox Jewish belief in the salvation of the *whole people* at a future time, Jesus taught the salvation of the *individual* here and now: "the kingdom of god is within you" (Luke 17:21). He not only performed miracles or magical feats himself; he exhorted his followers to emulate him: "Verily, verily I say unto you, he that believeth on me, the works that I do shall he do also; and greater [works] than these shall he do" (John 14:12).

Curiously, when Jesus is accused by the Pharisees of casting out demons by the force of Beelzebub—the ruler of demons—he replies only with an attempt to baffle them with apparently logical formulas (Matthew 12:24–27).

Perhaps the most interesting and compelling evidence is of a comparative nature. Assuming that Jesus was in some way a historical person who did things roughly answering to some of the accounts given in the Gospels, what kind of man would he have been? He fits perfectly the profile of a magician of his time and place. If Jesus *was* a magician, are there any corollaries to his magical activities elsewhere in the cultures of his exact time and region? Yes, there is much of it in the form of the Greco-Egyptian magical papyri.[14] Smith deals with this evidence in great detail. What emerges is a clear picture of a Hellenized Jewish magician—a magician who, among other things, claimed to be the son of a god, used verbal magical formulas to work miracles, and who did not send spirits or demons to do his work but rather contained or absorbed a divine spirit and exerted it directly.

Several papyri outline magical procedures for obtaining a spirit in order to become a son of a god. One of these says that the magician should purify himself, go onto a lofty roof and, among other things, blindfold himself with a "black Isis band." At one point in the ritual the band is removed and a "falcon will fly down" and drop a stone as a first sign of the manifestation of the spirit in the magician. This spirit, or *daimon,* becomes identified with the magician from an outsider's viewpoint so the magician in the words of the papyrus "will be worshipped as a god since [he has] a god as a friend."[15] Another papyrus (PGM IV:154–221) reads in part:

> . . . there will be this sign of divine encounter, but you, armed by having this magical soul, be not alarmed. For a sea falcon flies down and strikes you on the body with its wings, signifying this: that you should arise. But as for you, rise up and clothe yourself with white garments and burn on an earthen censer uncut incense in grains while saying this:
>
> > "I have been attached to your holy form.
> > I have been given power by your holy name.
> > I have acquired your emanation of the gods.
> > Lord, god of gods, master, daimon."
>
> Having done this, return as lord of a godlike nature which is accomplished though this divine encounter.[16]

The parallel between these magical rituals and the story of the baptism of Jesus (Mark 1:9–11), in which he receives a "holy spirit" in the form of a dove flying down from heaven, is remarkable. After this event he is able to perform magical feats by just "saying the word," namely some magical formula or "mantra."

A sorcerer who "had" a spirit or daimon might be called in the Greek of that day a *magos* (pl. *magoi*) and was often considered a "divine man." Such a magos was more than a mere *goês* (sorcerer), who could only command spirits outside himself. In Jesus's own time, some apparently thought that he had obtained the spirit of the executed John the Baptist and worked magic with it. But it is the "holy spirit"—the spirit of a god who Jesus the man seems to have invoked, internalized, and even become—which is the true agent of his miracles.

Because of his "divine nature," a magos can cause changes with his "word" (or directed, conscious will) alone. The papyri are full of verbal magical formulas, such as *ablanathanalba,* by which the magos may work his will. There is even one such word recorded in the Gospel of Mark (5:41), where Jesus heals a little girl with the (supposedly Aramaic) phrase *talitha koumi.*

For each of the miracles of Jesus, a parallel can be found in the magical literature of his day. Even the magical power of his own name was enhanced upon his death, since magic worked with the spirit (or "name") of an executed criminal was believed to be of special power. This is, of course, further bolstered by the knowledge that Jesus exhorted his followers to do this, saying that he would be in them always (John 14:23 and 15:4–9; Matthew 18:20 and 28:20).

Jesus was a deified man—just as every magos is. Among many magicians of the time, deification (and, with it, immortalization) was the highest goal of the art and practice of *mageia* (magic). Jesus's own declarations of his divinity correspond with the words from magical papyri in which the magician declares his divine qualities:

JESUS: "I am the Son of God." (John 10:36)

MAGICAL PAPYRUS: "I am the Son . . ." (PGM IV:535)

MAGICAL PAPYRUS: "I am the Son of the living God." (DMP XX:33)

JESUS: "I am . . . the one come from heaven." (John 6:51)
MAGICAL PAPYRUS: "I am the one come forth from heaven." (PGM IV:1018)

JESUS: "I am . . . the truth . . ." (John 14:6)
MAGICAL PAPYRUS: "I am the truth." (PGM V:148)[17]

But was Jesus a master of the left-hand path? From the most objective evidence and methods of investigation (filtering out the often self-serving redactions and interpretations of his followers), it would appear that the man and magos Jesus *was* a practitioner of the left-hand path. He was an antinomian, preaching an abrogation of the established Jewish Law, and was thought to be "Satanic" by his contemporary rivals and critics (charges that he did not directly deny). He taught the "salvation" of the individual apart from the collective, while practicing the *deification* of his own individual self. That so much of this comes through, despite the deliberate (and successful) attempt to transform his teachings into a right-hand-path doctrine, is remarkable.

The parallels between Jesus and Simon Magus also include the fact that Jesus (despite whatever later attempts may have been made to gloss over the circumstance) had as his consort a supposed prostitute, Mary Magdelene. This seems to be an essential component in the myth of the magus.[18]

In the final analysis, however, because Christianity as an institution was founded and promoted by men such as Saul/Paul (who was an avid persecutor of early followers of Jesus and who was never taught by the "master") and Jesus's own brother James (who rejected his brother as insane in his own lifetime), we cannot trust that any of the possible left-hand-path teachings of Jesus survived intact. If Jesus was a lord of the left-hand path, his teachings were at once betrayed by a group of his followers so that now no more of his true doctrines survive than do those of Apollonius of Tyana or Simon Magus. To risk stating the painfully obvious: all organized forms of orthodox Christianity—Eastern or Western, Catholic or Protestant—are monuments of right-hand-path intolerance and hatred of the individual spirit.

ISLAM AND THE LEFT-HAND PATH

In the southern (or Middle Eastern) tradition, no other system of thought more perfectly embodies the ideals of the right-hand path than orthodox *Islam*. The very word means "submission": submission to the laws of Allah. Philosophically, Islam is the most radically monotheistic of the religions of the Middle East. At the same time, this radical theology actually allowed for a great deal of free thought *outside* the confines of the religious life, which is why the Muslims of Persia, Egypt, and Moorish Spain were able to become such great collectors and interpreters of Hellenic philosophy, as well as innovators in many philosophical and scientific areas.[19] The Muslims collected and read the works of Plato, Aristotle, and the Neo-Platonists at a time when such works were considered to be pure diabolism in ecclesiastical circles in the Christian West.

Historically, Islam is another cult-form inspired by the Judaic or Hebrew mythology. It was founded by Muhammad (570–632 CE), who quickly spread his form of religion by military conquest. From the very beginning, this was viewed in terms of a Holy War (Ar. *jihad*). Within ten years following the Prophet's death, Islamic armies had conquered Egypt, Palestine, Syria, Mesopotamia, and much of Iran (Persia). By a century after Muhammad's death, the Moors were moving into France from Spain, which had already fallen into their hands. They were only stopped at the Battle of Tours in 732 by Charles Martel ("the Hammer"), although they continued to occupy the Iberian Peninsula for eight hundred more years.

The root essence of Islam lies in the formula known as the *shadah:* "There is no god but Allah, and Muhammad is the Messenger of Allah." Allah is derived from the same common Semitic name for god that we also find in Hebrew *El*. The Arabic form comes from *al-Ilah,* "The God." Submission to this creed and to the laws outlined in Muhammad's book, the Qur'an or Koran ("the Recitation"), is the essence of Islam.

However, and especially in the earlier culture of Islam, there were allowances for certain unexpected irregularities. Once a man's outer religious obligations were met in accordance with the rule of custom, he might be free—if only *secretly*—to pursue philosophical or magical interests liberated from moral restrictions or laws. This is how Islamic culture became a bastion of classical learning in the Middle Ages. The Islam of today has been greatly affected by fundamentalist Wahhabist reforms, which have blunted the cutting-edge intellectualism once enjoyed by the Islamic world. Secret (and sometimes non-Islamic) pursuits were most often carried out in certain heterodox sects or brotherhoods. The main category of such sects is known as Sufism. Within the context of Sufism, characteristics of the left-hand path are often developed. Two other Islamic sects that attract some attention in discussions of the left-hand path are the Ishmailis (or Hashashin) and the Yezidis.

Before exploring these sects, it would be helpful to understand the uniquely Islamic view of Shaitan (Satan), or Iblis, as he is also known. The name Iblis is derived from the Greek word *diabolus.* In Islamic mythology, Iblis refuses to bow down before Adam (humanity) as all Allah's other angels had done when commanded to do so (Qur'an II:34). It is for this transgression or rebellion that Shaitan is punished with rejection.

One Sufistic school, founded by Ibn Arabi, has another interpretation of why Iblis would not bow down. They say that Iblis represents the imagination, which would not prostrate itself to the intellect. "Imagination . . . both dissipates and concentrates the faculty of remembrance and seduces both to 'sin and rebellion' and to the vision of the divine-in-things."[20]

The term Sufi is used to describe a number of mystical sects within Islam. Sufism is an Islamic synthesis of mystical teachings often influenced by Gnosticism, Neo-Platonism, and other religious sects and traditions. However, it contains many original features based on Islamic and native Arabic or Persian ideas. Solid evidence for the Sufi movement dates from around 800 and continues as a viable part of Islamic culture today. It appears likely that these tendencies in Islam are largely the result of original Persian or Iranian influence. One tradition holds that its ultimate root is to be found in the personality of Muhammad's Persian barber, Salman al-Farisi, who lived in the Prophet's house. If there are left-hand-path characteristics to be discovered anywhere in the philosophically right-hand-path tradition of Islam, it should be in Sufism. And indeed there are important fleeting glimpses of sophisticated left-hand-path ideas in these sects.

To some Sufis, Iblis is seen as a manifestation of Allah's majesty. They say that he refused to submit to the God's command because he was totally focused on the Absolute and would not dilute that focus by worshipping anything else.

Islamic thought again brings up the topic of the dual heritage of the left-hand path, the carnal and the intellectual. A mystical view is that Iblis is the carnal soul (*nafs*): "The carnal soul and Satan have been one from the first. And both have envied and been an enemy of Adam."[21]

Iblis is said to have a special kind of link to the Absolute. This is due to the idea that he is the first model for the separate "I-consciousness" independent of the Absolute. In a way, then, Iblis disobeyed Allah for the sake of love and for the sake of his loyalty to his One Beloved (the Absolute). He is cursed and punished for his disobedience, but even in this he takes satisfaction at being separated out for unique treatment by the Absolute. The parallel between this and the psycho-cosmology of the Gnostic magus is obvious.

Ayn al-Qozat Hamadani, a Sufi who was executed for his thoughts in 1131, referred to those who have a special affinity for Iblis as "the separated ones": those who thrive in a state separate from Allah. Peter Lamborn Wilson writes:

> Ayn al-Qozat implies that separation-in-love is in some sense superior to union-in-love, because the former is a dynamic condition and

> the latter a static one. Iblis is not only the paragon of separated ones, he also causes this condition in human lovers—and although some experience this as "evil," the Sufi knows that it is necessary, and even good.[22]

As we will see in chapter 8, Aleister Crowley (or his "Holy Guardian Angel") will echo some of these sentiments in *The Book of the Law* (I:29), in which Nuit says: "For I am divided for love's sake, for the chance of union."

Al-Qozat goes on to develop the concept of Iblis as the guardian of an inner chamber of divinity wherein there is a Black Light. This is a realm beyond all duality; it is "darkness, but it is light just the same."[23] Al-Qozat declares: "hear the word of God: 'Praise be to God, who has created the heavens and the earth and has established darkness and light' ([Qur'an] VI:1). How can black be complete without white or white without black be complete? It cannot be so."[24]

The figure of Iblis even becomes a secret exemplary model for some Sufis. One rather notorious group, the *Malamatiya* (from Ar. *malama,* "blame") sect, practiced antinomianism reminiscent of the Ophite or Barbelo-Gnostic sects. Members of this sect believed that their nearness to a divine state was proven by the level of contempt shown to them by normal humanity. They totally neglected religious laws and regularly committed sinful acts.[25]

One of the earliest Sufi practitioners whose ideas bordered on the left-hand path was Abu-Yazid of Persia (d. 875). He came to realize that God was the equivalent of his own soul. He wrote: "Glory to Me! How great is my Majesty!" Technically, he was committing the intellectual sin of "incarnationalism" (Ar. *hulul*) by claiming to be God (or a god) incarnate. This seems to be a general tendency in Sufistic beliefs. Again we are reminded of the Gnostic sects, where a practitioner could exclaim at a certain stage: "I am Christ!"[26]

Al-Junaid (d. 910) developed the idea that man's separate existence from God is a result of God's own will. However, God tries to "overcome" this separateness by pouring out the fullness of his own Being.

This Sufi used the imagery of erotic love to articulate his theology of human separateness from God. The lover yearns for union but takes intense joy in the suffering caused by the separation.[27]

The most radical of the early Sufis was a student of al-Junaid, Mansur al-Hallaj (d. 922), who actually identified himself as a god, or perhaps *logos* incarnate. He equated himself with the *logos* of Truth. In his *Kitab al-Tawasin,* he wrote:

> If ye do not recognize God, at least recognize His signs. I am that sign, I am the Creative Truth (*ana 'l-haqq*), because through the Truth I am a truth eternally. My friends and teachers are Iblis and Pharaoh. Iblis was threatened with Hell-fire, yet he did not recant. Pharaoh was drowned in the sea, yet he did not recant, for he would not acknowledge anything between him and God. And I, though I am killed and crucified, and though my hands and feet are cut off—I do not recant.[28]

For writing these words, al-Hallaj was condemned to die. He had committed the gross blasphemy of equating himself with (a) god and, what was worse, he had used the model of Jesus Christ for doing so. For this, his mode of execution was that of his hero: crucifixion. Al-Hallaj is said to have reached a "Permanence of Self in the Real" (Ar. *baqa'*), by which he was able to ascend to Paradise after his martyrdom.[29]

THE ASSASSINS AND THE OLD MAN OF THE MOUNTAIN

Another faction with left-hand-path implications is the Ishmaili sect within Shi'a Islam of Persia. The Ishmailis are also known to history as the Hashashin, or "Assassins." This sect has its origins in 1074 when the Persian Hassan-i Sabbah was initiated into Ishmailism in Cairo. In 1094, he moved his headquarters to a mountain fortress in Persia called the Alamut ("Eagle's Nest"). This effected a division within the sect into two branches: the oriental branch, with its headquarters at Alamut in Persia, and the occidentals in Egypt and Yemen.[30] It was the *sheihk* or "elder" of the fortress of Alamut—the so-called Old Man of the Mountain—about whom Marco Polo reported in his book recounting his journey to the east.[31]

Hassan-i Sabbah developed and taught a system of spiritual hermeneutics called in Arabic *ta'wil:* "to take something back to its source or deepest significance." *Ta'wil* is used to penetrate beyond the exoteric limitations of the Law (*shari'ah*) and Path (*tariqah*) of religion to arrive at the esoteric Reality (*haqiqah*) behind the outer forms.[32]

It is interesting to note that a quite vibrant modern Western mythology has been built up around the figure of Hassan-i Sabbah. This largely stems from the romantic mystique of a secret, mountaintop-dwelling cult of hashish-using assassins,* whose watchword was a heretical statement allegedly uttered by Hassan-i Sabbah on his deathbed: "Nothing is true, everything is permitted." Despite the fact that the sentiment may or may not have any historical connection to Hassan-i Sabbah, these powerful words have had considerable artistic and esoteric impact in recent history. Quoted by Nietzsche in his 1887 work *On the Genealogy of Morals* in reference to the "Order of the Assassins" (which he calls "free spirits, *par excellence*"[33]), it was later further disseminated to subcultural circles by the artist Brion Gysin and his friend the "Beat" novelist William S. Burroughs, as well as by writer Robert Anton Wilson and the modern movement called "Discordianism." More recently, it has been applied as a practical technique in certain types of occultism, notably the "Chaos Magic" of Peter J. Carroll and the Illuminates of Thanateros (IOT).

In 1162, Hassan II (son of Hassan-i Sabbah) became the sheikh of Alamut. On 17 Ramazan (8 August) 1164, he declared the *Qiyamat:* the

*The word "assassin" indeed derives from Ar. *ḥaššāšīn,* which is the plural form of *ḥaššāš,* "hashish user." This was a pejorative term in the late medieval Arab world and may not have been a literal reflection of actual Ishmaili practices, but nevertheless colorful tales of the drug-crazed Assassins were already circulating in Europe from the reports of Marco Polo in the early fourteenth century.

Great Resurrection. In doing this, he proclaimed: "The chains of the Law are broken!" The inhabitants of the Eagle's Nest were free of obligations of Islamic religious laws and a perpetual holiday was declared. Hassan II can be said to have realized the "Imam-of-his-own-being"* and he then invited all his followers to participate in this.[34] With the Qiyamat, Hassan II maintained that the resurrection of the dead in physical bodies was possible *in life.* The Ishmaili initiate "'dies before death' when he comes to realize the separative and alienated aspects of the self, the ego-as-programmed-illusion. He is 'reborn' in consciousness but he is reborn in the body, as an individual, the 'soul-at-peace.'"[35] In 1166, Hassan II was murdered.

It seems likely that Hassan II took his followers too far, too fast. He had perhaps reached the spiritual "station" called Permanence (baqa'), but his doctrine of Qiyamat had been developed over several years through the gradual stages of Ishmaili initiation and based on the practice of ta'wil. But the stage that immediately precedes Permanence is said to be Annihilation (Ar. *fana'*).[36] This annihilation is not an end in itself, which may be the case in the right-hand path, but rather a phase to be passed through before individual Permanence is possible. Hassan II tried to offer this intoxicated state of Permanence to his followers in a direct and simple form, which they did not seem ready to accept or be able to achieve. From the left-hand-path perspective, he attempted to transform overnight a school of the intellectual, gradual transcendental path into one of the sensory, immediate immanent path. Ultimately, it did not work for all of the followers.

The Ishmailis came to believe that their Imam was divine, and following 1164, the time of Qiyamat, many of them maintained the possibility of a "pure spiritual Islam, freed of any legalistic spirit, of all servitude to the Law."[37] Far from submitting to "God's will," in the final state of Ishmaili initiation (the IX°) "every vestige of dogmatic religion has been practically cast aside, and the initiate is become a philosopher

---

*Imam (literally "leader" in Arabic) refers to a male spiritual and temporal leader or guide, often seen as divinely appointed.

pure and simple, free to adopt such system or admixture as may be most to his taste."[38]

In 1251, the fortress at Alamut was captured and destroyed by the Mongols, and the vast library there was burned. Afterward the Ishmailis found refuge in various Sufi sects.[39] In the nineteenth century, the Ishmailis reemerged under the spiritual leadership of the Aga Khans, and are today a wealthy sect headquartered in India.[40]

THE YEZIDI DEVIL WORSHIPPERS

To call the Yezidis an Islamic sect may or may not be correct. Nevertheless, it probably makes the most sense to discuss them within the cultural milieu of Islam. To call them "devil worshippers," which has so often been done,[41] also may or may not be correct. However, they have been called this so often that a discussion of their beliefs in the left-hand-path context seems necessary.

The Yezidis are a Kurdish people. Kurdish is a dialect of the Iranian branch of the Indo-European family of languages. They are not therefore part of the general Arabic population that has surrounded them in their homeland, which lies in and around the valley of Lalish near the sources of the Tigris and Euphrates rivers in the northern part of modern Iraq. Evidence for the Yezidi religion dates only from the fourteenth century. Its peculiar lore may be the result of ancient pre-Islamic tenets being grafted into Islamic religious terminology, or it may constitute an original creation.

Historically, the Yezidis trace the origin of their faith back to sheikh Adi ibn Musafir, who came to the valley of Lalish from the valley of Baalbek in Lebanon by way of Baghdad. Around the year 1100, he was in Baghdad, where he was associated with various Sufis, including Ayn al-Qozat Hamadani. Among the Kurds of Lalish he founded an order that was outwardly orthodox, but which secretly venerated Melek Taus: the Iblis of al-Hallaj.

The word "Yezidi" is probably derived from the Persian word *yaz(a)d-*, "supreme being," which is part of the Zoroastrian terminology. The term was used as a pejorative by the Shi'ite Muslims of Persia for whom it essentially meant "heathen" or "infidel."[42]

In Yezidi doctrine, the "First Cause" or God (*Khuda*) created the cosmos through the agency of seven angels. The first among these, Azaziel or Asa'el, refused to bow down before Adam (man) who had been created directly by Khuda alone. One of the reasons for his refusal, by the way, may be that Azaziel was formed of fire, while Adam was formed from clay—the angel refused to bow to a lower being.[43] However, Khuda subsequently forgave Azaziel, who is therefore not the spirit of evil that the uninitiated make him out to be. The Yezidis consider the name Shaitan (Satan) as an insult to Azaziel and refuse to use the term. If it is used by others in their presence, retribution is demanded.

The name Azaziel is also rarely heard among them. It has been largely replaced by a cognomen, Melek Taus: "the Peacock Angel." The Yezidis trust in Melek Taus and ask for his special knowledge and protection. They believe that Judgment Day is in the remote future and that the faithful live on through cycles of reincarnation (a belief also shared with other Ishmaili sects, including the Druzes). To the Yezidis, evil is a fact of *natural* life and not the work of a supernatural being. Melek Taus's role in the "fall" of man is not that of a tempter: he is revered as the brave provider of knowledge needed by mankind to survive.

One of the Yezidi holy books, called the *Kitab el-Aswad* in Arabic or the *Mas'haf Rish* in Kurdish (both meaning "Black Book"), tells that God created Adam (*only* the male) and placed him in Paradise but forbade him to eat of *wheat*. After a hundred years go by, Melek Taus asks God why Adam has not increased or multiplied. God responds by giving to the Peacock Angel administrative authority in the world. Melek Taus then instructs Adam to go against God's prohibition and eat of the grain. The Peacock Angel then *drives* Adam out of paradise. Only later is woman created (from under Adam's left armpit), and mankind is able to increase.[44] Here the positive, evolutionary role of Melek Taus is clear.

How this positive, evolutionary role is reflected in the spiritual lives of individuals is demonstrated by the words of a poem by sheikh Adi himself:

> *I am Adi of Shams (Damascus), son of Musafir*
> *In the secret of my knowledge there is no god but*
> *me . . .*
> *Praise be to myself, and all things are by my will.*
> *And the universe is lighted by some of my gifts.*[45]

With the Yezidis and Ishmailis, as with so many of the other apparently left-hand-path traditions, the essentially left-handed goal—immortal, independent existence of the self in a quasi-divine state—is not clear except at the highest levels of initiation or at the leadership level. It is probably for this reason that the leaders and past leaders of these sects seem to be "worshipped." They are in fact seen as pioneering spirits who have walked the path before the aspirant and thus serve as exemplary models. It is interesting to note that one of the shrines, or actual images, of the Peacock Angel (*sanjak*), in the Yezidi region is said to be dedicated to Mansur al-Hallaj, the Persian Sufi and apparent practitioner of the left-hand path executed in 922.[46]

It seems that the Yezidi tradition is the result of a syncretism of indigenous Kurdish beliefs (probably non-Zoroastrian Iranian sects), Iranian dualism, sheikh Adi's Sufistic teachings, Al-Hallaj's interpretation of Iblis, and perhaps Nestorian Christianity.[47] This synthesis may, however, only be a superficial one and perhaps the values and structures underlying Yezidi belief remain essentially ancient Kurdish ways. This is even alluded to in another of the Yezidi holy books, the *Kitab al-Jilwa* (IV): "The scriptures of strangers are accepted by me (Melek Taus) in so far as they accord with my ordinances and run not counter to them."[48]

It is curious to note that virtually all of the left-hand-path traits present in the Islamic cultural stream seem to flow ultimately from the Iranian world, whether it is the heretical Sufis, the Ishmailis, or even the Kurdish Yezidis. I would speculate that the reason for this is that the left-hand-path ideas were common (even if eternally controversial) in the pre-Islamic world and that these yearnings of the human spirit to attain an independent, immortal, and awakened state could not be stamped out entirely—even by the vigorously right-hand-path tradition of the way of "submission."

5
The Path of Satan

THE LEFT-HAND PATH IN THE WESTERN MIDDLE AGES
500–1500

In any given culture, the beginning of the medieval period may be marked from the time it officially accepts (by whatever means) the nominal authority of the Christian church. By the time of the advent of the Middle Ages in Western Europe, the basic church dogmas outlined by St. Augustine had become the standard of orthodoxy. However, the swarm of heterodox teachings, and even organized sects, remained unceasing until the present day. The orthodox call heterodox doctrines "heresies," and as often as not equate them with the work of the devil. At the same time, the "heretics" almost without exception conceive of *themselves* as true Christians who champion the true teachings of Jesus against the orthodox forces, which are sometimes characterized as being diabolical. Although there are some rare exceptions to the rule, for the most part the story of medieval spiritual dissent and warfare is one that takes places within the parameters of the right-hand path.

Augustine's dogmas of the Trinity, Original Sin, Free Will, and Grace became litmus tests for other doctrines. The seeds of many heterodox movements were planted early.

As we noted in the discussion of the conversion of Goths in

chapter 2, Arius (256–336), a priest in Alexandria, Egypt, taught that Jesus Christ was not god himself but a man who had become godlike. This teaching was condemned as heretical because it denied the dogma of the Trinity, the doctrine that the Father, Son, and Holy Spirit are/is coeternal and coequal. This Christological controversy perhaps ultimately stems from two Greek words used to describe Christ: *theotetos,* "having the substance of god," and *theomorphos,* "being akin to god." In actuality, Arius was trying to preserve the purity and simplicity of monotheism in his teaching. The orthodox elevation of Jesus to the level of God the Father did two things: it created a kind of duotheism (or tritheism), and it made Jesus ever more remote from humanity. As this happened, it became increasingly difficult for the Christian believer to see Jesus as an exemplary model for his own salvation, and at the same time it increased the power and necessity of the institutionalized church in the spiritual life of the individual. In the Middle Ages, things as apparently irrelevant to modern minds as Christology had a *direct* effect not just on the spiritual life of each individual, but also on the prevailing social, political, and economic conditions.

Another important heretical thinker was Pelagius (died ca. 420), who taught that every human was born free of original sin and that all individuals were responsible for their own moral actions. Pelagius was of Celtic heritage (either Irish or a native of Britain) and was most interested in the improvement of the moral practice of Christianity. Even in this early period, Christian moral practice was lax because there were always ways to shirk moral responsibility. Augustine taught that moral behavior was a sign of God's grace, while it might be held that immoral behavior was somehow "caused" by the devil; in either instance the individual is *not responsible.* Pelagius was condemned by the church and died in an unknown place in the Middle East.

Certainly neither Arius nor Pelagius could be called practitioners of the left-hand path. However, the main points of their teachings (the heroic view of Christ as an exemplary mythic model for self-development; the basic *freedom* of human beings and their *responsibility* for their own actions) are elements of any coherent left-hand-path philosophy.

The strongest exponents of this early form of Christian heresy were the various East Germanic tribes (Ostrogoths, Visigoths, Vandals, etc.) who converted to this Arian form of the faith. It is also very likely that their Gothic Christianity was mixed with elements of their native Germanic religion.[1] Nevertheless, this form of Christianity—linked as it was with the Goths—was annihilated in a series of wars waged on the Goths by the Pope and various secular kings in the sixth through eighth centuries.

Gnosticism was the root of the most powerful challenge to orthodoxy in the later Middle Ages. This branch of Gnosticism, however, had its direct root in the doctrines of Mani (216–277), a Persian holy man who was raised in the Judeo-Christian sect of the Elchasaites. In 240, he broke with the sect and founded his own movement as a result of messages he received from the "King of the Paradise of Light." Manicheanism is a synthesis of Iranian Gnostic thought with Judeo-Christian mythology and certain Buddhist teachings.

Mani taught that there are two principles—light and darkness—and three great epochs of cosmic history: a time when light was separate from darkness, this time in which the darkness attacks the light, and a coming time in which the darkness will again be separated from the light. A person can be saved from the world of darkness—or flesh—only through *knowledge* (gnosis) of this reality.[2]

From these Persian and Manichean origins sprang many heretical sects in Western Europe. Some of the sects were highly ascetic, such as the Cathars, while others went in the libertine direction, such as the Brethren of the Free Spirit. Indeed these are the same tendencies present in all Gnostic movements.

The church fought dissenters and protesters throughout the Middle Ages. Virtually all of those it oppressed, however, were also followers of the right-hand path, and often more aware ones at that. After the success of one of these group's movements—the Protestant Reformation begun by the German priest Martin Luther—interest in the possibility of secret underground diabolical movements increased. This was true both in the Protestant north as well as the Catholic south.

In the first half of the Middle Ages (i.e., until about 1200), the religious intolerance of the church was largely reserved for pagans (peoples adhering to their national native traditions) and national Christian religions (such as Gothic Arianism). These enemies were usually opposed in open warfare in an alliance between the Pope and relevant secular authorities—most often the French king or the Holy Roman Emperor.

A foretaste of what was to come occurred in 385 when Pricillian was executed in Trier for holding heretical beliefs. But the institutionalized persecution of heretics, witches, magicians, and the like did not begin in earnest until around 1200. By this time, all overt paganism in Europe had been stamped out, so the forces of intolerance and spiritual totalitarianism *turned inward* to begin the persecution of those who professed to be Christians but who did not meet orthodox standards of belief.

In a bull of 1199, Pope Innocent III formally established the church-wide institution of the Inquisition. By 1273, Pope Gregory IX had appointed the Dominican Order as the official Inquisitorial body. This was later modified to include the Franciscans.

The level of institutionalized violence and hatred embodied in the Inquisition has rarely been equaled in the course of human history. Its record is too well known—and too vile—to repeat here in any detail.[3] Our purpose in this book is not to recount the history of *evil,* for if such were the case then surely the history of the left-hand path would make a poorer subject than the history of the forces of institutionalized orthodoxy: Christian, Muslim, communist, or National Socialist. But in order to appreciate the level of resistance faced by spiritual dissenters of all sorts—including practitioners of the left-hand path—it is important to remember the nature of the forces bent on their destruction.

It is also noteworthy that the Inquisition of the Roman Catholic

Church was (or *is*—for the institution still exists under the name "Congregation for the Doctrine of the Faith") not the only body in Christendom that engaged in these intolerant and spiritually totalitarian practices. "Freelancing" Protestant witch-hunters or witch-finders, along with local Protestant clergy and secular authorities, persecuted those thought to be in league with the devil no less vigorously than the Catholics had done.

Although heretics of all kinds were considered to be at least indirectly in league with the Devil, it was not until the sixteenth and seventeenth centuries that widespread "Satanism" or "witchcraft" was suggested by the forces of orthodoxy (Protestant or Catholic). Not surprisingly, this is a time when we also find little in the way of true left-hand-path practice.

The whole "witchcraft scare" of the 1500–1600s seems to have been for the most part a malicious (and profitable) fantasy on the part of churchmen. In a brilliant study, Norman Cohn has shown how later Christians used earlier Roman descriptions of what they thought occurred at Christian *agapê* feasts and modified the descriptions over time to suit any heretical group that the churchmen wished to slander.[4]

Two examples of the process should be sufficient to illustrate the point. Concerning what Romans think Christians do in their services, Minucius Felix (active at the end of the second century CE) wrote:

> A child . . . is set before the would-be novice. The novice stabs the child to death. . . . Then . . . they hungrily drink the child's blood, and compete with one another as they divide his limbs. Through this victim they are bound together; and the fact that they all share this knowledge of the crime pledges them all to silence.
>
> On the feast-day they foregather with all their children, sisters, mothers, people of either sex and all ages. When the company is all aglow from feasting, and impure lust has been set afire by drunkenness, they twine the bonds of unnameable passion as chance decides. And so all alike are incestuous, if not always in deed at least by

complicity. . . . Precisely the secrecy of this evil religion proves that all these things, or practically all, are true.[5]

Some eight centuries later, around 1050, the Greek philosopher Michael Psellos wrote a dialog, *On the Operation of Demons,* containing what the orthodox Christians thought of the rites of the Bogomil heretics:

They bring . . . young girls whom they have initiated into their rites . . . and throw themselves lasciviously on the girls; each one on whomever first falls into his hands, no matter whether she be his sister, his daughter, or his mother. . . . When this rite has been completed, each goes home; and after waiting nine months until the time has come for the unnatural children of such unnatural seed to be born, they come together . . . on the third day after the birth, they tear the miserable babies from their mother's arms. They cut their tender flesh all over with sharp knives and catch the stream of blood in basins. They throw the babies, still breathing and gasping, into the fire to be burned to ashes. After which they mix the ashes with the blood in the basins to make an abominable drink . . . [6]

Let it suffice to say that the latter description is no more likely to be true than the former one. What is remarkable is that such descriptions could still be heard on television "news" programs in the 1980s and 1990s—including stories about women being "breeders for Satan" and infants being burned and devoured (although there was never any "evidence" for the crime).*

It is certain that we would learn little concerning any genuine left-hand-path schools, traditions, or philosophies by relying on medieval Christian descriptions of the activities of their adversaries—real or imagined. However, the *symbols* engendered during this period would

*See the appendix, "The Urban Legend of Satanicism."

serve to stir the rebellious imaginations of antinomian Romantics in the late eighteenth to twentieth centuries.

THE CHRISTIAN HERETICS

The Dualists

Even when we look to those who spiritually rebelled against the authority of the church during the Middle Ages we find mostly only other right-hand-path practitioners.

The great dualistic heresies, which have been referred to as being "Satanic" by orthodox theologians, had few left-hand-path tendencies. As can be seen from the "learned" description of their activities reported by Psellos, the orthodox believers really had no idea what the Bogomils or Cathars believed, and they were not interested in knowing. The orthodox wanted only their extermination. This extermination could only be completed by means of open warfare on the sects involved. This was the so-called Albigensian Crusade (1207–1221). Even after this campaign, it still took until about 1330 to wipe out the last vestige of the Cathar movement in Europe.

What did these "vile heretics" teach?

Derived ultimately from the Manichean tradition (probably in the "Paulician" or "Messalian" forms in Asia Minor), Bogomilism was founded around 950 by a village priest in Bulgaria calling himself Bogomil ("Beloved of God").

Bogomil preached that God (Slavic *Bog*) had two sons: Satanel and Christ. Satanel rebelled in heaven and caused one third of all the angels to follow him. As a result of the rebellion, Satanel created the material universe, of which he is god. Similarly to most Gnostics, Bogomil equated the Jewish God of the Old Testament with Satanel.

As a result, Bogomil believed all flesh, along with material things of all sorts, to be evil tricks of Satanel. The orthodox priesthood and its sacraments and miracles—all of which are works through matter—were thus held to be manifestations of evil.

The ultimate aim of the Bogomil believer was to unite with Christ, the good god. To do this he or she must lead an ascetic lifestyle, be vegetarian, and not indulge in wine, sex, marriage, or procreation. It is interesting to note that the English term "bugger," meaning "sodomy, anal or oral intercourse" is derived from *Bulgarus,* Bulgar. This is because the Bogomil heresy, with its prohibition against procreation, was so widespread among these people in the Middle Ages they became identified with such practices!

Most of the propaganda written against them (a sample of which appears above) is useless as evidence for what they really believed because it seems to be merely repetitions of charges made indiscriminately against any and all whom the church wished to slander and destroy.

The Bogomils were the object of frequent persecutions by the orthodox authorities. This in part caused them to send missions north of the Balkans and the west into Italy, France, and western Germany, where they developed into various movements, such as the Cathars or Albigensians, and the Waldensians.[7] By the beginning of the fourteenth century, the Bogomils were effectively suppressed as an open religion, and with the Ottoman conquest of the Balkans in the late fourteenth century, the religion disappeared. Most Bogomils eventually converted to Islam.[8]

The Cathars had a theology and cosmology almost identical to that of the Bogomils. However, they were much more successful in organizing themselves, especially in southern France or Provence.

Probably the chief reason for Cathar popularity in Europe was the widespread and thorough corruption of the Roman Catholic institutions. Catholic priests lived in carnal luxury. Many were married or simply lived together with concubines; they ran taverns and charged extra fees for all their religious services. This latter practice was necessitated by the need of priests to pay off their patrons within the church who had arranged for their appointments to office. The Cathars, on the other hand, seem to have been devoutly and *radically* spiritual in all that they did.

Cathar internal structure was simple. After a long apprenticeship, an adept entered the sect by means of a rite called the *convenza.* The second and last level of initiation was celebrated in a rite called the *consolamentum,* after which the initiate is called a "Perfect." These were the true *Cathari*, the "Purified Ones" (*Catharus* comes from the Greek *katharos,* "pure").

After one had become a Perfect, it was expected that one would sin no more. Although the Cathars were lenient on the laity, their standards of morality at the "Perfect" level were so harsh that many practiced the *endura* (self-imposed death by starvation) after the *consolamentum* rite. This was done in order that they might ascend into the realm of light without sin. For the Cathars, there was no hell below this world—this world of flesh and matter was the prison of the spirit and the true Inferno. Their ideal was to set into motion a process that would end the existence of humanity in this world, propelling it into a realm of pure spirit.

Although Manicheans, Bogomils, and Cathars would often be referred to as "Satanic" by orthodox propagandists, it can be seen that they have virtually nothing to do with the left-hand path. From the Cathar point of view, the Roman Catholic Church was in reality Satanic. This is the common charge/counter-charge tactic typical of the right-hand path. In the case of the Roman Church, however, such a charge might seem plausible when one reads a study such as *The Bad Popes* by E. R. Chamberlin.

The strict moral dualism of the Manichean kind—or even the implicit and elusive dualism of the orthodox variety—is simply not conducive to a true left-hand-path philosophy. In order to be true to left-hand-path premises, such dualism that does exist as a part of the analysis of the cosmic or human order must be accepted and *utilized* for the evolution of the self into an ever-more-perfected and godlike being.

PANTHEISTIC FREE SPIRITS

Another kind of Christian heresy especially popular in Germany, northern France, the Low Countries, and England was the so-called

Brethren of the Free Spirit. This movement existed throughout these regions from about the beginning of the 1200s all the way to the end of the 1600s. One of the reasons why the movement as a whole could continue beyond the grasp of the Inquisition is that it had no formal structure and the members tended to be both highly intelligent and mobile. Nevertheless, many were burned at the stake for their beliefs. "Spiritual Libertinism" was equally widespread among women and men. The sect often flourished *within* the social context of the wider communities known as the Beghards (men) and Beguines (women).

Their traditions tended to be *oral* and hence original texts are scarce. Three of the most important original sources for Free Spirit thought are *Schwester Katrei,* Marguerite Porete's *Mirror of Simple Souls,* and a tract by an English "Ranter" (a Free Spirit offshoot) called *A Single Eye.*[9]

The Brethren of the Free Spirit may indeed be said to belong to the more libertine branch of "Gnostic" thought, just as the Cathars represented an extreme form of the ascetic branch. However, extreme dualism is not a feature of their thought. It is more in keeping with the known facts to call the Free Spirit movement "pantheistic."

On the surface, the Spiritual Libertines—as they are also called—would seem to be prime examples of left-hand-path thought and practice, and be in many ways similar to the left-hand-path antinomian tantrics of the East. Norman Cohn says they represent "a system of self-exaltation often amounting to self-deification." If we delve beyond the surface, we can see some distinctions that bear emphasis.

The overriding cosmological feature of Free Spirit belief is the realization that "God is all that is" and that "every created thing is divine."[10] These formulas, as well as the essence of their practice, point to a Neoplatonic model of reality as the root of their beliefs. Cohn, however, suggests that their teachings seem to stem from the writings of Pseudo-Dionysius and John the Scot Eriugena, and do not appear to represent any greater attempt to homogenize Neo-Platonism into the Christian mainstream of orthodoxy.[11]

Another important influence on their understanding of the world seems to have been supplied, if indirectly, by the visionary Joachim of Fiore (1145–1202).[12] Joachim divided the history of the world into three phases or stages: that of the Father (or Law), of the Son (or Gospel), and of the Holy Spirit. The advent of the Age of the Holy Spirit would usher in a transformation of the world. The first Age was one of fear and servitude, the second of faith and filial submission, but the third Age "would be one of love, joy and freedom, when the knowledge of God would be revealed directly in the hearts of all men."[13] The Brethren of the Free Spirit had a similar doctrine in which they held that the Incarnation of the Son (Christ) was being surpassed by the Incarnation of the Holy Spirit in the bodies of the "Spirituals," the highest initiates of the Free Spirit movement. They could at that point declare: "I am the Holy Spirit!"[14]

The pantheism of the Spiritual Libertines comes to the forefront when we observe their attitudes toward the self of humanity, and Cohn concluded that the core of the Free Spirit system hinged on an attitude toward the self. The Spiritual Libertine believed he had attained perfection and so was *incapable* of sin. This awareness inevitably led to certain antinomian practices. It became a virtual requirement for the initiate to engage in forbidden acts.[15] In a world in which sexual pleasure was perhaps the greatest of forbidden pleasures, it was only natural for the practices of the Spiritual Libertines to gravitate in this direction. There is evidence for a tradition of "free love" among them, but little to no evidence for the public orgies often ascribed to them by their orthodox enemies.

Those who had realized their unity with the divine considered themselves to have returned to the *Adamite* state of being, free of sin and unashamed. The Free Spirits seem to have practiced ritual nudity as an expression of this realization.

But *how* did the Spiritual Libertines attain to this Adamite state of sinless innocence and immortality? Unfortunately, most of the texts that might have been used by the sect were destroyed by the Inquisition. In the fragments of the system that remain, however, a few things are clear.

The first phase of initiation, which may go on for years, involves self-abnegation and self-torture. There is the cultivation of absolute passivity and obedience (sometimes to a "master"). During this phase, one is not a true Spiritual Libertine, but as an apprentice one is being trained to receive the Incarnation of the Holy Spirit. The second phase is the actual transformation into God. At that point, one becomes Adamite (or Evite), restored to the original state of being.

The *Mirror of Simple Souls* describes a more detailed process of seven steps of initiation. The first three involve ascetic practices of self-denial and obedience. Levels four and five prepare the way for the state of exultation: one is blinded by the light of love, preparing the way for the recognition of one's own sinfulness at the fifth level. This *experience* of the immense gulf between the self and God allows the light and love of God to sweep into the self. The will of God becomes the will of the self. At the sixth level, one becomes a true Free Spirit—the soul is annihilated in the deity so that there is nothing but God: God = self. In the seventh and last level, the self rejoices permanently in the divine state of being.[16]

The Spiritual Libertine is not just united with God but becomes identical to God. This identity is furthermore permanent. Because of the evolutionary quality of Free Spirit theology, namely their belief that this phenomenon represents a new stage in the development of deity and humanity, the Free Spirit initiate could claim to be superior to God as understood in texts from previous Ages.[17]

As with many Gnostic sects, the Brethren of the Free Spirit considered this world to be the realm of hell and punishment. But it was not because it was made of matter, rather it was because of the existence of the gulf between man and God and the presence of man's feelings of guilt and conscience that torment him due to his ignorance of reality. By attaining identity with God, the Free Spirit is liberated from these pangs of conscience, which is tantamount to the liberation from the torments of hell.[18]

The praxis or spiritual technology of the Free Spirits, like those of so many sects—especially those of the left-hand path—can be dangerous if misunderstood. Spiritual liberation is not, in fact, something that one just suddenly decides is true and then acts upon. If this were so, it might easily become little more than an excuse for vile or criminal acts. (There is no record of such acts committed by true Free Spirits.) An actual process of self-transformation must be undertaken. This process will invariably involve a long period of discipline and self-denial, of spiritual and physical austerities.

A great deal of the Free Spirit sect's beliefs and practices certainly accord with the general characteristics of the left-hand path. They seem to deify the self, which is dynamic and evolutionary, and direct these efforts toward an immortal existence. Socially they are antinomian, but not particularly so when it comes to religious symbolism. They do not, for example, worship a devil. There is, however, an important and subtle difference between this and the other schools of the left-hand path. Left-hand-path philosophies emphasize the *individual* development and immortality. The emphasis is on the deification of the unique and separate self—each individual is "raised" to the level of deity (either in this lifetime or in some postmortem state). With the Free Spirits, the emphasis is quite different. The Holy Spirit descends and incarnates in individual humans, filling them individually and collectively with the undifferentiated substance of the Holy Spirit. Although the individuality appears to be preserved, this is only an illusion viewed from the outside. In reality, the individual soul has been annihilated and the self identified with the Holy Spirit in toto. This is similar to the more orthodox views of the state of jivanmukti (individual liberation) in Hinduism. For this reason, the Spiritual Libertines must ultimately be excluded from being called practitioners of the left-hand path.

Before leaving this topic, I would like to mention that many of the ideas underlying the Free Spirit movement were embodied in—and, in turn, influenced by—the contemporary German mystical theologians Meister Eckhart, Heinrich Suso, and Johannes Tauler.[19] The thought and writings of these and many of the other heretics of the medieval period often find much more sympathetic readings today than do the orthodox dogmas of either that time or our own. The reasons for this will become apparent later.

THE WITCH CRAZE

Anton LaVey's Ninth Satanic Statement reads: "Satan is the best friend the Church has ever had, as He has kept them in business all these years!"[20] This formula is true on many levels. It could be made both with regard to the definitions of the actual Satan (as a symbol of carnality or as the principle of isolate intelligence) or with regard to the fictional character of Satan hatched in the lurid imaginations of repressed churchmen, freelance witch-hunters, and hysterical members of the peasantry and middle class.

Once the great organized heretical movements were thought to be either demolished or under control, more widespread and deep-level spiritual dissent began to take root. This would bear fruit in the form of the Protestant Reformation. Heretics, whether Gnostic dualists or pantheistic Free Spirits, were always portrayed by churchmen as "Satanic," which simply meant they *opposed* the official orthodox and exclusively valid "party line" of the church's dogmas. By the sixteenth and seventeenth centuries, there were no great heretical movements or pagan nations left to conquer, so the churches turned *downward* to the grass roots of society to find their victims of "evangelism."

It is well known and well documented that the early church "diabolized" the native gods and goddesses of local populations as they converted them to Christianity. Given the monotheistic theoretical basis of the faith, this was not an altogether illegitimate attitude. The pagan deities could not be wiped away overnight—and, in fact, *were never fully eradicated* by the church. The lore, myths, rituals, and beliefs of Christianity actually had to accommodate themselves in many instances to pagan practices. Striking examples of this are found in everything from the adoptions of the pagan calendar of festivals to popular things such as the Christmas tree, Santa Claus, and the

Easter Bunny. Indeed, pagan forms and practices survived in syncretization with Christian customs both positive and negative. The old ways were canonized or sanctified in some aspects, and diabolized in others.

The *Indiculus superstitionum et paganiarum* (Index of Superstitions and Pagan Practices) is a remarkable document from early medieval Germany (around 740). The list must represent things that were still occurring in central Europe at the time the *Index* was published. The list reads:

1. On the sacrilege at graves and of the dead
2. On the sacrilege among the buried dead
3. On the purification festivals in February
4. On the little houses, that is, enclosures for the gods
5. On sacrileges performed in churches
6. On holy places in the woods, which are called Nimidas [*Nemeton* = Celtic word for sacred enclosure]
7. On the practices which they carry out on top of rocks
8. On services to Mercury [= Odin] and Jupiter [= Thor]
9. On sacrifices, which are given to a saint
10. On amulets and magical bands
11. On sacrifices at wells
12. On magical incantations
13. On auguries by means of birds or horses or from the manure of oxen or from their kidneys
14. On divination or sortilege
15. On fire produced by friction from wood, that is, the Need-fire.
16. On the brains of animals
17. On the heathen observations of the hearth-fire, or the ignition of these things
18. On uncertain places, which they hold sacred
19. On the bundle of straw, which the common folk call St. Mary
20. On the festivals, which they give to Jupiter [= Thor] or Mercury [= Odin]

21. On the waning of the moon, which they call *Vince Luna*
22. On tempests and horns and spoons
23. On the furrows around the yards
24. On the heathen meeting called *Irias* with torn clothes and shoes
25. On the belief that they consider every dead person a saint
26. On idols made from dough
27. On idols made from cloth
28. On idols which they carry across fields
29. On wooden feet or hands according to heathen practice
30. On the opinion that the hearts of people can be taken away according to the heathens, as women conjure the moon[21]

This primary evidence shows the nature and scope of continuing heathen practice. We can see that none of it is particularly "diabolical" in character—at least not by modern standards.

The shift from heresy to "witchcraft" as a basis for religious persecution was facilitated most of all by the publication of the *Malleus Malificarum* (Hammer of the Witches) in 1486.[22] It became the "witch-hunters' manual" and was reprinted in fourteen editions by 1520.[23] From this time to around 1700 was the period of the so-called witch-craze. Persecutions of people suspected of witchcraft and witch trials were sporadic throughout Europe during this time. It would die down in one place only to flare up again elsewhere. Even the British colonies were not immune. From the 1640s to the 1690s, witches were hung in the colonies of Connecticut, Rhode Island, and Massachusetts.[24]

The *Malleus Malificarum* appears to be largely a work of learned fiction, but a deadly fantasy it is. In it, we are told that witches will do four things: renounce the Catholic faith, devote themselves body and soul to evil, offer unbaptized children to the devil, and engage in sexual orgies. Of course, these were just variations on the same literary fictions invented by the Romans and repeated by early churchmen almost 1,500 years before the publication of this witch-hunters' manual.

Now the fact that the witch cult did not exist in *reality* was hardly a hindrance to the witch-hunters. Since there were no *obvious* suspects, anyone and everyone could be made suspect. This significantly broadened the social scope of the persecutions. Since "evidence" was almost always obtained under torture, the witch-finders could suggest just about any wild fantasy and have it affirmed by the delirious object of his cruel occupation.

The Protestant Reformation might have held out a more rational alternative to the Inquisition of the Roman Catholics. But Martin Luther's own obsession with evil and witchcraft, along with the Protestant cultural tendency to allow the laity to engage in witch-hunting activities for God and profit (here the "work ethic" meets the Inquisition), made the newly Protestant northern Europe no less likely to persecute witches than the conservative Roman Catholic south.

What does all this mean for our purpose of exploring the essence of the left-hand path? Ironically, and perhaps unfortunately, the vast storehouse of western European imagery relating to "devil worship," witchcraft, and "Satanism" is for the most part the invention of the church and witch-hunters. This leads us to conclude that the invented evidence is largely useless for the discovery of any true left-hand-path ideas current in this period. To rely on this evidence to discover anything about the Satanism of the period would be somewhat like trying to determine the actual character of modern Satanism from Dennis Wheatley novels and Hollywood horror films.

THE FAUSTIAN PATH

At the end of the medieval period in Germany, a whole tradition of magic arose that was associated with the name of Dr. Faustus. The tradition originated at a time contemporary with other great magical thinkers, such as Cornelius Agrippa von Nettesheim (1486–1535) and Theophrastus Paracelsus von Hohenheim (1493–1541), and the spiritual revolutionary Martin Luther (1483–1546). The study of the Faustian tradition is best understood on several levels. These include the actual historical man, probably named Georg Faust(us); the legends, which grew up around and attached themselves to his figure after his death (around 1540); and the subsequent complex artistic tradition, which actually continues to grow. Without doubt, since the demise of the ancient ways in the North, this man was one of the first new masters of the left-hand path—for through magic and dealing with the Dark Side, he managed to enter into myth and legend and has become thereby immortal.

The historical Faust was probably born in or near Knittingen in southwestern Germany in 1480 and died near there at Staufen in 1539 or 1540. He was born with the first name Georg (or Jorg). An early tradition changes the name to Johann(es) for some unknown reason. The name or title "Faust(us)" could derive either from the German name *Faust* ("fist" or "club") with the addition of the Latin ending *-us*, or it could be a later title from Latin *faustus* ("favored" or "lucky one").[25] (It has been noted that Simon Magus also went by that title in Latin.)[26] In one primary document, he also calls himself Sabellicus. This could be a mythic reference to the ancient tribe in Italy called the Sabellians—who were thought to be experts in magic—or perhaps it is only a Latinization of his ordinary name, which might have been Zabel.[27]

Whatever the man's name, there are some definite details of his life and travels, even if these details are scanty. He was reputed to be an expert—if only semi-learned—in magic, astrology, necromancy, and all the occult arts of his day. From about 1507 to 1513, he lived and taught on a freelance basis in Heidelberg. During this time he came to be known as "the demigod of Heidelberg." In 1513, he was active in Erfurt, where he conjured images of Homeric myth while giving lectures to awestruck students. In the 1520s, he lived in or near Wittenberg, the epicenter of Protestantism where Martin Luther had nailed his Ninety-Five Theses to the church door in 1517. At least at the beginning of this time (in 1520), he appears to have been employed by the Roman Catholic bishop of Bamberg, which, if true, suggests all sorts of intrigues.

A document from the city of Ingolstadt dated June 17, 1528, states that Faust was forcibly exiled from the city, but only after he had vowed not to take (magical) vengeance on the city leaders. It appears that Faust was often eventually ejected from cities where he made an impact. He always lived in university towns and taught and influenced students there, although never as a member of the official faculty. In terms of his magic, he claimed to have restored the lost teachings of Plato and Aristotle and to be able to equal the miracles of Christ.[28] In 1534 there is evidence that Faust wrote a set of predictions for the German explorer Philipp von Hutten before a voyage to South America. Von Hutten wrote to his brother in 1540 to confirm the predictions.[29] During his career Faust is said to have openly declared that his knowledge and power were the result of a pact he had made with the devil. Whenever he was exhorted to repent and return to the church, he would reply that he preferred to remain loyal to the devil because he "has fairly kept what he promised me and therefore I intend to keep fairly what I have promised and signed away to him."[30] Shortly before his death, Faust returned to his native region in southwestern Germany and was found dead in the city of Staufen. His enemies assumed he had been taken to hell; it was approximately thirty-three years after he first came on the scene as a disciple of the devil in Heidelberg in 1507.

In the years immediately after Faust's death, legends and tales about his life proliferated and grew in magnitude. Even in Faust's lifetime his exploits were being merged with those of legendary magicians. Within twenty-five to thirty years of his death, a Latin manuscript concerning him was written by an anonymous student in Wittenberg. A German translation of this text was made sometime in the 1570s and the Latin original was eventually lost. The German edition of the first *Faustbuch* (Faust Book) was published by Johann Spiess in 1587 at Frankfurt am Main. Its full title reveals much of its nature and purpose:

> *History of Dr. Johann Faustus, the Notorious Magician and Necromancer. How He Sold Himself to the Devil for an Appointed Time, What Strange Adventures He Saw in that Interval, Himself Inventing Some and Living through Others, Until He Received at Last His Well-deserved Requital.*

The book was immensely popular. It went through several reprintings that year and the text was exported at once to England, as well as France (1598) and Holland (1592).[31] A new edition of a *Faust Book* compiled by Georg Rudolf Widmann appeared in 1599; this contained more sensationalistic material and an even more moralistic tone. The main purposes of the early *Faust Books* appear to have been to make as much money as possible off of a lurid account of a wretched sinner and at the same time to preach with righteous indignation against the prideful excesses of the human spirit. This convenient combination of puerile fascination and religious intolerance, further mixed with a profit motive, is not foreign to our world today.

It has been noted that the books are of a strongly orthodox Lutheran bias with anti-Papal sentiments. In them, the evil Dr. Faustus is sometimes contrasted with the good Dr. Luther.[32] In this regard, the early *Faust Books* were reflections of the ordinary—and still medieval—prejudices of the masses of the sixteenth and seventeenth centuries.

The Faust legend as recounted in these books became the main source for later literary treatments. In the *Faust Book,* the hero—or "villain"—is portrayed as a peasant's son who inherits a fortune. He goes to Wittenberg to study theology. He is talented, but displays unusual characteristics that make him suspect. After a while, he abandons theology and takes up magic and medicine. In time, he becomes a great physician knowing the secrets of herbology and drugs. (This is undoubtedly a reflection of the historical figure of Paracelsus.) But all this soon leads to his conjuration of demonic entities, and ultimately to the signing of a pact with Mephistopheles. In an age when it was still thought that "seekers of knowledge outside the church were suspected of traffic with the minions of Hell,"[33] it was widely believed that such a quest would be expressed through just such a pact with the devil. This would be in the form of a legal contract in which the seeker promised his soul in return for a specific period of sinful indulgence (or knowledge). In most Faust stories, this period was one of twenty-four years.

After the pact is signed, Faust is indulged in all kinds of things. He receives food, drink, clothing, money, as well as knowledge about hell and the demons. He travels widely over all of Europe, relishing in playing practical jokes on the Pope in Rome and the sultan in Constantinople. Faust also visits Egypt and Asia, where he even sees the Garden of Eden. But Faust soon turns his attentions to love. He summons Helen of Troy and spends years indulging in sexual excesses. In the end, Faust is overcome with remorse and fear, and at a "last supper" with his students he exhorts them to follow Christ. But on his last night alive, Faust is indeed taken to hell by a horde of fiendish spirits.

In the earliest German *Faust Books,* the chief sins of the magician are his "speculative" interests, that is, his attempts to discover ways to enjoy the pleasures that medieval morality stigmatized as having their origins in the "seven deadly sins": pride, greed, lust, anger, gluttony, envy, and sloth.[34]

As we know, the Faust material at once went over to England where it struck a responsive chord. The poet Christopher Marlowe (1554–1593) began writing his drama *The Tragicall History: The Life and Death of Doctor Faustus* as early as 1588, and probably finished it around 1590, although it was not printed until 1604. Marlowe was the first author to write at all sympathetically about Faust and to connect the ideas of the Renaissance with his subject. In *The Tragicall History* it is clear that Faustus sells his soul not only for pleasure but for knowledge and power. It is his will to become an earthly god through magic and to be able to direct worldly politics by influencing the Pope and Holy Roman Emperor. Despite whatever sympathies Marlowe might have had with his subject, in the end Faustus is condemned (as he is in all the *Faust Books*). The complete "Faustian" treatment of Faust remained for a more Faustian man to complete: Johann Wolfgang von Goethe. We shall return to a transformed Faust in the next chapter.

The Faustian tradition is not limited to the historical personage of Faust or to artistic fictionalizations of his adventures. There is also a tradition of practical magical manuals or *grimoires* ("grammars"), which were reputed to be the very texts actually used by the magician to conjure spirits and demons. These are important because they show that the tradition was not merely literary but reflected an authentic school of magical operations. In German culture of the sixteenth, seventeenth, and eighteenth centuries, the Faustians were not only exhorted by literature to follow in the footsteps of their exemplary model—they were also provided with practical manuals purporting to tell them just how to do so.

There are a number of manuscripts referred to as Faustian grimoires, which were supposedly ones used or written by him. Most are composed in German, although some are in Latin. These were collected as early as 1846 in J. Scheible's series *Das Kloster.*[35] They bear titles such as *Doctor Faustens dreyfacher Hollenzwang* (Dr. Faust's Threefold Conjuration of Hell) or *D. I. Fausti Schwarzer Rabe* (D[r.] J[ohann] Faust's Black Raven). These works are part of the same general tradition that gave rise to the *Sixth and Seventh Books of Moses,* examples of which were also produced in Germany at about this time.

Almost all of these books appear to have been supplied with false dates and places of publication. The printed dates sometimes go back before Faust's time, while the places—which include Rome and Vienna—betray an interest in making the magical practices contained in them seem particularly Roman Catholic.

The type of magical practices reflected in these books is fairly standard for medieval sorcery. The magician draws a circle around himself that is full of prayers, names of God, or sacred symbols meant to protect him. Outside the circle there is a place—sometimes within a triangle—

where the sign (sigill) of the spirit to be summoned is placed. Then, through prayers, conjurations, and even threats, the magician calls up the angel or demon to his presence in the triangle outside the circle before him. Once he has succeeded, the magician deals with the entity, bargaining with it to try to obtain the particular gifts that correspond to the manifested entity.

Regardless of whether it deals with angels or demons, this kind of magic is essentially a right-hand-path practice insofar as it keeps the source of power and divinity (or diabolism) *outside* the self and the magician. In the final analysis, it will not be the power or gifts bestowed upon the Faustian magician that will lead to his becoming a god-man, but rather the breadth and depth of *experience* provided by this magic. It is what the Faustian magician *learns* from his quest into the realms of the unknown, beyond the limitations of time and space, that is the secret of the *Black Raven*.

The legends and even the motivation for the publication of the grimoires had a purely right-hand-path bent. The creators and publishers of the material were trying to hold onto medieval thinking and philosophical morality for as long as possible, keeping their societies in its thrall. One authority puts it well:

> Numerous are the legends built up around the personalities of men who defied the taboos of their times and sought to probe the unknown nature of man and the universe. Their strength lay in their "magic," their power over the "right" word; their weakness lay in their isolation, which invited distrust and condemnation.[36]

The Western Middle Ages were singularly inhospitable to left-hand-path philosophy because of the essentially antihuman bias of official church dogmas that tended to dominate the period. The Renaissance would partially, but only partially, compensate for the cultural losses incurred during the medieval epoch. It would not be until the twentieth century that the spiritual baggage of the Middle Ages could be dispensed with completely. But even now the medieval period casts a shadow that can be seen in the shapes ranging from modern-day witch-hunters to TV evangelists. Nothing that has made an impact on the course of human culture ever seems to disappear totally. Indeed, the spirituality of the Middle Ages is alive and well, and can be seen on American cable television on a regular basis.

6
Lucifer Unbound

THE MODERN AGE AND NEW UNDERSTANDINGS
1433–1900

Presaging the birth of the historical Faust in northern Europe, certain social circles in southern Europe, and especially in Italy, were undergoing radical transformations. The northern Italian cities of Florence, Milan, Genoa, and Bologna became the cradles of the Modern Age in that period of cultural renewal we call the *Renaissance*.

Throughout the intellectually depressed period of the Middle Ages, the spiritual treasures of the humanities—the writings of Plato, Aristotle, and other pagan philosophers—had been grudgingly preserved in monasteries or cultivated in the intellectual haven provided by a more tolerant Islamic culture. In the West, these treasures were not appreciated for the ideas they contained, but only for their utility in bolstering Christian dogmas or their usefulness as linguistic or rhetorical textbooks for classical studies.

In the decades immediately before and after the watershed year of 1500, the Western world underwent a number of "revolutionary" changes. Throughout the fifteenth century, northern Italian guilds and trade associations, using newly refined financial institutions or banking, had been able to build up powerful trading empires with connections to the eastern Mediterranean. There they did business in centers such as Tyre, which was at the end of trade routes reaching eastward to India and China. The wealth of this new class of men and families—such as the Medicis, Borgias, and Sforzas—allowed them to create a new culture separate from that dominated by the church or the old aristocracy. With this new power came new interests in pagan national traditions and pagan rational philosophy. The powerful families of the Florentine Renaissance became interested in "things that worked." It was this pragmatism that motivated much of their patronage of the arts and sciences.

It is ironic that the most lasting result of the Crusades—the church-inspired wars designed to "liberate" from the Muslims the sites in Jerusalem holy to Christians—was an opening of Christendom to the economic and cultural influences of Islam and other "eastern" civilizations. The "Holy Land" remained ultimately in Muslim hands.

Besides the Crusades, which sent tens of thousands of Christians to their horrible and useless deaths, the church had committed a number of other acts that corroded its previously unquestioned position of spiritual authority. The excesses of the Inquisition, and the widespread institutional corruption of the priesthood and sacraments of the church, contributed to increasing doubt about the veracity of church authority and dogmas. Major cosmological underpinnings of the medieval world were also turned upside down through such world-shattering discoveries as Columbus's reports of a "New World" (a place unrecorded in the Bible, which previously had been seen as a "universal book of knowledge") in 1492 or Copernicus's theory that the sun, and not Earth, was the center of the planetary system. The final blow to the Middle Ages came with the success of the Protestant Reformation (beginning 1517). For the first time since the beginning of the medieval period, the absolute ideological authority of the Roman Catholic Church had been challenged effectively in the West. Within a generation, all of northern Europe had broken with Rome.

The early Renaissance flourished in the protected, yet often volatile and fragile, havens for learning and the human spirit provided by the northern Italian families of patronage. It was a time of true rebirth. Some were so bold as to attempt the overt revival or renewal of the pagan Greco-Roman cult,[1] but the main purpose of most thinkers was to attempt a synthesis of sophisticated pagan philosophy with medieval Christian symbolism. The dominant philosophy emerging from the Florentine Renaissance was Neoplatonism. In its Renaissance form, this philosophy was to be a pagan system of thought gilded with Christian imagery for the sake of the consumption of the masses and of churchmen. It might be a shocking revelation to some, but the most renowned art treasure of the Vatican itself, the frescoes of the Sistine Chapel created by the "divine" Michelangelo, actually represents Neoplatonic allegory using Biblical scenes.[2]

The greatest exponents of Neoplatonism in the Italian Renaissance were Marcilio Ficino (1433–1499) and Giovanni Pico della Mirandola (1463–1494). What was most relevant to the further development of the left-hand path in Renaissance thought was the newfound stature of the individual human being and of humanity in general.

Ficino wrote an essay called "Five Questions Concerning the Mind" (1495),[3] in which he makes it clear—in keeping with pagan philosophy—that the human mind or will is able, through rational means, to liberate and enlighten itself. So far, he is only in agreement with most other pagan systems, East or West, that do not posit the necessity of God's *grace* in this process. The aim of the mind could still be either belonging to the right-hand path (seeking ultimate union with the divine) or with the left-hand path (seeking permanence and divinity for itself).

Perhaps one of the most inspirational documents of the Renaissance relevant to the redevelopment of the left-hand path in the West is Pico della Mirandola's "Oration of the Dignity of Man" from 1486.[4] In this "oration," which was to be the inaugural speech for a series of disputations concerning his 900 Theses at the university in Florence, Pico discusses two major themes: the nature and dignity of humanity, and the pursuit of the "unity of truth." In the latter, he began syncretizing all philosophical and religious systems to find the unity holding them all together in truth. It is, however, the first theme that concerns us most.

The "Oration" contains a passage in which Pico has the Creator say to Man:

> The nature of all other beings is limited and constrained within the bounds of laws prescribed by Us. Thou, constrained by no limits, in accordance with Thine own free will, in whose hand We have placed Thee, shalt ordain for Thyself the limits of Thy nature. . . . Thou shalt have the power, out of Thy soul's judgment, to be reborn into the higher forms which are divine.[5]

Pico holds that humanity finds itself in this world in an unfinished or *indeterminate* state of being. Humanity stands at the center of creation: it can evolve to the divine or devolve to the bestial. The soul of an individual is what is responsible for these transformations. It is precisely because of this "self-transforming nature" that mankind can be seen as noble. Man is the only creature not determined by *nature* but by *will* or consciousness; he *can* exist outside the hierarchy of Nature and God in a separate order.

"OLD NICK"

Another side of the Renaissance was shown by the first master of modern politics, Niccolo Machiavelli (1469–1527). His most famous book, *The Prince* (written in 1513, but not formally published until after his death), develops a political philosophy radically at odds with the Christian theory. Instead of deriving all power from God, Machiavelli sees that dealings with God must be based on pure faith, while political aims must be pursued in an atmosphere of pure reason, in order that the rational and *virtuous* ends of government may be achieved. The morality of the means used to realize these ends is measured purely in terms of their effectiveness. The ends justify the means. As a ruler, Machiavelli concludes, it is better to be *feared* than to be *loved,* "since love depends on the subjects, but the prince has it in his own hands to create fear, the wise prince will rely on what is his own."[6]

His cosmology, at least for political purposes, did not place God in a central position. He saw political affairs as largely the result of the interplay between *virtue* and *fortune* (or "fate").

The ideas and theories of Machiavelli had a profound effect on the advent of the modern world. His words have echoed throughout history since his death, for he dared to write what others only kept hidden in their hearts.

Machiavelli did not attack religion or Christianity directly, and always focused his attention on the practice of *virtue* and "the Good," but because he largely *ignored* the importance of the church and God in his political theory, he was seen as a threat to the power of the religion. This may have earned him his cognomen "Old Nick."

The Renaissance represents the infancy of the Modern Age, which would eventually allow for the practice of more left-hand-path philosophies. This Modern Age, with its increased interest in the stature and nobility of the individual human spirit and of human reason, coupled with a new valorization of nature or physicality as the matrix of divinity (rather than a barrier or hindrance to it), led to later developments in the left-hand path.

LUCIFER AND THE ENLIGHTENMENT

In reality, the Renaissance was as much or more a revival of ancient things and a continuation of medieval ones than it was an innovation of new forms of thought. More radical solutions were sought by the liberated minds of the seventeenth and eighteenth centuries. Tradition of all sorts was suspect of gross error and *scientific* methods were pursued by which each individual could prove the nature of himself and the world (seen and unseen) around him. If Satan—the Adversary of God—is ever to be equated with the independent, incarnate, human mind in a rationally enlightened state of being, then it is in the Enlightenment that he finds his first home since the advent of Christianity in Europe.

The foundations of the Enlightenment rest with such thinkers as Francis Bacon (1561–1626) in England and René Descartes (1596–1650) in France. In his major work *Novum Organum* (1620), Bacon championed a purely inductive method of reasoning that challenged all forms of received or "revealed" knowledge. Intellectual or spiritual authority was questioned more radically than ever before. Descartes, on the other hand, attempted to create a mathematical system of deductive reasoning. His most famous formulation, *cogito ergo sum* (I think, therefore I am), is in fact one of the keystones to any left-hand-path philosophy. What can be known with the most certainty about reality is our existence as individual entities. This brings psychecentricism again to the forefront of Western thought. Descartes himself realized the "diabolical" implications of his ideas on some level and tried for much of his life to reconcile his system with Christianity. But the genie was out of the bottle. By 1687, Isaac Newton (1642–1727) had published his *Mathematical Principles of Natural Philosophy,* in which he presented a unified, rational, coherent theory of the mechanics of the universe as known in his time.

TO RULE IN HELL

The English poet John Milton (1608–1674) gave expression to some of the new religious attitudes and paradoxes in his epic work *Paradise Lost* (1667). Milton's Protestant subjectivism allowed him to *feel* his way into the mythological figures in the Old Testament tale of the rebellion of Satan so deeply that when he gives voice to Satan and other demons of the pit, heroic and highly sympathetic characters emerge. This is especially true in the first part of the poem.

In the Second Book of *Paradise Lost,* Mammon speaks, giving expression to the grievances of the minions of hell:

> *Suppose he should relent*
> *And publish Grace to all, on promise made*
> *Of new Subjection; with what eyes could we*
> *Stand in his presence humble, and receive*
> *Strict Laws impos'd to celebrate his Throne*
> *With warbl'd Hymns, and to his Godhead sing*
> *Forc't Halleluiahs; while he Lordly sits*

Our envied Sovran, and his Altar breathes
Ambrosial Odours and Ambrosial Flowers,
Our servile offerings. This must be our task
In Heav'n, this our delight; how wearisom
Eternity so spent in worship paid
To whom we hate. Let us not then persue
By force impossible, by leave obtained
Unacceptable, though in Heav'n our state
Of splendid vassalage, but rather seek
Our own good from our selves, and from our own
Live to our selves, though in this vast recess,
Free, and to none accountable, preferring
Hard liberty before the easy yoke
Of servile Pomp.

(II: ll. 237–257)

Perhaps unconsciously, Milton gave voice to the Romantic rebellion against conventional moral and religious authority in the generations to come.

As the Age of Reason seemed to be moving away from traditional images of God, there was also a move away from the images of the traditional devil. Bolstered by the scientific theories of Newton, a new school of religious thought called Deism arose. Deists posit that a perfect and good God would only—and *could* only—create a perfect and good universe. From this it may be seen to follow that all apparent "evil" is actually misperceived good. This is the essence of the philosophy of Optimism championed by Gottfried W. Leibniz (1646–1716) and the English poet Alexander Pope (1688–1744), who wrote in his *Essay on Man:*

All nature is but art, unknown to thee;
All chance, direction, which thou canst not see;
All discord, harmony not understood;
All partial evil, universal good;

And, spite of pride, in erring reason's spite,
One truth is clear, Whatever is, is right.
(Epistle I:X, ll. 289–94)

However, there was also a more rebellious side to the Enlightenment, one that saw the political, religious, and philosophical establishment—all predicated on the Christian concept of God—as an ideological foe. More than most, such rebels might tend to see the image of the old Christian devil as a hero and role model. This rebellion of reason on earth was seen by some to be a reflection of the Rebellion in Heaven undertaken by Lucifer—who could now be restored as a figure bearing the light of reason and liberty. As we will examine later in this chapter, some hundred years after the Enlightenment, anarchists such as Mikail Bakunin will also see Lucifer in this same role.

THE HELLFIRE CLUB

One of the organizations of the past widely thought to be Satanic in nature was the so-called Hellfire Club in England. This group has been repeatedly discussed in dozens of books on Satanism and black magic from the 1700s up to lurid accounts written in this century. In his book *Dashwood,* Eric Towers discusses and refutes most of these accounts in some detail.[7] The Hellfire Club was supposed to have had wild orgies and Satanic black masses as a regular part of their activities. The true nature of the club was much more complicated—and ultimately much more dangerous to the establishment—than mere debauchery and blasphemy against the Roman Catholic Church.

Historically, there were two separate and apparently unrelated groups to which the name "Hellfire Club" was attached. Only the first of these, the one founded by Philip the Sixth, Duke of Wharton in 1719, ever called itself by that name. The purpose of the club was "to proclaim a profound contempt for established morality, thought, and theology."[8] This club met in the Greyhound tavern near St. James Square. They named the devil himself as their president and three of the leading members went by the names "Father, Son, and Holy Ghost."[9] This association attracted a great deal of attention to itself and was eventually banned and disbanded (in 1721) after much bad publicity. Philip went on to found the "Schemers," a sort of society of rakes who occasionally got together for sexual escapades in the company of women who were customarily masked. This masking was ostensibly because the ladies were reputed to be of high stature in society.[10]

However, it is usually the group founded by Sir Francis Dashwood (1708–1781) to which the name Hellfire Club (and the most sensationalistic activities) have been ascribed. Dashwood founded two relevant societies: the Society of Dilettanti in 1736, and then a club that met near his estate of West Wycombe at Medmenham Abbey after about 1751. The Dilettanti group was set up for the social gatherings of young Englishmen who had traveled to Italy. They would meet on the first Sunday of the month at the Bedford Head tavern in Covent Garden to dine and have learned and ribald discussions about their adventures in Italy. The actual name of the latter society is uncertain, but it seems to have been formed from Sir Francis's first name as an irreverent pun on the Catholic Order of the Franciscans: the "Friars of St. Francis" or the "Society of St. Francis" are possible conjectures.[11] The "Friars" group is the one erroneously referred to as the "Hellfire Club" in popular literature.

Although Dashwood was a Member of Parliament, even becoming Chancellor of the Exchequer in 1763, and remaining a government official until his death, the good "Friars of St. Francis," as we will call them here, were mostly well-to-do local friends of his and not especially high-placed government officials. Dashwood was a close acquaintance of Dr. Benjamin Franklin of Pennsylvania, but their association appears to have been more of an official nature. There is no evidence for Franklin being one of the "Friars." Franklin did visit West Wycombe in 1773, and at one point Dashwood gave him a copy of a draft of a new version of the *Book of Common Prayer* that Dashwood had written. In it, Sir Francis had deleted all references to the Old Testament and made the whole work more brief. He said of the Old Testament: "[It] is allowed to be an accurate and concise history and, as such, may and ought to be read at home . . . It is a Jewish book, very curious, perhaps more fit for perusal of the learned rather than suited to the capacitys [*sic*] of the general illiterate part of Mankind."[12]

Dashwood was certainly not a "Satanist." But his true person was perhaps more damaging to the cultural establishment than any occult antics would have made him. Like his acquaintance Ben Franklin, and like many of his Age of Reason contemporaries, Dashwood was outwardly orthodox but inwardly a Deist. This allowed for many divergent intellectual and spiritual views in Dashwood's life. His interest in classical antiquity and its spiritual values is reflected in his (what at first seems whimsical) construction of temples to Apollo and Bacchus (Dionysius) on his West Wycombe estate. Dashwood had perceived the divergent tendencies of rationalism (Apollo), and of intuition and ecstasy (Dionysius) in Greek religion a full century before that other "Antichrist," Friedrich Nietzsche, did so in his *Birth of Tragedy.*[13]

Another curiosity in the history of magic is reflected in the inscription Dashwood had placed over the entrance to the Abbey: *Fay ce que voudras,* "Do what you will." This was lifted directly from a reference to the "Abbey of Thélème" in the sixteenth-century humorous work *The Life of Gargantua and Pantagruel* by François Rabelais.[14] This motto was, of course, again taken up in the twentieth century by the English magician Aleister Crowley as "Do what thou wilt" (see chapter 8). The Abbey at Medmenham, by the way, had been a genuine Cistercian establishment in the thirteenth century. The building ruins were in the Gothic style that was further enhanced by Sir Francis, who wished to have a "Gothick"—or northern—aesthetic to complement the classicism of the temples to Apollo and Bacchus.

Unfortunately, Dashwood did not leave behind extensive writings detailing his philosophies, or if he did they were destroyed. If such writings had been preserved, however, it is certain that they would have contained little serious discussion of Satanism.

The late eighteenth century was a time of violent and bloody revolution. In America, the king of England, George III, who held himself to rule by Divine Right, by the Grace of God Almighty, was indicted by Thomas Jefferson of Virginia as a gross violator of Natural Law. On the principles of reason and Natural Law, the revolutionaries declared their enmity to the Divinely ordained tyrants of eighteenth-century Absolutism. In the much extoled—yet now little-read—"Declaration of Independence," Jefferson wrote:

> When in the Course of human events, it becomes necessary for one people to dissolve the political bonds which have connected them with another, and to assume among the powers of the earth, the separate and equal station to which the Laws of Nature and of Nature's God entitle them, a decent respect to the opinions of mankind requires that they should declare the causes which impel them to the separation.

George's defense would be that he, as king, was placed in his position by the Grace of God—and that to oppose the will of the king was tantamount to opposing that of God.

The revolutionary republicans of America and France were seen by the authorities as agents of the devil trying to "import" the otherworldly revolt in heaven to the political systems of the states of the world. In principle, the establishment of the day was correct, and events of the twentieth century have recorded at least a partial victory for this temporal revolt. Revolutionary republicanism goes against every idea of medieval Christian political theory, which is essentially based on the Pauline formula "there is no power but of God" (Romans 13:1) coupled with strictly authoritarian hierarchical theories of political organization inherited from Middle Eastern sources through Roman Imperialism. Republicanism, without abandoning the pagan ideals of an aristocracy of merit, attempts to pluralize the power centers of society. From the viewpoint of medieval Christian sentiment, this would amount to a "Pandemonium."

Although Satan was little championed among the republicans, the authority of the church was widely and vigorously challenged in the name of Deism and Pietism. The point of view was usually taken that Jesus was a good and noble man and teacher of great moral values and truths who had been betrayed in death by unscrupulous followers. Thomas Jefferson went so far as to compile a text he called *The Life and Morals of Jesus of Nazareth.* Now more commonly known as "The Jefferson Bible," this volume consisted of the story and words of Jesus extracted from the rest of the Biblical narrative, which Jefferson rejected and literally excised (using a razor, he cut out the sections he disapproved of), leaving a slim volume of eighty-four pages.[15] The Old Testament was roundly rejected by Deists in toto. The great American patriot Thomas Paine wrote a scathing attack on the Bible in his controversial work *The Age of Reason.*[16] In this book, Paine lampoons the whole Christian story of Satan. After first observing that the story of Satan's rebellion and exile from Heaven seems borrowed from pagan mythology, Paine makes the following analysis:

> The Christian Mythologists, after having confined Satan in a pit, were obliged to let him out again to bring on the sequel of the fable. He is then introduced into the Garden of Eden, in the shape of a snake or a serpent, and in that shape he enters into familiar conversation with Eve, who is no way surprised to hear a snake talk; and the issue of this tête-à-tête is that he persuades her to eat an apple, and that eating of that apple damns all of mankind.
>
> After giving Satan this triumph over the whole creation, one would have supposed that the Church Mythologists would have been kind enough to send him back again to the pit; or, if they had not done this, that they would have put a mountain upon him (for they say that their faith can remove a mountain), or have him put *under* a mountain, as the former mythologists had done, to prevent his getting again among the women and doing more mischief. But instead of this they leave him at large, without even obliging him to give his parole—the secret of which is, that they could not do without him; and after being at the trouble of making him, they bribed him to stay. They promised him ALL the Jews, ALL the Turks by anticipa-

> tion, nine-tenths of the world beside, and Mahomet [Muhammed] into the bargain. After this, who can doubt the bountifulness of the Christian Mythology?[17]

The even more radical French revolutionists were not satisfied with the rationalistic Deism of the Anglo-Americans. Many among them wanted the official demise of the church and its replacement with a neo-pagan religion or simply with pure reason. More and more, the image of Lucifer and the idea of reason will be associated with one another as the conflict between "faith" and "reason" becomes ever sharper in the Modern Age.

In the "mainstream" of divergent eighteenth-century thought—whether Neo-Classicist or Romantic—the invocation of a new sacred formula, "Nature," usually called to mind an orderly, benevolent (or at least neutral), and even "rational" system. Whether it was the Natural Law of the Neo-Classicist or the "back-to-nature" sentiment of the Romantics, Nature was the New God (or Goddess) defining the best aspirations of an enlightened mankind.

THE DIVINE MARQUIS

At least one man stood against this all-pervasive sentiment: Donatien Alphonse François Marquis de Sade (1740–1814). Although the "Divine Marquis"[18] was not what we might call a true Satanist, for reasons that will soon become apparent he has been widely seen as a paragon of evil and even called "Satan's Saint." (This is the title of a novel based on de Sade by Guy Endore.) But was his philosophy, which remained immature, one of the roots of the modern left-hand path?

Philosophically, the Marquis de Sade was a radical materialist. In this idea he was following his countryman Julien Offray de La Mettrie (1709–1752). La Mettrie held that the soul—or any other previously thought to be "spiritual" part of man—was in fact entirely physical or chemical in its nature. In this idea he was, of course, following the philosophy of the ancient Epicureans. He acknowledged this philosophical debt in his 1750 book *The System of Epicurus.* These ideas were so radical for his time that he was exiled from France and his books burned. One of his most important books was *Man a Machine* (1748). La Mettrie eventually found his way to the court of the Prussian king Frederick the Great, who became his patron. Two of La Mettrie's ideas that would influence Sade profoundly were that the imagination—the image-forming ability—is the chief function of the soul and that there is a close correspondence between a person's appearance and his or her character.[19] These same ideas also appear to have influenced Anton LaVey in the twentieth century.

The works of the Marquis de Sade are hardly sexual or "pornographic" documents in the sense that is widely assumed by those who have never read them. They are truly works of philosophy or "anti-theology." Every page that Sade writes is redolent of his deep rage in the face of the Roman Catholic God of eighteenth-century France. This rage stems from the same idealism that moved the Deists. All theological evidence of God, be it from the Bible or from pious churchmen, objectively pointed to a cruel and despotic God whose agents hypocritically claimed his omnibenevolence. The God of the Bible and church is manifestly wicked and villainous. But in this Age of Reason, this conclusion did not necessarily lead to the idea that the enemy of God, Satan, must be a hero. The whole Judeo-Christian tradition tended to be rejected as superstitious nonsense.

On occasion, the devil is spoken well of in Sade's works. One passage of *Philosophy in the Bedroom* (1795) sums up Sade's attitude toward God and the devil and is spoken by the character Dolmance:

> Had man been formed wholly good, man should never have been able to do evil, and only then would the work be worthy of God. To allow man to choose was to tempt him; and God's infinite powers very well advised him what would be the result. Immediately the being was created, it was hence to pleasure that God doomed the creature he had himself formed. A horrible God, this God of yours

a monster! Is there a criminal more worthy of our hatred and or implacable vengeance then here! . . .

More powerful than this villainous God, a being still in possession of his power, forever able to brave his author, the *Devil* by his seductions incessantly succeeds in leading astray the flock that the Eternal reserved unto himself. Nothing can vanquish the hold this demon's energy has upon us.[20]

At first Sade sees Nature as a neutral force, the true creatrix of the world. She is the actual *first cause,* not "God." But Sade soon discovers what he determines to be the actual meaning of Nature for Man: corruption and destruction. This is made explicit in a passage in *Juliette* (1794), which could be taken as Sade's manifesto on Nature. With fitting irony, he places the words in the mouth of the Bishop of Rome. The Pope says:

No earthly creature is expressly formed by Nature . . . all are the result of her laws . . . very different creatures probably inhabit other globes . . . But these creatures are neither good nor beautiful, precious nor created . . . they are the result of Nature's unthinking operations.

Once cast, man has nothing further to do with Nature; once Nature has cast him, her control over man ends; he is under the control of his own laws that are inherent in him . . . [T]hese laws are those of his personal self-preservation, of his multiplication . . . laws which are . . . vital to him but in no way necessary to Nature, for he is no longer of Nature, no longer in her grip, he is separate from her. If man destroys himself, he does wrong—in his own eyes. But that is not the view Nature takes of the thing. As she sees it, if he multiplies he does wrong for he usurps from Nature the honor of a new phenomenon . . . [O]r multiplication . . . is therefore decidedly detrimental to the phenomena whereof Nature is capable.

Thus those that we regard as virtues become crimes from her point of view. . . The most wicked individual on earth, the most

> abominable, the most ferocious, the most barbarous, and the most indefatigable murderer is therefore but the spokesman of her desires, the vehicle of her will, and the surest agent of her caprices.[21]

Sade sees Nature as a mechanical creatrix possessing only the will to propagate herself. But she is limited by her own laws, so this cannot occur as long as the creatures already formed continue to live and multiply. Therefore, she cannot propagate herself anew until the present creatures have been eliminated. When a human therefore undertakes to destroy life, to degrade and defile it, he or she is doing Nature's will.

Humanity is now separated from Nature's will and control, but when humans act in accordance with the hidden "will" of Nature, they are rewarded with pleasure *and* success. When they act contrary to the will of Nature, they are visited with pain and failure.

The human faculty of imagination is the key to Sade's psychology. "Imagination is pleasure's spur . . . directs everything, is the motive for everything; is it not thence that our pleasure comes?"[22] In Sade's grand scheme, of course, it is the imagination that spurs man to act in accordance with the destructive desires of Nature. However, even if one rejects Sade's cosmology, his psychology remains of interest. It is here that his ideas concerning the erotic enter his philosophy most directly. Ultimately, Sade holds that the pursuit of pleasure is the object of human life, and that physical satisfaction is more noble than the merely mental. Happiness depends on the greatest possible extension of pleasure. This is done by enlarging the scope of one's tastes and fantasies. It is only through willful imagination that the possibilities for pleasure are extended. Social or *religious* conditioning prevents this in most cases. Finally, happiness is not so much found in the enjoyment of pleasure as in the desire itself and in the destruction of obstacles in the way of its accomplishment.

Sade posited that there were essentially three kinds of people, erotically speaking:

1. Those who are of weak or repressed imagination, courage, and desires—and who live without remarkable incident.

2. The "natural perverts," who act out of obsession which is usually congenital in origin.
3. Libertines, who consciously develop their fantasies and who set about to realize them.

It is this third category, the libertines, which Sade saw as the apex of humanity. By active use of the imagination, libertines transform themselves through acts of will, in accordance with Nature. For Sade, the greatest pleasures were to be found in overcoming things that may have at one time inspired fear or disgust.[23]

Whether in the sexual or the more abstract philosophical sphere, the truest definition of Sadism (or perhaps we should use the term *Sadeanism* instead, to distinguish it from the pathological terminology of modern psychiatry) is: "The pleasure felt from the observed modifications on the external world produced by the will of the observer."[24] It should not be overlooked that this definition could serve equally well when describing the pleasure artists feel when working in their media.

The importance of the "Divine Marquis" to the modern left-hand path lies not so much in the most essential aspects of his philosophy as in its reception—especially its erotic component—by Anton LaVey in the twentieth century (see chapter 9). Sade's philosophy is to a great extent underdeveloped. His philosophical writing career only lasted some fifteen years, and his considerable time spent in prisons and asylums was hardly conducive to the development of a reflective system. There seems to be an inherent internal antagonism between Sade's professed radical materialism and the assigned role of the *will* and *imagination* in the process of transforming human beings into his idealized libertines. While Sade rightly rejected the whole notion of the Christian God as purely expedient illusion, he also saw a dark side to the face of Nature so extolled by Neo-Classicists and Romantics alike. For him, there was a demonic side to Nature that he only reluctantly and sparingly would ever identify with the devil. He was right not to do so, for the *thing* that he glimpsed seems closely akin to the substance of Yahweh Elohim—the dark demiurge of the Gnostics and the "sadistic" creator of the material universe.

Enlightenment thought rejected both the traditional God of the church and the devil in favor of Nature and a perfect creator God—one who is perfect in his reason. These ideas are further refined in the Neo-Classical period, which will again be more hospitable to images from the past, at least as literary motifs.

THE DAWN OF THE FAUSTIAN AGE

Although the Middle Ages had ended in a historical sense during the 1500s, elements inherent in medieval culture, such as political Absolutism, continued to be a part of the established cultures until the early nineteenth century. The legacy of the Middle Ages still continues to haunt us on the brink of the twenty-first century, but it is in the theme of Faust, inherited from medieval literature of the propagandistic intolerance, that we can see the cultural transformation from those times into a kind of universal "Faustian Age." Whether the pact our culture signed will have its desired effects waits to be determined.

Whenever I have the opportunity to teach *Faust* in a literature or humanities course, I like to point out a certain attitudinal fact to the students. First, I tell them of the origins of the Faustian literature and how it had been written to warn would-be dabblers in the "black arts" away from seeking three things forbidden by orthodox cultural authority in the Middle Ages: knowledge, power, and pleasure. But, I ask of my bright-cheeked students, are these not the three culturally legitimate reasons you are sitting in this class today? Perhaps it is for the idealistic reason of gaining *knowledge,* perhaps it is for the pragmatic reason of potential career advantages that a higher degree will bring (*power*), or perhaps it is for the pure *fun* of learning. None of these reasons would have been found short of sinful to the medieval mindset. We live, for better or worse, in a Faustian Age—and some might go so far as to call it a "Satanic" one. By this I do not wish to imply that the times are in any intrinsic way *evil.* They are, however, times of transformation and change.

GOETHE AND FAUST

The greatest single poetic monument describing the spiritual position of humanity in the Modern Age is *Faust: Eine Tragödie* by Johann Wolfgang von Goethe (1749–1832). Goethe was himself the paragon of the "Faustian Man" as he defined (or redefined) it in his work. It could have been no less, because the poetic drama of *Faust* was actually a kind of "spiritual autobiography" of the poet himself. The work appeared in two parts. Part I was published in 1808 and part II, only finished just before his death, was published in 1832. But the poet actually began to work with the Faust material as early as 1770–1775. In his old age, Goethe said that he worked on *Faust* "without plan and without a break."

On one level, Goethe follows much of the outline of the traditional Faust literature in crafting his drama. His work is on the surface more fragmentary, yet it is possessed of an inner level mirroring the same coherence and archetypal unity as the author's own soul.

Goethe was no mere poet. He was a philosopher and a talented scientist, as well as a professional statesman. He may have been one of the last truly "Renaissance Men." Beginning around 1768, he studied alchemical and magical texts intensively. But his spirituality would always remain a highly individualistic one. A family friend, Susanna von Klettenberg, introduced the young Goethe to pietism and spiritism. Ultimately, Goethe's philosophy and spirituality was a unique synthesis of the ideas of his time coupled with his own inner vision. Throughout his life, Goethe built an enormous reputation for himself through his writings. By the time of his death, he had reached the level of a living culture hero of international stature.

Goethe's *Faust* begins with a "Prologue in Heaven," in which the Lord wagers with Mephistopheles that he cannot tempt Faust—the representative of all Mankind—to ruination. This exchange is, of course, based on the beginning of the biblical book of Job. Meanwhile, Faust is a highly dissatisfied man. He has attained all the knowledge available in the world—yet he thirsts for more. So he turns from scientific pursuits to *magic*. With the aid of magical grimoires, he first conjures the

Earth-Spirit and then attempts to conjure the devil. At first, he is apparently unsuccessful, and therefore concludes to end his life. However, just as he is about to drink poison, he is startled to new life by the tolling of church bells on Easter morning. This demonstration of the depth of his commitment—to both life and death—coupled with the magical formulas is successful in bringing the Demon to him, at first in the form of a stray black poodle who follows him home.

Faust forms a pact with Mephisto unique in the Faustian literature. Because Faust believes himself incapable of satisfaction—and does not desire it—he concludes a pact:

> *Werd' ich zum Augenblicke sagen:*
> *"Verweile doch, du bist so schön!"*
> *dann magst du mich in Fesseln schlagen*
> *dann will ich gern zugrunde gehn.* (I, ll. 1699–1702)
>
> (If I ever say to any moment: / "Remain—you are so beautiful!" / then you may put me in fetters / then I will gladly go to my death.)

This pact is unlike others in the Faustian literature in that it is not based on a time limit. Each party to the pact believes this to be to his own advantage: Mephisto believes he can "satisfy" Faust quickly (so he will not have to wait years to obtain his soul), while Faust believes that nothing can satisfy him (so he will have the devil's services forever).

After the signing of the pact (in Faust's blood), Faust and Mephisto set out on many adventures. In Part I, they explore the mysteries of the microcosm; in Part II, those of the macrocosm. These include the seduction and eventual moral and physical destruction of an innocent milkmaid named Margaret or "Gretchen." (The name Margaret means "pearl" in Greek, and Goethe's own first love was named Gretchen.) Part I ends with Margaret about to be executed for the murder of her illegitimate child fathered by Faust.

Part II is so fantastic in its scope that it has only rarely been staged.

Central to this half of the tragedy is Faust's conjuration of, and union with, Helen of Troy: the eternal ideal of feminine beauty. In the end, after many years of Mephisto's attempts to satisfy Faust's hunger for power and knowledge, that moment does come when Faust says of it, "*Verweile doch, du bist so schön!*" (II, l. 11582) This occurs while he is involved with claiming land from the sea in Holland, in imitation of God's separation of the earth from the waters. In the end, the Heavenly Host and the Infernal Legions fight over Faust's soul. A member of the Heavenly Host, "a Penitent, once named Gretchen," intercedes on behalf of Faust's soul and saves it from damnation. The final lines of the poem sung by the "Mystical Choir" read:

> *Alles Vergängliche*
> *Ist nur ein Gleichnis;*
> *Das Unzugängliche,*
> *Hier wird's Ereignis;*
> *Das Unbeschreibliche*
> *Hier ist's getan;*
> *Das ewig Weibliche*
> *Zieht uns hinan.* (II, ll. 12104–111)
>
> (Everything that is transitory / is only an image; / the inaccessible [there] becomes actual here; / the indescribable [there] / is enacted here; / the Eternal-Feminine / draws us onward.)

Faust, an almost fluid document produced continuously throughout the poet's life, is the most vivid representation of Goethe's philosophy. To be sure, he made this philosophy more explicit elsewhere in more prosaic forms. The keyword to Goethe's philosophy is said to be *Werden* (Becoming) or *Wandelung* (Transformation).[25] True to the *Zeitgeist* of the Age of Reason, Goethe saw "Nature" as an all-encompassing matrix of reality. For him, Nature was "a reality of matter and mind, a synthesis of substance and energy, in which the *geprägte Form* [characteristic form] of any existing being was the necessary result of its intrinsic purpose."[26] For Goethe, *Life*—or existence—was a synthesis of substance and energy "held together by an unbroken nexus of continuous change ('*Werden*')."[27] His primary interest was the discovery of hidden archetypes or first forms; secondary to this, but linked to it, was the observation of isolated "forms" in Nature. Man's ability to discern the archetypes is dependent upon the intellectual or spiritual development (*Bildung*) of the individual. In this view, man cannot become a fully objective observer of a continuously dynamic process of which he himself is a part.[28] This is essentially the *modern* synthesis of the ancient dichotomy of psychê and physis. It is clear that Goethe and his contemporaries struggled with some of the same questions Plato had over two millennia earlier. For Goethe, the form is revealed by its particulars, each contributing to understanding the form.

There are, of course, many different kinds of interpretations of Goethe's *Faust.* The most convincing and eternally valid and useful, however, is one that sees the *whole* as the story of the transformations of the soul of Modern Man—it is, after all, the spiritual and poetic story of one exemplary model of one such man, Goethe himself. Such an interpretation would see each of the major "characters" as archetypes within a single evolving soul. Faust, Mephisto, Gretchen, and Helen are all internal to the soul. The drama is the story of the complex interactions of these archetypes within the soul through time.

The figure of Faust represents the self or I-consciousness, that is, the complex psychological essence of Modern Man. Faust says of himself (I, ll. 1112–17):

> *Zwei Seelen wohnen, ach! in meiner Brust,*
> *Die eine will sich von der anderen trennen:*
> *Die eine hält, in derber Liebeslust*
> *Sich an die Welt mit klammernden Organen;*
> *Die andere hebt gewaltsam sich vom Dust*
> *Zu den Gefilden hoher Ahnen.*

> (Two souls dwell, alas, in my breast, / one desires to

> separate itself from the other: / the one clings to the world with clutching organs / in a dogged lust of love / the other lifts itself forcibly from the gloom / toward the fields of sublime ancestors.)

This is indicative of the dichotomy of the strivings of modern man: one toward material life and accomplishment, and one toward intellectual advancement. This echoes the dual nature of the "sin" of mankind reflected in Judaic lore: one fleshly, one intellectual. Furthermore, it foreshadows the two predominant schools of the postmodern left-hand path.

Faust is a *positive* figure. He is a "yea-sayer" to life and all things in it. Yet there is—as there *must* be—a void, an unrealized *negative* space in the soul, a shadow or darkness, into which the soul may grow and evolve. This is the function of Mephisto. The demon is the contrary, the adversary, to whatever is posited—the antithesis to Faust's thesis. The drama unfolds in the ongoing dynamic (*werdende*) synthesis of the two. Mephistopheles says of himself:

> *[Ich bin] ein Teil von jener Kraft*
> *Die stets das Böse will und stets das Gute schafft.* (I, ll. 1336–37)

and:

> *Ich bin der Geist, der stets verneint!* (l. 1338)

> ([I am] a part of that force / that always desires what's evil, yet always works for the good. . . . I am the spirit, which always negates.)

The negation, or counterforce, of Mephisto is necessary to the dynamic process of becoming. From within, Faust is driven by a mysterious force—that manifests itself in his sense of dissatisfaction, and is drawn onward by an equally mysterious force dwelling outside his normal field of consciousness: "the Eternal-Feminine."

This Eternal-Feminine is embodied in the figures of Margaret

(Gretchen) in Part I (the microcosm), and Helen of Troy in Part II (the macrocosm). These are the two aspects of the mysterious archetype that is the object of the seeker's eternal longing. Gretchen is the earthly reflection of the ideal Helen. But, through suffering, Gretchen too is lifted into the realm of the archetypal and becomes the agent of Faust's salvation. The left-hand-path connotations of this philosophy should be obvious from the discussion of the role of the feminine in the left-hand-path systems of Hinduism and Buddhism.

Faust is the modern exemplary model of spiritual heroism. He is complex and doomed to freedom and to the quest for knowledge and power. Although some aspects of Goethe's *Faust* seem to be "Christian" in nature, neither the religion of Goethe nor the character he created out of himself could be called "orthodox." When Gretchen poses her famous "Gretchen Question" (I, l. 3415)—*"wie hast du's mit der Religion?"* ("What's your position on religion?")—Faust answers, in part:

> *Schau' ich nicht Aug' in Auge dir,*
> *Und drängt nicht alles*
> *Nach Haupt und Herzen dir,*
> *Und webt in ewigem Geheimnis*
> *Unsichtbar sichtbar neben dir?*
> *Erfüll davon dein Herz, so gross es ist,*
> *Und wenn du ganz in dem Gefühle selig bist,*
> *Nenn' es denn, wie du willst,*
> *Nenn's Glück! Herz! Liebe! Gott!*
> *Ich habe keinen Namen*
> *Dafür! Gefühl ist alles;*
> *Name ist Schall und Rauch,*
> *Umnebelnd Himmelsglut.* (ll. 3446–58)
>
> (Does my eye not gaze into your eye, / and doesn't everything / press itself into your head and heart / and weave in eternal mystery / the invisible made visible beside you? Fill your heart with it, as great as it is / and

> when you are completely happy in that feeling, / call it what you will, / call it happiness! heart! love! God! / I have no name / for it! Feeling is everything; / A name is sound and smoke, / obscuring the glow of heaven.)

To this, Gretchen rightly replies (1. 3468): "... *du hast kein Christentum*" ("you have no Christianity"). In this, of course, she is right in so far as *orthodoxy* is concerned. Faust, and Goethe, have developed their own religion, a modern synthesis of all that has gone before them.

In many ways with the modern Faust, we return to the ideal man of pagan antiquity. If, in keeping with the Socratic philosophies, we say that everything in the world has its special function, and to fulfill that function is the *Good* of that thing, then Faust (as the steadfast *seeker of knowledge and power*) may be seen as the exemplary model of human *Good*, not "evil," since mankind's apparent *unique* function is to gain increasing consciousness and organize increasing potencies. As long as Faust is *true to his quest,* he does Good—and it is this innate truth that "saves" him in the end. He is saved by the eternal object of his own subjective quest: the mysterious Eternal-Feminine.

To some extent, Goethe revolutionizes the left-hand path in the West. But was he himself a lord of the left-hand path? The answer, given our criteria, must be a reluctant "no." On the one side, the overriding implications of his great work, *Faust,* would seem to indicate a left-hand-path orientation. However, his unequivocal philosophical position on the role of man in nature and his decidedly ambiguous stance vis-à-vis the imagery of culturally traditional "evil," show him to be a manifestation of one of the "doubting angels" who took neither side in the battle between Lucifer and the Trinity.[29]

THE CLASSICAL DEVIL

Although Goethe is often viewed as a proto-Romantic by cultural historians, the fact that he considered himself a Classicist seems to sum up his general assessment.

Classicism was the final flowering of the ideologies spawned in the Enlightenment, the so-called Age of Reason. In cultural history, it may be said to be characteristic of the time period from about 1700 to 1800. With Classicism, philosophy and aesthetics began to return to the established *forms* of Greco-Roman ideals, although this was synthesized with the Enlightenment concept of questioning and/or rejecting all forms of received knowledge. The paradox here is obvious. The thoroughly *modern* split between the signifier and the signified, or between the symbol and what it symbolized, was complete. Things could be regarded in a much more detached, "scientific" way.

In many respects, Goethe fashioned the character of his Mephistopheles, which was rational, aloof, and ironical, after the spirit of the Age of Reason. He was perhaps inspired in this regard by the character and temperament of the French philosopher Voltaire.

Because at the time of the Enlightenment and Classicism popular and political culture were still thoroughly dominated by the spirit of Absolutism, there was some room in rational circles for revalorizing the "spirit of contradiction" (the devil) as the spirit of rationality. From our virtually postmodern perspective today, it is clear that here we have the beginnings of the split between the image or "sign" of the devil and that which he had signified in the premodern (medieval) world, in other words, "evil." From this time period on through the remainder of the Modern Age, serious attempts to deal with the devil will come more and more from the artistic rather than the theological world.

In reality, the true devil, the exemplary model of the magician on the left-hand path, is fully liberated again from the theological dungeon of medievalism with the advent of Classicism. The gate was opened during the Renaissance, and his chains were broken by the Enlightenment, but only with Classicism does he begin to walk the earth freely again. The true essence of this devil is, of course, the principle of isolate intelligence made aware of this material embodiment. The classical devil is the human spirit exercising its freedom and rationality, its fleshly existence and sense of beauty, its objectivity and sense of humor against the grain of cultural and political Absolutism, which continued to wrap itself in the armor of divinely righteous justification.

The sense of humor displayed by the classical and enlightenment devil is a powerful aspect. It at once tells us that the dungeon of medievalism had not dampened the devil's wit, and that he remained clever enough to use his most devastating of weapons. It also points to a certain disidentification between the image of the devil and the world he begins to find so ironically humorous.

From the point of view of the left-hand path today, there is something important to note with regard to the dawn of the Modern Age: here the eternal values or principles that characterize the left-hand path in any age or in any culture were in reality merely liberated (and then only partially) to be able to effect some of the work they had done in previous ages of Western culture.

SATAN IN THE NINETEENTH CENTURY

The Devil and the Romantics

In most things, the Romantics sought after the same ends and goals as the Classicists, and they held many of the same ideals. But they went about it all in a precisely contrary fashion. The Romantics reacted to the perceived sterility and rigidity of Classicism and wanted to infuse human life with more emotion and vitalism. The essential hallmark of Romantic thought is an "inwardness" (G. *Innerlichkeit*) or subjectivity. This is in contrast to the objectivistic trait of Classicism. The Romantics would extol feeling over thought. Jean-Jacques Rousseau (1712–1778), the French father of Romanticism, said in his *Confessions:* "I felt before I thought."[30] Where the Classical aesthetic had praised what is simple, clear, exact, and complete, the Romantic aesthetic acclaimed what is complex, obscure, approximate, and fragmentary.

In many ways, Romanticism represents the final vital synthesis of Western culture. Although aesthetically and emotionally it extols the virtues of a return to bygone nights, to "medievalism," and to the inner world of dreams (and nightmares), the scientific methodology and Classical modes of intellectual analysis are not rejected totally. But instead of the physical universe being the favored object of inquiry, as with the Classicists, now the history of human culture in all its aspects of life—and especially the mysteries of the mind and soul—retake center stage.

Whereas the Classicist had celebrated the bright and clear virtues of southern European culture, that of ancient Hellas and Rome, the Romantic would celebrate the dark and misty inner landscapes of the North, both ancient and medieval. "Romanticism" is, in fact, such a product of the Northern mind that it has been revalued as "Germanticism" on occasion. Perhaps a better term would be "Gothicism," which the Romantics *themselves* favored at the time.* On a greater scale, the inward turning of Romanticism was conducive to nationalism as this subjectivity was expressed throughout the organic collective of individual *nations*. But on the scale of the individual person, this inward turn often manifested as an interest in the "demonic."

With regard to our subject, the greatest effect of the Enlightenment, of "modernism," had been the permanent separation of the *idea* of evil from the *image* of the devil. Once this modernist separation was complete, the image of the devil, or Satan, was liberated to undergo revalorization in the hands of essentially Romantic artists and thinkers, who in many instances proved to be powerful magicians on the stage of the history of ideas.

The Romantic revalorization of Satan, or the devil, was primarily the work of the English Romantic poets William Blake (1757–1827), George Gordon Lord Byron (1788–1824), and Percy Bysshe Shelley (1792–1822). Every Romantic seems to have had a slightly different feeling about the mythopoetic place of Satan, or Lucifer, in the scheme of things.[31] But there are some important themes that hold most of them together as well.

---

*While this term took on multifaceted connotations in wake of the Romanticism with which it was associated, its origin is of course in the name of one branch of the old Germanic tribes: the Goths (discussed in chapter 3).

To begin with, "God" and "Satan," or other medieval theological terms, had become essentially literary symbols for the modernist Romantics. This is not to say they were not real. At first, this may seem to trivialize the entities referred to by the terms (this especially would seem to be the case for medievalistic apologists such as Jeffrey Burton Russell). In fact, Satan is not "trivialized" by the poets, but rather the *symbol* is revaluated and redeemed by making it again relevant to human experience. The essence of the meaning of human existence is to be found not in a system of supposedly supernatural laws presided over by institutionalized authority, but instead in the experience of the individual heart and soul. Because the medieval mind holds mankind to be in a sense "trivial," all things that symbolize and embody mankind and its faculties are thus likewise (de)valued.

The Romantics see the devil as a complex being or symbol. He is neither all evil nor all good. He is a mixture of complex and ambiguous characteristics—as is the human soul, of which he is perhaps a projection. Mythically, the Judeo-Christian figure of Satan was combined with the Hellenic figure of Prometheus. This combination is a natural one, just as Prometheus is in many ways the prototype of the Christian devil (see chapter 3).

None of the Romantics could as yet call themselves "Satanists," though they were often called this by an outraged, middle-class populace. Essentially drawing upon Milton's portrayal of him in *Paradise Lost,* the Romantics did make Satan a heroic figure worthy of human emulation. They admired him for his act of rebellion against legalistic and organized authority (= God) and for his sublime existence, majesty, and stubborn courage against all odds. They could empathize with Old Nick.

Romantics are, however, obsessed with the concept of love. Although they could see Prometheus as a lover of mankind, they still preferred to use the symbol of Jesus as the paragon of love in their mythopoetic systems. This is not, however, the Jesus of historical Christian tradition, but one that they claimed as the *true* Jesus. They may or may not have a basis for this in the evidence, as we saw in chapter 4.

While the northern Romantics were engaged in creating new syntheses and in some cases harkening back to premedieval mythology to explore the demonic, the French tended to delve into more traditional diabolical imagery and feelings. Early French literary Romanticism, founded by François-René Chateaubriand (1768–1848), was highly sympathetic to the spirit of the Middle Ages, and it was against revolutionary thought. (It was quite the opposite in the North.) Most French Romantics remained firmly in the grip of Catholic mythology, medieval aesthetics, and antirevolutionary sentiments. Demonic imagery was principally used for its ironic impact or horrific effect. Victor Hugo (1802–1885) eventually developed a prorevolutionary, antimedieval position within French Romanticism. His ideas are imaginatively explored in his historical novel *Notre-Dame de Paris* (1831), better known perhaps under its popular title in translation, *The Hunchback of Notre-Dame*. The devil becomes a symbol for rebellion as well as alienation or separation from God, with God being seen Platonically as the Good, or as Being. Thus, God of the traditional churches is rejected and replaced by the idea of infinite love. Satan is seen as an exemplary model of the human condition: a mixture of good and evil.

The Romantic with the fondest emotions for the devil seems to have been William Blake. In his *Marriage of Heaven and Hell* (1790), Blake depicted Satan as a symbol of vital creativity who struggles to be free of a coercively passive God.[32] Blake, who in a section of this same work says of Milton that he was of the "Devil's party without knowing it" (because he wrote of freedom when he wrote of the devil and of limitations when he wrote of God),[33] took Miltonian subjectivism one step further. Blake invented his own religion and his own mythology, and in this sense he presaged various schools of thought in the twentieth century. In Milton and Blake, we also see the roots of the twentieth-century movement called the Process Church of the Final Judgment.[34]

In the midst of all this Romanticism, one of the major roots of the coming occult revival was being laid by Alphonse Louis Constant (1810–1875), who wrote seriously about the idea of true Satanism. Constant is better known under his pseudonym Eliphas Levi. He tended to portray the devil in a positive light: when Levi supported revolutionary change (mainly in the 1840s), Satan was the rebel, but later, when Levi came to advocate the establishment of law and order, Satan was portrayed as the model ruler. In any event, Levi's positive valuation of an occult Satan must be viewed as the forerunner to current philosophical left-hand-path thought in the West.

In France, the dark side of the Romantic movement developed into a variety of sometimes bizarre pseudo-Catholic sects on the one side, and the artistic-literary traditions of Symbolism and Decadence on the other.

The father of the French Symbolist movement was the Romantic poet Charles Baudelaire (1821–1867). In his writings, Baudelaire drew on the early American tradition of darkness found in Nathaniel Hawthorne, Edgar Allen Poe, and Charles Brocken Brown. Although he wrote such poems as "The Litanies to Satan" in his 1857 collection entitled *Flowers of Evil,* Baudelaire could in no meaningful way be described as a Satanist. The poet was one of those unfortunate souls who believed in the traditional ideas of God and sin, and who was unable to prevent himself from committing sin. Nevertheless, Baudelaire's words later became a gateway to darkness for a number of diverse twentieth-century figures that include the surrealist artist Kurt Seligmann, the fantasy writer Clark Ashton Smith, and avant-garde singer Diamanda Galás.

Among the Decadents, Isidore Ducasse (1846–1870), who used the literary pseudonym Lautreamont, is perhaps the most interesting from a Satanic viewpoint. His *Les chants de Maldoror* (1868) is a neo-Sadean celebration of cruelty. Both Baudelaire and Lautreamont were moved by a deep sense of outrage against hypocrisy, both within themselves and in the world around them. It is this opposition to hypocrisy, together with a courage to face even the darkest aspects of the human soul, that makes the Decadents interesting from a left-hand-path perspective. Lautreamont is noteworthy for his connection of alienage with evil, foreshadowing such modern writers as H. P. Lovecraft or Don Webb.

The essentially aesthetic and artistic context of the Symbolists and

Decadents makes them difficult to study from a philosophical viewpoint. James Webb puts this larger movement in the arts into an occult context when he writes:

> [Symbolists] set out, . . . with assumptions which were anti-rationalist and anti-materialist, to produce anti-naturalist art. Because this approach was based on a total rejection of the world it may be legitimate to call it "spiritual." Whether it led to "Satanism," or the cult of the Beautiful, the face this reaction presented to the public was uniformly rebellious.[35]

Whereas the aesthetic writers and painters present us with obscure ideas beautifully wrought, the pseudo-Satanic sect leaders demonstrate their doctrines quite clearly, or at least as clearly as they are able. There were essentially two types of these sects: one clung to medieval metaphysics and considered itself generally Christian, while the other was more in line with the Decadence of the literati.

In August of 1839, Eugène Vintras (1807–1875), a manager of a cardboard-box factory in Tilly-sur-Seule in Normandy, France, had a vision of the archangel Michael; later the Virgin Mary and St. Joseph appeared to him. From these experiences he founded his own sect, the "Work of Mercy" (*Oeuvre de la Misericorde*). This sect was soon linked with the political interests of the "Royalist Party" (which wanted to restore a king to France), a shady operation spearheaded by one Ferdinand Geoffroi, an acquaintance of Vintras in Tilly. The sect grew rapidly, but ran afoul of establishment government officials and the highest levels of the Catholic church, despite the fact that it was supported by some local priests. The sect was declared heretical by the Pope in 1848, a situation that only spurred its development: Vintras now became the Pope of his own movement with his own priests. Women were also admitted to the priesthood. The sect spread to England, Italy, and Spain.[36]

The visions of Vintras have been compared to those of William Blake or Emmanuel Swedenborg, in that they involve the perception of the dichotomy between extremes of heaven and hell.[37] But the rather unsophisticated Vintras could conceive of this only in terms of what he had absorbed from Catholicism. So he cannot see the necessity of reconciling the two extremes; instead, he sets out to destroy what he identifies as the "church of Satan." There is every reason to believe that by this Vintras meant the official orthodox Roman Catholic Church.

At the same time, it is curious to note Pope Pius IX issued the *Syllabus of Errors* in 1864 in a theological attempt to cast all efforts toward radical, social, or cultural change in the mold of a Satanic force in the world. Freemasonry was especially targeted, but so too were other occult movements.[38]

Vintras died in December of 1875. At this point one of his controversial priests, Abbé Boullan, who had earlier that year been defrocked by the orthodox church, declared himself as his successor.[39] As we will see, Boullan is perhaps most famous for the supposed magical cause of his own death in 1893. The Work of Mercy had been fighting the forces of evil marshaled all around it for decades. These forces had come to include the Roman Catholic Church, along with other occultists now engaged in what the Work of Mercy held to be "black magic." Then, as now, these sinister forces tend to reside not in the objective universe, but in the paranoid fantasies of the accusers.

In any event, there was a cadre of occultists of darker aspect active in France in the late nineteenth century. This group became the target of the accusations of the self-proclaimed "white magicians" of the Work of Mercy.

The principal two occultists of this kind active in France at that time were Joséphine Péladan (1858–1918) and Stanislas de Guaita (1860–1898). It will become clear that neither of these is a true left-hand-path magician nor a Satanist. They are merely decadent eccentrics.

Péladan was the son of a schoolmaster who edited a fanatically pro-royalist and Catholic paper (*Le Châtiment*). Péladan's father also made somewhat of a business of his mystical speculations about the "sixth wound of Christ"* as a trade had built up around selling religious trinkets commemorating this newfound wound. Péladan ran afoul of the law as a protester against decrees banning unauthorized religious congregations in 1880. In 1883, he went to Paris and entered artistic circles. He held himself to be ultra-orthodox and at the same time a "magician," by which he meant "someone who is totally in control of himself."[40] In 1884, he published his major work *La Vice suprême.*

Guaita had also come to Paris in 1880 and made his reputation as a poet and writer. He published *La Muse noire* in 1882. As a result of Péladan's book, Guaita met him in 1884, and the two formed an alliance that would last until 1890. In 1888 the two in partnership founded the Ordre Kabbalistique de la Rose-Croix. Guaita was greatly inspired by Baudelaire, whom he identified as the "Satanist" poet. It seems to be Baudelaire's use of drugs, however, that most influenced de Guaita, who used morphine, cocaine, as well as hashish in his "occult" experiments. Guaita also cultivated eccentric habits that drew attention to himself: he slept by day and only went out at night, his apartment was draped in red, and he usually dressed in robes of that color as well.[41] Guaita is most notorious for having been accused of causing the death of Abbé Boullan by magical assassination in 1893. This accusation was probably nothing more than the product of paranoid rumors. Guaita himself denied it; furthermore, he was on record in his book *Le Serpent de la Genèse* as condemning the Vintras sect and the Abbé Boullan as being the ones who were "Satanic."[42] In the final analysis, it seems we have nothing more than a paranoid fanatic and a drug-deluded aesthete playing a game of "you're one too!"

In 1890, Péladan broke with Guaita and subsequently founded his own independent Rose-Croix Catholique. This schism was referred to as "the War of the Two Roses." Péladan adopted the Assyrian title and name "Sâr Merodack" (King Marduk). He began to issue mandates to

*This "sixth wound" had allegedly been inflicted on Christ's shoulder by the cross when he fell on the way to Golgotha. This was in addition to the traditional five Holy Wounds that were suffered in the hands, feet, and chest.

the world (and especially to the artistic and occult worlds), which was in keeping with his newfound stature as "king." The Sâr conjured a highly original and creative synthesis of occultism and Catholic tradition. No matter how outré the Sâr's behaviors or theories became, he was unable and unwilling to put his fanatical Catholicism behind him. The first rule in the Rose-Croix manifesto states the goal "to restore the cult of the IDEAL in all its splendour, with TRADITION at its base and BEAUTY as its means."[43] Péladan's Rose-Croix organization had widespread influence among artists in Paris.

The Sâr's Rose-Croix order did not survive his death in 1918. Guaita died in 1898, blind and shattered in body and mind, an end that had been undoubtedly hastened by his brand of "pharmaceutical occultism." However, his order was continued by Gérard Encausse (1865–1916), who wrote prolifically under the name "Papus."

The Bohemian or Decadent artistic movement runs parallel to the occult revival taking place in Europe during the same time period. As much as these aesthetes loathed the modern age, they were utterly the product of it and their "magic" was essentially a modern construction—albeit a "Romantic" one. The Decadents, by using every artistic medium of communication available to them, sought to undermine the positivistic, rational materialism that had come to dominate the upper levels of Western civilization by the latter half of the nineteenth century. They nevertheless fought this battle on a field defined by the positivists, that is, in the world of the senses.

LE DIABLE AU XIXE SIECLE:
Leo Taxil and the Anarchistic Art of Hoaxing

In the latter half of the nineteenth century, and especially in France, the devil had become a figure of enormous entertainment value as well as a symbol of spiritual and political rebellion (especially among fanatic or conservative Catholics). "Black Masses" were performed in Paris as dramatic tourist attractions, and the figure of the devil—

then as now—was always a good vehicle for stirring up sensationalistic expectations. But since the issuance of the *Syllabus of Errors* by Pope Pius IX in 1864, conservative Catholics also had a new impetus for considering all forms of progressivism and change as essentially diabolical in origin.

Freemasonry had been especially identified by the church as a Satanic force. In his 1879 encyclical *Humanum genus,* Pope Leo XIII claimed that Freemasonry intended to overthrow Christianity and reestablish paganism. A Jesuit Archbishop wrote *La franc-maçonnerie, synagogue de Satan,* in which it was claimed that the Grand Master of the lodge in Charleston, South Carolina, was the Vicar of Satan and that it was the intention of Masonry to destroy Christianity and establish a Satanic Empire.[44]

These two tendencies—to see "Satanism" as both high entertainment and as a serious threat to the establishment—were woven together in one of the most elaborate hoaxes in history. The apparent purpose of the hoax was the exposure and weakening of the conservative cause. The means used for this operation were the popular press and popular literature on the subject of Satanism. The ironic thing is that much of the literature created for this hoax (which one could also term a "disinformation campaign") or its derivations is still being used today in lurid descriptions of supposed Satanic goings-on.

The mastermind of the hoax was Gabriel Jogand-Pagès, who wrote under the name Léo Taxil (as well as under the name Dr. Bataille). Jogand was born in 1854 and began his education under the Jesuits, but began to call himself a "freethinker" by the age of fourteen. He was exposed to the ideas of Masonry through a book he obtained from a friend at school. His rebelliousness eventually led him to try to run away to Italy, and as punishment he was sent to a juvenile prison for eight months by his father. This incident was apparently further fuel for his sense of rebellion against authority throughout his life.[45]

In 1870, he joined the military and served in Algeria. After this, he began to publish anticlerical and Republican journals in his native Marseilles. As a result, he was convicted of, and fined for, "blasphemy and outrages against religion," but his journalistic subversion continued nevertheless.

In 1878, he moved to Paris, where he founded radical journals of tremendous popularity. By 1881, he actually joined a Freemasonic lodge. He spent a total of twelve months in the brotherhood and must not have been very highly initiated (although by this time most Masonic "secrets" were available to the learned public anyway). After his departure from the lodge, he "mysteriously" began to write exposés of the sinister secrets of Masonry and to make alliances with clerical forces. In 1887, he published his *Confessions d'un ex-libre-penseur* (Confessions of an Ex-freethinker), which won him an audience with Pope Leo XIII.

"Taxil" then proceeded to *create* and publish anticlerical and anti-Catholic literature, including periodicals ostensibly emanating from the Satanic "Palladium." First he set about fabricating the personality of Diana Vaughan, who was supposedly the descendant of a line going back to a union between the English alchemist Thomas Vaughan and the goddess Astarte! (Incidentally, Diana Vaughan finishes up her career as a fictional character when Arthur Machen borrows the name for a character in his novella *The Great God Pan,* published in 1894.)

At the same time he was creating the artificial reality of the "Palladians" and their head "Diana Vaughan," Taxil was also busy publishing exposés of the Satanic cult. In 1887, he claimed that Diana Vaughan was now in hiding from the Palladists—but could not show herself for fear of reprisals. He exhorted good Catholics to pray and have masses said for her conversion from her religion of evil to the true church. Astonishingly, Jogand/Taxil would continue exploit this hoax for *ten more years*. At a certain point, he had Diana finally "convert" to Roman Catholicism—and even had her writing devotional literature that was praised by the Pope himself! In 1892, Jogand issued his *magnum opus* under the name Dr. Bataille called *Le Diable au XIXe Siècle* (The Devil in the Nineteenth Century). "Dr. Bataille" was another alternate persona used by Jogand—sometimes to whip up the Satanic scare, sometimes to decry it as a fraud. Jogand was, by the way, aided in his work by his female secretary, who in fact was the actual writer of some of the "Diana Vaughan" material.[46]

Jogand/Taxil was indeed a magnificent sorcerer. He spun a web of mass illusion at the highest ranks of society for well over a decade. It was just after Easter, 1897, that he called down the final curtain. Diana Vaughan was set to appear for the first time in person before an audience gathered at the Geographic Society in Paris, but only Jogand appeared. He read a statement to the crowd in which the whole hoax was laid out.[47] He had made fools of the masses in demonstrating that they were ready to believe the most outrageous neo-medieval nonsense imaginable!

Although apologists would try to claim that the revelations about the Satanic Palladium, Masonry, and all the rest were really true, (and that Jogand had been paid off by the evil conspirators to falsely confess that he had made it all up—an "explanation" that even further stretches credibility), a more likely interpretation is that Jogand was practicing a form of journalistic sorcery—and anarchy—at the expense of the church and the Masons both. He was just continuing his lifelong rebellion against authority of all kinds.

The story of nineteenth-century French "Satanism" is important to us because it sets the stage for subsequent developments in the left-hand path in America in the late twentieth century. The interweaving of religion and philosophy with art and entertainment would become a hallmark of the LaVeyan Satanism that begins in the 1960s, and it continues to the present day. In the final analysis, however, there is little in the world of French Decadence of the late nineteenth century that can be seen as furthering the philosophical aims of left-hand-path philosophies. Because they tended to hang onto medieval imagery—conditioned by their thoroughly Catholic cultural milieu—the French Satanists (of fact and fiction) actually seem to have retarded the renewal of the philosophy of the transcendental branch of the left-hand path in the West. By the same token, however, they provided the heart and soul of the *imagery* upon which the redevelopment of the immanent branch of the path would rest.

THE RED DEVIL

While the Satan of the Decadents and the Neo-Romantics was being manifested in the world of the arts, another image of Satan was being revalued in the political sphere. The Satan of Judeo-Christian tradition—as developed by Milton and the Romantics—was a highly suitable symbol or embodiment of rebellion in the revolutionary period of the mid-nineteenth century. Even the materialist/positivist revolutionaries saw Satan as a hero of sorts.

Almost in a revival of the ancient debate between Epicureans and Stoics, the mid-nineteenth century saw the growth of a new form of materialism. This had been theoretically pioneered by La Mettrie and Sade, but it was now projected into the world of economic and political action. In essence, however, the assertion that the material universe is all that exists and any notion of a metaphysical realm is purely an aberration or delusion, is, in and of itself, a matter of faith in something unseen or unapparent. In practice, radical materialism is just as "mystical" as spiritualism, and history has shown it to be no more "scientific" than theology and not nearly as effective.

The materialists of the nineteenth century were uniformly revolutionaries; they were intellectual as well as political rebels. They revolted against an establishment that had universally wrapped itself up in the mantle of religious authority. God Almighty, King of Heaven, ruled there in the same continuum as the Czar, Kaiser, or King ruled in Russia, Prussia, or England. Therefore, it is not surprising that if and when the antiestablishment rebels couched their thoughts in Biblical metaphors, they might tend to show an overwhelming amount of sympathy for the devil.

Whether it was the communism of Marx, the anarchism of Bakunin, or the Bolshevism of Lenin, each had their special relationships with the devil and each saw him as they saw themselves—cast in the glow of a red light. In their minds, the battle lines were drawn between the spiritual and material, the bourgeois and proletariat, the "haves" and the "have-nots."

THE DEVIL AND KARL MARX

Over the past century and a half or longer, for conservatives ranging from Pope Pius IX to John Birch and beyond, the ideas of revolutionary communism have been virtually synonymous with a cosmic Satanic conspiracy. Before these apparent ravings are dismissed out of hand, however, we might find it interesting to explore the philosophies of Marx and other socialist/materialist thinkers from a left-hand-path viewpoint.

Karl Marx (1818–1883) did not invent communism or historical materialism, but he was an original synthesizer and codifier of a range of philosophical, economic, and socio-political ideas into a theoretically coherent whole. This ideology could then be more forcefully disseminated than had been the case with the loose association of concepts that marked any related, pre-Marxist movements.

Marx was born in Trier, Germany, on May 5, 1818, to an ethnically Jewish family.[48] His father, Heinrich, had converted to Lutheranism just the year before. Karl was brought up entirely in the Lutheran faith. In 1835, he went to study law at the University of Bonn, but transferred to Berlin the following year, at which point he was quickly "converted" to philosophy under the influence of the "Young Hegelians," a group of intellectuals engaged in the transformation of Hegel's historical idealism into historical materialism.

Marx had planned to become a university lecturer. He wrote his doctoral dissertation on the philosophy of Epicureanism. By 1841, however, the Prussian government clamped down on the Hegelian left, which caused all job prospects for Marx to evaporate. Back in the western part of Germany, in Saarbrücken, Marx met a communistic Zionist publicist named Moses Hess who was able to "convert" him to a communist philosophy. Hess was also responsible for converting Friedrich Engels, Marx's future collaborator. Marx soon became the editor of a liberal newspaper, the *Rheinische Zeitung,* which he quickly radicalized. In April 1843, the paper was suppressed by the government and Marx emigrated to Paris. He was expelled from France in 1845, eventually settling in England in 1849. The year before, in 1848, he wrote (in collaboration with Engels) one of his two major works: *The Manifesto of the Communist Party.* He was to live the rest of his life in relatively obscure circumstances in London.

In 1864, the "First International" (more precisely, the International Workingman's Association) was organized in London. This was a federation of unions and radical organizations. Marx was able to exert his influence on this group. In place of nationally organized and loosely affiliated, vaguely liberal unions, Marx imposed his vision of an international, disciplined, federated, radical organization bent on the utter destruction of capitalist society. Because of his authoritarian principles, Marx was opposed in the International by the almost equally prestigious Mikhail Bakunin.

In 1867, the first volume of Marx's magnum opus, *Das Kapital* (Capital), appeared. By this time, his thought had reached its full maturity and he could only defend the doctrines he had already developed. His support for the short-lived, violently insurgent government known as "the Commune" in France in 1871 earned for Marx the popular title of "the Red Terrorist Doctor."

Due largely to the chaotic influence of Bakunin in the organization, the International died in obscurity in Philadelphia in 1876. In his latter years, Marx developed closer ties with Russian communists. But before these ties could be exploited, he died in London on March 14, 1883. He is buried there in Highgate Cemetery. It would be over three decades before his theories would begin to be put into practical use after the Russian revolution of 1917.

Marx's attitude toward traditional religion was that it is "the opiate of the masses." However, it is equally clear that he intended his philosophy to be a total replacement for religion. His antipathy toward religion started shortly after he began his university studies. He and his associates at the *Doktorklub*—the Young Hegelians of Berlin—set out on an atheistic program to destroy the superstructure of conservative authority, which they saw in religion. Although he later concentrated on certain economic theories coupled with historical materialism, the young Marx had a vision of the "total redemption of humanity,"[49] as he wrote in the introduction to his *Contribution to the Critique of Hegel's*

Philosophy of Right (1844). The whole of Marx's philosophy has been seen as a sort of "prophetic politics" that first envisions and then promotes a total transformation of the world.[50]

The early ideas of Marx—in which the roots of his motivations may be found—have been analyzed as being Faustian/Promethean by at least one scholar.[51] Even the casual observer will have noticed the quasi-religious features of Marxism, both as a theory and in the manner it has been practiced in various countries in the twentieth century. This perhaps has its origins in the nature of Marx's own initial impetus during his Berlin period. All this is best revealed in his own early, precommunist, writings, such as the epic drama *Oulanem* (1837) and his poetry. In one of these poems, "*Der Spielmann*" (The Fiddler, written in 1841), he writes:

> *Was, was! Ich stech', stech' ohne fehle*
> *Blutschwarz den Sabel in Deine Seele,*
> *Gott kennt sie nicht, Gott acht' nicht der Kunst*
> *Die stieg in den Kopf aus Höllendunst,*
> *Bis das Hirn vernarrt, bis das Herz verwandelt:*
> *Die hab' ich lebendig vom Schwarzen erhandelt.*
> *Der schlägt mir den Takt, der kreidet die Zeichen;*
> *muss voller, toller den Todtenmarsch streichen . . .*
> (ll. 17–24)

> (Behold, my blood-blackened saber shall stab / Without fail into your heart. / God neither knows nor does he honor art. / It rises into the brain as vapors from Hell. / Until my brain is deluded and my heart transformed: / I bought it while still alive from the Dark One. / He beats the time for me, he gives the signs; / must more boldly, madly rush in the March of Death . . .)

It is curious that even toward the end of his life, overtly Satanic images were used to describe Marx's appearance, even by his close associates. His son-in-law, Paul Lafargue, said of him: "he himself was known as the Moor or Old Nick on account of his dark complexion and sinister appearance."[52]

In the final analysis, Marxism is a system of mystical materialism. He posits that history has an organic structure and that its evolution is driven not by the mind of God, as Hegel would have had it, but by exclusively material considerations (such as purely economic factors or human behavior) along with the change caused by struggles between economically determined classes in society. Throughout all of history, classes of people—as determined essentially by economic status—who were without power would, by the inevitable force of the "historical dialectic," wrest power away from those who have it at present. Thus the proletariat would, by the sheer force of history, overcome the overripe capitalist establishment.

Marx claimed that his theories were purely "scientific" or rationally based, that he merely had the clearest view of historical change and its causes. But as it turns out, his work had an effect less like a prophecy and more like a sorcerous incantation. Essentially, Marx's view of history appears uncannily like that of Judeo-Christian tradition, only its causal agent has been revaluated from "God's Plan" to "historical dialectic." In the former, there is an initial Edenic period that is broken by man's transgression against God's law. This is followed by a long period of tribulation ended first by the incarnation of the Messiah, who brings the program for salvation (the *Evangelium*, or "good news") that is to be enacted by his earthly followers (the church). Once this program has been spread worldwide, evil will be vanquished and a new paradise will be established on earth. The Christian version of this is, of course, highly spiritualized, while the Judaic version remains largely materialistic. The Marxist view similarly posits an early period of primitive communism, broken by the institution of private property (= Original Sin) and slave labor. This is followed by successive economic stages of feudalism and capitalism. The beginning of the end of the capitalistic phase is heralded by Marxist theory as a program for "redemption" (operating through the process of the historical dialectic), which is to be enacted by socialist revolutionaries (the International). Once revolution is spread worldwide, capitalism will be vanquished and the classless, perfected communist society will be established on earth. Such parallels between Marxist and Christian and/or Judaic views of history have also been pointed out by several scholars in the past.[53]

Although Marxist theory may be increasingly discredited (as political systems based upon it fail and prove to be programs for ever more inefficient and intolerant systems than those the theory was designed to overthrow), elements of Marxist thinking have definitely permeated into popular political culture in the form of such things as notions of "political correctness." The concept of "political correctness" (even the connotations of the phrase) stems from Marxist orthodoxy and is based on the premise that there is an ongoing struggle by a variety of suppressed groups who are at present viewed as being relatively powerless (such as women, African Americans, Hispanics, the physically challenged, etc.). It is their collective aim (as well as each group's individual one) to wrest socioeconomic power from those who have it at present. This is Marx's "class struggle." Furthermore, those groups are assured by Marxist theory of fighting the good fight, the moral fight, because the historical dialectic (or the Marxist "God") is on their side. Their morality and their future victory are assured by the very fact that they are *currently* powerless. This is why, for example, blacks cannot be considered "racists," or women "sexists," at least according to this theory based in the Marxist historical dialectic.

THE ANARCHISTIC DEVIL

"If God really existed it would be necessary to abolish him."

MIKHAIL BAKUNIN

In his fragmentary work, *God and the State,* the Russian anarchist Mikhail Bakunin (1814–1876) at one point assesses humanity in terms of the Edenic myth and says: "[Satan] makes man ashamed of his bestial ignorance and obedience; he emancipates him, stamps upon his brow the seal of liberty and humanity, in urging him to disobey and eat of the fruit of knowledge."[54] As Bakunin saw it, humanity—as an essentially bestial creature—was "endowed in a higher degree than the animals of any other species with two precious faculties—*the power to think and the desire to rebel.*"[55] His understanding of humanity—his *anthropology*—held that collectively and individually the development of man was characterized by three principles: human *animality, thought,* and *rebellion.*

For Bakunin, Satan is "the eternal rebel, the first freethinker and emancipator of worlds."[56] Like most anarchists who derive much of their theory from Rousseau's idea of the "noble savage," civilization and its institutions are the chief evils in the world. They must be struck down so that the innate nobility of humanity may emerge as a matter of natural course once it is freed of all socially determined conventions.

Bakunin was himself more of an activist revolutionary than a writer or philosopher. He said, "I cleave to no system, I am a true seeker."[57] He is alleged to have had a love for the mysterious and the irrational. This put him at odds with those who followed the more systematic philosophy of Marx and whom he called "doctrinaire communists." Both of these philosophies are, however, based on a positivistic materialism. "God" was firmly identified with the idea of "spirit," so the devil, God's opposite, must be—if we choose to use this language—tantamount to the idea of matter. The property of "intelligence" can, however, be ascribed to matter due to its "dynamic nature and evolutionary quality," according to Bakunin.[58]

This dichotomizing of "matter" and "spirit" is, of course, typical of the modern era. Where such dichotomies can be generated, one aspect must be accepted and the other rejected—or so goes conventional thought. All this is modern, all-too-modern. From a left-hand-path perspective, it is perhaps interesting to remember that ancient Hebrew mythology identified as "Satanic" *both* the existence of the flesh (nature/matter) and the presence of intelligence (as a result of rebellion).

While the ideas of Bakunin lived on in a vague obscurity—and continue to do so today among dedicated anarchists who oppose authority in all its forms—the ideas of Marx have had a much more doctrinaire and institutionalized history. This history was to be played out not in the industrialized capitalist strongholds of western Europe, but in the still largely feudalistic, preindustrial Russia.

THE BOLSHEVIKS AND THE "EMPIRE OF EVIL"

The Slavs in general, and the Russians in particular, have a special place in their national traditions for the devil or devils. Russian popular religion on the very eve of the 1917 Revolution was still a mixture of orthodoxy and rural demonology; there was indeed still a true "dual faith" (Rus. *dvoeverie*).[59] This only goes to show how extraordinarily conservative (in the sense of holding onto archaic cultural traditions) the Russian peasant was. The structure of this faith had remained virtually unchanged from the period when the Russians converted to Orthodoxy nine centuries before.

But besides the "normal" culturally conservative peasants who believed in the magical power of saints (who embodied their old Slavic gods) and the powers of devils great and small, there was a variety of extraordinary sects or cults in late nineteenth- and early twentieth-century Russia, which must be understood in order to comprehend the spiritual dimension of the phenomenon of Bolshevism.

Most of these sects rejected orthodox spirituality in favor of their own teachings, many of which were heavily tinged with Gnosticism and most of which held out the promise of the advent of an earthly paradise (as opposed to the more orthodox promise of a heavenly one). Many of these sects were rationalistic and materialistic in their ideas and prophesied a time when mankind, as a collective entity, would become godlike. Sects such as the Raskolniki, the Molokans, Duckobours, Stundists, Neo-Stundists, the Nyemolyaki (nonprayers), Medalyshchiki and Nyeplatelshchiki (nontaxpayers), and several others all taught of the evils of private property and the Russian Orthodox Church. They were for the universal brotherhood of humanity and the advent of an earthly paradise in the name of true Christianity. They were against the privilege of private property, the Orthodox Church, and Satan.[60]

Other sects in Russia from this period that are perhaps better known include the Khlysty ("whippers") and an offshoot of the latter called the Skoptsy ("the mutilated"). The Khlysty practiced a libertine form of mysticism, which involved flagellation and sexual orgies. The Skoptsy, however, believed in extreme asceticism and practices of corporeal mortification, including mutilation of the sexual organs and amputation of limbs. Their leader was typically believed to be the reincarnation of Christ, and sometimes the Czar would "humor" the Skoptsy by crucifying them on the Kremlin wall![61] These sects have many tendencies in common with the Gnostic cults from the first few centuries of the Common Era.[62]

It seems likely that the famous rogue holy man, Grigori Y. Rasputin, was closely allied with the teachings of the Khlysty, at least in spirit. However, the majority of hard evidence (such as his own writings) points to him being a rather naive, simple peasant in most of his outlook on life. Certainly he was no follower of the left-hand path,[63] despite the fact that he is listed as one of the major influences on Anton LaVey on the dedication page of *The Satanic Bible,* and despite the popular image of him as a "devil worshipper" (see chapter 9). Often the myth—or *image*—of a man in history far outweighs any factual data on him.

It is amid this cultural backdrop—one of widespread popular demonology, sects preaching the advent of "heaven on earth," and cults practicing extreme forms of libertinage and asceticism—that the Bolsheviks of V. I. Lenin step upon the stage of Russian history.

Vladimir Ilyich Lenin (1870–1924) founded the Bolshevik (majority members) faction of the Russian Social-Democratic Workers' party in London in 1903. This wing opposed the Menshevik (minority members) faction. Lenin, born Ulyanov, became a Marxist revolutionary after the execution of his brother who was implicated in a plot to assassinate the Czar. Lenin was later arrested and sent to Siberia in 1895. In 1900, he fled to western Europe to organize socialism internationally. In 1905, he returned to Russia to participate in the abortive revolution of that year, but fled again in 1907. Lenin returned to Russia after the outbreak of the 1917 revolution in March of that year, and led the Bolshevik overthrow of the provisional government in November (October in the Old Style Russian calendar, hence the "October Revolution"). As chairman of the Council of People's Commissars, he became the virtual dictator of Russia. From then until his death in 1924, Lenin worked to establish the professional revolutionaries of the Bolshevik party as the ruling elite of the country, while suppressing all internal opposition to himself and working to spread communist revolution worldwide. One of his closest associates was Joseph Stalin.

Lenin's opponents often saw in him the Antichrist.[64] Certainly he was an "apocalyptic" figure who attempted to transform a whole culture in a very short period of time. He was as successful as he was because of his mystical vision of a primitive culture transformed into an ultra-modern, electrified, totally efficient machine. The *machine* was Lenin's god.

Each individual worker or peasant—each individual human being—was essentially a machine, and so too was the collective entity of all workers and peasants. Lenin's inner task was to make the whole work as an efficient, perfected machine. This is why science and technology were virtually sanctified in Soviet Russia: the New Man, the New Machine—the *Homo Sovieticus*—would be created from the scientific communist programs of the Bolsheviks. These programs were indeed set into motion by the party. These activities amounted to the dismantlement of orthodox religion replaced by the new faith of communism.

THE RITES AND RITUALS OF BOLSHEVISM

No source informs us more about the early cultural history of Soviet Russia then René Fülöp-Miller's *The Face and Mind of Bolshevism* (1926). As time goes on, we can expect more internal evidence to surface about the quasi-religious and even "magical" aspects of Soviet culture. It is clear that the early Bolsheviks had an extremely radical "plan," implicit in the Marxist-Leninist philosophy, for the transformation of the human species into a collective godlike machine. But *how* was this to be done in practical terms? First, the vestiges of the old system, the bourgeois society and culture, had to be destroyed utterly. As institutions, the church and state could be eradicated or controlled in a relatively easy manner—through brute force. But the psychological and cultural (collective psychological) hold of the old ways would require a second phase: the institution of new cultural and quasi-religious forms to replace the old ones.

In the efforts of the first phase, the communist youth organizations, especially the Komsomol (Communist Youth League), were instrumental. There were massive campaigns to debunk the Russian Orthodox religion and every cultural aspect of that church. The public was rationally "educated" against belief in icons or the miraculous powers of relics of the saints. In the former effort, for example, comic antireligious icons were produced in magazines such as *Bezbozhnik* ("*The Atheist*"), an example of which is reproduced as figure 6.1.

"Red Masses" were held in the old churches. These lampooned the orthodox faith with comic mockeries of their ceremonies. Churches were turned into museums of atheism and the hammer and sickle replaced the orthodox cross atop the spires. Belief in the curative powers of the miraculously preserved bodies of saints was debunked with rational and scientific explanations of how the bodies were preserved by artificial means. It is rather ironic, but consistent with the nature of cultural continuity, that Lenin's body was preserved the way it was—as a miraculous example of "Soviet Sainthood."

Soon after the revolutions of 1917, the Soviets set out to create a replacement for the "opiate of the masses." The negative campaign against religion in general could only take them so far in transforming the society. Certain rites and customs were created in the time of Lenin to act as positive answers to the human need for such things. There were rites for "baptism," marriage, and funeral.

The most interesting of these is that of the baptism, or naming, of a new "comrade." The names given to children were sometimes selected by collective action in the factory or party offices. A whole new type of names began being given in Russia—ones that reflected revolutionary values, for example, Revolutia or Oktyabrina (in honor of the October

Figure 6.1. An antireligious illustration on the cover of Bezbozhnik

Revolution) for girls and things such as Rem (an acronym from the Russian phrase for "Revolutionary Electrification Program") for boys. The naming was done in a "Red Baptism" presided over by local party secretaries in party facilities. Usually children were named in group ceremonies. The meeting hall was draped in red, the gathered workers sang "The International," the hymn of international communism, and the parents swore to bring up the child as a good communist. The official naming was done ceremonially with these words:

> *We the undersigned herewith confirm that into the union of the Socialist Soviet Republic a new citizen* ________________ [here the first and last names are inserted] *has been received. As it is that we give to you your name in honor of* ________________ [here an explanation of the socialist significance of the first name is given], *we greet you as a future worker and founder of Communist society. May the ideals of Communism henceforth form the content of your long-lasting life! May you become one of those who will lead the great task of the proletariat to its conclusion! You shall step beneath the red flag! Long live the new revolutionary citizen!*[65]

The Soviets thought that the new, younger generation would be the true transformers of humanity. Instrumental in this transformation of the species would be a new sexual morality. Until the advent of Stalinism, there was a red sexual revolution following in the wake of the political revolution. Both marriage and divorce were made easier, requiring no involvement with ecclesiastical sacraments. Abortions were also easily available, but not encouraged. Certain aspects of the new red sexuality suggest possible links with the Khlysty sect, at least in spirit.

In the *Pravda* newspaper, a female ideologue, Smidovich, published an article on this new morality pertaining especially to the young members of the Komsomol. She wrote that the more primitive ("animalistic") the rules of conduct for sexual life are, the more communistic they are. The youth must not place restrictions on their sexuality. No female should refuse the sexual advances of a male member of the Komsomol. In the Komsomol itself, orgies called "African Nights" were organized in which there were approximately 70 percent men and 30 percent women.[66]

These institutions did not survive the development of Stalinism. Lenin only lived until 1924, at which time Joseph Stalin (1879–1953) began to consolidate his power from his position as General Secretary of the Communist Party. By 1929, with the exile of Leon Trotsky, Stalin's hold on ideological power was complete. Stalin reinstated a high level of cultural conservatism and virtually every shred of the avant-garde characteristics of the Revolution was suppressed. To his citizens, Stalin became a devil incarnate, perhaps liquidating as many of his countrymen as would be killed in the "Great Patriotic War" with the Germans. Any and all popular deviations from the strict, atheistically puritanical code of Stalinist authoritarianism became impossible.

The demise of the Soviet system in the early 1990s indicates nothing more than the failure of one more totalitarian regime to sustain the common welfare. The theoretically Marxist-Leninist line of thought was utterly (if covertly) rejected by Stalin during his tenure as Soviet dictator. For all intents and purposes, the Marxist-Leninist experiment died in the Stalinist purges. What replaced it was the ever-popular form of simple tyranny.

From a left-hand-path perspective, there are essentially two kinds of political structures. One is the tyrannical structure in which the leader is virtually deified (or demonized) and worshipped. In such a structure, the only possible practitioner of the left-hand path would be the leader himself or herself; all others would have to practice the right-hand-path value system of self-annihilation before the will of the leader. The second left-hand-path political structure involves the relative deification of a variety of individuals in various spheres of influence, with each individual epicenter of consciousness on the perimeter of other surrounding spheres.

Both structures have their representatives. The latter structure is more complex and subtle, of course. It is seen in the models of pagan antiquity (whether that of the national traditions, Indian tantrism, or Platonic systems) and in modern organizations such as the Temple of Set. The former model is more evident in modern movements of ideological or political totalitarianism where the leader understands himself to be the universal "god"—or standard—of the "world" in which he reigns. This is usual in many occult organizations, and it is often the case among modern Satanic groups. A case in point is the Church of Satan, in which the personality of Anton LaVey defined its essence in toto.

The question as to the true left-hand-path significance of Marxist theory and practice is fairly clear. Theoretically, Marxism assumes a possible perfection (deification) of humanity *as a species.* But this perfection is only possible on a collective rather than individualized basis. The nature of this collective is determined by materialistic/economic criteria and the process of perfection is governed by a transpersonal force in history. The idea that the human can become (a) god is essentially a left-hand-path premise, but the fact that the process by which this occurs in Marxism is *collective* and *not willed* (but rather inevitable, according to historical dialectic) means that the ideology cannot ultimately be considered as a left-hand-path system. Plato or Pythagoras would have told Marx that any deification must be based on *individuality.* It is perhaps this truth that Lenin and Stalin realized in their final stages of personal development.

"Collective perfection" is a notion inherited from Judaic and perhaps Iranian ideology. The idea that a selected *group* of humans will gain knowledge, power, and immortality passes into institutionalized Christianity and can be found in "political" ideologies such as Marxism or National Socialism. Such ideologies are always dependent on *linear* models of history: the group as a whole must progress through time until the advent of collective perfection (or "salvation"). For the National Socialist (Nazi) or Jew (from whom the Nazi derived the idea), the collective is deified in terms of an ethnic group. For the Marxist or Christian, the collective is determined on a more voluntary ethical basis. But it is also somehow "predestined" (by historical dialectic here, by "God's Plan" there). A comprehensive analysis of "Satanic politics" still awaits some future investigator.

THE WILL TO POWER

Nietzsche: the Antichrist

Friedrich Nietzsche (1844–1900) is a philosopher with a sinister reputation. For the most part, this is because Hitler is supposed to have liked him. This is also why Richard Wagner is an "evil composer." If they were capable of perceiving the truth, the popular pundits responsible for such ludicrous reasoning would have much more to fear from both of these men than even they can imagine.

Nietzsche's objectively productive period spanned from 1872 (when *The Birth of Tragedy* was published) to 1889 (when he becomes either insane or divine—after this time he referred to himself with a variety of "divine epithets" including Dionysius, "the Crucified," and Apollo). Among his last works was *The Antichrist,* which was a full-force frontal attack on Christianity. In an early section of that book, he writes:

> What is good? Everything that heightens the feeling of power in man, the will to power, power itself.
>
> What is bad? Everything that is born of weakness.
>
> What is happiness? The feeling that power is *growing,* that resistance is overcome. Not contentedness but more power, not peace but war, not virtue but fitness (Renaissance virtue, *virtu,* virtue that is moraline-free).
>
> The weak and the failures shall perish: first principle of *our* love of man. And they shall be given every possible assistance.
>
> What is more harmful than any vice? Active pity for all the failures and all the weak: Christianity.[67]

The comprehensive philosophy of Nietzsche is too complex to discuss extensively in this forum. His cosmology was an entirely materialistic one, and his view of man one that would be closely imitated by Anton LaVey. Man's only distinction from "other animals" is his ability to build "horizons"—to overcome limitations imposed upon him and which he imposes on himself.

The most mysterious of Nietzsche's ideas is his doctrine of Eternal Recurrence (*ewige Wiederkehr*).[68] It was *this* idea that he himself thought was the essence of his teaching. Three ideas—the Will to Power, the Overman, and Eternal Recurrence—are bound together in a mysterious triad. Recurrence is the law, the Will to Power is the method, and the Overman is the aim.

Nietzsche saw himself, and the readers who would *understand* him, as "Hyperboreans"—those of the ultimate North, separated from the rest of humanity by their characters. They are to be *Übermenschen* ("overmen"), those who have "overcome by going-under" (see *Thus Spoke Zarathustra,* Prologue 1). Nietzsche's philosophy is based on the force of the empowerment of the individual will or consciousness. It is a philosophy of *Diesseitigkeit* ("this-sided-ness"). It is the individual, carnal ego, which is to empower its will in order to become the *Übermensch.* This evolution into the Overman—this "self-deification"—takes place under the direction of the will. Essential to the *technique* of Nietzsche's active philosophy is the *Umwertung aller Werte:* "the Revaluation of all Values." This virtually defines a modern school of secular antinomianism instituted for the sake of the evolution of the will into a unique and potent entity.

Obviously, many of Nietzsche's ideas correspond to the philosophy of the left-hand path. The elements that appear to be lacking are a theory of "magic" and a system of "initiation," although Nietzsche's ideas were to be developed in this direction by such magical philosophers as Aleister Crowley (who seems to have based his philosophy on Nietzsche's Will to Power), P. D. Ouspensky, Gregor A. Gregorius, and Anton LaVey. We will examine all of them in subsequent chapters.

From the time of the Renaissance—in other words, the dawn of the Modern Age—there has been a steady development toward secularization, rationalism, and even materialism within the establishment of Western culture. This has manifested itself in everything from the growth of free-trade capitalism, to representational democracy, to "secular humanism," to Marxist political theory. But at the same time, during the course of the most recent and accelerated phase of modernism (from about 1880 to the present), there has been a growing "occult revival" running below the surface of established norms. The keys to the current manifestations of the left-hand path can be found in this counter-cultural phenomenon. It will be found, too, that these keys help to unlock various mysteries housed in the establishment culture—mysteries that were in many cases spawned from intersections of modernist rationalism and occultist magic and mysticism.

7

An Interlude in the Absolute Elsewhere

Adolf Hitler and the Modern Mythologizing of Evil

In Western culture during the latter part of the twentieth century and into the twenty-first, no other man is personally more identified with the idea of evil than Adolf Hitler, no symbol more emblematic of evil than the swastika, and no organized body of men more vilified than the "Nazis." In fact, it often seems as if Hitler has replaced Satan as the very image of evil in our popular culture. In the great historical sweep of things, this will surely prove to be nothing but a passing fad, but it is, for now, a collectively perceived subjective reality.

The origin of this image lies in wartime propaganda produced during the course of the Second World War. The prime example is Lewis Spence's 1940 book, *The Occult Causes of the Present War,* which makes claims such as: "From the first Germany has been a region favourable to the suggestions of the powers of evil."[1] Spence goes on to write chapters with titles like "The Satanic Element in Nazism," "The Satanic Power in Old Germany," "The Satanic Power in Modern Germany," and "Nazism and Satanism." Each chapter contains assertions whose shrillness is exceeded only by their vagueness and obscurity. Few written or verifiable sources are ever cited for Spence's information about the "Satanic Church" that has supposed to have been in control of Germany since time immemorial—but, after all, none are needed because the work is a work of pure wartime propaganda.

A whole modern mythology of "Nazi Occultism" grew up in the years after the war. The common denominator in the literature that fed this mythology was the idea that the National Socialists were somehow really and truly in cahoots with the devil in one guise or another, and were involved in all manner of occult practices.

The "occult classic" of the 1960s by Louis Pauwels and Jacques Bergier, *Le matin du magiciens* (translated into English as *The Morning of the Magicians*), set things into even higher gear with a chapter entitled "A Few Years in the Absolute Elsewhere." The contents of this chapter can best and most charitably be described as an effort in modern mythologizing. Few objective facts are present.

Then, in the early 1970s, a writer named Trevor Ravenscroft wrote a book entitled *The Spear of Destiny.* This was largely based on the ideas of his teacher, Walter Johannes Stein. In an apparently learned style, Ravenscroft weaves a tale of reincarnation and evil in which Adolf Hitler is the reincarnation of a historical personage, Landulf II, who was, in turn, the basis for the character of Clinschor/Klingsor in the Parzival/Parsifal legend. The "Spear of Destiny" is the spear supposedly used by Longinus to pierce the side of Jesus as he hung on the cross. Because this spear thrust was necessary to fulfill biblical prophecies concerning the divinity of Jesus, it is said that Longinus "held the fate of the world in his hands" with that spear. So, too, will any other man who holds the spear: it is a talisman of world power. As a young man, Hitler saw it on display in the treasure room at the Hofburg palace in Vienna, and later had it brought to Germany after the annexation of Austria by Germany in 1936. This spear (which can again be seen today at the Hofburg) does indeed have many legends attached to it, including perhaps that of Longinus. However, it cannot have actually been that spear. The spear in question is not of Roman origin; in fact, it was not made until around 700 CE, and is certainly of Langobardic manufacture. (Spears, symbolic of the magical weapon of the high god Wotan, served as royal scepters of the old Germanic kings.)

Ravenscroft (and perhaps Stein) are shown to have created "facts" out of thin air on many occasions.[2] To put it as charitably as possible, *The Spear of Destiny* is a work of "poetic" history and/or cosmic propaganda. But its story seemed so compelling that it spawned a whole new wave of "occult Nazi" books, such as J. H. Brennan's *The Occult Reich* (1974), Jean-Michel Angebert's *The Occult and the Third Reich* (1974), and Francis King's *Satan and Swastika* (1976).

Each of these works has some pet theory to espouse as to just why and how the Nazis were mixed up with "dark forces." The only work to make any real sense of this period, however, is Nicholas Goodrick-Clarke's study *The Occult Roots of Nazism.* Its only somewhat occult concept is its own thinly disguised Marxist theoretical base, but that does not obstruct the facts nearly so markedly as the theories and claims abounding in the other works.

In the following presentation, I will concentrate as much as possible on aspects of Nazism that might be construed as having left-hand-path tendencies. For most writers on this subject, there is hopeless confusion with respect to the topics of paganism, the occult in general, and "Satanism." My forthcoming book, *Nazi Occultism,* clarifies these topics in a comprehensive manner.

THE FACTS BEHIND THE MYTHOS

There is an important question to raise here: if the Nazis were *not* actually involved in the Satanic affairs the propagandists and popularizing occult writers would have us believe, then why is such mythologizing so appealing and why does it continue to "sell"? One of the reasons is that the Nazis *did* play the role of villains so well—at least as villains were supposed to appear to the Anglo-American world. They wore austere uniforms and had great rituals and indulged in celebrations of vital existence. To the wide-eyed Anglo-American observer, it was all just very intense. To argue, however, that their practice of exterminating whole populations somehow made them "diabolical" in any traditional sense is absurd. If it were true, then we would also have to classify the Roman Catholic Church as being equally "diabolical." The claim that the acts of the Nazis were somehow historically unique is equally absurd. The Stalinists, the Ethiopian communists, the Khmer Rouge, and dozens of other parties, factions, and states carried out similar programs in the twentieth century alone.

No, there is something archetypal about the *style* of the Nazis that makes them so singular. This style, together with a philosophy that is a curious mixture of the barbaric, the medieval Christian, and the futuristic/scientific, gave rise to an image distinctly out of step with the norms of the twentieth century.

There is a whole range of types of approaches that have contributed to the mythologizing of the Nazis and the occult. These are laid out—and largely debunked—in a comprehensive way in the second edition of *The Secret King: The Myth and Reality of Nazi Occultism.*[3] This book is a study of the life and writings of Karl-Maria Wiligut, one of the few genuine occultists who had some documentable influence in the Third Reich.

NAZI IRRATIONALISM AND PAGANISM

It is widely believed that the Nazis were heavily involved in neo-Germanic religion (tantamount to diabolism in orthodox Christian circles). This was not really the case. Among the top Nazi leaders, for example, only Himmler and Rudolf Hess ever resigned from their Christian Church affiliations.

For many decades preceding the arrival of National Socialism, Germany had been swept up in a neo-Romantic fever for all things *Germanic.* Wagner's operas, especially the *Ring of the Nibelung* tetrology and *Parsifal,* were the rage. Guido von List and others had instituted a new runic mysticism,[4] and neo-Germanic religious and cultural groups were springing up all over Germany and Austria from the late nineteenth through the early twentieth century.[5]

The fact is, however, that the God of Hitler was *not* Satan or Wotan. When Hitler spoke of his own religious conceptions, he spoke entirely in terms of a Christian God (as he understood it). All of Hitler's expressions concerning religion have been collected by Manfred Ach and Clemens Pentrop in their 1977 study *Hitlers 'Religion': Pseudoreligiose Elemente Im Nationalsozialistischen Sprachgebrauch* (Hitler's "Religion": Pseudo-Religious Elements in the National Socialist Use of Language). Hitler tolerated and made use of the widespread neoheathenism in Germany because he thought it provided "unrest" in the populace—unrest that he could direct toward his own ends. "These professors and obscure men who found their Nordic religions corrupt the whole thing for me," he stated.[6] This is the *documented* reality of the personal attitude of Hitler toward neoheathen religion. He could hardly be called a Satanist or Wotanist!

As we will see, the Nazis attempted to institutionalize a new religion based on their own party's doctrines and given shape by religious and magical pageantry with symbolism drawn from the established churches, but also from Imperial Rome and, to a lesser degree, what they knew of ancient Germanic cult. Many of the leaders of the Nazi hierarchy had unusual beliefs, but there appears to have been no "master plan" for integrating these ideas. Hitler merely allowed these leaders to indulge their passions, as long as they moved his major agenda items forward.

NAZI MEDIEVALISM AND SCIENCE

The deeper motivating factors for the Nazis' actions are not rooted in magical or pagan ideas. They are rooted in the hatreds and fears first conjured in the Christian Middle Ages. The obsession with the Jews and the belief that they were agents of evil in the midst of the good Christian folk of Germany, and ultimately responsible for every social, political, and economic ill suffered by the people, is all thoroughly medieval. Such ideas were part and parcel of establishment thinking in the Christian Middle Ages. The only direct root for Nazi enmity toward the Jews is in the medieval Christian hatred of them as "Christ killers." The only modern addition to this is that the Nazis now augmented the theological argument for the Jews being an "evil race" (an idea introduced by the Christian church fathers) with scientific and pseudo-scientific arguments stemming from Darwinist and even Theosophical doctrines.

A careful study of all the facts regarding the true nature of Nazi ideology reveals that the whole "occult Nazi mythos" is bogus in character, and misses the whole point of any real black magical, or left-hand-path aspects that might have been occurring in the National Socialist movement. For the most part, the Nazis thought of themselves as being on the side of Nature, and their mission was seen as being an entirely "hygienic" one: they would rid Nature and the world of its diseased and degenerate segments and cultivate and nurture the healthy and wholesome wherever they could find it.

Final answers on the actual character of any occult or magical practices undertaken by the Nazis are impossible to arrive at because the records of such practices, if they ever existed, would have been destroyed at or before the end of the war. In the absence of any hard evidence, we are reduced to inconclusive speculations. The records that do exist of Nazi investigations into occult, religious, and magical matters can be found in the archive in Koblenz, and in the Library of Congress where photographic copies of that material are stored. A review of that material shows no traces of Satanism or black magic in the usual sense.

THE LIFE OF ADOLF HITLER

The Wolf Unbound

Hitler—whose nickname, or code-name, was "Wolf"—was born in Braunau am Inn, Austria, on April 20, 1889. His given name, "Adolf," means "the Noble Wolf." Evidence indicates a troubled childhood in an authoritarian household. He left school when he was sixteen, dreaming of becoming a painter. In 1907, he made his way to Vienna where he led a bohemian lifestyle until 1913.

It was in this Viennese milieu that he received his education in politics and in the racial and perhaps mystical doctrines that would shape his future philosophy. Of course, the hatred of the Jews and the Marxists was an important part of this worldview. It was at this time that he was exposed to the doctrines of Jörg Lanz von Liebenfels, and perhaps also Guido von List.

In 1913, Hitler moved to Munich, Germany. Shortly thereafter, war broke out in Europe, and he joined the German army and served courageously on the front. After the war, he worked as a domestic spy for the German army. He ended up joining one of the groups he was supposed to investigate, the German Workers' Party, which had about forty members at the time. The party soon thereafter changed its name to the National Socialist German Workers Party, colloquially known as the "Nazis." By 1921, Hitler had been elected chairman of the party and had personally chosen its symbol, the swastika or *Hakenkreuz* (hook cross).

By November 1923, Hitler's party and other nationalist groups were ready to try to conduct a putsch against the Bavarian government. In the resulting street battle, sixteen of the nationalists were killed and the putsch failed. Hitler was arrested and sentenced to prison. While in Landsberg prison, he dictated his book *Mein Kampf* (My Struggle) to his associate Rudolf Hess. It was in prison that he also underwent a personal transformation from a rabblerouser into a cunning politician.

After nine months in prison, he was released. By 1926, he had rebuilt the disintegrated NSDA. From that time to his final election as chancellor of Germany in January of 1933, Hitler undertook a relentless campaign of political organization. Once in power, he consolidated that power through various maneuvers until he was the absolute dictator of Germany by the next year.

Subordinates Heinrich Himmler, Hermann Goering, Josef Goebbels, and (to a lesser extent) Alfred Rosenberg were allowed to control certain aspects or segments of this new "Third Reich."

By 1935, Hitler had begun to build up German military power and in 1938 Austria was finally made a part of Greater Germany. He met with success after success in domestic and foreign affairs. The outside world, as well as the Germans themselves, seemed to both fear and admire him.

In September of 1939, the Germans invaded Poland using blitzkrieg tactics and the Second World War was underway. For the first three years of the war, from late 1939 to mid-1942, the Germans were virtually unstoppable. But from the middle of 1942, with the Americans now in the war, the Germans began to suffer defeat after defeat on both the eastern and western fronts. The final moments came for Hitler when he committed suicide in his bunker in Berlin on *Walpurgisnacht* (April 30) 1945, with the Red Army entering the now all-but-flattened city above.

THE LIFE OF HEINRICH HIMMLER

Lord of the Black Knights

Himmler was born October 7, 1900, in Munich. His father was a pious Roman Catholic school teacher. He served in the German army just at the end of the First World War and from 1918 to 1922 he attended the Munich Technical University. During his less-than-successful business career after this time, he became involved with a nationalist organization and participated in the 1923 putsch led by Hitler and the NSDAP. From 1925 to 1930, he was propaganda leader of the Party, and in 1929 was appointed as leader of the *Schutzstaffel* (protection squad; often referred to simply by its initials: SS), which at that time was a two-hundred-man bodyguard of the *Führer.* By 1933, the scope of the organization had expanded in many directions and SS membership stood at 52,000.

Himmler envisioned the SS as an elite corps of modern knighthood. Its members would serve as the cutting edge in the generation of the long-awaited superman, or master race. This SS superman would be leader, scholar, warrior, and administrator all in one.

In his position as the *Reichsführer-SS,* Himmler was given progressively greater powers during the National Socialist reign. He became the supreme commander of a private army. An SS subdivision of militarized units called the *Waffen SS* was given complete control of all the eastern territories occupied by the German *Reich.* Over time, the SS thus became the head of all political and state police forces both inside and outside Germany.

The center of Himmler's worldwide SS empire was to be Castle Wewelsburg in Westphalia. There the SS was to have its magical headquarters where the knights of the "order" would be educated and trained, and where they would hold their rites of chivalry. Other castles, called *Ordensburgen* (order castles), were also instituted.

The branch of the SS most responsible for its reputation as an "occult order" is the *Ahnenerbe* (ancestral heritage), which was instituted to study ancient Germanic culture and religion, including runes, astronomy, architecture, and other occult traditions that fascinated Himmler. If Himmler had not been so involved in matters of this nature, the case for the more overt forms of "Nazi occultism" would be extremely weak.

Two members of the SS who greatly affect our views of the Nazis and the occult are Karl Maria Wiligut (1866–1946) and Otto Rahn (1904–1939). Wiligut was a visionary occultist who designed rituals and symbols for the SS and Rahn was a grail-seeker with gnostic predilections. Rahn saw Lucifer as a positive, light-bringing figure, and this assessment opened the door to much later misinterpretations that his views somehow reflected a "Satanic" component in Nazism.

Himmler's SS became a "state within a state" in Nazi Germany. At the end of the war, Himmler attempted to negotiate separately with the Allies in the west in hopes of stabilizing that region so he could carry on the fight against communism in the east. In the final moments of the war when Hitler found out about Himmler's actions, the Führer denounced him and removed him from his official positions. Shortly after Himmler was captured by the Allies in the west, he committed suicide by means of a poison capsule on May 23, 1945.

SOURCES FOR THE STUDY OF THE NAZIS AND MAGIC

The major primary sources for the study of the magical or religious aspects of the National Socialist movement in Germany would be the

Ahnenerbe archives, as well as the many official publications of the SS, the Rosenberg Office, and other branches of the NSDAP. Other primary sources include the esoteric articles of Karl Maria Wiligut[7] and the writings of Otto Rahn,[8] since both of these men held official rank in the SS.

The most valuable secondary studies have been provided by Klaus Vondung (1971), Michael Kater (1974), and Ulrich Hunger (1984). The roots of what was to become, at least in part, the NS ideology can be studied in the works of Jörg Lanz von Liebenfels, Guido von List, and dozens of others. It must be stressed, however, that these neo-Romantic mystics were not "Nazis," nor were their ideologies identical to those of the later Nazis. Some of their ideas were simply used by the founders and developers of NS ideology. One of the most important studies of this aspect is Wilfried Daim's 1958 book *Der Mann, der Hitler die Ideen gab* (The Man Who Gave Hitler His Ideas). This is an exhaustive treatment of Lanz von Liebenfels and his possible influences on Nazi ideology.

NAZI COSMOLOGY

The cosmology underlying Nazi ideology is reminiscent of Manichean dualism. The important factor is that there is an ongoing *conflict* in the world: a conflict between the forces of darkness and evil (embodied in the subhuman species of mankind) and the forces of light and good (embodied in the embattled Aryan). The Aryan is good—not by virtue of his actions or beliefs, but by his very nature and organic essence. By the same token, the subhumans are evil by reason of their organic inferiority. The cosmic struggle is an organic one between the Aryans and subhumans whose agenda it is to destroy the human Aryan race before it has a chance to evolve into the superhuman race of the future. These ideas of conflict are essential to Nazi cosmology. This is also one reason why the apparently pseudo-scientific theories of Hans Hörbiger (1860–1931) concerning cosmic fire and ice were so attractive.

Many believed that the Aryan man had a "divine spark." This spark was more evident in ancient times, but it had become clouded due to deleterious effects throughout history: under the influence of Judaized Christian culture, backward steps had been taken in the evolution of the superman. On the most magical level, the National Socialist agenda was to aid this further evolution of the *Volk* (the most advanced of the Aryan race, the Germanics). Instead of the economically driven historical dialectic of the Marxists, the Nazis had an organically (nationally) determined evolutionary dialectic. The end result would, however, be similar in both cases: there would be a paradise on earth ruled by a perfected species of man. For the Marxist, this would be achieved through revolution, "education," and strict planning of the economy so as to provide for all the material wants of the people. For the Nazi, this paradise would be brought about through conquest, hygiene, and eugenics—selective breeding that would lead to the evolution of the superman. In the case of both Marxism and National Socialism, the cosmological model is probably evolved from the Judeo-Christian model. Table 7.1 comparatively shows the cosmological relationships among these ideologies.

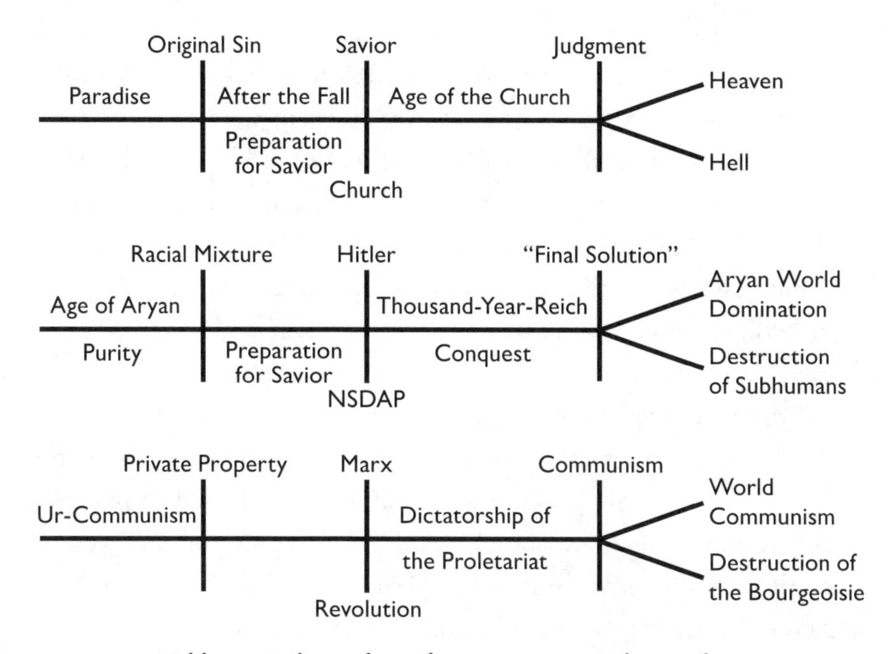

Table 7.1 The Judeo-Christian, National Socialist, and Marxist Cosmologies

NAZI METHODOLOGY

We can speak of a form of Nazi "magic" with a definite aim: the divination of the Volk. Its methodology is, however, something other than what the many books on "occult Nazism" might lead one to believe. Attempts to categorize Nazi magical methods with those of mainstream Western occultism (Crowley, Gurdjieff, and so on) completely miss the mark. Nazi magic is rooted entirely in an organic model. There is a mysterious element—a hidden or occult component—that goes beyond established genetic sciences, however. Poetically or mystically, this might be referred to as "the blood," but more analytical minds might want to designate it as some particular DNA pattern.

The methods described here must be interpreted as "magical" because they are intended to cause changes in conformity with will and they are making use of theories that exceed or stand outside of the established science of their day or ours.

Four main magical methods are used: hygiene, eugenics, war, and ritual. Each supports the other, makes the other possible, and each is necessary until the final perfection of the superman has been achieved.

Hygiene is the maintenance of health and the prevention of disease. In the magico-racialist sense used here, it concerns increasing refinement toward purity and the prevention of further mixed breeding between "Aryans" and "non-Aryans." This became the object of laws established in Germany in 1935, the so-called Nuremberg Laws. This hygienic stage, which is essentially an operation to separate the "good" from "evil," is somewhat passive. It only "restores health and prevents disease."

Beyond the hygienic stage is the more active eugenic stage. With eugenics, the work becomes one of actually improving, or evolving, the Volk (now *elected* through hygienic measures) into the willed object of the operation. This more complex and delicate phase of the method was only partially undertaken in the Nazi regime. Eugenics attempts to select specimens for reproduction that display elements most similar to the desired final form that is being aimed for.

Himmler indeed envisioned establishments that would correspond to the much-invoked horror of "breeding camps," although his version would have sounded much more "romantic." Programs such as the *Lebensborn* ("Well of Life") initiative were designed to ensure that Aryan women had Aryan children, and that Aryan orphans would have shelter and safe haven from the war. SS men were chosen for their racial characteristics, and German women were encouraged to have children by them (as many as possible) before they were sent off to war (probably to die). Since the offspring would be those of brave warriors, in this way the racial stock was not only maintained but was also improved.

War and conflict are important to the whole process for a number of reasons. War is necessary to protect and defend the Aryan racial stock and to help destroy the subhuman genetic elements that threaten it now, or may threaten it in the future. War and conflict of all kinds help to harden the basic Aryan stock and select out of that stock the fittest and most powerful. War can be the final proving ground, in an objective way, for the superiority of the superman. War is also, in and of itself, a kind of meta-ritual. It organizes and focuses the attention of a whole culture on an enormous undertaking. This is obviously necessary when one is trying to revolutionize a culture at the root level, and it was true for Marxist revolutionary societies as well. If there is no actual war going on, one needs to be created in fact or in propagandistic fiction.

The importance of ritual and spectacle, public and private, is obvious to anyone who has seen films of Nazi rallies, parades, and so on. The National Socialists were modern masters of symbolism and ritual, of what would come to be called "lesser (black) magic" in left-hand-path circles today. (Nowadays only rock concerts and sports events remain as pathetic attempts at this kind of spectacle.)

The ritual was necessary to focus attention on the cause, and its shape and nature, on a day-in, day-out basis. As individuals can be transformed by rituals, whole cultures can also be metamorphicized through collective participation in such rituals. Even marginally effective ones, if repeated often and long enough, will have some result. But it may take only one good jolt from a highly potent rite to have a profound and lasting effect. The Nazis used both kinds.

THE RITUALS OF NAZISM

Although the NSDAP and all its various groupings, such as the SS and the Hitler Youth, had many kinds of rituals and festivals, we will concentrate here on the more public ones. A fair amount of documentation of these has been recorded. Of the more secret rites, little to nothing remains for us to draw upon for analysis. A lengthy discussion of National Socialist liturgy can be found in Klaus Vondung's 1971 study *Magie und Manipulation*.

From the calendrical rites we can form a well-rounded picture of the kind of rituals the Nazis were developing. Besides the "Ceremonies of the Reich and the Course of the Year," other liturgical formats used by them were: "Morning Ceremonies" (*Morgenfeiern*) also called "philosophical hours of celebration"; "Ceremonies of Life" (rites of passage); and the dramatic celebratory plays and so-called *Thing*-plays.* This latter type of ritual was an effort to create a mass drama in which the audience, or congregation, participated in poetic chants with actors or choral groups. A number of special open-air theaters called *Thingstätten* ("Thing steads") were built for this purpose in the early years of the Reich.

From the beginning, we want to avoid the mistake of assuming this liturgy was a standardized one, or that it was ever fully developed during the short history of Nazism. Some features were developed only late (after the war had begun), and others fell away in the early years. Some ceremonial forms were practiced only in certain segments of the Party, which, despite the *Führerprinzip* (The "Führer principle"), was far from a monolithic entity. There was a deep aesthetic-ceremonial rift between proponents of a Romantic-Germanic style (favored by Himmler and Rosenberg) within the SS and the Hitler Youth, and a Neo-Classical style favored by Hitler (and hence the "mainstream" of the Party). The latter tendency was also partly shared by the Minister

*The word "Thing" here refers to the name for the old Germanic tribal assemblies (e.g., the Icelandic Althing, which was an annual assembly of all the chieftains and freemen to discuss and settle legal, religious, and other matters).

of Propaganda, Joseph Goebbels, although he also leaned toward more modern aesthetics.

Ceremonies of the Reich and Course of the Year

It was clear from the beginning of the Third Reich that the Party was actively trying to displace orthodox Christianity. One of the most significant ways it set about doing this was through the institution of its own "sacred calendar." The main days celebrated were:

January 30: Day of Coming to Power

The main liturgical act was a nighttime torchlight parade as a reenactment of the one held on that night in 1933. Its significance was the final victory of the Party.

February 24: Proclamation of the Party Program

In the early years, this was celebrated by Hitler and the "old guard" with private ceremonies in Munich at the Hofbräuhaus, the beer hall where Hitler had first proclaimed the program of the party on this date in 1920. This was only briefly a special day of public celebration (1934–1935). Its significance was the mythic foundations of victory, which would come to fruition on January 30, 1933.

March 16: Heroes' Memorial Day

This holiday for mourning the dead of the (First) World War was taken over from the Weimar Republic. It was originally called the "Day of Popular Mourning" (*Volkstrauertag*) but was Nazified into a day of heroic celebration for those who fell in battle.

Last Sunday in March: Pledging of the Youth

This was analogous to confirmation in the Christian churches. It was the day on which the fourteen-year-old boys and girls could transfer to the Hitler Youth (*Hitler-Jugend*) or League of German Girls (*Bund deutscher Mädel*) from the corresponding "junior leagues" of these organizations. Although this was an individual rite of passage, it had national significance as a time of celebrating the commitment of youth to the National Socialist movement.

April 20: Hitler's Birthday

Only once was this a legal holiday, but three important liturgical events took place on this day: the acceptance of ten-year-olds into the German *Jungvolk* and *Jungmädel* (the aforementioned junior leagues of the HJ and BDM, respectively), military parades, and the swearing-in of Political Leaders of the Party. This latter event was staged in full liturgical splendor at night in the Königsplatz in Munich, illuminated with torches and vessels of fire.

May 1: National Day of Celebration of the German Folk

This was an ancient festival, which through Marxist influence had acquired the connotation of a "labor day." The Nazis combined these ideas to celebrate the worker as well as "joy over the victory of eternally new life." Goebbels declared it the highest holiday of the German people.

German Easter and High May

Two days that had taken on Christian importance, Easter and Pentecost (which comes fifty days after Easter and is called "High May" in the folk tradition), were "repaganized" by the National Socialists. These were celebrated with neo-Germanic festivities and had the function of focusing the attention of the folk on their national heritage as distinct from the internationalist form of Christianity.

Second Sunday in May: Mothers' Day

After the war had begun in 1939, the Nazis instituted ceremonies in which mothers who had borne a certain number of children would be invested with a Cross of Honor, and those mothers who had lost children in the fighting were escorted by flower-bearing members of the Hitler Youth to ceremonies where they received places of honor.

June 21: Summer Solstice

This was especially celebrated by the Hitler Youth and the SS, the groups most interested in Germanic traditions. In the SS, it was the time when good Aryan marriages were made, and other neo-Germanic festivals were held. After 1937, Goebbels arranged a more neoclassical ceremony in Olympia Stadium in which a giant solstice fire was ignited to symbolize the victory of the Aryan race. As usual, this ceremony was held at night.

First Half of September: Party Day of the Reich

This was the most important celebration of the full power of the Party—the triumph of its will, as it were. It in fact consisted of an entire week of political and ritual events. In 1934, these were recorded by Leni Riefenstahl in her famous film *Triumph des Willens.*

Beginning of October: Harvest Thanksgiving Day

As May 1 was the workers' day, this was the day to honor the farmer, who was held in high regard in the "Green" Nazi *Blut und Boden* (blood and soil) ideology promoted by Walther Darré and others. The Harvest Festival Rally was held in the 1930s in the town of Bückeberg near Hameln. Hundreds of thousands of farmers were brought to this festival, which also had a set liturgy, the high point of which was the presentation of the harvest-crown to the Führer. This symbolized the presentation of the harvest to the entire Volk.

November 9: Memorial Day for the Fallen of the Movement

This is the anniversary of the failed putsch of 1923. By all accounts, this was the most religiously loaded cultic affair of the party. In the ritual, the "Old Guard" (those who had been there on that day in 1923, and who had been invested by Hitler with a special medal, the *Blutorden*) gathered with the Führer in front of the Bürgerbräukeller beer hall and marched toward the Feldherrnhalle, where sixteen of their number had been felled by gunshot in 1923. This march was led by member of the Blutorden bearing the famed "Blood Flag," which had been carried on the original day and was stained with the blood of the martyrs. As they marched, they passed pylons upon which were written the names of 240 "fallen of the movement." As the "Blood Flag" passed by each pylon, the name of the martyr was called out. Throughout the entire procession, the *"Horst-Wessel-Lied"* (the "Horst Wessel Song," written by an early National Socialist "martyr"; it effectively became the anthem of the Party) blared out through loud-speakers. When they reached the Feldherrnhalle, sixteen canon shots rang out. Hitler laid a wreath on the memorial stone of the martyrs as the *"Lied vom guten Kameraden"* ("Song of the Good Comrade") played, followed by the *"Deutschlandlied"* (the "Song of Germany," more commonly known by its first line *"Deutschland, Deutschland über alles . . ."*), which swelled in intensity as the marchers continued their way to the Königsplatz, where the martyrs had been entombed in the "Temple of Honor." Here a speech was made, usually by Goebbels. The names of the martyrs were read out as the gathered Hitler Youth responded "Here!" in unison after each one, followed by a three-gun salute. The "Horst Wessel Song" was again played, followed by the "Badenweiler March" (Hitler's favorite) and a final repetition of the *"Deutschlandlied."*

December 21 and the "Holy Nights"*—Winter Solstice

Although already largely pagan in form, the German Christmas festivities became a target for Nazi liturgical reinterpretation. Himmler was especially interested in "re-Germanicizing" the festival as the Yule Fest. Goebbels and Rosenberg both used more subtle means. In all cases, however, since this festival always had been (even in pagan times) a private family or clanic and not a public affair, it did not become a candidate for massive Nazi liturgy. It also posed a new problem: how to develop National Socialist traditions in private homes. It was not until 1942 that these festivities began to take on any set form outside of the SS (where Himmler's version of the Yule Fest had long been practiced). The festival was to consist of three major celebrations: that of

*The German word for Christmas, *Weihnachten,* literally means "holy nights."

the "troop" (i.e., within the NS organizations, military groups, etc.), that of the community, and that of the family. During the Christmas seasons of 1943 and 1944, the Ministry of Propaganda issued a book called *Deutsche Kriegsweihnachten* (A German Wartime Christmas), which gave a full private liturgy with songs, poems, customs, and legends. This went so far as to present the legend of the dead soldier who returned for the "Holy Nights" to participate invisibly in the celebrations of the family.

There were many kinds of ritual used by the Nazis, but a common underlying structure can be discerned that clearly defined many of them. This was a sixteen-point working outline, divided into three parts:

PART I

Fanfares

1. Marching-In of the Banners and Flags
2. Common Song
3. Poetic Invocation
4. Chorus of the Troops (ritualized chants)

PART II

5. The Eternal Watch (the words of the Führer)
6. Chorus of the Troops
7. Address of the Highest Ranking Official
8. Honoring of the Fallen
9. Oath of Obligation (to the dead, to the Volk, etc.)
10. Honoring of the Dead (ancestors, heroes, etc.)
11. Chorus of the troops

PART III

12. Solemn Vows
13. Common Song

14. Honoring of the Führer (threefold *Sieg Heil*!)
15. National Hymns (i.e., the "Horst Wessel Song" and the "Deutschland Song")

Fanfares

16. Marching-Out of the Banners and Flags

As a form of "lesser magic," these rituals had many functions. Among them were the forging of a focused "mass will" of the Volk, the creation of a deep sense of self-consciousness as an organic entity, the bonding of that entity to a set of symbols, and the projection of the entity through those symbols back in time to the ancestors and forward in time to the descendants.

The ritual devices were often complex and manifold, but they generally consisted of these elements: ritually shaped space, motion within that space, color, sound (music), and the spoken word. All this was played out in a pattern of dynamic tension between the individual and the gathered mass. Nowhere is this more symbolically clear than with the sight of the Führer addressing the faithful troops at Nuremberg.

As we can reconstruct it today, the magical methodology of the National Socialists extended from private chambers to mass rallies, from traditional folk festivals to high-tech electronics, from the rites of war to the rites of spring. As with all magic, however, the *aim* must be kept firmly in focus when attempting to understand it. In this instance, the aim was the forging of the Master Race: the Volk made divine. The methods involved the attempt to separate the genetic basis for this massive working from the rest (for this, hygiene and war were necessary), and the subsequent transformation of that genetic basis (for which ritual and eugenics were needed). The biggest obstacle the Nazis faced was cultural in nature: how to motivate millions of the most modern, well-educated people in the world to cooperate in the most radical social and magical experiment in history? The attempt to manipulate the mass-mind to these ends was the underlying factor in much of what we can readily identify today as real "Nazi occultism."

THE NAZIS AND THE LEFT-HAND PATH

The closest comparison to the National Socialist doctrines with regard to the left-hand path would be those of Marxism. Whereas Marxism proceeds from a materialistic cosmology and looks to social and economic factors in creating its ideology for the perfectibility of the human species, National Socialism proceeds from a mystically organic model and looks to racial and military factors in creating its model for the deification of the elected Volk.

In the final analysis, we must again ask ourselves whether the Nazis are in any real sense to be aligned with the left-hand path. On the essential element of self-deification, the Nazis present a mixed picture. The Führerprinzip—the idea of an absolute ruler of godlike power—is, in a sense, consistent with left-hand-path ideas. But this is institutionalized in a statist form, which is an anathema to the general practice of the left-hand path focused on the individual. Figures such as Hitler and perhaps Himmler may have been able to practice the path of the left-hand, but few below them did so. (And it is highly doubtful whether either of these men understood themselves in this capacity.) The deification in Nazism is contained not in the individual, and not in the whole of the human species (as with communism) but in the particular organic strain of humanity known as the Aryans. It is the Volk as an *organic* construct that will reach the state of divinity in the National Socialist model.

The Nazis intended to separate this new "god" from all others, and develop it to a new level of being. If there is a crux to the issue of the nature of "evil" with regard to the National Socialists, or to the question of whether they practiced any sort of "black magic," surely this is it. The Nazis represent a race-based, nationalistic rebellion against the natural cosmic order (or perhaps the modern "conventional order"), just as the true black magician represents that rebellion in the individual ego.

This fact negates the viability of the essential individualistic component to the practice of the left-hand path. The individual is almost totally irrelevant in the ideology of Nazism, except as a mythic heroic model for behavior suited to the aims of the State.

The National Socialist penchant for rank and status and for hierarchical command structures is not unique in any way. This should not be confused as a sign of magical initiation. A higher rank in an organization indicates the level of service that person is capable of rendering the organization, but is not intended to indicate the level of *being* or essence attained by that individual as a human being. The most "magical" aspect of National Socialist "rankings" would have to do with the relative "purity" of a person's "blood." The more pure the person's blood, the closer he or she came to being *a part of* the divine ideal. Since genetic—or eugenic—magic was the major Nazi methodology for working in the field of magical reality (the genetic structure of the Volk), "initiatory progress" in this could hardly be measured in individual terms, but only in familial ones.

Indeed, the Nazis did use *magic* of a most sophisticated and modern kind. Their "lesser magical" use of symbolism and spectacle to manipulate and direct the masses is only to be rivaled by Madison Avenue today.[9] On a higher level, when it comes to magic used to transform the self into the image of the divine, it is also clear that there was much magic in the practices of the Third Reich. These are most pronounced in the chivalric mythology and methods of the SS and in the metaritual of racial transformation. The degree to which these methods could be called black magic is open to interpretation. Since the aims were usually collectivist and thought to be "ordained by Nature," they would seem to be more "white magical." But seen from the level of the *selected* (separated and independent) "folk group," the picture becomes darker. The separated group, with its own idiosyncratic characteristics, imposes its will on the environment around it—contrary to the "natural" flow of convention and historical development.

Antinomianism is also a complex issue when analyzing National Socialism. The Nazis never embraced conventional symbols of evil, and never identified themselves with Satanic imagery. Their antinomianism was of a far more *modern* kind.

Nazi ideology went against the grain of history; it opposed modernism in many of its forms. This was not because the Nazis feared *change* or were "conservative" in the usual sense. They were even more radical in their desire to embrace the *future* than their Marxist counterparts. They opposed trends of modernism they felt to be embodied in materialism, positivism, internationalism, and Marxism. In this process, the Nazis did adopt some features of medieval ideology, such as anti-Semitism, although this was a concession to conventional beliefs rather than a radical departure from social norms of the day.

The great trend of cultural history was toward egalitarianism, materialism, rationalism, and the belief that all problems have essentially socioeconomic and environmental causes. Today we, as a society, stand firmly in the midst of these opinions and sentiments. Many among us even worship these values as if they were God Almighty. It is against this God that the Nazis rebelled, and it here that they exhibit a fundamental contrast to Marxism.

In terms of our study, National Socialism might best be described as a uniquely postmodern, organic school of the left-hand path. They have an organic, collective basis (the Volk), together with a gradual (and quasi-initiatory) perspective on the transformation of the entity in question from its mundane base into its divine state using magical means—a triumph of the will.

8
The Occult Revival

Against the grain of growing rationalism and scientism in the late nineteenth and early twentieth century, there was a groundswell below the surface of establishment culture. This occult movement had its roots in ancient traditions as they had been revived in the Renaissance and early modern era. The deep-level appeal of Satanic imagery to this movement is perhaps best accounted for in the fact that it was essentially a countercultural force. As the historian James Webb has put it, this constituted a "flight from reason."[1]

From a modernistic, evolutionary perspective, this "flight from reason" may seem to constitute some kind of flaw or cultural sin. *Progress* is, after all, the *summum bonum* of the modern mindset. The left-hand-path elements of the occult revival are therefore quite fitting. A revival of the occult in an age in which the light of pure science was to shine brightest and show the way to a rational future is a powerful antinomian statement.

One aspect of this scientific revolution had to be accounted for in the occult revival: evolution. Charles Darwin published his *On the Origin of the Species* in 1859. The compelling idea that man had *evolved* from lower life forms, rather than that God had *created* mankind, was revolutionary and presented a great challenge to traditional religious cosmologies. The occult revival, however, seemed to embrace the concept of evolution, albeit as a part of its own mystical model.

The occult revival can be dated from 1875, the year of the foundation of the Theosophical Society (and, coincidentally, the birth year of Aleister Crowley). It effectively comes to an end, or reaches the end of its first phase, at the close of World War II. This revival was characterized by a myriad of organizations, societies, orders, and schools. But the most important ones from a left-hand-path viewpoint were the Theosophical Society, the orders of Aleister Crowley and their derivatives, the magic of Austin Osman Spare, and the teachings of G. I. Gurdjieff.

HELENA PETROVNA BLAVATSKY AND THE THEOSOPHICAL SOCIETY

Perhaps no other figure is more responsible for the twentieth-century occult revival than Helena Petrovna Blavatsky (*née* von Hahn). The daughter of an officer in the Russian army, she was born in the Ukraine in 1831. Her mother and grandmother provided female role models of nonconformity with upper-class values. Helena's mother wrote novels under the pseudonym Zenaida R-Va. These novels concerned the social position of women in revolutionary terms. Her grandmother, Helena Pavlovna de Fadeef, was an informed correspondent of famous scientists of her day with a keen interest in geology and botany. She even has a fossil named after her, the Venus Fadeef.

In childhood, Helena Petrovna was known for her active imagination. She was able to spin wild yarns and create whole worlds out of her mind even at a young age. In 1847, just before she turned seventeen, she was married by arrangement to a forty-year-old man, Nikifor Blavatsky. Blavatsky was to be the vice-governor of Yerivan in Armenia. After only a brief time, Helena abandoned Nikifor and made her way to Constantinople.

For approximately the next twenty-five years, there is little concrete evidence for what Blavatsky's life was like. Regarding these years, which must have been formative for her intellectual development, historian Bruce Campbell has determined four major characteristics:[2]

1. She is known to have traveled throughout Europe, the Middle East, and North America.
2. She was involved with spiritualism and knew the "Coptic magician" Paulos Metamon in Cairo and spiritualist D. D. Home in England.
3. She led a generally "Bohemian" existence, took drugs (especially hashish), had affairs with several men, and perhaps bore as many as two children out of wedlock.
4. She was possessed of a certain feeling of *mission* about her own life.

In 1871, she founded her first organization, the Societé Spirite in Cairo. After some further travels, she eventually emigrated to the United States in 1873. In New York she worked at various jobs, including the manufacture of artificial flowers. The next year she met Henry Steel Olcott, a journalist and occult enthusiast, at a farmhouse in Chittenden, Vermont, which was famous for its "spiritualistic" phenomena. Olcott and Blavatsky became friends, and in 1875 they founded the Theosophical Society with a number of others interested in spiritualism and ancient wisdom teachings. Blavatsky was not the sole leader of the group at first, serving instead as its "corresponding secretary." Her talents were not administrative, but it was her charisma and writings that attracted and held most Theosophists to the "cause."

Shortly after founding the society, Blavatsky went to Prof. Hiram Carson's house in Ithaca, New York. She went there to help the professor make spiritual contact with his daughter, who had recently died. It was there that she began to write her first major work, *Isis Unveiled.* Together with Olcott she continued writing this two-volume opus in New York City. The work was published in 1877. Even then, shortly after its publication, it was noticed that a large amount of it had been plagiarized from about a hundred books on the occult commonly available at that time. William E. Coleman found about two thousand plagiarized passages lifted verbatim from these books.[3]

Fraud, trickery, and plagiarism were common traits of Blavatsky's method of operation. How much of her efforts in these directions can be ascribed to the motives of the left-hand-path Buddhist conjurer and how much to the motives of the confidence (wo)man is left for others to decide.

For the first few years, the Theosophical Society stagnated and membership dwindled as it tried to find its own identity outside spiritualism. In 1878, there was a brief official merger between the society and the Arya Samaj, an Indian organization promoting a return to archaic Vedic, Aryan (Indo-European) values and customs. This was the beginning of a long-standing close relationship the Theosophical Society was to have with Indian society and politics. At the very end of 1878, Blavatsky and Olcott set sail for India. In February of 1879, the headquarters of the Theosophical Society were moved first to Bombay, later to Adyar. Theosophy became more and more open to increasing amounts of Indian teachings, both Hindu and Buddhist. Over a hundred chapters of the society were opened in India at that time.

It is only after this time (1879) that the Mahatmas ("great-souled ones"), or Masters, became an integral part of Theosophical teachings, although Blavatsky would later claim that she had been taught by them in Tibet back in that obscure, pre-1873 period in her life. But it seems most reasonable to conclude that the whole story of the Mahatmas was fabricated as a common sorcerer's ploy to gain prestige, power, and charisma, much like Anton LaVey and Carlos Casteneda would do in the 1960s and 1970s.

Blavatsky translated her mediumistic talent for communicating with people's dead relatives to one for communicating with "Hidden Masters." Here, too, is the root of the late-twentieth-century craze for "channeling" bazillion-year-old extraterrestrials. In 1884, Blavatsky's "phenomena" were investigated by the somewhat skeptical Society for Psychical Research and found to be fraudulent. While Blavatsky was in England, her methods were also exposed by a former confidant in Adyar.

Blavatsky eventually moved back to England to stay in 1887. The last five years of her life were devoted to writing *The Secret Doctrine*

(1888) and articles for her own journal *Lucifer,* which she founded at that time. She was also engaged in a power struggle with Olcott for control of the Theosophical Society. As a part of this struggle, she founded an "Esoteric Section" as a kind of "inner order" within the society.

In May of 1891, Helena Blavatsky died. But there can be no doubt that her vision and her voice, as heard through her writings, have been the guiding principles for the Theosophical Society through several generations of its existence.

One of the chief contributions of the Theosophical Society to the general occult revival was the profound connections it made between Eastern and Western occult or religious teachings. Blavatsky would on numerous occasions make statements to the effect that both Eastern and Western traditions were derived from the great "secret doctrine," the common source of Hindu and Greek wisdom schools.[4] This is, of course, true, but the *factual* reason for this—the common Indo-European heritage of both traditions—was still obscured from popular knowledge in Blavatsky's day. This is somewhat ironic, since one of the other legacies of the Theosophical Society to the occult revival was an infusion of at least a "faith" in scientific methods and terminology. The Theosophical Society was, to some extent, an attempt to bridge the gap between medieval faith and modern science by harking back to "ancient wisdom."

The flow of popularized esoteric information from the East began through the conduit provided by the Theosophical Society. It was in this body of information that the ideas of left-hand-path tantrism and right-hand-path mysticism entered into the Western world on a wide scale.

THEOSOPHY AND THE LEFT-HAND PATH

The relationship of Theosophy to the left-hand path is highly ambiguous and in many ways foreshadows the same ambiguities found in the magical career of Aleister Crowley, who was only sixteen when Helena

Blavatsky died. Blavatsky was often quick to identify her movement with the "White Lodge" or the "Great White Brotherhood," which is occasionally contrasted with the "Black Lodge." Blavatsky is usually anxious to claim to be a part of the *White* Brotherhood, while at the same time her works are replete with positive references to Satan and Lucifer. Even her own magazine that she published in the final years of her life was called *Lucifer.* Adding to the ambiguity, she asserts that, in theory, the aim of human development or initiation is the loss of the spark of individuality in the larger fire, the drop within the ocean. Individuality must be stamped out as the "self of matter," the "bud of personality," is crushed so that the SELF of spirit—beyond individuality—may thrive.[5]

But in examining her system in action we do not—even theoretically—see selfless souls devoid of personality, but rather "hidden" and ascended masters (many of whom are said to be still living in human bodies) in the company of great individuals in the history of mankind from Pythagoras to Jesus, and from Confucius to Mesmer. The implicit *reality* of the Theosophical myth is, even by its own definitions, left-hand path. The personality and individual consciousness is not obliterated, but rather these individuals ascend to a level of consciousness, individuation, and immortality otherwise reserved for gods and goddesses.

We are also reminded of the spiritualistic roots of Theosophy. Spiritualism is a sort of cult of at least quasi-immortal personalities, although these entities are largely impotent in their dealings with the living. The Masters, by contrast, virtually control the living, or could do so if they wished.

To some extent, we must look at Blavatsky's ideology or system in much the same way we would look at the staging of one of her "phenomena." They are both appearances with hidden realities and with a hidden agenda, which comes back to an empowerment of the sorcerer who creates the appearances—and perhaps, if he or she is observant, the enlightenment of the one who looks on.

Any *traditional* right-hand-path practitioner, whether Hindu or

Christian, Buddhist or Jew, will quickly see in Theosophy a system that glorifies the individual, promotes the biological interests of the Aryans (Indo-Europeans), and posits a rationally willed method of self-transformation. Any one of these aims would constitute a theoretical reason to condemn Theosophy as "left-handed" or "sinister." But perhaps because of the innate fear and loathing most humans have of the full implications of the left-hand path—knowledge (for ignorance is bliss), consciousness, power (for with it comes responsibility), and individual immortality (for in it there is no peace)—the structures of the left-hand path are hidden and disguised behind semantic sorceries such as "And now thy Self is lost in SELF, thyself unto THYSELF, merged in THAT SELF from which thou first didst radiate."[6]

HELENA P. BLAVATSKY AND THE "LIGHT-BEARER"

The fact that Blavatsky named her personal magazine *Lucifer* is a positive indication of her attitude toward that idea and figure in the traditions of humanity. *Lucifer* was published during the last years of her life at about the time she was writing *The Secret Doctrine,* so the title cannot be dismissed as a youthful indiscretion.

Her understanding of Lucifer-Satan (whom she equates on one level)[7] is clearly a variant of the Ophite-Gnostic interpretation. When referring to Hebraic tradition, she equates Jehovah Elohim with the demiurge who created the world and man's physical aspect, and she sees the true god who liberated man and gave him his divine aspects as Lucifer-Satan. This divine aspect is one of dynamic spiritual immortality, as opposed to the static physical immortality offered by Jehovah.[8]

Blavatsky made no apologies for her positive valorization of what orthodox Christian theologians called "devils," nor for her negative opinion of those "ignorant and malicious" theologians and their God and his angels. The "devils" she sees as the true, higher, more spiritual aspects of the gods (or God).[9]

The God of orthodox theologians is, for Blavatsky, the source of true evil in the world, which is equated with "an antagonizing blind force in nature; it is *reaction, opposition,* and *contrast.*" But even in this she can see that in reality such things can be "evil for some, good for others."[10] From the esoteric doctrines of Hinduism and Buddhism she seems to have absorbed the principle that the "good" involves an understanding of duality and the necessity of its preservation, while "evil" is concerned with the destruction of one aspect (either/or) of the duality by the other.

In *The Secret Doctrine,* she writes:

> In human nature, evil denotes only the polarity of matter and Spirit, a struggle of life between the two manifested Principles in Space and Time, which principles are one per se inasmuch they are rooted in the Absolute. In Kosmos, the equilibrium must be preserved. The operations of the two contraries produce harmony, like the centripetal and centrifugal forces which are necessary to each other—mutually inter-dependent—"in order that both should live." If one is arrested, the action of the other will become immediately self-destructive.[11]

Blavatsky sees in humanity—*or at least a portion of it*—the actual incarnation of the divine spark. In her interpretation of the conflict between Satan and Jehovah, she sees that Satan "claimed and enforced his right of independent judgment and will, his right of free-agency and responsibility." This is the true nature of the "fallen angels."[12] A "fallen angel" is then an *agathodaimôn* (Gk. "good spirit") as opposed to Jehovah and his obedient angels, each of which is a *kakodaimôn* (Gk. "evil spirit"). The "fallen angels" are an older creation possessing free will, who rebelled against the *natural order* of Jehovah.[13] One of the revolutionary ideas contained in *The Secret Doctrine* is that the gift of the divine spark is the result of actual *incarnation* of the "fallen angels" in human bodies through sexual reproduction. Some of these ideas were later picked up and expanded by Jörg Lanz von Liebenfels in works such as *Theozoologie.*

Whether it is in the Hebrew tradition, where she interpreted the myth of Eden recorded in Genesis 2–4, or the in the Greek myth of Prometheus, Blavatsky sees metaphors portraying the transformation of "fallen angels" into physical bodies, thus inseminating carnal humanity with a spark of the divine. Jehovah, or Zeus, created the flesh—senseless and without a mind—but Lucifer, or Prometheus, "represents the intellect infused into humanity."[14] In this way, *terrestrial* man is (or can be) made divine.[15]

Prometheus (and Satan) is seen to break the natural order of strictly preserved cyclic development and to put the divine gift into a weak physical vessel. There arises a tension between the physical vessel and the divine spirit.[16] Again the disharmony between these two dualistic poles is emphasized.

Blavatsky makes it clear that the divine spark is stronger in some people than others. She writes that in a certain portion of humanity, "the 'sacred spark' is missing . . . mankind is 'of one blood' *but not of the same essence*."[17] The portion of humanity in which the "fallen angels" incarnated "preferred free-will to passive slavery, intellectual self-consciousness pain and even torture to inane, imbecile, instinctual beatitude."[18] All of this relates to the essentially evolutionary aspect of Theosophy's esoteric teachings.

The Secret Doctrine contains a whole cosmogony that outlines the predetermined evolution of "root races" on this planet. There will be seven of these. At the apex of present human evolution is the Fifth Root Race, the "Aryans." We are now in the twilight of the Aryan epoch ruled by the Anglo-Saxons, but it will be out of that group that the next root race will necessarily appear. Incidentally, she located the appearance of the next evolutionary stage as being in North America.[19] The story of the first root races was one of a "descent into matter." During the course of the Fourth Root Race, the balance was tipped in favor of a spiritual evolution, as the species of humanity defined by the divine spark began its ascent back to a state of deity. This describes the evolutionary path of each individual, as well as that of the species as a whole.

The rhetoric of Theosophy—especially in later years among

Theosophists who were active after Blavatsky's death—is peppered with references to "black magic" or the "left-hand path." These are often used so loosely as to mean nothing more than "un-Theosophical." But it is clear that for Blavatsky herself, Lucifer (by whatever name) was her God, and that evolution to an immortal state of independent enlightened existence was her goal. This may be sufficient to consider her a "lady of the left-hand path"—even though she might not like the terminology.

Theosophy and *The Secret Doctrine* created untold ripples throughout the occult revival. Theosophical ideas, while themselves evolving (or devolving), were absorbed to some degree either directly or indirectly into virtually every occult school in the Anglo-American and central European worlds. Studies of the initiates of the Golden Dawn and its offshoots show the extent of Theosophical ideas present in Germany.[20] Not only did the German Secretary of the Society, Rudolf Steiner (1861–1925), break away to form his own successful Anthroposophical Society, but the important German magical order *Fraternitas Saturni* also shows significant Theosophical influence.

THE GREAT BEAST

Aleister Crowley

No man is more enigmatic in the history of the occult revival than Edward Alexander Crowley (1875–1947), better known as Aleister Crowley. He is so enigmatic because although opinions of him and his work are often strong, they hardly ever agree. What makes matters even more knotty is the fact that Crowley himself seems to have been somewhat unsure of his own nature: was he the "Great Wild Beast" or the "World Teacher"—or both?

Most discussions of Crowley quickly descend into recounting various legends and anecdotes concerning his exploits. These may be found in numerous books, for example John Symonds's *The Great Beast* (1972), as well as Crowley's own *Confessions.* My intention here is to concentrate on the *ideas* of Crowley as they possibly relate to the left-hand-path system of magical philosophy.

Crowley's father was a well-to-do beer baron and member of a fundamentalist Christian sect known popularly as "the Plymouth Brethren." His father died in 1886, and Crowley's future exploits were largely financed through his inheritance. As a young man, his avocations were poetry and mountain climbing. In the last month of 1896, while in Stockholm, he was awakened to the possibilities of magical philosophy. Two years later, on November 18, 1898, he was initiated into the "Hermetic Order of the Golden Dawn." By 1900, he had been initiated to the *Adeptus Minor* grade in the G.·.D.·.,* but he was soon thereafter alienated from the organization and began an independent career in magical studies.

In April of 1904, Crowley conducted a series of magical workings in Cairo, Egypt, in which he received the words of a text entitled *Liber AL vel Legis: The Book of the Law* from a discarnate entity called Aiwass (sometimes spelled Aiwaz). In Crowley's own mythology, this event (and the transformation it brought about in Crowley himself) is said to have ushered in a new Aeon in human history. It was this event, and the product of it—*The Book of the Law*—that would certainly reshape the rest of Crowley's life. In 1907, he founded his own magical order, the Argenteum Astrum (Silver Star; A.·.A.·.). In 1909, Crowley claimed to have attained the magical grades of initiation referred to as *Adeptus Exemptus* and *Magister Templi* in the G.·.D.·. system. But his claims were for his own magical order, the A.·.A.·..

In 1912, he began an alliance with a pseudo-Masonic German lodge, the Ordo Templi Orientis (Order of Eastern Templars; O.T.O.). The O.T.O. teaches forms of sexual magic akin to Indian tantrism, and Crowley was to become absorbed in this kind of magic for the rest of his life.

On his birthday in 1915, he claimed the initiatory grade of *Magus*, assuming the motto or magical name *Tô Mega Therion,* "the Great Beast" (see Revelation 13:1–18). The last initiatory grade was claimed

---

*The triangular devices of three dots used in the abbreviations for the names of certain occult orders derive from Masonic usage.

in May 1921, that of *Ipsissimus* (Latin for "his very utmost self").

The "Great Beast" died in relative obscurity in Hastings, England, on December 1, 1947, in the fullness of seventy-two years of age. But even more so than during his lifetime, in the latter half of the twentieth century his personality and his ideology—or mythology—cast a shimmering shadow over the entirety of the Western magical world.

SOURCES FOR THE STUDY OF THELEMISM

Crowley's philosophy, which might best be termed Thelemism (after his Aeonic Word: Gk. *thelêma,* "true will") or magick (after his method of attaining and exercising this will), is amply documented in the written works of Crowley himself. For our purposes, the most important of these are: *Book of Lies* (1913), *Liber Aleph* (finished 1918, first published 1961), *Magick* (1929), *The Equinox of the Gods* (1937), *The Book of the Law* (1938), *Eight Lectures on Yoga* (1939), *The Book of Thoth* (1944), his own autobiographical *Confessions* (1930), and the periodical *The Equinox* (originally published 1909–1913). Also among the most important primary sources for "Crowleyanity" or "Theriology" are two published diaries, *The Magical Record of the Beast 666* (1972) and *The Magical Diaries of Aleister Crowley* (1979). The secondary material on Crowley is voluminous, though much of it is sensationalistic or sectarian in its approach. The most useful works of this kind seem to be John Symonds's *The Great Beast* (1971), Israel Regardie's *The Eye in the Triangle* (1970), and Colin Wilson's *The Nature of the Beast* (1987). With all the books and sections of books written on Crowley, however, no objective study of his ideas has yet been produced.

CROWLEY'S MAGICAL ORDERS

Crowley was involved deeply with three magical orders during his lifetime. His association with the Hermetic Order of the Golden Dawn was brief, yet formative of many of his ideas. The G.·.D.·. was founded by a group of British Freemasons in 1888. It appears to have been greatly influenced by the Theosophy of Madame Blavatsky, although in many regards it is just an eclectic product of the same occult revivalist milieu of late-nineteenth-century Western civilization. However, other than the practice of magic for purposes of individual empowerment and enlightenment, there seems to have been little of the left-hand path about the G.∴D.∴.[21]

The initiatory philosophy of the A.∴A.∴ will be discussed further below when I analyze the initiatory theory of Crowley's Thelemism. It is useful to realize that the A.∴A.∴ was to initiate its individual members in the magical curriculum of the order so that they might better serve the progress of mankind, and that Crowley believed magick, the spiritual technology of the A.∴A.∴, was ultimately a thoroughly scientific discipline. Crowley designed the A.∴A.∴ as a vehicle of his Aeonic Word (thelêma). Theoretically, the design seems well suited to this purpose, but Crowley himself must have found the A.∴A.∴ and its magical methods in some sense less than viable, because in 1912 he formed an alliance with the Ordo Templi Orientis. The principal method of magical working in the O.T.O. is sexual. It is known that Crowley had experimented with sexual magic as early as 1902,[22] but he was doing no more than poking around in the dark until his contact with the O.T.O. His diary entries from 1914[23] express his insecurities and doubts concerning his effectiveness with this new magical form, despite the fact that he had claimed the initiatory grade of Magister Templi in 1909.

In contrast to the coherent and predictable curriculum of the A.∴A.∴, the O.T.O. system is significantly more mysterious. This is because the secret of sexual magic was to be withheld from the public at large and even from initiates of lower degrees within the O.T.O. The history of this order is better discussed elsewhere.[24] Crowley incorporated A.∴A.∴ ideas into the structure of the O.T.O., which was seen as a valuable tool for the dissemination of his teachings. From a left-hand-path viewpoint, one of the most interesting aspects of the O.T.O. is its use of magical technologies similar to those of Hindu and Buddhist tantra.

CROWLEY'S COSMOLOGY

Crowley's cosmology—the way he understood the universal order and his place in it—was dominated by the structures of the Kabbalah.[25] He had first absorbed or internalized this system, and been predisposed toward acknowledging its prestige and supremacy, during his training in the G.·.D.·.. The principal cosmological tool of the Kabbalah is the Tree of Life (see figure 8.1).

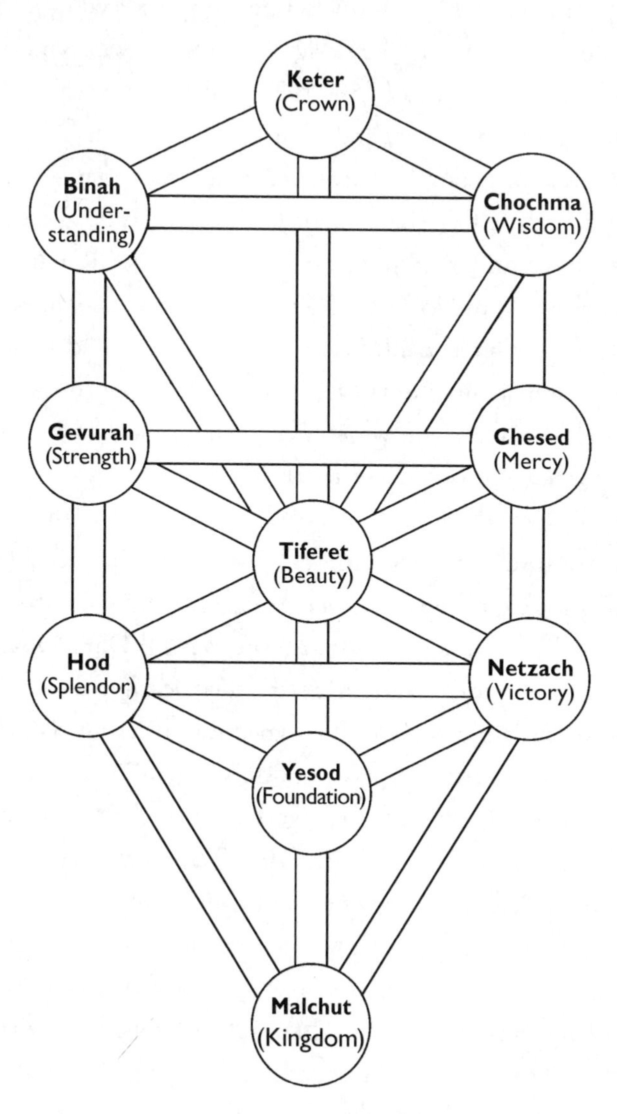

Figure 8.1. The Kabbalistic Tree of Life

In *Magick,* Crowley wrote: "The Qabalah maps ourselves by means of a convention. Every aspect of every object may thus be referred to the Tree of Life, and evolved by using the proper keys."[26] The Tree of Life presents the entirety of the cosmos—the universe—as a series of numbered emanations from the Absolute to the mundane or material universe. From the magical point of view, this "map of the cosmos" is supposed to provide a system of correspondences between and among all things in the universe. Thus, if one wishes to invoke Venusian qualities into one's life, a ritual would be designed using objects symbolic of the seventh *sephira* of the Tree of Life: the number seven, the color green, the sign and image of Venus, and so forth. By no means did Crowley invent this mode of thought, of course. It has its origins in prehistory; it was already codified by the time of Pythagoras, Judaized by mystical medieval rabbis, and again pioneered by Florentine Renaissance philosophers such as Marsilio Ficino. The system was expanded upon by occultists from Agrippa to Eliphas Levi and formulated in the system Crowley inherited from the G.·.D.·. This philosophy posits a unified field of continuous reality in which everything that exists is in one way or another connected to every other thing.

Another essential element of Crowley's magical cosmology is the theory of evolutionary stages in the history of the development of humanity. This general idea was very much in vogue due to the influence of Blavatsky's *Secret Doctrine* and the general Darwinist scientific fashion, perhaps coupled with Marxist theories. Crowley's tripartite doctrine of historical evolution (or dialectic) posits an older, matriarchal Aeon, ruled by the Egyptian goddess Isis, followed by a patriarchal one ruled by her husband, the god Osiris, which reached its end with the dictation of *Liber AL* in 1904. This new Aeon is ruled by their son Horus, "the child crowned and conquering."[27] This transition from the aeonic rulership of one god to another is what constitutes the "Equinox of the Gods." Crowley's tripartite aeonic progression had been anticipated by Joachim of Fiore (1145–1202), as well as by the heretical Brethren of the Free Spirit that flourished in Germany from the thirteenth to seventeenth century. For the Brethren, the three ages were ruled over successively by the Father, Son, and Holy Spirit (see chapter 5). The premise of a primeval matriarchal age had also been put forth in J. J. Bachofen's anthropological theories.[28]

Sexuality was, however, fundamental to Crowley's outlook on life and the world. This is reflected in the theo-cosmology contained in *The Book of the Law.* There we read of the sexo-cosmological and sexo-psychological interaction of two entities (or qualities): *Nu*(*it*), which is feminine, and *Had*(*it*), which is masculine. In his 1938 Introduction to *The Book of the Law,* Crowley wrote:

> This book explains the Universe.
> The elements are Nuit—Space—that is, the total of possibilities of every kind—and Hadit, any point which has experience of these possibilities.[29]

Here we have symbols of the Absolute, the universe, and the subjective universe defined by the individual psyche. In his "New Comment" (1920) on *The Book of the Law,* in regard to the opening line "Had! The Manifestation of Nuit" (*AL* I:1), Crowley claims that "The theogony of our Law is entirely scientific. Nuit is matter, Hadit is motion, in their full physical sense . . . Our central truth—beyond other philosophies—is that these two infinities can not exist apart."[30]

Crowley's symbols—or those of Aiwass—are chosen from a pseudo-Egyptian storehouse of images. Nuit was the Egyptian goddess of the vault of the night sky. But there is no god called "Hadit" (which Crowley identified with the familiar winged sun disk). The name Hadit seems to have been taken from Arabic *hadit,* "tradition." In any event, the concepts are clear enough. The closest analogs to these basic elements of cosmogony and cosmology are the yin and yang concepts of Taoist thought, and the concepts of *prakriti* (the unmanifested basis) and *bindu* (the universal seed principle) in Indian tantrism.

The universe is a continuous essence for Crowley. The psyche is a part of it, a part of Nature. Attainment is in the end the melding of any one manifestation of self with all else that exists:

> Each one of us has thus an universe of his own, but it is the same universe for each one as soon as it includes all possible experience. This implies the extension of consciousness to include all other consciousness.[31]

This is the essence of the Law of Thelema:

> "Do what thou wilt shall be the whole of the Law." (*AL* I:40)
> "Love is the Law, love under Will." (*AL* I:57)
> "Every man and every woman is a star." (*AL* I:3)

Crowley often comments on these formulas in ways that make them seem to partake of both right-hand-path and left-hand-path concepts. However, it is usually clear that he wishes his work to be understood as being of the right-hand path, and the true teaching of the "Great White Brotherhood."

PHILOSOPHY OF MAN

Understanding of Thelema (True Will) and the progress of its discovery in the individual is the kernel of Crowley's philosophy of man, his anthropology. Technically, the Law of "Do what thou wilt" is fulfilled upon the "Attainment of Knowledge and Conversation of the Holy Guardian Angel." Concealed in this rather ambiguous and quaint language is the idea that the individual magician becomes fully and constantly aware of the divinity or "higher self" within, or above, his everyday consciousness.[32] From that moment forward, the magician can be informed and transformed by this magical contact. This attainment, and subsequent willed actions informed by "conversation" with this entity, is the core of the exhortation "Do what thou wilt." The will is not the base desire, but the divine or true *Thelema*. From Crowley's own theoretical viewpoint, then, the notion that the Law of Thelema is a forerunner of "Do your own thing," or "If it feels good, do it," is misguided and inaccurate (but such "Laws" can never be understood by the masses, who will always degrade them to their level of perception).

"Love is the Law, love under Will": this aspect of Crowley's formula is nowhere more succinctly expressed than in *Eight Lectures on Yoga* (1939). Here he posits that "all phenomena of which we are aware take place in our own minds, and therefore the only thing we have to look at is the mind."[33] He also goes on to affirm that all human minds are essentially similar and that differences are the product "of systematic sectarian training."[34] He posits an important premise when he states, "all bodies, and so all minds, have identical Forms."[35] Crowley defines "love" quite precisely as "the instinct to unite and the act of uniting." But he tempers this with the admission that this must be done "'under will,' that is, in accordance with the nature of the particular units involved."[36] This love (Gk. *agapê*) is the act of the union of one thing with its (naturally determined) opposite.

So, for Crowley, the will toward union and the act of uniting with the *natural* opposite of the individual self (i.e., the Absolute, or universe) is the measuring stick for what the *True Will* is. Of course, Crowley is well aware of the essential distinction between the left-hand path and the right-hand path, black magic(k) and white magic(k), and so is always philosophically "correct" in his discussions of these matters. In *Eight Lectures on Yoga,* he makes statements that are among the most straightforward in occult revivalist literature about the aim of right-hand-path magick:

> It is therefore incumbent upon us, if we wish to make the universal and final Yoga with the Absolute . . . to train ourselves in knowledge and power to the utmost; so that at the proper moment we may be in perfect condition to fling ourselves up into the furnace of ecstasy which flames from the abyss of annihilation.
>
> . . . [U]ltimate [union] . . . destroys the sense of separateness which is the root of Desire [= Love] . . . [and] . . . is to be made by the concentration of every element of one's being, and annihilating it by intimate combustion with the universe itself.[37]

Crowley constantly seems to champion the concept of *liberty.* He states, for example, that "the Law of Thelema is the law of liberty."[38] This liberty is most directly expounded in *Liber LXXVII* (*OZ*), which is essentially:

> *There is no god but man.*
> 1. Man has the right to live by his own law . . .
> 2. Man has the right to eat what he will . . .
> 3. Man has the right to think what he will . . .
> 4. Man has the right to love as he will . . .
> 5. Man has the right to kill those who would thwart these rights . . .[39]

Viewed from an orthodox and exoterically law-bound system such as Christianity or Islam, this championing of pure liberty appears to be the epitome of the left-hand path and hence a moral framework for black magic. However, our assessment must in fact be tempered by Crowley's own interpretation of such formulas. Although the Law of Thelema posits no universal code of morality, it does insist upon the idea that for each individual soul there is one right or natural path, and that all such right paths lead to one goal: annihilation of the self. From a purely left-hand-path perspective, this is a disqualifying factor. All this clearly puts Crowley in a "gray zone" when it comes to our topic.

CROWLEY'S THEOLOGY

A definitive theology is difficult in Crowley's case. Certainly he held that Man, and the human mind characterizing the species *homo sapiens,* is the primary creator of gods and goddesses, angels and demons. Man "creates" them by *naming* them (i.e., categorizing them and discriminating between and among them). On the one hand, for Crowley, "Gods are but names for the forces of Nature themselves."[40] But he also says that "God [is] the Ideal Identity of man's inmost nature."[41] In Crowley's thought, the supreme God would then be one's own Holy Guardian Angel.

The discarnate entity that dictated *Liber AL* to Crowley in 1904 might at first be thought of as being a type of god-form by some. Others might see it as Crowley's own Higher Self. In *The Confessions,* Crowley himself comes to the conclusion that Aiwass and his Holy Guardian Angel were one.[42] The discarnate spiritual aspects of incarnate human beings can be true god-forms, if they are *invoked often* by means of the "spiritual technology" of magick. In this regard, Crowley has merely returned to the model of *daimonology* as held by the ancients. Primarily, the magician is his own god, but normally this god-form is hidden from his consciousness. He must learn and develop techniques for becoming aware of its existence and its characteristics, and absorb them into his everyday consciousness.

In Crowley's magical universe, however, there was also a hierarchy of discarnate entities (in some cases perhaps still incarnated in human bodies according to their wills). These were the "Secret Chiefs." Crowley had, of course, assimilated this conception from the G.·.D.·. (with analogs in the Theosophical Society and other occult groups). These virtual demigods play a pivotal role in Crowley's understanding of the conscious entities that motivate change in the world and in Crowley's life. In his *Confessions,* he definitely indicates that the ushering in of the New Aeon and his role in it is the work of the Secret Chiefs.[43] The very concept of entities such as the "Secret Chiefs" is tinged with left-hand-path connotations. These are not "gods" per se; they are humans who have become as gods, or godlike, in their immortality, power, and wisdom. It is not within the purpose or scope of this book to undertake a discussion of the reality or actual nature of these entities. But for Crowley they existed. Positing one's self as the prophet of a New Aeon, as the Great Beast, is a lonely task. It is more convenient to assume that one is being "ordered" from "higher up," so the Secret Chiefs constitute a kind of pantheon of quasi-divine beings who take a personal interest in the enlightenment of humanity and in the sponsoring of individual magicians.

The use of Egyptian god-forms in *The Book of the Law* appears arbitrary.[44] The fact that Crowley was in Cairo when *Liber AL* was dictated, coupled with the popularity of Egyptian god-forms in the G.·.D.·., probably best explains their usage. The divine and demonic symbols he tended to use were drawn from every culture and from his imagination and experience.

To be sure, the "god-form" that would interest us most for this study would be Satan, or perhaps Set. Crowley repeatedly, if poetically and sometimes ambiguously, equates himself—and his own "Holy Guardian Angel" Aiwass—with Lucifer or Satan.[45] He, of course, also liked to envision himself, at least "magickally," as an entity from conventional demonology. Two of his initiatory mottos are also figures from traditional demonology: Baphomet and Tô Mega Therion, the Great Beast or the Anti-Christ (= Satan). Satan is, in turn, equated with Set, the Gnostic god-form Abrasax (or Abraxas), and even with Adam.[46] This latter equation is important with respect to the position of man in Crowley's system.

But what is the real significance of Satan (by whatever other name) in Crowley's theological/daimonological formulas? He is quite clear on this:

> "The Devil" is, historically, the God of any people that one personally dislikes. This has led to so much confusion of thought that THE BEAST 666 has preferred to let names stand as they are, and to proclaim simply that AIWAZ—the solar-phallic-hermetic "Lucifer" is His own Holy Guardian Angel, and "The Devil" SATAN or HADIT of our particular unit of the Starry Universe. This serpent, SATAN, is not the enemy of MAN, but HE who made Gods of our race, knowing Good and Evil; He bade "Know Thyself!" and taught Initiation. He is "the Devil" of the Book of Thoth and His emblem is BAPHOMET, the androgyne who is the hieroglyph of arcane perfection.[47]

To understand completely what Crowley is saying, we must refer to his general cosmology, which is monistic: all apparent *opposites* are unities in reality. This is how Horus is united with Set (see chapter 3). They are the light and dark opposites within the same unity.

"[T]he true magick of Horus requires the passionate union of opposites."[48] This is clearly how, for Crowley, this is the Aeon of Horus, but its root formula is "ShT" (rendering Satan, Shaitan, Set, etc.).[49]

Here, as elsewhere, Crowley is using the familiar practice of antinomianism. In *Liber V vel Reguli* (Ritual of the Mark of the Beast), Crowley lays out his antinomianism and its practice:

> This is in fact the formula of our Magick; we insist that all acts must be equal; that existence asserts the right to exist; that unless evil is a mere term expressing some relation of haphazard hostility between forces equally self-justified, the universe is as inexplicable and impossible as uncompensated action; that the orgies of Bacchus and Pan are no less sacramental than the Masses of Jesus; that the scars of syphilis are sacred and worthy of honour as such.[50]

He goes on to explain:

> The Magician should devise for himself a definite technique for destroying "evil." The essence of such practice will consist in training the mind and body to confront things which cause fear, pain, disgust, shame and the like. He must learn to endure them, then to become indifferent to them, then to analyse them until they give pleasure and instruction, and finally to appreciate them for their own sake, as aspects of Truth. When this has been done, he should abandon them if they are really harmful in relation to health or comfort. Also, our selection of "evils" is limited to those that cannot damage us irreparably. E.g. one ought to practice smelling asafoetida until one likes it; but not arsine or hydrocyanic acid. Again, one might have a liaison with an ugly old woman until one beheld and loved the star which she is; it would be too dangerous to overcome the distaste for dishonesty by forcing oneself to pick pockets. Acts which are essentially dishonourable must not be done; they should be justified only by calm contemplation of their correctness in abstract cases.[51]

In Crowley's "theology," the results of the application of this antinomianism are that opposites, such as the Beast and the Lamb (Revelation 13:8) and the Whore of Babylon and the Woman clothed with the Sun (Revelation 12:1), are only *apparent.* From a higher perspective, they are unities or equivalencies (Beast = Lamb; Whore = Woman).[52]

The very existence of the conventional "Devil" (as a positive and objective entity of *evil*) is rejected by Crowley.[53] *Evil,* such as it is, is seen as a product of subjectivity and ignorance in humanity: "Satan [is] regarded with horror by people who are ignorant of his formula, and, imagining themselves to be evil, accuse Nature herself of their own phantasmal crime."[54]

Despite the fact that antinomianism is usually characteristic of the left-hand path, Crowley uses it toward the aims of the right-hand path. Indeed, *tools* or techniques such as antinomianism are essentially neutral and can be used toward a variety of ends. The core of Crowley's *magical* philosophy is the willed dissolution of opposites in greater unity (agapê, love):"Let there be no difference . . . between any one thing and any other thing."[55] On the left-hand path, antinomianism points to the separateness or isolation of the self or individual intelligence from oppositional categories, but the dissolver remains intact and independent of its dissolutions. The right-hand path turns antinomianism upon the opposition of self/not-self, or psychê/physis, or subjectivity/objectivity as such.

THE TECHNOLOGY OF MAGICK

Crowley's theology can only be understood fully in terms of his system of magick or initiation. Magick is Crowley's technique for practicing "the Science and Art of causing Change to occur in conformity with Will."[56] This "science and art" is to be most properly applied to the discovery and exercise of the True Will, which is unique, but also "natural and necessary" for each individual. Magick, then, is a program for individual transformation according to the individual True Will of the one being transformed. Crowley wanted to postulate magick as a new *scientific* discipline. As such, he knew that certain universal principles and patterns should apply. This is another factor that distinguishes Crowley from the separative left-hand path, wherein the distinction between the limited and nature-bound character of science (dianoia) and the unlimited rational intuition (noesis) is clear.

However, for the understanding of the structure of the left-hand path as practiced in the contemporary world, the theories of Aleister Crowley are important. He provided a sophisticated definition of the character of the left-hand path and what he called black magick.

According to Crowley, "black magick" is characterized by "any will but that to give up the self to the Beloved"[57] (i.e., the universe, which is the opposite of self-consciousness), or any deviation from the straight line leading to the "Single Supreme Ritual" of "the attainment of Knowledge and Conversation of the Holy Guardian Angel."[58] But he also calls "black" any renunciation for "an equivalent in personal gain,"[59] the use of "[magical]" powers if the object can possibly be otherwise attained,[60] or "the use of spiritual force to material ends."[61] Presumably, because Crowley had undergone the "Supreme Ritual" and was in fact a Magus, he could regularly perform magick of the kind in his *Magical Record:*

> 1. Dec. 4 p.m. [1916]
>
> Anna Grey [woman with whom Crowley performed an act of sexual magick]
>
> [object] Wealth
>
> Operation: difficult but success great as to Object. Elixir, nothing special—good, though when duly mixed
>
> Result: $45.00 next day.[62]

BROTHERS OF THE LEFT-HAND PATH

In the initiatory system Crowley devised for his A.·.A.·., he described a certain advanced moment in the process when the initiate could choose to follow the left-hand path. Until that moment, according to Crowley, all initiates are on the same basic path (see figure 8.2 on page 275 for the initiatory system of the A.·.A.·.).

The initiate begins as a *Student,* who studies various systems of spiritual attainment from a list of books. Next he becomes a *Probationer,* who undertakes whatever magical practices he wishes making a record of them for one year. After this he becomes a *Neophyte* and acquires "perfect control over the Astral Plane." He then becomes a *Zelator,* who perfects himself in basic yogic techniques of the body and breathing. Next he becomes a *Practicus* and completes intellectual training and study of the Kabbalah. Following this he becomes a *Philosophus* and completes his moral training and is tested for his devotion to the order. He then becomes a *Dominus Liminis,* who masters the yogic techniques of *pratyahara* (withdrawal of senses from external objects) and *dharana* (concentration). After this point he becomes an "outer" *Adeptus Minor* and performs the Great Work attaining the Knowledge and Conversation of the Holy Guardian Angel. (Here the Adept can be said to have become aware of his own True or Higher Self.) Upon completion of this the initiate is an "inner" *Adeptus Minor* who enters the "College of the Holy Ghost" or the "Order of the Rosy Cross." Next he becomes an *Adeptus Major,* who masters practical magick, but he does not necessarily understand the true nature of his work. There follows the grade of *Adeptus Exemptus* wherein the initiate becomes a leader of a school of thought. The Adeptus Exemptus is a "separate being . . . from the rest of the Universe."[63] He eventually transits into the "Abyss," into a zone of negation, wherein he may either:

1. Annihilate himself and become an embryonic "Babe of the Abyss"—or—

2. Remain in the Abyss isolated from the universe and become a Black Brother.

It is here, and really only here, that Crowley distinguishes between the right-hand path and the left-hand path. Beyond the Abyss, the "Brother of the Right-Hand Path" will be reborn as a Magister Templi who has annihilated the personality that had previously limited and oppressed his true self. He "is pre-eminently the master of mysticism . . . his Understanding is entirely free of internal contradiction or external obscurity." His work is to understand "the existing Universe in accordance with His own Mind." The Magus is the "Master of Magick . . . his will is entirely free from internal division or external opposition; His work is to create a new Universe in accordance with His Will." The Magus does this by uttering a Word of an Aeon or by making "personal progress equivalent to that of a 'Word of the Aeon.'" Beyond the Magus is the Ipsissimus who is "the Master of all modes of existence . . . entirely free from internal or external necessity. His work is to destroy all tendencies to construct or to cancel such necessities." Further, Crowley says: "The Ipsissimus has no relation as such to any Being: He has no will in any direction, and no consciousness of any kind involving duality, for Him all is accomplished."[64]

The Black Brothers, or Brothers of the Left-Hand Path, are those "who 'shut themselves up,' who refuse their blood to the cup, who have trampled Love in the Race for self-aggrandizement."[65] They refuse to exit the Abyss and remain there, retaining their own gathered powers. These powers will, according to Crowley, eventually dissipate, and with them the existence of the Black Brother.[66]

The system of the A∴A∴ shows a "logical" progression with two virtually obligatory critical junctures for those who would proceed through the grades normally. The first is the "Ritual of attaining Knowledge and Conversation of the Holy Guardian Angel." Here the initiate gains awareness of self and receives the power inherent in this self-knowledge. The second critical juncture is the experience of the Abyss. Here the initiate must chose the right-hand path or the left-hand path.

Although Crowley admits to the possibilities of the practice of "black magick," for him this has little to do with the pursuit of the left-hand path. Whereas in most areas he is anxious to annihilate the distinctions between categories, such as between the Beast and Lamb, or Set and Horus, he seems equally anxious to preserve the distinction between (white) magick and black magick. Any possible explanation for this incongruity is perhaps to be sought in Crowley's own character or needs. He has no objection to dealing with demonic forces,[67] but it is possible for him to explain lack of success in magick by positing interference from the "Black Lodge."[68] Certainly he also could point the finger at magical rivals (such as Gurdjieff), or former teachers (such as S. L. Mathers), or former protegés (such as Austin Osman Spare) and call them "Black Brothers" if it suited him.

VISION

It is clear that Crowley's most ambitious intention in life was the establishment of a new universal religion: a "new law" that would replace Christianity, Judaism, Islam, and all the religions of mankind. His vision was one of universal transformation ushered in by the "equinox of the gods" and helped along by his own work. Crowley would often return to the theme of the *universal progress* of humanity. At the same time (e.g., *AL* II:25), the Beast recognized a difference between the "chosen" (or elect) and the "people" (or mob), "which refuses to admit its deity."[69] This attitude is typical of Crowley; he wants it both ways after all. His system is both universalistic, as are the right-hand-path religions he sought to replace, and electoral (elitist), as are the mysteries of antiquity, Gnostic sects, and most occult organizations.

Was Crowley a lord of the left-hand path? Crowley himself sends a variety of mixed signals. He clearly defines what the left-hand path is in his own terms and carefully explains how he is not a "Black Brother." So we must take him at his word that he was not a treader of the left-hand path.

In my opinion, the key to Crowley's attitude can be found in his self-image. He thought of his "mundane personality" as a fiendish demon; he often called it "the demon Crowley." He saw himself as limited and insignificant, but his True Self he saw as godlike. So the idea of self- or personality-annihilation and rebirth in the True or Higher Self appealed to him greatly. Analysis of his life shows, however, that the personality of Aleister Crowley appeared to be just as strong emerging from the Abyss (on December 3, 1909) as it was going into the Abyss earlier that same year. Of course, our eyes may be deceived.

From the outside looking in, it appears that Crowley meets all of the criteria be a lord of the left-hand path. He practiced antinomianism with a vengeance—but within a theory of strict monism (certainly inspired by his Buddhistic leanings). *Self-deification* is clearly his goal, as he defines it in his own *initiatory* system. It is fundamental to his work that this deification is that of the individual self and that it is accomplished by the will of the individual magician by means of *magick.* So, as I have established the criteria, Crowley is a lord of the left-hand path, though not by his own estimation or evaluation.

One of the major theorists and practitioners of the left-hand path in the latter twentieth century, Dr. Michael Aquino, analyses Crowley's vision of himself and his work as being confused or "perplexed."[70] Given Crowley's criteria for initiation in the A.·.A.·., coupled with Crowley's continued, and even heightened, manifestation of self and personality, a paradox exists. At the level of Magister Templi, the *individual* self and its capacity to discriminate between one thing and another (i.e., logical thought) has supposedly been annihilated. If this is the case, how then can he "Understand the existing Universe in accordance with His own Mind"?[71] Dr. Aquino writes: "The inevitable conclusion is that there is no Right-Hand Path to the initiatory level of *Magister Templi* (at least not as prescribed by the original G.·.D.·. and A.·. A.·.). There is *only* the Left-Hand Path, and it is fraught with danger—not a one-time crossing of the Abyss test, but a continuous peril that exists from the moment the individual completely realizes him-Self as a Magister."[72] Aquino's analysis is essentially that Crowley *was* a Black Brother who, because of his unique position and Aeonic Work, could not clearly see that fact himself.

THE SATURNIANS AND GREGOR A. GREGORIUS

The Great Beast was a goat who spawned a thousand young. Numerous sects and orders based on, or inspired by, Crowley's system arose in the latter half of the twentieth century. The most stable and continuous of the groups independent of Crowley's direct legacy is the Fraternitas Saturni (Brotherhood of Saturn; henceforth FS). The group was initially led from 1927 to 1963 by Gregor A. Gregorius, whose mundane name was Eugen Grosche. The FS appears even more eclectic than Crowley's systems, and it seems also to embrace the traditional symbols of darkness even more enthusiastically than the Beast did.

Sources for the study of the FS have been limited and unsystematic, especially for those who do not read German. Despite whatever limitations it may have, my book *Fire and Ice* (1990; since republished in 2006 as *The Fraternitas Saturni*) was actually the first systematic treatment of the FS in any language.[73] Other than this English-language discussion, there are several collections of original documents. The most extensive of these is the complete collection of the journal *Blätter für angewandte (okkulte) Lebenskunst* published between 1950 and 1963. There are also the *Magische Briefe,* many of which have been reprinted by the German occult publisher Schikowski. Because a former Grand Master sold manuscripts of FS material in 1968 to a German professor of folklore, who in turn published them, a floodgate of original FS documentation and some limited secondary material opened on the German market.[74] Some of this is valuable, especially a study called *Die Fraternitas Saturni: Eine saturn-magische Loge* written by Aythos, another former Grand Master whose order name was Jananda (= Walter Jantschik).

HISTORY OF THE FRATERNITAS SATURNI

The internal tradition of the FS holds that the brotherhood has roots going back to Scandinavian lodges and to the Polish magician and mathematician Joseph Maria Hoëne-Wronski (1776–1853),[75] but its direct ancestry goes back only as far as the Pansophical Lodge and the O.T.O.

The Pansophical Lodge was headed by Heinrich Tränker (Recnartus) and counted among its initiates Eugen Grosche (Gregor A. Gregorius), Karl Germer (Saturnus), and Albin Grau (Pacitus). Grau was an architect and set designer for the German UFA studio in Berlin, where he worked on various films including F. W. Murnau's *Nosferatu*. Germer would go on to become more closely associated with Aleister Crowley, eventually becoming his magical heir. Tränker had derived his Masonic organizational authority from Theodor Reuss (Merlin/Peregrinus) who was the "Outer Head" of the O.T.O. from 1905 to 1922. In the years just after the First World War, Tränker founded a variety of magical organizations, some of which seem to have existed on paper only, and all of which had "pansophical" in their names. The background of these organizations seems to be one in common with the O.T.O.

The O.T.O. itself derived its organizational lineage from charters obtained from an English Mason named John Yarker. A Viennese industrialist and Mason, Carl Kellner, is said to have founded the O.T.O. around 1896, but no mention of it occurs in print before 1904.[76] Kellner is supposed to have pioneered a system of sexual magic. According to tradition, he is said to have traveled to the East, like the fabled Christian Rosenkreuz, and learned the techniques from masters in India and Arabia. It appears more likely that his teachings were derived from a French branch of the school of the American occultist Paschal Beverly Randolph (1825–1875).[77]

These two already closely related streams of German occultism came together for a time at the so-called Waida Conference in 1925. This meeting was held at Tränker's home near Waida, Germany, and its purpose was to bring Aleister Crowley together with German leaders that they might accept his Law of Thelema. The conference was only a qualified success for Crowley. The participants accepted the Law of Thelema, although some shortly thereafter rejected it. Gregorius then went on in 1928 to establish the Fraternitas Saturni as an order. The

FS accepted and worked with Crowley's Law of Thelema, but remained completely independent of involvement with the Beast personally.

The work of the order was, of course, interrupted by the Nazi years. In 1950, Gregorius reorganized the FS and it enjoyed a very productive phase from that time until his death in 1963. After that, there was a period of unsettled leadership until 1971, when the Brotherhood reconstituted itself. The magical philosophy of the FS I examine here is the one that was presided over by Gregor A. Gregorius between 1928 and 1963.

SATURNIAN COSMOLOGY

The cosmological doctrine, or cosmosophy, of the FS is based on dualities and the interplay of dualities: light and darkness, inner and outer, male and female. This echoes Crowley's "monistic dualism" and his polarity between Hadit and Nuit. The synthesis of polar opposites is a much stronger theme in Saturnian teachings than it is in the writings of Crowley.

From the theories of the "heretical" astrophysicist Hans Hörbiger, Gregorius gleaned a doctrine of the cosmic tension between centripetal and centrifugal forces—between the forces of repulsion/expansion and attraction/contraction. The center of the cosmos is symbolized by the center of the sun, while the outer limits of it are embodied in the orbit of the planet Saturn. (In ancient astronomy and astrology, Saturn was the outermost planet as the others were not visible.)

Saturnian teachings give *primacy* to darkness. Darkness is said to precede light and to provide a matrix for the manifestation of the light: without darkness there is no light![78] The "dualism" of the FS does not seek to destroy one pole in favor of the other, but rather it seeks to go beyond the polarities through experience of both extremes.

Gregorius places more emphasis on astrological (or "astrosophical") factors than Crowley. For Gregorius, the New Aeon was to be as much determined by the transition into the much-anticipated Age of Aquarius as by the "Equinox of the Gods" perceived by the Beast. In traditional medieval astrology, the zodiacal sign of Aquarius is ruled by the planetary force of Saturn. (In modern forms of astrology, the planet Uranus is given primary rulership over that sign.) The Kabbalah played a significantly smaller role in Saturnian teachings about the nature and structure of the cosmos than it did in the G.·.D.·., A.·.A.·., or the O.T.O.

For the Saturnian, the cosmos seems to be a much harsher and more severe place to survive in than it does to the more "orthodox" Thelemite. The Law of Thelema was in fact modified or extended by Gregorius to conclude: "Love is the Law, Compassionless Love" (G. *Mitleidlose Liebe*). This compassionless, or "pitiless," love is derived in part Crowley's *Book of the Law* (*AL* II:21):

> We have nothing with the outcast and the unfit: let them die in their misery. For they feel not. Compassion is the vice of kings: stamp down the wretched and the weak: this is the law of the strong: this is our law and the joy of the world.

But the Saturnian formula seems more directly based on the philosophy of Friedrich Nietzsche, who equated pity (G. *Mitleid*) with self-annihilation in his seminal work *Thus Spoke Zarathustra*.[79] For the Saturnian, rejection of "pity" is the magical equivalent of the rejection of self-annihilation. In looking at the Saturnian initiatory path, it will be noted that there was no hint of the Abyss phenomenon or the exhortation to destroy the mundane self so that a new one may be reborn from its ashes.

HUMANITY IN THE DARK LIGHT OF SATURN

In an address entitled "Der Mensch in seiner höchsten Erkenntnisreife" (Humanity in its Fullest Intellectual Maturity),[80] delivered at the Easter Lodge of the FS in 1961, Gregorius discussed the nature of humanity in a way reminiscent of Pico della Mirandola's "Oration." As an individual being, Gregorius sees the human as an entity caught between two opposing poles of life or creativity, and death or destruction, between knowledge and ignorance. But Gregorius does not view these as "good" versus "evil": both poles are necessary to the evolution or initiation of the individual. Only an elite, however, will ever see beyond the dualities or will be able to utilize both poles for the evolution of the self.

Ignorance or "Agnosis" (G. *Nichtwissen*), when recognized as such by the subject, is a true spur to real knowledge or understanding. Here we are reminded of the declaration of the oracle at Delphi that Socrates was the wisest of men in all Greece because he claimed "to know nothing." All knowledge begins with an assumption of ignorance. But the ignorance is like a great weight on the spirit and soul; only the strong will be able to use this resistance to enlightenment for the purpose of initiation. The all-pervasive ignorance of the masses is a testing mechanism. The masses, which are incapable of true knowledge (gnosis), become prisoners of unconsciousness. As a result, external god-forms are projected in order to allay the humans' fear of having to doubt. The Saturnian elite, however, recognize that they are their own gods: they must be, for there simply are no others. Gregorius writes that the Saturnian initiate "should elevate himself upon the pedestal of a godlike entity, despite his profound knowledge that there is no personal God—just as there is no Devil."[81] Gregorius poetically expressed this idea in his 1943 poem "Thou Art Thine Own God":

> *1. Thou must affirm the God in Thee, for every*
> *doubt takes power from Thee.*
> *Every hour of Thy divine knowledge brings*
> *Thee a step higher in Thy journey.*
>
> *2. Thou canst unfold the spark,*
> *that God bestowed on Thee, to a pure flame*
> *that makes worlds fall and rise again,*
> *God is in Thee!—Thou art Thyself God!*
>
> *3. Thus Thou canst have Gods enthroned in Thee*
> *build altars, ignite sacrificial flames,*

for every dream—and form of thought is
Thy power,
and every force of desire takes a form and
shape.

4. Thus art Thou the shaper of transcendental
worlds,
imaginative creator of Thine own realm,
Thou art priest, magus, royal lord
and prince in Thy soul's expanse.

5. Cyprus groves stand round Thy palaces of
thought
and blue waves lap at the marble steps
and ships fare out upon the seas,
for Thee, who wearest the purple.

6. The Earth is Thy sorrow that shaped the
knowledge
and bitter fruits of Thy Golgotha—
And nevertheless the call rings out to Thee:
Lo! I am here![82]

SATURNIAN "THEOLOGY"

Despite the insistence on the initiated individual as the true measurement of the divine, certain apparently objective figures of godlike dimensions play a part in the Saturnian cosmology. These apparent divinities are, however, not gods in the traditional sense. They are either objective concrete phenomena (following the way Crowley described the true nature of Nuit and Hadit) or psychogonic projections of individual or collective human minds.

To the former category belong entities such as Saturnus, the creative agency of the cosmos, or demiurge, as well as Lucifer and Satan(as), the so-called higher and lower octaves of the Saturnian sphere. To the latter category belongs the GOTOS, the egregore of the FS. This entity has been built up through the ages as a result of Saturnian magical work by individual magicians and the FS as a whole. The Grand Master of the order stands in a special relationship with this entity as it is identified with the 33° of the order, the *Gradus Ordinis Templi Orientis Saturni* (G.O.T.O.S.).

The archetypes such as Saturnus and Lucifer become models for the evolution of the magician. They are the patterns of existence in the objective universe, which initiates use to shape their own paths of transformation. But the entities that are the pure products of human will are utilized as tools for the creation of certain magical effects. The GOTOS holds together and empowers the FS in a general way and lends its power to individual members who know the keys to gaining access to that power. The creation of such egregores or psychogones (entities generated by the human psyche or will) is a common magical technique in the FS even on a much smaller scale. In many ways, the magical teachings of the FS seem to be a return to the extremely archaic practices of priests like the Vedic Brahmins, who worship the gods that they themselves have created.

THE INITIATORY PATH OF SATURN

The structural framework of initiation in the FS is provided by the 33 degrees based on the system of the Ancient and Accepted Scottish Rite. This becomes a vast training curriculum for the acquisition of magical skills and techniques.[83] To a greater extent than in the teachings of Aleister Crowley, the system of the FS and Gregor A. Gregorius emphasizes a wide range of magical and meditative techniques and methods as being necessary to progress. This progress is seen as a continuum through the 33 degrees with no annihilation of the self being a part of it.

The path of Saturn is constantly being called one that is both lonely and fraught with danger and suffering, all of which is taken on as a matter of self-determined volition. There is intentional suffering, as Gurdjieff might call it. The role of antinomianism in the FS curriculum is great. Not only is there an emphasis on dark and foreboding images and experiences, which is meant to weed out those unfit for Saturnian initiation, but there is also the common training principle of going against the grain of the initiate's natural inclinations. For example, if the person is naturally oriented toward intellectual and analytical pursuits, that person might be directed to emphasize emotive and intuitive methods in training.[84]

The magical methodology created by Gregorius for the FS hinges on *experience* and *knowledge:* the experience of the Saturnian life and of the sacraments of the brotherhood and knowledge of the Saturnian "cosmosophy" or wisdom concerning the cosmic order. Solitude is cultivated so as to isolate the true subject of the transformation, the individual self. The transformational process follows along a path defined by the 33 degrees leading from Earth to the core of the Saturnian sphere. In that sphere, according to Saturnian cosmosophy, is the true reality of the "Solar Logos." The Sun is the polar opposite of Saturn. But because the core on one extreme contains the essence of its opposite, the path to Saturn is the surest path to the Sun. In this way, the alchemical "lead" is transformed into "gold." Standard Western magical symbolism ascribes lead to Saturn and gold to the Sun. This is the initiatory application of the cosmosophical doctrines of polarization.

For the individual, the chief function of the brotherhood in this process is that the group builds and maintains a constant bond with the Saturnian sphere in the form of the egregore GOTOS. The egregore is the product of concentrated, collective thought-forms built up throughout the years by the FS. The bond with this egregore both aids in the "re-polarization" of the individual toward the Saturnian sphere and provides energy for effecting practical magical ends.

THE SATURNIAN VISION

Because the FS has as one of its main teachings that the world is passing into an Aquarian-Uranian Age, a fairly developed picture of the envisioned future emerges. It only bears a fleeting resemblance to the much publicized "Age of Aquarius" made popular in the 1960s and 1970s. The astrological sign Aquarius is traditionally ruled by Saturn with his dark and distant aspects. Only in more modern times, with the discovery of the planets outside the orbit of Saturn, was Aquarius assigned to the planet Uranus.

This Aquarian-Uranian Age, ruled by Saturn, will be one in which a spiritual elite will be increasingly powerful. Because the initiatory process of this *Saturnian* spiritual elite takes place on a very individualized basis, however, cooperation or fellowship between and among initiates will be a great challenge. This is part of the significance of the Brotherhood of Saturn itself. The individuals seek solitude for their spiritual development, but the physical basis needed to sustain the spiritual solitude requires social cooperation. One unrealized, yet definite part of the Saturnian vision was the establishment of a "monastery" for initiates. This monastery would serve as an educational center (and vacation site) for most members of the order, while it would be staffed by a group of high-grade initiates who would live there.[85] The monastery would provide the kind of physical and spiritual isolation conducive to Saturnian initiation.

GREGOR A. GREGORIUS AND THE LEFT-HAND PATH

As compared to the writings of Aleister Crowley, those of Gregorius are much more filled with direct evidence of a self-conception of his FS as being something of a "dark brotherhood." The association of Saturn with Lucifer/Satan (as the higher and lower octave of the planetary sphere) is freely made and antinomianism is even a part of the training theory promoted by Gregorius. Of course, magic is the chief tool in FS practice and this tool is used mainly for the purpose of initiation or transformation of the brother or sister through the 33 degrees of the Saturnian system. Finally, Gregorius overtly promoted the idea of self-deification as the end of the Saturnian path. That this is a highly individualized path, and an essentially *solitary* one, is emphasized by the nature traditionally ascribed to Saturn. Perhaps more than any other single figure in the first half of the twentieth century, Gregor A. Gregorius exemplifies a true lord of the left-hand path.

AUSTIN OSMAN SPARE

The Lover of the Self

One of the most uncanny figures of the occult revival was Austin Osman Spare. Spare is odd in that he founded no organized group and wrote little (and what he did write was often obscure and muddled). He was most particularly a graphic artist, not a thinker or philosopher. Spare's magic wells up from the unconscious, from a realm of images swirling in the right hemisphere of the brain.

Perhaps the main reason for discussing Spare as a possible lord of the left-hand path is that apparently Aleister Crowley once called him a "Black Brother." The reason Crowley gave for this is that he thought Spare's practice amounted to a "cultivation of self-love through pleasure."[86] This comment alone—if it is reliable—necessitates the examination of Spare's ideas for this study. A major problem with the study of Spare's magic is that more has been written and spoken about it than Spare himself ever put into words. We often remain dependent on the interpretations of others—especially those of the English occultist Kenneth Grant (1924–2011)—for some important data. Grant, too, categorized Spare as a magician of the left-hand path, which Grant defines as the "path of those who use the energies of sex for gaining control of unseen worlds and their denizens."[87] This definition, which seems influenced by Buddhistic attitudes, is far too limited and simplistic for our study. Nevertheless, it is yet another assessment of Spare as a practitioner of the left-hand path.

Spare was born in 1886, the son of a London policeman. He became a graphic artist and edited and published several magazines and books between 1905 and 1927. His most important works are *Earth: Inferno* (1905), *A Book of Satyrs* (1909), *The Book of Pleasure (Self-Love)* (1913), *The Focus of Life* (1921), and *The Anathema of Zos: The Sermons to*

Hypocrites (1927). In 1910, he joined Crowley's A.·.A.·., but soon left the order. Spare became increasingly alienated from "normal" society, so that by 1930 he had completely dropped out of his usual circles. He lived in a South London slum until his death in 1956.

Kenneth Grant met him in 1949 and knew him until the time of his death, whereupon Grant became his literary executor. Spare, chiefly through Grant's efforts, became more well known in death than he ever had been while alive. Not only has Grant's "branch" of the O.T.O. been influenced by Spare's magical ideas, but two other contemporary orders that first became active in the mid-1980s owe significant debts to Spare's "system": the Temple of Psychick Youth (TOPY), which was established by Genesis P-Orridge and Peter Christopherson, and the Illuminates of Thanateros (IOT) founded by Peter J. Carroll and Ray Sherwin.

Spare's cosmology and theology are one and the same because he has a pantheistic view of reality. For Spare, there is a universal self called Kia, which is also the "primal power" of the universe analogous to the Chinese Tao or the Kabbalistic *ain soph*. Spare theorized that the Kia became bored in its monotonous existence and so "condensed itself," or part of itself, into "matter." The planets are used by Kia as staging grounds for the evolution of life. Living creatures are thought to be the "sensory organs" of Kia. The whole physical universe is seen as the product of Kia's will to generate a love object within itself: Kia's will is that of self-love. Therefore, conscious human existence has as its highest purpose the generation of experience for Kia to enjoy: "We love Kia by self-love."[88] When self-love dominates in the awareness of a human being, that person's motivation is harmonized with that of Kia itself.

Thus, in Spare's view, humans are not creatures separate from the natural order, but merely sentient extensions of an absolute reality otherwise cut off from experience of itself. The task of mankind is not to differentiate itself from the natural order through the love of the individual self, but to imitate Kia's cosmic self-love by means of mankind's own communion with the unconscious. Following contemporary psychological theories of Freud and Jung, Spare held that a person has a conscious mind (which is ignorant of experience of Kia) and an unconscious mind. The latter component is the link between the person and Kia, or reality. The unconscious is thought to be inhabited by "elemental automata" or "atavisms," which have their ultimate sources in the deepest levels of Kia. These psychic atavisms are said to be the actual means for Kia's self-awareness. When humans gain experience of these atavisms, Kia gains wider experience in the world of matter.

Like many of his contemporary magicians, Spare seems fundamentally to have been a materialist. In *Earth: Inferno* (1904) he implies that the realm of the flesh, or the natural order, is all that really exists. Thoughts to the contrary are illusions.

From a left-hand-path viewpoint, the most interesting aspect of Spare's system is not his highly subjective cosmology and "theology," but his magical technology. The cosmology is essentially a right-hand-path system, albeit an idiosyncratic or solipsistic one. But his method of working his own magic is so subjective that it must be considered an exercise in at least one kind of left-hand-path *practice,* if not theory. Spare created his own personal magical system independent of any known tradition. In addition, there is no evidence that he really tried to imply that his system was anything other than just this own personal idiosyncratic praxis with no necessary universal value. Spare created a totally arbitrary magical symbology. This involved his representational graphic artwork and a peculiar set of symbols he called the "Alphabet of Desire." He never presented or explained this "Alphabet" in a complete or systematic way. It is a series of glyphs or ideograms, each representing an eternal identifiable element in Spare's own unconscious.

Spare's method of linking the conscious mind (the material world) with the unconscious (Kia) was to create images consciously and then suppress them into the unconscious, where they must be forgotten by the conscious mind. Then they will be free to affect the "flow of fate" and cause the desired effects in the material or conscious world. This process is what Spare called "making the desire organic" or "fleshing" it.

An example of the way Spare "fleshed" desires is provided by the magical technique of "sigilization." This involves the creation of unique graphic forms to act as anchors to sink desires into the deep unconscious and to fix them by an unseen chain to the material world. The most intelligible explanation of Spare's use of various kinds of sigils is found in Frater U.·.D.·.'s book *Practical Sigil Magic.*

Ultimately, the only reason Spare would deserve Crowley's designation of him as a "Black Brother" can be found in his practice of creating an entirely subjective, personal, and unique cosmology and technology for dealing with it. In this regard, Spare *practiced* a separation from the environment even if he did not promote this idea in *theory.* In Spare's theory, self-love is not a turning away from the absolute (Kia) but the only possible direct way to embrace it.

The main problem in interpreting the left-hand-path contents of Spare's ideas is that we are sometimes led astray by the interpretations of other writers. Spare wrote relatively little himself and often what he wrote was unclear and ambiguous. He was a highly undisciplined and virtually unedited writer. When reading Spare, it is sometimes difficult to shake off the nagging feeling that one is simply trying to unravel the ravings of a man half-mad by his own design.

Austin Osman Spare makes for an interesting comparison with Anton LaVey, whom we will meet in the following chapter. Both are essentially creative artists, and both artistically create their subjective experiences based on a carnal mysterium. Spare tended to project the vision more and more *inward,* while LaVey projects his *outward.*

THE FOURTH WAY AND THE LEFT-HAND PATH

If we were to measure the magnitude of "occult leaders" by the greatness achieved by those whom they taught or in some positive way influenced, then certainly the greatest such teacher of the twentieth century would be George Ivanovitch Gurdjieff. He was the principal teacher of P. D. Ouspensky and several others who went on to form their own independent groups within what is known as "the Work" (see figure 8.2). Gurdjieff's teachings have formatively influenced people as diverse

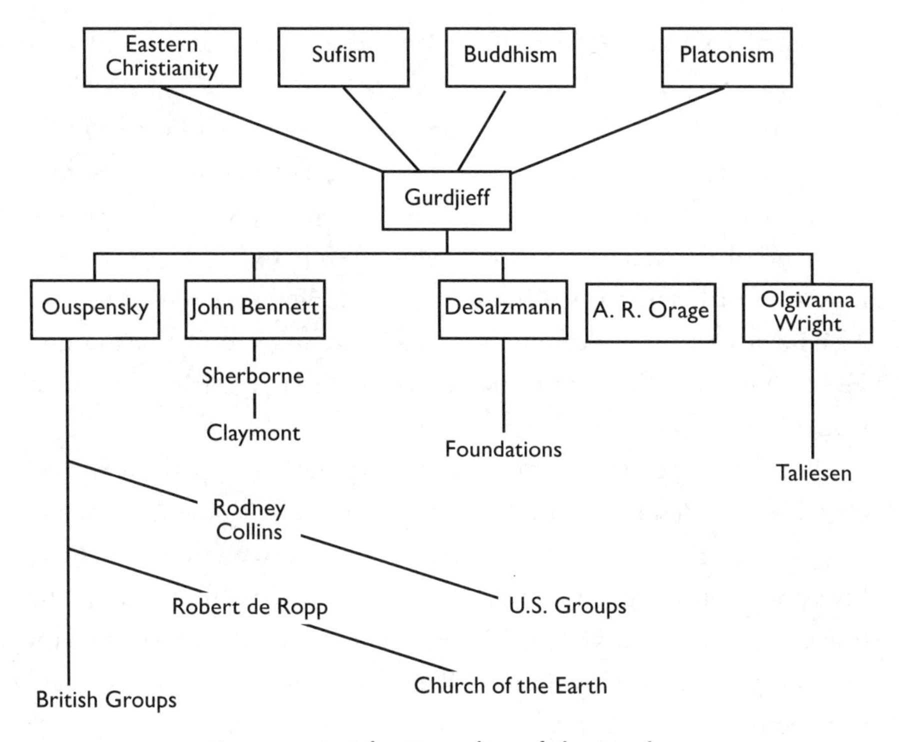

Figure 8.2. The Branches of the Tradition

as architect Frank Lloyd Wright; painter Georgia O'Keefe; film makers Alejandro Jodorowsky and Peter Brooks; authors Katherine Mansfield, J. B. Priestley, and Kathryn Hulme; as well as musicians as diverse as Thomas de Hartmann, Alexandre de Salzmann, and Robert Fripp.[89] Despite his unabashedly "esoteric" status, Gurdjieff has even exerted direct influence on some schools of "orthodox" psychology (e.g., Gestalt psychology), and his ideas are often held in high regard in the academic world.

Gurdjieff is also an unusual figure in the occult revival because when he came upon the scene publicly in Russia for the first time, it was for the express purpose of combating the "occult revival," which he characterized as a "psychosis."[90]

At the same time, "Mr. G.," as he is often affectionately referred to by his followers, is generally shrouded with a mantle of sinister reputation and dark mystery himself. Like others with cultural roots in the lands of eastern Christianity, he seemed to feel little compunction about occasionally associating himself the "the benevolent Devil." Gurdjieff's greatest literary work, *Beelzebub's Tales to His Grandson,* again places Mr. G. in the Devil's lineage. Such references would, however, be nothing but poetic flourishes or deliberate attempts to obfuscate the hidden truths in the absence of more positive evidence. Gurdjieff also has his share of detractors. Louis Pauwels's 1972 book *Gurdjieff* is a collection of such sinister depictions of Mr. G. He was supposed to have been involved with Hitler and the Nazis, as well as with Joseph Stalin.[91] He is supposed to have been able to stimulate an orgasmic response in women by his gaze alone.[92]

But despite his contemporary sinister reputation, or perhaps *because* of it, even his detractors often ended in extolling his power and sometimes carrying on his essential teachings. Mr. G. often frequently ended his association with former pupils in an abrupt or offensive way—he had to drive them away in disillusionment in order for them to gain their own independent existence. Behavior patterns such as these are just one more obstacle in the path of any would-be biographer of G. I. Gurdjieff.[93]

REMARKABLE MEN

The Lives of G. I. Gurdjieff and P. D. Ouspensky

Gurdjieff was probably born in 1874,[94] perhaps on January 13 (New Year's Day in the Old Style Russian calendar), in Alexandropol (later called Leninakan) in the present-day Republic of Armenia. But even these basic data are controversial and subject to mythologizing. The whole of Gurdjieff's early life up until 1912 is shrouded in mystery and self-created myth. The most objective biographical treatment seems to be that of James Webb, *The Harmonious Circle* (1980).

His mother was Armenian and his father was an emigré from Greece. The family's original name was probably Georgiades, which was Armenianized to Gurdjian, and when the region became part of the Russian Empire the name was Slavicized to Gurdjieff. In 1877, the family moved to Kars, closer to the Turkish border. It is there that Gurdjieff grew up.

Gurdjieff's earliest teacher appears to have been his father, who was an *ashokh:* one steeped in traditional ancestral lore. During his formative years, he was exposed to a rich mixture of Greek, Armenian, and Russian Orthodox Christian spirituality. These Eastern sects of Christianity are not only more open to what might be called "occult" ideas and practices in the West, but they are also much less intolerant of divergent spiritual paths. It is even possible that Gurdjieff spent some time training for the priesthood in the Greek Orthodox tradition.[95]

Around the year 1892, when he would have been eighteen years old, Gurdjieff underwent a turning point in his life. He decided to seek knowledge and truth no matter what the cost. Shortly after this, in 1895, Gurdjieff tells us that a group of young fellow investigators formed an association they called the "Seekers for Truth." It was around this time that he would have been eligible to be conscripted into military service for the Tsar. There is good evidence to suggest that the young Gurdjieff fulfilled his military obligation to the Tsar in the field of espionage and later even diplomacy in foreign lands to the south and east of Russia.[96] This period of service most likely lasted from 1892 to 1904 or perhaps 1910. He was wounded by gunfire on at least three occasions during this period; the first time in Crete in 1896 while he was apparently involved with Greek nationalist interests on that island opposing the Turkish forces there.

Most of Gurdjieff's travels and assignments seem to have been concentrated in the *east*—in the regions of present-day Turkestan, Afghanistan, Tibet, and Mongolia. While traveling under an assumed identity at this time, he even appears to have become an intimate of the court of the Dalai Lama in Lhasa. These activities on behalf of Russia and Tibet continued until at least 1904. From that time up to around 1910, it is said he studied hypnotism and healing arts in the Central Asian region of Turkestan. The timing of his return to Russia from Central Asia coincides with the Chinese invasion of Tibet in 1910, which effectively put an end to the interest Russian intelligence had in that country.

With his career in the intelligence service at an end, Gurdjieff, at the probable age of thirty-six, began to bring together what he had learned over the past eighteen years. He moved to St. Petersburg in 1910, and in 1912 began his new career in teaching his unique system to a select circle of pupils. In 1914, he moved to Moscow, and in the spring of 1915 he met a man who would become his most influential student: P. D. Ouspensky.

The "orthodox" Gurdjieffian mythology would have it that Mr. G. spent the years up until 1910 traveling from teacher to teacher, especially in the Middle East, eventually becoming highly initiated in a major international Sufistic brotherhood. This brotherhood then sent him to undertake the enlightenment of the West using a method and system appropriate to the present culture of the Occident.

From the truly *objective* viewpoint—using the word "objective" as Gurdjieff himself might have used it—it does not matter which version, if either, is factually true. It matters only which one brings the individual *subject* of the search for *truth* closer to his goal.

By the winter of 1916, the chaos caused by the First World War and the onset of revolutionary activity prompted Gurdjieff to move south with his students to the ancient Armenian town of Essentuki on the northern side of the Caucasus mountains. There they remained together through the difficult circumstances occasioned by the Bolshevik Revolution of 1917. In January 1919, they moved on to Tiflis on the southern side of the Caucasus near Gurdjieff's family home. There he founded the Institute for the Harmonious Development of Man, but the harsh political conditions forced it to be dissolved in the spring of 1920. By June of that same year, it was clear that Gurdjieff and his pupils would have to immigrate to the West, as so many other subjects of the Russian Empire had been forced to do. First they went to Constantinople (Istanbul), where the Institute was reopened for a year. But this was only a temporary stopover for a more ambitious mission to Western Europe. The group's first stop was in Berlin, where they stayed from the summer of 1921 to the summer of 1922.

During the stay in Germany there was contact with the artistic communities of Berlin and Hellerau (near Dresden), where Gurdjieff briefly attempted to gain control over a facility earlier abandoned by the founder of "Eurhythmics" (*Rhythmische Gymnastik*), Émile Jaques-Dalcroze.[97] There is no evidence to show that Gurdjieff had any contact with the then-subversive National Socialists; if this did ever occur, it would have been during the period of Gurdjieff's many trips to Germany in the late 1920s.[98]

Paris became Gurdjieff's final destination in the West, as it had for so many other refugees from the Bolshevik Revolution. In 1922, he bought an estate, later named the Prieure, in Fontainebleau near Paris. He reestablished his Institute for the Harmonious Development of Man here, and it was here that Gurdjieff's reputation in the West was made. Students came from everywhere, but especially from America.

One famous visitor was Aleister Crowley, who showed up as a weekend guest in 1925. After Gurdjieff had fulfilled his obligations as a host, he ejected Crowley with a flurry of invectives. Perhaps Mr. G.'s ire had been raised when Crowley told a group of children at the Prieure that he was raising his own child "to be a devil."[99]

Despite the fact that many students were attracted to Gurdjieff's teachings, his manner and means of teaching drove almost as many away after some period. Ouspensky finally broke with him in 1924, and his most dynamic Western pupil, Alfred Richard Orage (1873–1934), was driven off by 1931. Even Thomas and Olga de Hartmann, who had been with Gurdjieff since the beginning of his teaching in Russia, were driven off—all by impossible, irrational demands made on them by their "Master." Over time, this situation led to financial disaster for the Prieure, which eventually had to be sold in 1933. From then until the outbreak of World War II, Gurdjieff lived in transit in various locales in Europe and the United States. It was also during this period that he wrote his major literary productions.

Strangely enough, when war did erupt in Europe, Gurdjieff returned to Paris, where he lived out the war years mostly under German occupation. According to him, he sold rugs, owned a company that made false eyelashes, and made "deals" with many people to get along.[100] This is just one more of the verifiable facts concerning Gurdjieff's life and political dealings that invite sensational speculation.

After the war, he again took up an itinerant existence teaching certain pupils and continuing to write and rewrite *Beelzebub's Tales.* Gurdjieff died on October 29, 1949.

Just two years earlier, on October 2, 1947, Gurdjieff's most influential single student, Pyotr Demianovich Ouspensky, had died in London. Ouspensky's life had been vastly different from that of Gurdjieff. He was born in Moscow on March 5, 1878 (Old Style), to a well-educated, Westernized family. His father was an officer in the Russian Survey Service and an amateur mathematician. His mother was a painter and an amateur student of French and Russian literature. In 1888, his parents took young Pyotr to France to see the Paris Exposition.

Ouspensky appears to have been one of those personality types—common among geniuses and "okkultnik nincompoops" alike (though the two types should not be confused)—who can muster no motivation to learn and study things that do not interest them intensely at that very moment. The result of this in Ouspensky's case was that he failed out of university preparatory school when he was about sixteen years old. He then became an auditor in lectures at Moscow University. He read Nietzsche around this time and was greatly influenced by the German philosopher's ideas of the overman. From 1896 to 1905, Ouspensky traveled widely seeking hidden knowledge. His "search for the miraculous" had begun. At the age of twenty-seven, he began his career as a journalist writing for both newspapers and magazines. In 1907, he discovered Theosophy, with which he was never quite satisfied. It surely lacked the precision he was looking for.

Ouspensky entered into the social milieu of the literary Symbolists and the avant-garde. He became a freelance journalist and lectured on occult subjects in the years between 1909 and 1912. In 1912, his first book, *Tertium Organum,* was published. This is a valuable record of the nature and quality of his thought before exposure to Gurdjieff's ideas. He spent most of the years 1913 and 1914 in India, where he visited the headquarters of the Theosophical Society in Benares. He found nothing miraculous there.

Another "pre-Gurdjieffian" work, *Talks with a Devil,* written in 1914 in India and Ceylon, is of interest to us because in it we learn of Ouspensky's particular attitudes toward the devil and evil rooted in Slavic folklore as well as in the spirit of his own time and place. For Ouspensky, the devil is the embodiment of matter. Logic and science are his tools and he uses these to entrap mankind into remaining enslaved to matter. The devil could be said not to exist in any real sense, but is instead the creation of man through ignorance of the nature of matter and the lack of knowledge concerning the reality beyond material appearances. In this metaphor, Ouspensky is firmly on the side of God, as an embodiment of spirituality and against the devil who is the embodiment of "GREAT MATTER."[101] Ouspensky's attitudes can be compared to those of his contemporary countryman, Lenin, who took the other side in this cosmological debate.

Upon his return to Russia in the following year, he met Gurdjieff and became one of his pupils. Intensive work with Gurdjieff lasted until 1918, when a combination of revolutionary chaos and some misgivings caused him to go his separate way during the migrations Gurdjieff and his students made before eventually settling at the Prieure.

Ouspensky finally immigrated to England in August of 1921 and at once began teaching the ideas of Gurdjieff. He gathered students around himself and set up a school that would pursue a course independent from that of Gurdjieff himself. Although Ouspensky's school was essentially "Gurdjieffian," he did tend to attempt to reduce Gurdjieff's teachings to generally intelligible principles. In the last weeks of Ouspensky's life, however, it is reported that he repudiated Gurdjieff's teachings as a whole and advised his students to make a fresh start in their individual quests.[102]

The "orthodox" Gurdjieffian evaluation of the split between Ouspensky and Mr. G. (although this reason is nowhere made explicit) is that Ouspensky wanted to reduce the "system" to general principles, which is impossible because the "system" is only applicable to individual persons, times, and places as determined at critical moments by a living teacher: a "Man Who Knows." The major problem with this interpretation is that it leaves the whole Gurdjieffian movement—or "the Work"—in a hopeless situation upon the death of their Master. This would be at least one reason for Gurdjieff uttering his reputed last words to his followers at his deathbed: "I'm leaving you all in a fine mess!"

SOURCES OF STUDY

Many of Gurdjieff's students, and their students, have written copiously on "the Work." Perhaps the best general introduction is Kathleen R. Speeth's *The Gurdjieff Work* (1976), while the best in-depth introduction to the basic ideas remains Ouspensky's *In Search of the Miraculous* (1939). Several other studies by Ouspensky continue to be invaluable for understanding Gurdjieff's basic system. These are: *A New Model of the Universe* (1931), *The Psychology of Man's Possible Evolution* (1947), and a posthumous collection of shorter works and lectures entitled *The Fourth Way* (1957). The direct approach to Gurdjieff through his own writings—*Herald of the Coming Good* (1933), *Beelzebub's Tales to His Grandson* (1949), *Meetings with Remarkable Men* (1963), a series of early talks collected in the volume *Views from the Real World* (1973), and *Life Is Only Real Then, When "I Am"* (1975)—would be bewildering without the guidance of either secondary sources or a teacher in the Work. This is only to be expected, since all of Gurdjieff's own books were written with the main intention that they would be read as a part of guided work within his system.

THE ORGANIZATION OF THE WORK

Before Mr. G.'s death, of course, the true center of the Gurdjieff Work could be easily focused on him and his Institute for the Harmonious Development of Man, at least until the closing of the Prieure in 1933. But other major teachers of Gurdjieff's system did emerge, even in his own lifetime. These included P. D. Ouspensky's group in London as well as groups around A. R. Orage. After Gurdjieff's death, however, the Work splintered into many schools with many former students founding their own branches. These are delineated on the bottom half of the diagram below. The most direct line of the tradition would appear to be the Gurdjieff Foundations instituted by Jeanne de Salzmann after Gurdjieff's death; it is said that in the days before he passed away, Mr. G. instructed her on how to carry on his Work.

The typical Gurdjieff Foundation group works under the guidance of a teacher and elder students. They have weekly meetings, which usually involve a question/answer format (students pose questions and the teacher answers them). After a while, the physical exercises or "movements" are studied as well as the writings of Gurdjieff. Also typical of these groups is that they will acquire some piece of property where the group will labor on the physical structure of the property as a form of exercise.

There are no provisions for formal initiations or recognitions of various levels of development in the Gurdjieffian school, although theoretically such levels of initiatory development are clearly articulated in the system itself. It seems that perhaps behind some of Mr. G.'s apparent "antics" was the hidden agenda to "shock" advanced students into venturing out on their own after the Work had done all it could for them. The "initiatory system" of Gurdjieff verged on the Darwinian as only the fittest survived and thrived within and beyond the confines of the Work.

THE WORK

Gurdjieff's Work is predicated on a definite anthropology—an understanding of man—or "psychology." But to call it a psychology may be going too far when being very precise about what Gurdjieff taught. Literally speaking, psychology is the understanding of the *soul,* which is something Gurdjieff categorically denied that the "normal," average man even has (or needs).

Mr. G. taught that normal man is *asleep* and completely *mechanical* in his actions. He is nonconscious and therefore can *do* nothing. Events *do* him, so to speak. "Things just happen." Normal man is impotent. His "I-consciousness" is *fragmented.* Normal man is not just one, but many. Many "I"s vie for focus in the normal man, with no central controller present. "*Man is a plurality.* Man's name is legion."[103] (This is an obvious reference to Mark 5:9 where Jesus asks a demon in a man what its name is and it answers: "Legion is my name, because we are many.") Normal man is *mortal,* having no *soul* (or *essence*) to survive in the *postmortem* state. Gurdjieff used the Platonic metaphor of man being imprisoned.[104] His goal is to escape to freedom. Like Plato's men in the cave, however, normal men need the help of those who have escaped before—they need the help of "Men Who Know."

In contrast to the normal man, the extraordinary man, the "Fourth Man," is free, and he is *immortal.* This is due to the fact that he has been able to build up an essence (or a true soul) in himself, which comes from a crystallization of a unified I-consciousness. This kind of man then becomes *potent* in the world around him. He can actually *do* things rather than having things "do" him. The Fourth Man is no longer mechanical (except when he wills himself to be so); he is awakened and no longer asleep.

The following table contrasts the characteristics of the "normal man" and the "Fourth Man."

Normal Man				Fourth Man
asleep				awakened
mechanical				nonmechanical
impotent				potent
fragmented				unified
mortal				immortal
imprisoned	→	escape with help of those who have escaped before	→	free

Gurdjieff taught a definite structure of the individual consisting of four "bodies":

1. Physical or Carnal Body (body)
2. Astral or Natural Body (feelings, desires)
3. Mental or Spiritual Body (mind)
4. Causal or Divine Body (I-consciousness, will)

Not all men have all four bodies. Only the first body is possessed by all. The other bodies must be developed in some way through the Work. Even mastery of the Carnal Body requires Work, however.

There are, according to Gurdjieffian teaching, four *ways* of working:

1. The Way of the Fakir, who develops power over and through the Carnal Body.
2. The Way of the Monk, who develops unity in himself through his emotions or Natural Body.
3. The Way of the Yogi, who develops power through knowledge and even understanding, that is, the Spiritual Body. The Yogi often attempts to enter the fourth state of the Divine Body, but finds this difficult because equal mastery of the first and second bodies must be gained also.
4. The Way of the Sly Man—the *Fourth Way*—in which all sides of the individual (physical, emotional, and mental) are developed in a balanced and harmonious way.

These are the *only* ways of working. Each of these ways develops some or all of man's hidden potentialities. This development is not, however, part of a natural law. "The law for man is existence in the circle of mechanical influences, the state of 'man machine.' The way of the development of hidden possibilities in a way *against nature, against God*."[105]

To explain how these four bodies are (or can be) linked together in the life of an individual, Gurdjieff drew upon an old Indo-European metaphor, used by both Plato and the philosophers of the Indian *Upanishads,* which compares the carnal body to a chariot, the soul to a horse, the mind to the driver, and the consciousness to the will of the driver.[106] The problem with normal man is that he is driven by his chariot, rather than having his will in control. Gurdjieff's position is that normal man is driven by the chariot itself or by the horse, whereas only the will or consciousness of the Fourth Man is truly in control of the lower bodies. The contrast between these two extremes was shown in diagrams that Gurdjieff produced for his early students in Russia (compare figure 8.3).[107]

THE SEVEN MEN

The Concept of Initiation in the Fourth Way

The aim of development in the Gurdjieffian system is the potent immortality of the *individual.* Gurdjieff taught that *individuality* (a permanent and unchangeable I-consciousness) and *immortality* are qualities that *can* belong to man, but that *do not naturally* or normally belong to him.[108] Furthermore, this development is only possible for a *few* individuals. This is partly due to the fact that the knowledge needed for such development is in limited supply.

Mr. G. taught that as far as the mass of humanity is concerned, *nature* controls the level of development. Man only evolves as it serves the purposes of nature to allow him to evolve.[109] "Changes likely to violate the general requirements of nature can only take place in separate units."[110]

"Carriage"	"Horse"	"Driver"	"Master"
Body Desires	Feelings	Mind	I-Consciousness or Will
Carnal Body	Natural Body	Spiritual Body	Divine Body

Figure 8.3. The Horse and Driver

"Humanity neither progresses nor evolves."[111] As the human species exists for the needs and purposes of nature on this planet, evolution of the species beyond a certain point is detrimental and actually impossible.[112] Evolutionary possibilities do exist for *separate* individuals only. "Such developments can take place only in the interests of the man himself against, so to speak, the interests and of the planetary world."[113] Forces seem to resist the evolution of large masses, but individuals can slip past the resistance. "What is possible for individual man is impossible for the masses."[114] Gurdjieff further insisted upon the idea that mechanical or unconscious evolution is impossible. "The evolution of man is the evolution of consciousness. *And 'consciousness' can not evolve unconsciously.*"[115]

Mr. G.'s system outlining the stages of such development in the Fourth Way comprises a seven-level scheme which is a systemic part of his overall cosmology (see figure 8.4). The First Man has his center of gravity, or focus of consciousness, in his physical or instinctive center. The kind of knowledge he can be said to have is imitative. The Second Man has his focus in the emotional center, and the type of knowledge he has is based on his likes and fondnesses. The Third Man has his center of gravity in his intellectual center, and his knowledge is that of subjective logic. The tendencies toward being one of these three types is innate in each individual. The Fourth Man develops in an extraordinary way. He develops a *permanent* center of gravity and his knowledge is increasingly objective; it is also knowledge that he must have received from someone at the fifth level. The Fifth Man makes his knowledge whole and indivisible. All his knowledge belongs to a unified I-consciousness. This knowledge must have been gained from a man at the sixth level. The Sixth Man possesses all knowledge possible for man, but it could still be lost; it also must have been gained through contact with a Seventh Man. The Seventh Man has perfected his knowledge, which has become both purely objective and permanent with an immortal I-consciousness.[116]

Despite this well-articulated system of initiatory development, these levels do not seem to be recognized within Gurdjieffian schools themselves. The system is a description of a process but not a scheme for the recognition of "degrees." It would appear that when individuals within a school or group reach the fourth or fifth level, it is inevitable that they would leave the group to form their own schools. This is perhaps the secret behind the vigorous and high-level spread of Gurdjieffian groups in the world.

Ouspensky clearly indicates that all real initiation is *self*-initiation: "Systems and schools can indicate methods and ways, but no system or school whatever can do for a man the work he must do himself. Inner growth—a change of being—depends entirely upon the work a man must do on himself."[117]

COSMOLOGY

Fourth Way cosmology is closely linked with its "psychology." Everything that is, or that develops, does so in a certain way or pattern. In many ways, Mr. G.'s system is, like so many others generated in Eastern Europe in the late nineteenth and early twentieth century, a *materialistic* one. By this, he seems to have meant that there was only one continuous, ultimately harmonious universe bound together with definite, even if mysterious, laws. There is not one mundane world and another heavenly one that absolutely transcends it. He again follows Plato in this model, although more precisely he reflects a Pythagorean universe.

Gurdjieff taught the primacy of two laws in the cosmos: the Law of Three and the Law of Seven. These two cosmic laws are harmonized by the octave, exemplified in the most recognizable device of the Fourth Way, the enneagram (see figure 8.5).

The Law of Three is based on a concept apparently common to all Indo-European traditions. It is also demonstrated in the Indian doctrine of the *gunas: rajas, tamas,* and *sattva* (activity, inertia, and being). For Gurdjieff, the three principles are the active, passive, and "neutralizing." This latter term can be misleading. In fact, according to Fourth Way teaching, the active and the passive alone tend to cancel each other out unless and until the "third force" acts as a catalyst that they may create something new. The Absolute is characterized by these

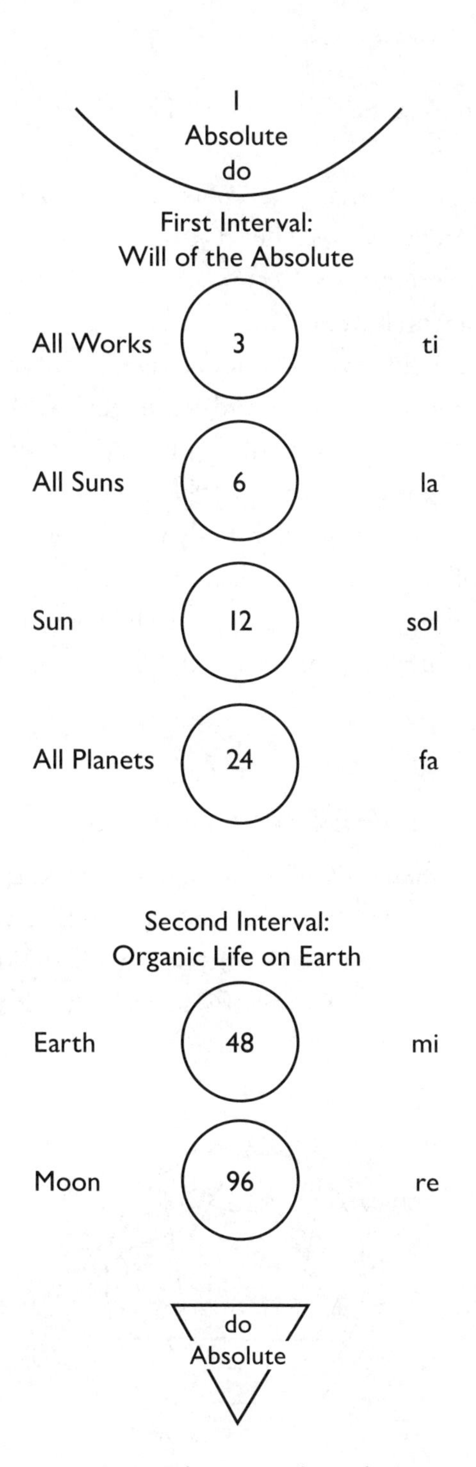

Figure 8.4. The Cosmological Octave

three principles or qualities. The Law of Three becomes a creative force through the octave.

In the octave, the Pythagorean roots of the Fourth Way system are again evident. Gurdjieff showed how the octave of the musical scale corresponded to the cosmological octave (see figure 8.4).

The developmental progress of an individual is linked to his relative freedom in the universe. The fewer laws the individual is subject to, the freer the individual is. According to Mr. G., the physical body is subject to the forty-eight laws of this planet, the astral body is subject to the twenty-four planetary laws, the mental body is subject to the twelve solar laws, while the Fourth Body is only subject to the six laws of all the suns of the universe. When an individual is liberated from the lower laws and thus becomes progressively more free, immortal, and potent, this is because there are fewer and fewer laws constraining the individual.

THE ENNEAGRAM

In *Meetings with Remarkable Men,* Gurdjieff ascribed the symbol of the enneagram to a legendary "Sarmoun Brotherhood." This appears to be pure mythologizing on Gurdjieff's part, but that has nothing to do with its usefulness as a symbol. Gurdjieff said of it that it rendered books

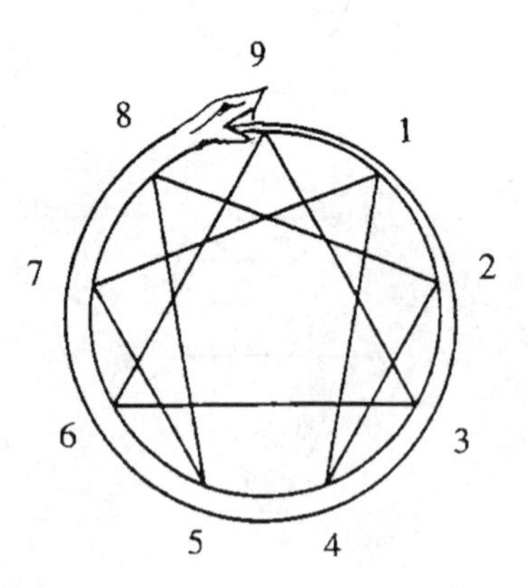

Figure 8.5. The Enneagram

useless because it contained all the wisdom necessary to human development. The ninefold cosmology is common among Indo-European mythologies—most prominently among the Germanic peoples with the "nine worlds" contained in the cosmic tree called Yggdrasill.

The enneagram describes the harmonization of three dissimilar processes: linear progression, dynamic cycle, and static coalescence. All three are necessary and none is reducible to one of the others. Figure 8.5 shows all three properties. This is how the Law of Three and the Law of the Octave are harmonized and it is by understanding how this works that progress in development and mastery over events in one's life are gained.

The serpent of sequential linear time, Chronos, describes the apparent eternal progress of events, while the dynamic (and nonlinear, from the perspective of the sequence 1–9) recurrent cyclical rhythm of 1-4-2-8-5-7 is demonstrated by the complex "hexad" within the circle and the static coalescence of 9-3-6 is indicated by the static triangle.

A FOURTH-WAY THEOLOGY?

There is no theology in the Fourth Way. "God" or "gods" appear to be virtually irrelevant to the concerns and methods of the Sly Man. It is here that the close relationship between the Fourth Way and Buddhistic ideas is quite apparent. In all of Gurdjieff's writings there is only fleeting reference to what he once called "*esoteric* Christianity." Gurdjieff seems to have created a myth wherein the teaching of Jesus was passed "from generation to generation" reaching "the present time in its original form."[118] If this is true, however, then this "esoteric Christianity" appears to be just another way of saying "non-Christianity" or Christianity without God or Christ. Nowhere in Gurdjieff's original teachings is there anything that resembles traditional religious concepts or practices found in either early Christianity or Orthodox Judaism. However, most of Gurdjieff's prominent followers (including Ouspensky and Bennett) tried to make Gurdjieff's teachings appear more "Christian" than they originally were by using examples or illustrations of his teachings drawn from Christian sources.

THE METHODOLOGY

Gurdjieff taught according to no discernible set methodology. Neither did he leave behind any such method. Part of the essence of the disagreement between Gurdjieff and Ouspensky revolved around the latter's desire to seek and formulate a universal coherent methodology of the Fourth Way and Gurdjieff's steadfast insistence on the primacy of the specific teacher-pupil relationship at a particular and unique time and place.

It seems that Gurdjieff's primary concern in this was that the pupils be guided in a way that would balance their development and maintain that balance. If a pupil was overly intellectual, Gurdjieff might recommend physical or emotional Work, and so on. This understanding of the teacher is, however, dependent upon the essence of the teacher and cannot be quantified or regularized.

There are, however, *general* lines of development in the Work. Essential to practical progress is involvement with a school and the help of a teacher (i.e., One Who Knows).

The first line of Work is focused on the self, the individual. One must first practice *self-observation.* Gurdjieff told the members of his early Russian group to write an autobiography without suppressing anything. This was seen as a test for further progress.[119] The pupil is given exercises in self-observation, in seeing themselves as objective beings. Everything from bodily habits and movements, to emotional reactions, to patterns of thought are observed without any attempt at first to control or change anything. This process usually is enough to learn directly about the multiplicity of "I"s within the personality. Self-observation may evoke flashes of *self-remembering.* Self-remembering is the most important part of the first line of the Work. In self-remembering, all three centers—the thinking, feeling, and moving centers—are active. One is hyper-aware of self and environment with one's full attention.

Attention is developed to a high level. One of the common exercises for the development of attention and preparation for self-remembering is sitting in quiet meditation every morning before daily activity begins.[120]

As the first line of Work is focused on the individual, the second line is centered on how that individual relates to other individuals. Gurdjieff said "To endure the manifestations of others is a big thing. The last thing for a man. Only a perfect man can do this."[121] The "manifestations of others" provide the *friction* necessary to the further development of essence. Gurdjieff advised pupils to learn to endure the "manifestations" of people they could not ordinarily bear without nervousness or discomfort. Suppressing the outward expression of negative emotions provides a friction for the development of a person's internal essence over the personality acquired through external experience.

The third line of Work is devoted to the school in selfless service. This is only truly possible once a high level of essence—or consciousness—has been developed and the fragmented personality is relatively disarmed.

In the Gurdjieffian system, *essence* is built up through all practical exercises. The exercises cause friction between a person's essence and personality. The essence is what is real or relatively permanent about an individual; the personality is the product of outside influences. The Work of developing essence must be pursued in a way balanced among all the centers. Imbalanced development is, according to Gurdjieff, the usual cause of the cessation of development of the essence. Most of what a person appears to be is nothing but an accumulation of personality traits. The development of the individual pursued in the Work is the development of the essence. Not all essences of individuals are noble, and the personality is not "demonized." On the contrary, the personality contains the information or tools the essence will need to develop itself.

"EVIL" AND THE FOURTH WAY

Although this is not a study in evil per se, our overall subject matter makes it desirable for us to know what a teacher like Gurdjieff thought "evil" was. On one level, he noted that for normal (or subjective) man, "evil is everything that is opposed to his desires or interests or to his conception of good."[122] A permanent idea of good and evil is "connected . . . with the idea of man's development through conscious efforts."[123] Everything that promotes this development, or awakening, is good; that which hinders it is *evil.* Gurdjieff maintained that good and consciousness were so closely bound to one another that *no conscious act of evil is possible.* He once set his pupils the task of committing an act of "conscious evil" and none could do it.

Gurdjieff also addressed the problem of "black magic." If you return to the definition of black magic given in chapter 1 ("black magic is for the exercise of independence from the universe and pursuing self-centered aims"), you will note that the main aims of the Work accord with that definition. However, Gurdjieff did not use the language of black magic and Satanism, or did so on a limited basis, so his definitions are quite different. According to Gurdjieff, black magic "is the tendency to use people for some, even the best of aims, *without their knowledge and understanding,* either by producing in them faith and infatuation or by acting upon them through fear."[124] In terms of the left-hand-path philosophy, this is a perfect description of most institutionalized forms of the right-hand path! Black magic is not evil magic, it is simply magic that works on others unconsciously. With regard to magic in general, in the same context Gurdjieff says: "there is neither red, green, nor yellow magic. There is mechanics, that is, what 'happens,' and there is 'doing.' 'Doing' is magic and 'doing' can be only of one kind. There cannot be two kinds of 'doing.'"[125]

IS THE FOURTH WAY LEFT-HAND PATH?

From a structural and methodological standpoint, the Fourth Way generally presents a picture in complete harmony with those of the left-hand path. It is only in the lack of recognition of the historical and archetypal analogs of the system within Satanic symbolism that the

Fourth Way may fall short of the criteria of being a school of the left-hand path, but this is practically a matter of aesthetics.

Fourth Way teachings, and even its very methodology, are often antinomian. There is a constant "going against the grain"—of nature, of God, of the mechanism of the universe. Its aim is the attainment of an awakened, independently existing intellect and relative immortality (self-deification). This is individualistic, it comes in initiatic stages (the "seven men"), and its chief technology is *doing:* the use of the will to cause the mechanism to conform to its volition (i.e., "magic").

Gurdjieff was, in many ways, a more pure practitioner and teacher of the left-hand path than Aleister Crowley or any other reputed "black magician" of the early occult revival—a movement Gurdjieff saw himself as actually fighting against.

MODERN WITCHCRAFT AND THE LEFT-HAND PATH

Witchcraft, or "Wicca," is an area of the contemporary occult revival that often comes up in discussions of Satanism, and by inference, the left-hand path. Current adherents of "Wicca" are usually at great pains, however, to point out that their new religion has nothing to do with the worship of the devil. They maintain that such assumptions are carry-overs from the propaganda of the medieval and early modern churches, which saw all heretics or heterodox worshippers as ipso facto Satanists. If such heretics worshipped or venerated anything but the Holy Trinity, they were worshipping an image *contrary* to God and were therefore *Satanic.* This included not only unconverted or apostate pagans or heathens, but also Muslims and Jews. Many modern witches claim they are reviving or preserving ancient pre-Christian (but not necessarily anti-Christian) practices and beliefs. From the standpoint of orthodox religious authority, however, all that is merely another way of defining Satanism in its most virulent form.

Modern "Wiccans" can trace the origin of their neopagan religion back to the late 1930s. Most attempts to ascertain the origins of the Wiccan belief system end up focused on the personality of Gerald Brosseau Gardner (1884–1964). Gardner had little formal education and spent most of his adult life employed with the commercial branch of the British Civil Service in the Far East until he retired in 1936. In his retirement, Gardner returned to England and slowly began to create the religious system called by the name "Wicca" today. Although the particulars of the system evolved or changed over the years, the essential elements remained relatively stable.

The most useful written sources for the study of the historical foundations of modern Wicca are Ronald Hutton's *Triumph of the Moon* (1999), Aidan Kelly's *Crafting the Art of Magic* (1991), together with Doreen Valiente's *Rebirth of Witchcraft* (1989). Primary sources for "Gardnerianism" are his "Book of Shadows" (*Ye Bok of ye Art Magical*) coupled with his own published works *High Magic's Aid* (1949), *Witchcraft Today* (1954), and *The Meaning of Witchcraft* (1959). For most of its developmental years, however, Wicca remained a system the essence of which was only transmitted through oral coven teachings and ceremonial experience.

From its putative beginnings in the late 1930s, the "Wiccan Movement" has grown to shape the spiritual lives of several hundred thousand practitioners, mainly concentrated in the Anglo-American world. It virtually exploded over the span of half a century with no central organization or leadership. That, if nothing else, should speak to the power of the *essence* of Gardner's vision.

The ideal Wiccan organization is the "coven" made up of six male/female couples headed by a high priest or priestess. Originally, since Wicca was supposed to be a survival of an ancient cult of nature and fertility, only heterosexual couples could be admitted. However, the more recent demographics of the movement would show that a large percentage of Wiccans in general and their coven organizations now have a specifically homosexual orientation. The "clergy" or priesthood in a given region or tradition may form a "council," but for the most part each coven is an independent entity ruled by its priestess or priest.

Wiccan initiation consists of three levels or degrees, the most advanced of these being that of "High Priestess" or "High Priest." Once this level is attained in the coven, it is customary for that person (and perhaps his or her consort) to "hive off" and create a new coven. This is the traditional way the Wiccan movement spread according to a sort of "apostolic succession" from Gardner.

A study of the aims and methods of modern witchcraft or Wicca will show it to be nothing other than a universalistic, duotheistic cult of sexuality. This cult is focused on the establishment of ersatz families in an urbanized, largely rootless civilization, and on the practice of methods that are felt to reconnect the individual and the group with some natural source of power housed in nature and especially in sexuality. Although there may be many outward similarities here with the tantrism discussed in chapter 2, this could not be legitimately characterized as having anything to do with the left-hand path.

The only reference to any kind of self-deification comes in the form of the belief that the priest and priestess can, for a time, incarnate the God and Goddess respectively in order to carry out the "Great Rite" (ritual coitus). They do not embody unique or individual divinities, but rather *the* God and *the* Goddess, who are universal. Of course, modern witches do use techniques of initiation and magic. However, the initiation is actually most often a path of preset training in coven and craft lore, and ritual technique, rather than a program of the transformation of the essential being of the initiate. Magic is mostly used for critical needs (healing, personal worldly advancement, love, etc.), and then only rarely. Wicca is truly a new *religion* with all the expected hallmarks of a religion. Within the cult, all are said to be *equal* on an essential level. This is the basis for at least one explanation of their practice of ritual nudity.

There are several antinomian aspects of Wicca: the taking of the name "witch" (categorically an antisocial label), use of sexuality and nudity (and, in its pure and original form, flagellation), and the antimodern stance of looking *backward* in time (real or imagined) to find its value system. Most of these antinomian characteristics offend not against the old religious establishment, but against the new "creed" of positivistic modernism.

Taken as a whole, however, the Wiccan system is clearly a right-hand-path one. Its main purpose is the reintegration of the individual into an organic model of society (in this case, the symbolic coven) and nature and the cycles of nature, and the integration of the group into a universal scheme of nature embodied in the God and Goddess. In its most authentic form in Western European culture, modern *wiccecræft* is essentially (and unwittingly) a revival of the ancient Indo-European cult of the third function (see chapter 2).

Since the 1960s, there has been a good deal of friction between self-professed Satanists and Wiccans. The Wiccans generally see the Satanists as bad for their image with the public and usually spend a fair amount of time explaining why their Horned God is not the "Christian" devil, and how they are not Satanists but rather gentle nature worshippers desiring only to "Harm none." Satanists, on the other hand, tend to have little respect for Wiccans, whom they see as cashing in on the glamor of the sinister imagery of devilry while claiming in essence to be no different than any other religion. The *real* source of this friction has nothing to do with "imagery," however. It stems from the *reality* that Wicca is a right-hand-path system (along with orthodox Christianity, Islam, and Judaism) and philosophical or "religious" Satanism is usually a true left-hand-path system. While Satanism and Witchcraft may *appear* to be similar, in fact they are worlds apart. The friction is simply the result of ordinary people's inability to distinguish between image and substance.

The occult revival has had two significant phases. In many ways, Gerald Gardner's Wicca can be seen as the bridge between the two phases. The first phase, which has been the subject of this chapter, was relatively restricted to certain levels of society and was taken relatively more seriously than the average "New Age" thinker, cult, or philosophy is now, at the dawn of the twenty-first century. This seems largely to be the result of socioeconomic changes following World War II. Magical systems and the occult traditions have become consumer goods marketed to the masses right along with the latest soap or automobile. Of course, here we are again speaking only in terms of *appearances.* In reality, no matter how secrets are sold, they cannot be possessed now in any other way than they were at any time in the past—through hard individual work. Anything to the contrary is an illusion. The current practitioners of the left-hand path seem to have grasped this reality, and it usually forms a part of their philosophies.

9
Anton Szandor LaVey and the Church of Satan

By the latter half of the twentieth century, the first occult revival had run its course. All of its major prophets—Blavatsky, Crowley, Gardner, Spare, Gregorius, and Gurdjieff—were dead. But by the culturally tumultuous mid-1960s, a new cycle of the occult revival loomed on the horizon, and it was one that would be played out on the popular level as never before.

Into this new occult theater there stepped a mysterious man with a message for his time. That man called himself Anton Szandor LaVey

Figure 9.1. The Sigil of Baphomet

(1930–1997). The philosophy he expressed over four decades represented the first major breakthrough of a purely left-hand-path form of thought in the modern Western world. Whereas others such as G. I. Gurdjieff or Gregor A. Gregorius might have had structurally left-hand-path philosophies, they did not overtly combine their philosophies with culturally accepted images of the demonic. LaVey synthesized external demonic imagery and a coherent focus on the independence of the individual. He brought a mass of new information into the model of the left-hand path from areas of human thought previously (and subsequently) ignored by occultists. But we will see how he synthesized all this into a unique, if often pessimistic, weltanschauung.

LaVey's ideas are well documented. However, facts concerning his life and background are often shrouded in mystery, as they were even in his own lifetime. This, it turns out, was a self-created mystery and one that was really a part of the magical philosophy of the man. In this book, as much as possible, I focus on the *ideas* of the lords of the left-hand path and eschew as much as possible the "soap-opera" aspects of biography that only tend to distract us from the central meanings of people's lives. With LaVey, however, it is important to understand how his philosophy revolved around the way he was able to recreate himself out of self-chosen images. It is in this respect, hidden though it usually is, that LaVey exercised his most godlike power.

There were other people who contributed toward making the Church of Satan the institution it was in its early years, but the philosophy underlying the Church, and which gives the Church its continuity, has always been the personal philosophy of Anton LaVey. As a general practice, I will address the central personal philosophy of LaVey, rather than trying to fit any other elements into the overall Church philosophy.

THE LIFE OF ANTON LAVEY

The life story of Anton LaVey is a complex one. Central to any understanding of this story is an awareness of its mythic components and of the tension between mythology and historical facts. If it has not become apparent in the contents of this book already, it should be explicitly mentioned now: often the *myth* (i.e., the idealized and eternal essence) of a person's life is more important for us than the *biography* (i.e., the historical data of external existence). It is more important because it is more likely to be relevant to our individual existences and more likely to be of some *use* to our individual situations than bare factual biography. Rarely do we get so much opportunity to gain a glimpse into the myth-making process as we do with Anton LaVey.

The chief published sources for the LaVey legend are *The Devil's Avenger* (1974) by Burton Wolfe and the more recent "authorized" biography *The Secret Life of a Satanist* (1990) by Blanche Barton. Both of these works appear to have been approved word for word by LaVey himself and so must be considered as much self-portrayals as anything else. They provide the canon of the myth. Few treatments of LaVey can be called both objective and informed. A most revealing, if all-too-brief, account is provided by the journalist Lawrence Wright in an article for the September 1991 issue of *Rolling Stone* magazine. This was later republished as a chapter in Wright's 1993 book *Saints and Sinners*.

Essential to the nature of the myth of any figure such as LaVey are the influences that shaped that figure's thought and action. LaVey himself provided a core list of such influences on his thought on the dedication page of the original printings of his seminal text *The Satanic Bible* (1969). In some editions of the book, this list was omitted.

On that list appear nineteen primary personages with twenty more given a sort of "honorable mention." (There is also one animal, LaVey's famous pet lion Togare, as well as the "Nine Unknown Men.") Almost seventy other names appeared in a similar list in his *Satanic Rituals* book. These, too, were removed in some later editions of the book. Space does not permit me to discuss each one of these personages in any detail, but the primary list is extremely important to understanding LaVey's Satanic philosophy. The nineteen primary men are (in the order he listed them): Bernardino Nogara, Karl Haushofer, Grigory Yefimovitch Rasputin, Sir Basil Zaharoff, Allesandro Cagliostro, Barnabas Saul, Ragnar Redbeard, William Mortensen, Hans Brick,

Max Reinhardt, Orrin Klapp, Fritz Lang, Friedrich Nietzsche, William Claude Dukinfield, Phineas Taylor Barnum, Hans Poelzig, Reginald Marsh, Wilhelm Reich, and Mark Twain. After the names of each of these men, LaVey characterized them with a dedicatory phrase. These are given in quotation marks in the discussions below.

Bernardino Nogara (1870–1958), "who knew the value of money," was a savvy treasurer to the Vatican in the first half of the twentieth century. Presumably, LaVey's cynical appreciation of Nogara, who himself held no adherence to Catholic doctrine, is similar to his esteem for Basil Zaharoff (see below).

Karl Haushofer (1869–1946), "a teacher without a classroom," was the founder of the theory of "geopolitics" and a professor of geography at the University of Munich. He was sympathetic toward National Socialism and exerted influence on its ideology, especially through one of his students, Rudolf Hess.[1] However, LaVey's image and admiration of him comes through the modern mythologizing contained in *The Morning of the Magicians,* in which the authors have Haushofer involved in various occult goings-on in Tibet and with the infamous *Thule Gesellschaft* of Rudolf von Sebottendorf. There is, however, no historical evidence for these more "occultnik" connections.

Rasputin (1872–1916), "who knew the magic of a child," was much admired by LaVey because he saw the Russian "mad monk" as a lusty manipulator of people (especially women) and power—all traits respected by LaVey. As we saw in chapter 6, however, Rasputin was not likely to have had anything really "Satanic" about him. LaVey was most certainly inspired by more lurid accounts of Rasputin[2] and by the film *Rasputin: The Mad Monk* (Hammer 1965).

Sir Basil Zaharoff (1850–1936), "a gentleman," was an arms merchant who sold weaponry and encouraged his customers to use their purchases—all while not only becoming wealthy but being knighted by the king of England, too!

Cagliostro (1743–1795), "a rogue," was the assumed name of an Italian magician and alchemist named Guiseppe Balsamo. He billed himself as a "Count" and the "Grand Kophta" of the Egyptian Lodge, but what was less known was that he had been expelled from several countries due to his fraudulent dealings. He was popular with the people and a supporter of revolution, but ended his life in the dungeons of Pope Pius VI.

Barnabas Saul, the "link with Mount Lalesh," was the first "scryer," or medium, employed by the Elizabethan mage John Dee (1527–1608). After leaving Dee's service, Saul disavowed his visions. Mount Lalesh (or Lalish), one of the so-called Seven Towers of Satan, is a sacred site for the Yezidis (see chapter 4). Whatever "link" exists here seems to be a personal association in LaVey's mind.

Ragnar Redbeard (1842?–1926?), "whose might is right," is a story unto himself. "Redbeard" was perhaps the pseudonym of Arthur Desmond, an atheist and social Darwinist street-philosopher from whose book, entitled *Might Is Right,* LaVey used whole sections to create the "Book of Satan" portion of *The Satanic Bible* (pages 30–35).

William Mortensen (1897–1965), "who looked . . . and saw," wrote a photography manual entitled *The Command to Look* (1937). The psycho-optical theories contained in it greatly influenced LaVey's approach to art and to images and the way they can influence the human mind. It must be considered a keystone of LaVeyan Satanism.

Hans Brick (1889–1972?), "who knows the law," was a German-born animal trainer (notably of big cats) whose autobiographical book *The Nature of the Beast* (1960; published in England as *Jungle, Be Gentle*) recounts his experiences training circus animals of all sorts. The "law" referred to in LaVey's remark is the *lex talionis* (Lat. "law of the talon"). Observations on animal behavior were a formative influence on LaVey's social philosophy, especially as contained in the "Eleven Rules of the Earth." Brick's descriptions of training big cats would have also been relevant to LaVey's own handling of these animals.

Max Reinhardt (1873–1943), "a builder of dreams," was born Max Goldman in Austria and became famous as a theatrical director who specialized in staging huge spectacles.

Orrin Klapp (1915–1997), "the walking man," is a sociologist whose works *Heroes, Villains and Fools* (1962) and *The Collective Search for*

Identity (1969) were greatly influential on LaVey's ideas of social movements and change.

Fritz Lang (1890–1976), "who made moving blueprints," was an Austrian film director who made such classics as *Die Nibelungen* (1924), *Metropolis* (1926), and *M* (1930).

Friedrich Nietzsche (1844–1900), "a realist," was a German philosopher and forerunner to the existentialists. His ideas of the *overman* (or "superman") and the "will to power," as well as his ideas concerning the existence of natural "masters" and "slaves," are greatly admired by modern philosophical Satanists. (For more on Nietzsche, see chapter 6.)

William C. Dukinfield (1880–1946), "who saved me a journey to Tibet," was the real name of the actor W. C. Fields.

P. T. Barnum (1810–1891), "another great guru," was the American showman famous for his exhibits of freaks and establishment of circuses. Barnum's supposed basic philosophy of "There's a sucker born every minute" was taken to heart by LaVey and used as a mainstay of his worldview.

Hans Poelzig (1869–1936), "who knew all the angles," was a German architect who specialized in grandiose and imaginative structures. An example is the Grand Theater in Berlin, also called the Max Reinhardt Theater (1919). He was also the set designer for the film *The Golem* (Deutsche Bioscop 1914).

Reginald Marsh (1898–1954), "a great artist," was an illustrator, scene designer, and painter of gritty street scenes. He was much admired by LaVey, who was himself a painter of unusual subjects.

Wilhelm Reich (1897–1957), "who knew more than cabinet making," was a German psychologist who held that there was a material force called "orgone" that worked in conjunction with the human orgasm. This force could also be collected in "cabinets" called "orgone accumulators."

Mark Twain (1835–1910), "a very brave man," was the pen name of the great American writer Samuel Langhorn Clemens. LaVey much admired Twain for his works *Letters from the Earth* (1962) and *No. 44, The Mysterious Stranger* (1969). In an early Church of Satan document,

LaVey praises Twain as "one of the greatest of the Devil's advocates in history" and as "the most noble embodiment of the Satanist."[3]

This list of influences provides invaluable insight into the formation of LaVey's philosophy and outlook on life. Of the sixteen identifiable men, fully half of them are artists of one kind or another. Of these, five dealt with the creation of visual imagery, and two, W. C. Fields and P. T. Barnum, were best known as "trickster" figures. The idealization of *image makers* should provide some clue as to the true nature of LaVey's philosophy and magic.

Beyond these influences there are at least three others that are known but which remain relatively unacknowledged by LaVey: the horror writer A. Merritt (1884–1943), the magician Aleister Crowley (see chapter 8), and the philosophical writer Ayn Rand (1905–1982).

Merritt wrote a novel called *Seven Footprints to Satan* (1928), which contains a characterization of Satan—who is ultimately shown to be a carnal being—upon which LaVey seems to have based his own living portrayal of the Prince of Darkness. In that novel, Satan is a conspiratorial mastermind who draws in followers and subjects them to a tortuous game of chance in which they must ascend a staircase without stepping on seven predetermined steps. If they succeed, they can have any wish fulfilled; if they fail, they will become the slave of Satan. His zombie-like followers become addicted to a drug called *Kheft,* which he distributed to hold them in thrall. Satan also espouses a philosophy of life in which he claims that only three things are worthwhile: amusement, beauty, and "the game" (which supposedly involves chance). A fourth component, *power,* is also mentioned. This provides the rationale for a sort of "meta-game" beyond the apparent staircase game, which is in fact *rigged* in Satan's favor.

Although LaVey viewed Crowley as a deluded, drug-addicted adventurer, he admired "the world's wickedest man" for having lived a full life. In *The Devil's Avenger,* Crowley is mentioned as an early influence on the adolescent "Tony LaVey."[4] Indeed, Crowley does appear to have been a role model for LaVey, as perhaps Gerald Gardner was as well. LaVey saw Gardner as following in Crowley's footsteps—after Crowley had "made it safe" to be an occult leader by taking the heat of negative publicity in the early part of the century. Crowley had been a villain, but was transformed by historical developments into a hero—a pioneer of liberated thought—and men like Gardner and his imitators (such as Alex Sanders, the English Wiccan high priest known as the "King of the Witches") were riding his historical coattails in the more tolerant 1950s and early 1960s, and usually being portrayed as "fools." The parallels between the development of Gardner's publicity campaign (including his "witch museum" and tabloid coverage) and the one mounted by LaVey in the mid-1960s to early 1970s is remarkable and worthy of further study. "Occult leaders" such as Crowley appear to have been less magical or philosophical role models and more strategic ones for LaVey. In the Church of Satan, serious consideration of Crowley's magical philosophy would only be given by Michael Aquino, who wrote a study of it for the Church publication *The Cloven Hoof.*[5]

The Russian expatriate philosopher Ayn Rand's books were recommended on the Church of Satan reading list in the early 1970s. In subsequent years, her influence was not touted too highly. But her impact was apparently formative to the most succinct presentation of LaVeyan Satanism, "The Nine Satanic Statements." A 1987 article by George C. Smith points out the obvious parallelism between the number and order of these statements and a speech given by John Galt, the protagonist in Rand's novel *Atlas Shrugged* (1957).[6] However, the rhetorical style of the "Statements" also seems drawn from that of Ragnar Redbeard's *Might Is Right.*

The fact that most of LaVey's ideas are not "original," and that his philosophy is largely made up of bits and pieces of the philosophies of others, which he recomposed according to his own tastes and style (unique to himself and to his time), might also be said of some of the other subjects in this study. We could say the same of anyone who ever created a religion, whether Gautama the Buddha or Gerald Gardner. What made LaVey somewhat unusual in this respect is that he often seemed to insist on the idea that he *invented* a way of thinking, that his Satanism was something akin to a product upon which he had a copyright of some sort. But more remarkable than the idea that LaVey invented his Satanism out of bits and pieces of obscure philosophies is the fact that he actually reinvented *himself* out of the depths of his own mind where these various ideas had been distilled.

THE MYTH OF DR. LAVEY

No other figure in the second wave of the "occult revival" has had anecdotes about certain aspects of his life more widely recorded than Anton LaVey. Is this record mere history or is it more remarkably the outer form of an act, or "working," of lesser (black) magic? If one wanted to write a full and factual biography of Anton LaVey, it would require much research, and commercially published works would probably only provide the mytho-magical backdrop to the all-too-human—or all-too-demonic—drama lurking below the surface.

The first significant effort at separating fact from myth was made by Lawrence Wright. At present, however, a clear separation of myth and fact remains impossible—and this may always be the case. I will recount here briefly the reported events of LaVey's life as given in *The Devil's Avenger* and *The Secret Life of a Satanist,* both of which are authorized biographies, supplemented or commented upon by data gathered by Wright and other sources. It is not the purpose of this book to delve into "tabloid" aspects of the lives of the personalities studied, but it is important to understand the way a magician might use and invent "history" as a source of personal power. Anton LaVey appears to be *the* outstanding modern example of such sorcery.

Howard Stanton Levey, who was later to be reinvented by himself as Anton Szandor LaVey, was born in Chicago on April 11, 1930. His parents' names were Michael and Gertrude, although he liked to refer to them as "Joseph" and "Augusta" in his biographies. Michael Levey became a successful businessman in the liquor trade. Not long after Howard's birth, the family moved to northern California.

Although predominantly Jewish, his family contained a variety of religious and ethnic backgrounds. Religion in any formal sense seems not to have been emphasized in Howard's early years.

"Tony," as he was nicknamed, apparently discovered art and music at an early age. When he was fourteen, he found a copy of William Mortensen's *The Command to Look*. In this "how-to" manual of photography (originally published in 1937), Tony saw a key to magic and to the manipulation of others. He would use these principles later in his own paintings. He also must have begun to learn a great deal about music and the playing of various instruments.

In the "authorized" biographies, it is reported that Tony went with one of his uncles to Germany in 1945 just after the war ended.[7] He has often claimed to have been, at fifteen, the youngest musician to have played for the San Francisco Ballet Orchestra as second oboist. This seems unlikely as, according to the research of Lawrence Wright, there was no orchestra by that name, nor a musician by his name in any San Francisco orchestra.[8] The next year, at sixteen years of age, Tony dropped out of high school.

One of the most important factors in the LaVey legend is his association with the circus as a lion tamer. It is widely claimed that he worked for the Clyde Beatty Circus beginning in the spring of 1947.[9] Again, no record exists of anyone by his name ever working for the Beatty Circus.[10] From there, he claimed to have begun a career playing a variety of keyboard instruments in various places ranging from carnivals to nightclubs and strip joints.

It was at one of the latter type of establishments in Los Angeles that Tony claimed to have met, and had an affair with, Marilyn Monroe in 1948.[11] Serious biographers of Monroe have expressed extreme doubts about her employment in strip shows and her association with LaVey.[12]

From Los Angeles, Tony moved back to northern California. In 1949, he is supposed to have enrolled in City College of San Francisco for courses in criminology, and from this to have developed a second career as a police photographer. It was as a photographer of scenes of senseless brutality and violence that LaVey was supposed to have confirmed his dim assessment of human nature.[13] Again, however, public records show no trace of him under any name at City College or on the payroll of the police department.

In 1950, he met Carole Lansing and in 1951 they were married in Reno, Nevada. The record of this marriage is the first appearance of the name "LaVey."[14] Their daughter, Karla, was born in 1952.

It was apparently around this time that LaVey began to become more deeply interested in magic and occult culture. He is said to have made contact with the "Church of Thelema" headed by Francis Israel Regardie, a onetime personal secretary to Aleister Crowley. LaVey's contacts with groups, however, remained informal. He appears to have pursued his interests in magic—as he had all his personal interests—privately and unconventionally. Throughout the 1950s, it seems he mainly supported himself and his family through his many jobs playing piano and organ in various nightclubs and theaters in the San Francisco area. Throughout this time he was also said to have acted as a "psychic" investigator and professional hypnotist.

Beginning in the mid-1950s, LaVey began living in a house then owned by his father, Michael Levey, at 6114 California Street in San Francisco. Eventually, this was to become the infamous Black House. This 1905 house was, sadly, condemned and demolished in 2001 to make way for a new duplex.

In 1960, LaVey became interested in a seventeen-year-old movie theater usherette named Diane Hegarty. He eventually had her move into his house and soon thereafter he began giving Friday night classes in various occult subjects. During the early 1960s, regular visitors to LaVey's house coalesced into what became known as the "Magic Circle." This "circle" included the avant-garde film maker Kenneth Anger, anthropologist Michael Harner, the locally famous "mad countess" Carin de Plessen (who was indeed a member of the Danish peerage), as well as writers, doctors, lawyers, prominent nightclub people, and some members of the police force.

In 1962, LaVey divorced Carole, but never officially married Diane. On November 19, 1963, Diane bore Anton a daughter whom he named Zeena Galatea LaVey.

Starting as early as the mid-1960s, Anton had been drawing attention to himself locally by keeping big cats as pets and often walking them in public on a leash. The first of these, Zoltan, was a black leopard. Zoltan was killed by a car near the Black House in 1964. Soon thereafter, LaVey acquired Togare, a ten-week-old Nubian lion.

In that same year, a local American Humane Association television production for children called *The Wonderful World of Brother Buzz* gave a glimpse inside the house and of its occupants Anton, Diane, Karla, Zeena, and Togare. The program shows the interior of LaVey's private world much the same as it would appear four years later, after the founding of the Church of Satan, in the 1968 documentary *Satanis: The Devil's Mass.* This film is important for the understanding of the genesis of the Church of Satan.

THE EARLY CHURCH OF SATAN
1966–1970

"To 1966, The Year One!"

New Year's toast from *Rosemary's Baby*

A member of LaVey's Magic Circle, Edward M. Webber, who was experienced in publicity and financial matters surrounding churches and nonprofit organizations, suggested to Anton that he found a church based on his teachings.[15] This was done in a rather informal ceremony on April 30, 1966. April 30 is the date of Walpurgisnacht, a traditional German witches' festival made famous in literature by Goethe's *Faust.* The year 1966 was declared the Year I, *Anno Satanis,* and Anton LaVey declared himself the High Priest of Satan and Exarch of Hell.

The more conservative and socially influential people in the "Magic Circle" seemed to have supported this development and wanted the Church and the Black Pope to move on to more serious and substantial ground. But LaVey appears to have taken a different direction of development by seeking the most lurid kind of publicity. He put on a "Topless Witches Review" in a theater in San Francisco. One of his witches was

Susan Atkins, then using the stage name Sharon King. She would later go on to become one of the "Family" gathered around Charles Manson.

The Black Pope, it appears, had his own vision of what he was doing. Institutions of any kind had always been an anathema to him. In the years between 1966 and 1970, the Church existed as a more or less local San Francisco phenomenon. The wider publicity it gained was chiefly through the personality and activities of Anton LaVey himself. He continued with topless witches' shows and with his public lectures at the Black House. The lectures were usually punctuated by a theatrical, or psychodramatic, ritual demonstration. On February 1, 1967, LaVey presided over a wedding ceremony between writer John Raymond and socialite Judith Case. On December 8, the High Priest of Satan officiated at the funeral of Navy Seaman Edward D. Olsen, which was conducted complete with honor guard. These public acts outraged and fascinated elements of the mass media and their audience.

According to the official biographies, the High Priest was asked to be a "technical advisor" for Roman Polanski's film version of Ira Levin's novel *Rosemary's Baby* in 1967. This was the beginning of several cinematic advisory roles LaVey was to have, including *The Devil's Rain* (1975) and *Dr. Dracula* (1976). This latter film contains some obviously LaVeyan ideas on the possibilities of immortality.

During the years of 1966 and 1967, LaVey carried on an ambiguous personal relationship with the film actress Jayne Mansfield. Accounts of this relationship vary from those provided by LaVey (which show the actress as a sexually masochistic worshipper of the masterful High Priest)[16] to those provided by Mansfield's biographer May Mann and others (which show her being pursued by an aggressive LaVey and somewhat repelled and perhaps a bit frightened of him).[17] In any event, Anton and Jayne's lawyer and confidant, Sam Brody, did not like one another. For a variety of causes, so the legend goes, the Black Pope put a curse on Brody. On June 29, 1967, Jayne Mansfield and Sam Brody were killed in a car wreck in Louisiana. After Mansfield's death, LaVey spoke more provocatively about her involvement with the Church. (Only years later would LaVey begin to tell how his curse had worked its magic: it had operated in an unintentionally tragic way on the actress, when he was only trying to get the lawyer.)

The summer of 1968 saw the release of Polanski's *Rosemary's Baby.* LaVey, whose eyes allegedly had a bit part in the film playing the devil who impregnates Rosemary, was also employed in publicity for the film's premier at the Marina Theater in San Francisco. At that premier was a young Second Lieutenant, shortly bound for active duty in Vietnam, named Michael A. Aquino, who would have a significant role within the Church in the following years.

THE GREATER CHURCH OF SATAN
1970–1975

The Satanic Years V to X were a high point of the life of the Church of Satan. This period was ushered in with the publication and release of *The Satanic Bible* in January of 1970 as an Avon paperback. Now the sensationalistic publicity was backed up with a succinct expression of LaVey's Satanic philosophy that was available in every neighborhood bookstore. The Church would no longer remain the local San Francisco phenomenon it had been. In 1968, Church membership had been only 50–60.[18] Despite the enormous surge in worldwide publicity generated by the release of *The Satanic Bible,* however, actual membership only grew to number in the hundreds by 1975.

Over the five-year period from 1970 to 1975, the Church gained members from all over the world. Local Satanists wished to organize and hold rituals in emulation of events at LaVey's Black House. Now the Church needed an administration. Much of that administration was handled by Diane, who often responded to correspondence under the name "Lana Green." During this period, another important administrative role was taken on by Michael Aquino. Upon his return from Vietnam in 1970, he was named a Priest of Satan and a member of the Church's ruling body, the Council of Nine. From late 1971 to midsummer 1975, he was the editor of *The Cloven Hoof,* the chief in-house publication of the Church.

Also in 1971, LaVey's second book, *The Compleat Witch, or What to Do When Virtue Fails,* appeared. At first glance, this might seem to be a rather extremist book for women on "how to get men." It contains all sorts of advice that many find outrageous, such as telling women to save portions of their sanitary napkins or tampons in a pouch and to use the subtle odor from it as a perfume-talisman to attract the erotic interest of men.[19] But this was not only the first self-help book of the "me-generation" 1970s—it was also a manual of the principles of what LaVey called "lesser magic." Most of LaVey's magic has been of this type: sometimes on a grand scale (such as the publication of *The Satanic Bible* or the generation of media attention to cause shifts in public opinions or attitudes) and sometimes on a small scale (such as when he would charm or frighten individuals in his immediate environment).

Late in 1972, LaVey's third book—and last one for more than two decades—appeared in the bookstores: *The Satanic Rituals.* This is a collection of rituals, some of which are originally by LaVey. A number of the texts were, however, written by others: "The Black Mass" was by Wayne West, then a Priest in the Church; "The Call to Cthulhu" and "The Ceremony of the Nine Angles" were both by Michael Aquino, as was a portion of the "Adult Baptism" ritual.[20] Now the Church's literary base was in place. All of this continued to generate attention and publicity for the High Priest.

Outside of San Francisco, the Church structure continued to grow. Local groups of the Church, called "Grottos," were established in various places. By 1975, a total of around a dozen Grottos had been established in the U.S. and abroad. These sometimes caused problems for the "Central Grotto" in San Francisco. There appears to have been an increasing underlying friction between the centralized personality cult surrounding Anton LaVey in San Francisco and the more widespread, transpersonal Church throughout the country during this period.

Several regional gatherings, called "Conclaves," were held, mainly in the northeast, between the years 1971 to 1974. The last one was held in Windsor, Ontario, in August of 1974. No national or international

Conclave was ever organized for the Church of Satan, and Anton LaVey never attended any of these regional Conclaves.[21]

During this era of the Church of Satan's history, an initiatory structure was worked out, although it seems to have come only as an afterthought to the foundation of the Church. These initiatory grades are discussed in some detail below. LaVey's attitude toward initiation, grades, and so on appears to have been subjective at first. If he felt a person was worthy of being named—or "elevated," as he liked to call it—to the priesthood or Magistry, he simply "elevated" them on his personal authority as High Priest. Organizationally, this remained possible because the "Church of Satan" was never actually incorporated as a *church,* but rather remained more or less an assumed name for Anton LaVey's business purposes. He was actually philosophically opposed to the tax-exempt status enjoyed by churches.

This tendency toward informality reemerged in LaVey in 1975 when he, after previously authorizing and endorsing the idea that the priesthood of the Church has to be recognized on merit alone,[22] reverted to the idea that it could be acquired through donations to the "Church" of one kind or another, or merely according to his personal judgment.[23] The resultant fallout from existing members of the clergy led to what might be called a Church schism, in the wake of which a large percentage of the non-San Francisco membership and clergy resigned. It was also at this time that Michael Aquino claimed to have assumed the "Infernal Mandate"—a term not used by LaVey himself—and with it formed the Temple of Set (see chapter 10). For a time, this event seemed to bring an end to the wider experiment known as the Church of Satan—as it, and its leader, happily returned to the reclusive existence deep within the recesses of the Black House.

THE WITHDRAWAL OF DR. LAVEY

The Church of Satan 1975–1986

LaVey's public pronouncements had placed Church membership at more than 25,000, and eventually claims would be made into the millions.

In fact, active Church membership probably never exceeded more than several hundred. That is not to say LaVey has not influenced millions of people—sales of his books would indicate such numbers. The schismatic events of 1975 caused the Church of Satan for a time to return to being mainly a personality cult gathered around LaVey.

Publicity surrounding the Church of Satan and its founder dwindled and became more and more infrequent throughout the late 1970s and early 1980s. *The Cloven Hoof* continued to be published, however, with its contents revealing a High Priest less interested in the techniques of magic and more interested in social commentary and the maintenance of a reclusive and unique lifestyle. But because of the refocusing, his writings from this period are even more distinctive than anything earlier. Post-1975 accounts of the Church and LaVey emphasized the idea that the organization had "gone underground" or entered a "second phase," but continued to be strong.[24] Little more was heard of LaVey on the public scene until the mid-1980s.

Perhaps due to the legacy of a large segment of America's culture moving toward ultraconservative—often borderline medieval—positions on issues of "religion" or "social values," by the middle of the 1980s there was a renewed interest in Satanism. This time, however, it was not in the open and inquisitive spirit of the late 1960s and early 1970s, but rather in the narrow and bigoted one of the 1980s. These new medievalists sensed that something had gone deeply wrong with American society, and who else could be at fault but S-A-T-A-N.

DR. LAVEY RISES AGAIN

The Church of Satan 1986–1997

A combination of this renewed negative interest and the internal struggles going on within the Black House itself led to a reemergence of Dr. LaVey. The first portrait of the resurrected High Priest came in a story about him in the edition of *The Washington Post Magazine* from February 23, 1986.[25] In the intervening years, he and Diane had gone their separate ways (in 1984) and LaVey had acquired a new "girl Friday,"

Blanche Barton. In partnership with her, the Church was revitalized in the late 1980s and early 1990s. On November 1, 1993, Blanche gave birth to LaVey's son, Satan Xerxes Carnacki LaVey.

There was also during this time a resurgence in LaVey's public exposure, as is evident from the number of resource materials published between 1988 and 1992. But the life story of Anton Szandor LaVey by this time had no real events to recount. He had completed his magical transformation from Howard Stanton Levey and lurked within the recesses of the Black House, truly transformed into something akin to one of the Black Brothers as described by Aleister Crowley (see chapter 8). The story of Howard S. Levey may be a fascinating tale of human travails, but in fact Anton LaVey made that tale irrelevant as he redesigned himself and isolated that self from all that would disturb it. Within LaVey's own magical system and universe, it is not important what he *did,* but only what he *WAS.*

LaVey died on October 29, 1997. After his death, there was some internal consternation over the rights to his works and legacy. Blanche Barton emerged as the new High Priestess of the Church of Satan. On Walpurgisnacht of 2001, an orderly transition was made to the High Priesthood of Peter H. Gilmore.

SOURCES FOR THE STUDY OF ANTON LAVEY

Primary Sources

To understand the Black Pope, one must start with what he himself has either written or adapted. His major published works are *The Satanic Bible* (1969), *The Compleat Witch* (1971; reissued in 1989 as *The Satanic Witch*), and *The Satanic Rituals* (1972). In addition to these books are LaVey's numerous articles printed in *The Cloven Hoof,* the internal organ of the Church of Satan. *The Cloven Hoof* was begun as an in-house newsletter in 1969, and was published regularly in one format or another until 1988. It resumed publication between 1995 and 1997, and further issues, edited by Blanche Barton, appeared in 2003 and 2010. In

1992, LaVey's long-unpublished manuscript, *The Devil's Notebook,* was made available by Feral House. Some of the essays in this book had been published over the years as *Cloven Hoof* articles. The versions of LaVey's essays printed in *The Devil's Notebook* are, however, sometimes abridged or reedited versions. Most of this material presents a serious and erudite man of broad learning and unique tastes. LaVey's final book, published after his death, is *Satan Speaks!* (Feral House, 1998).

Approximately at the same time *The Satanic Bible* appeared, LaVey also began writing often humorous columns in the tabloids *The National Insider* and *The Exploiter.* These ran under the banner "Letters from the Devil." The columns were collected in a facsimile edition of the same title in 2010. Another document that has to be considered a primary source is John Fritscher's *Popular Witchcraft: Straight from the Witch's Mouth* (1972; 2nd edition, 2004). The book features a lengthy interview with LaVey in which he comments on a wide variety of topics.[26]

Secondary Sources

Few, if any, institutions of the second occult revival have had as much written *about* them as the Church of Satan.[27] It has been covered widely in all communications media. LaVey was a frequent guest of nighttime talk-show hosts from Joe Pyne to Steve Allen, stories about the Church appeared in every major newspaper, and perhaps hundreds of magazine articles have been written about LaVey and his Church.

These secondary sources must be divided into two categories. The first category consists of those works over which LaVey seems to have exerted direct and final control. A highly sympathetic account of the Church was given by Arthur Lyons in a book entitled *The Second Coming: Satanism in America* (1970). Lyons was at the time a I° member of the Church and remained friendly with LaVey through the years. His later book, *Satan Wants You* (1988), essentially repeats only information that seems to be personally approved by Dr. LaVey himself.

Even more extreme is the case of the first "biography" of the Black Pope by Burton Wolfe (also an on-again, off-again "member" of the Church) entitled *The Devil's Avenger* (1974). Michael A. Aquino reports that early in 1974 he read a draft of the proposed book by Wolfe that was *totally different* from the one finally published in November of that year. Aquino is convinced *The Devil's Avenger* is really more an autobiography than anything else.[28] Finally in this category are two more recent books by Blanche Barton: *The Secret Life of a Satanist* and *The Church of Satan* (both 1990). All of these are valuable as portrayals of LaVey and his organization as he would have others view him and it.

Another category of secondary sources is made up of those uncontrolled by LaVey. One group of these consists of academic or scholarly studies. However, even in these we find that the authors have been very friendly with LaVey on a personal level. Randall H. Alfred studies the Church from 1968 to 1969; in the course of his study he also became a member of the Church and its ruling council.[29] His resulting article was not published until 1976 in a volume entitled *The New Religious Consciousness.*[30] Another scholar, Edward J. Moody, joined the Church in San Francisco and participated in ritual activities and eventually became a Satanic Priest himself. His active involvement lasted from October 1967 to August of 1969. Later he published two articles, "Urban Witches" (1971) and "Magical Therapy: An Anthropological Investigation of Contemporary Satanism" (1974). Another scholar and longtime friend of LaVey, Marcello Truzzi, wrote about the Church in 1972 in an article for *The Sociological Quarterly.*[31] These studies are valuable as alternate perspectives on LaVey and his philosophy, but in all cases the authors are still under the spell of LaVey's considerable personal charisma.

The other category of secondary material is journalistic in nature. Such journalistic accounts of LaVey and the Church of Satan abound.[32] Most of these are superficial and repetitive of often-heard anecdotes about the Black Pope's exploits. However, there have been a few reports that have provided some important information. The most significant of these is the already mentioned 1991 article by Lawrence Wright in *Rolling Stone.* Others of some importance include Walt Harrington's essay for *The Washington Post Magazine* in 1986, Grant Harden's widely syndicated newspaper piece in October 1978, and Dick Russell's article in *Argosy* in 1975.

Two interesting film documentaries exist: one is the comical *Wonderful World of Brother Buzz* episode (1964); the other is the Ray Laurent documentary *Satanis: The Devil's Mass* (1970). This latter film is the source continually used for file footage in television reports relating to Satanism. It provides for a great deal of insight on the public perception of LaVey in the local San Francisco area during the early years of the Church. The film consists of ritual sequences and interviews with LaVey and other members of the Church as well as with LaVey's neighbors, who provide some of the most interesting and amusing perspectives. Those who look closely will see young Isaac Bonewits—a later would-be druid—having his "member" blessed by the High Priest.

Beyond a doubt, the most important single document chronicling the Church, especially from about 1969 to 1975, is the mammoth and privately printed volume entitled *The Church of Satan* by Michael Aquino (various editions between 1983 and 2009). As Aquino was an important Church official and confidant of LaVey's during the years covered intensively, the work gives a special insider's view. Aquino includes almost four hundred printed pages of text and well over that number of pages of primary documentary evidence in the form of appendices. This book is not published commercially, but is available on the Internet.

THE ORGANIZATION OF THE CHURCH OF SATAN

In its more than thirty years of existence, the Church of Satan has operated under several different organizational plans. However, one set of principles outlined fairly early in the history of the Church seems to have guided it more than anything else: "The position held by Anton LaVey as High Priest is monarchial in nature, papal in degree, and absolute in power."[33] This was essentially because LaVey incorporated the Church as a sole proprietorship: as a "business" of which he was the *boss*. (Note that this is how LaVey believes *all* churches and religious organizations should be required to do business; this is the second point of his Five-Point Program of Pentagonal Revisionism.)

The origins of the Church of Satan as an organization are controversial. According to LaVey, the idea for the Church came to him in a "blinding flash" of initiatory awakening.[34] He then evolved the Magic Circle (also secretly known as the Order of the Trapezoid) into the governing body of the Church. This became known as the Council of Nine (or, alternatively, the Order of the Trapezoid).[35] Other sources indicate a more mundane inspiration. One of LaVey's longtime neighbors appears in the film *Satanis* saying, "According to Mr. Webber, a publicity man whom I met, he and Mr. LaVey came upon the idea that, with LaVey owning a lion, a Satanist church would be a wonderful offshoot since he did evidently believe in the devil." A later interview with that "publicity man" basically confirmed this view.[36]

As with all organizations, from a historical perspective, the "facts" only tell a part of the story. Though they may be relevant to complete understanding, they only convey external appearances. As often as not, the outward appearances conceal more enigmatic realities. If the historical *facts* were known, the cynic might be tempted to dismiss Moses as a political opportunist, Jesus as a manipulative, power-mad sorcerer, and Muhammad as a bloodthirsty conqueror. In the cynical scope of things, the supposed "factual sins" of Anton LaVey don't seem so bad after all.

The chief officers of the early Church were that of High Priest held in perpetuity by Anton LaVey and that of High Priestess held exclusively by Diane LaVey. The Church was essentially a "papa and mama shop." The Council of Nine met on regular occasions, but was always strictly advisory in its capacity.[37] For the reasons made clear above, no official provision ever existed for the removal of LaVey from his position.

Most interesting for the purposes of this book is the degree system of the Church of Satan. Its structure has remained more or less intact from the early days of the Church, although the criteria for "elevation" through the degrees have undergone some changes. This system would later become the basis for the Temple of Set degree system as well, so it is of essential importance in understanding the process of initiation for these two influential organizations on the left-hand path.

PRE-1975 DEGREE SYSTEM OF THE CHURCH

For the Church of Satan, there are definitely two eras or epochs with regard to the degree system: pre-1975 and post-1975. The earlier system was geared for the development and maintenance of a "sacred" organization separate from the mundane world, while the later system has been geared for a more "secular" form of Satanism.

The original degree scheme consisted of five levels, at least externally. These were signified by Roman numerals I–V together with an appended degree symbol (°). They were also given dramatic titles, such as Warlock and Enchantress. Three important articles from the pre-1975 *Cloven Hoof* are the basis of the following discussion: "An Explanation of the Various Degrees of the Church of Satan" (1970), "What is a Satanic Master?" (1971), and "Official Degrees of the Church of Satan" (1972).

I° *Apprentice*, or "Active Member," is one who is *formally committed* to the philosophy of Satanism. Members remain at this level perpetually unless they resign or are expelled by the Council of Nine.

II° *Warlock* (male) or *Witch* (female) is one who has passed a formal examination on Satanic philosophy and magic. These could then become leaders of local Grottos in preparation for the priesthood.

III° *Priest* (male) or *Priestess* (female) is one who has established and maintained an authorized Grotto while upholding the dignified image of the Church. This "image" would include things from the kind of car the person drives, to their living quarters, to economic stability, to personal appearance. Members of the clergy would represent the Church in the media and so they had to have a high level of communication skills. In addition to these external requirements, the prospective Priest or Priestess had to take a written examination relevant to the degree. The imperative here was that the Satanic priesthood would be made up of the kind of people who would be successful in all phases of life and not just those who were entering into the occultic world to gain the recognition they were not able to gain it in the *real world*. LaVey was very serious about the necessity of high standards for the priesthood of Satan: "[T]he Priest of Satan must be better read, more self-aware, more achieved for his years, more articulate, more genuinely dedicated to his chosen faith than are the clergy of any other religion known to man."[38]

IV° *Magister* or *Master* is one who has built up his Grotto to the level where additional members of the Priesthood are necessary in the area. Magisters act in a way similar to that of Bishops, Archbishops, or Cardinals in the Roman Catholic Church. This administrative attitude toward the Magistry was short-lived—a peculiarity of the optimistic atmosphere of pre-1975 Satanism in America.

Beyond this administrative function, to be appointed as a Master by the High Priest, the Priest or Priestess would be evaluated according to criteria that were later kept secret. However, in the 1971 *Cloven Hoof* article on the subject, the High Priest defined a Satanic Master as someone who, by *conscious* application of certain principles, has created something that has significantly influenced or modified the lives of great numbers of the world's population.[39]

This definition in many ways bleeds over into the definition given in an earlier article of the Fifth Degree.

V° *Magus* is the degree conferred on members of the Magistry "who have discovered and brought forth a new magical principle and utilized it in a manner that profoundly affects the activities of the world." Mysteriously, LaVey, writing here as John M. Kincaid, alludes to "four additional degrees" beyond that of Magus.[40] These are never discussed again, although the Temple of Set was to develop the VI° Ipsissimus. These and whatever other criteria pertinent to the degrees of Magus and Magister were also made secret at a later date. LaVey himself was the only person ever recognized as a Magus in early years of the Church of Satan. Incidentally, the official form of address for a Magus is "Doctor," and it is for this reason that LaVey was sometimes so addressed by his followers, not because he claimed to have an actual academic Ph.D. from an accredited university.

It is clear that in the early days of the Church, LaVey considered himself a unique historical "embodiment of Satan," who was the Satanic Magus of the present "Age of Fire," which began in 1966/Year I. His task was the "bringing of Satanism into the world as an organized, legitimate, above-ground persuasion—and with it restoring the dignity of man's own godhead."[41]

POST-1975 DEGREE SYSTEM OF THE CHURCH

Following the watershed year of 1975, the degree system changed in some essential ways, yet the basic validity of the five degrees of Satanism is still upheld.[42] LaVey stated that the degree system as it had been was an experiment in seeing how far Satanists could be organized. As he came to see it, however, true Satanists remain nonjoiners and are virtually impossible to organize.

A concrete example of the results of this realization comes in the form of the official color designation of the ceremonial medallions worn by members of the Church. According to a *Cloven Hoof* article published early in 1976, there was originally no official policy on the colors of the medallions worn by members of the Church at various levels of initiation.[43] Then, with increased standardization in later years, official policy required that I° members word a black Sigil of Baphomet against a red background, II° members wore black ones against a white background, III° members of the priesthood had white Baphomets on black backgrounds, while IV° members of the Magistry originally wore specially designed silver pentagrams (later this was changed to a Baphomet on a blue background). The one and only V°, LaVey himself, was to wear a free-standing silver pentagram. In the case of LaVey, as the High Priest of Satan, this was struck through with a lightning bolt. But the 1976 article abandons all of that formality in favor of the reported individual freedom of the early days. In celebration of unconventional Satanic aesthetics, colors such as "peacock green" and "opalescent pink" even became available for a time.

The post-1975/Year X degree system has become keyed to an alternative scheme of development, which is said to describe not only the historical evolution of the Church of Satan, but personal initiation as well. This is the schemata of the five (or six) *phases* of Satanism:[44]

First-Phase Satanism is characterized by the key concept of *Emergence.* In the history of the Church of Satan, this is when the Satanic Age was crystallized into reality and made manifest in society. LaVey sees this being the equivalent of the I° Apprentice level in the original initiatory scheme as applied to individuals. At this stage, an outward show of Satanism with public rituals, and so on, may be important to help the individual break down social or psychological barriers to development.

Second-Phase Satanism is marked with the key idea of *Development.* Historically, this is the period of public expansion by the Church. It is also seen as a stage of distillation in which the Satanic "ideal" is separated from all that does not meet its criteria.

Third-Phase Satanism is distinguished by the key concept of *Qualification.* This involves the development of respectability and an image of prestige to the outside world.

Fourth-Phase Satanism is marked with the key idea of *Control.* "Ideal" elements isolated in Phase Two are stratified and further isolated into a separate and definite social structure. In personal initiation, this is the stage where mastery begins. There is an isolation from the general environment in which true individuality can manifest itself.

Fifth-Phase Satanism is indicated by the key word of *Application.* Techniques developed through the first four phases are employed as the "Myths of the Twentieth Century" are understood and exploited. At this end of the initiatory spectrum, LaVey says: "we still have Magisters and Magistras who divorce themselves from the mainstream as much as possible and arrange their lives to earn money at things that entail a minimal amount of contact with or input from the herd—artists, directors, writers, performers, entrepreneurs of various kinds."[45]

For LaVey, these phases ended in a posited *Phase Six*, which involves "the development, promotion, and manufacture of artificial human companions." This will be discussed at further length elsewhere in this chapter, but at this point it is important to note the initiatory logic of Phase Six. As an essential part of left-hand-path initiatory technique involves the *separation* of the subject from his or her environment in order that a true individual essence can be distilled, LaVey's decidedly sociological and materialistic brand of the left-hand-path ideology virtually demands a progressive isolation from the influences of other people. As Sartre said in his play *No Exit:* "Hell is other people." In an inversion of this, LaVey maintains that "other people" must be artificially replaced in accordance with the will of the magician in order that an "Infernal Paradise" can be created.

MAJOR DOCTRINES OF THE CHURCH OF SATAN

There have been three major doctrinal documents issued by LaVey since the inception of the Church of Satan in 1966. They typically have come in the form of enumerated aphorisms, some of which can be understood on various levels. These official doctrines should be allowed to shape our primary understanding of LaVey's teachings and hence of his Church of Satan.

THE NINE SATANIC STATEMENTS

(Ca. 1966, first published in *The Satanic Bible* in 1969)

These statements are the mainstays of the philosophy of the Church of Satan, and have often been reprinted in journalistic discussions of LaVey and the organization.

The first six of the statements are couched as contradictory formulas: Satan represents indulgence, vital existence, and undefiled wisdom instead of abstinence, spiritual pipe dreams, and hypocritical self-deceit. There is a "this" *instead of* "that"—not only is a positive affirmation given, but also an accompanying negative assertion. This is partially indicative of LaVey's particular form of dualism, which will be explored below.

The likely origin of the formulaic presentation of the Nine Satanic Statements in the work of Ayn Rand has already been noted above.

The first statement, inspired by the Redbeard text *Might Is Right,* extols indulgence as the essence of LaVeyan Satanic philosophy. In chapter VIII of *The Satanic Bible,* LaVey is careful to distinguish between indulgence and compulsion, that is, between consciously and willfully practicing an act that gives one pleasure and fulfills a natural desire, and unconsciously and uncontrollably committing an act that one "can't help but do." Indulgence is the fulfillment of a desire with its origins in one's essential human nature. Compulsion is outside one's conscious control. LaVey sees natural indulgence in all the so-called seven deadly sins of Christianity: greed, pride, envy, anger, gluttony, lust, and sloth. Each of these he views as a possible catalyst for positive and natural human activities or attitudes, such as ambition, self-respect, self-preservation, material or physical well-being, and pleasure of all kinds (see *The Satanic Bible,* chapter III). A powerful argument for the presence of a Satanic Age lies in the fact that the whole "Western industrialized economy" today is really *driven* by the desires of the masses to indulge in all of the seven deadly sins.

Abstinence is seen as the unhealthy, coerced cessation of natural human aspirations, or the belief that these are somehow evil or bad, and that a moral person should abstain from them.

The crucial factor in distinguishing between or among indulgence, compulsion, and abstinence is the actual will or nature of the individual. One should not have to *work* at what one wishes to indulge in; it should come naturally and be pleasurable.[46]

The second statement relates to LaVey's essentially materialistic, epicurean philosophy of life. "Vital existence"—the power of living flesh—is not only extolled over things "spiritual," but spirituality itself is relegated to the category of a "pipe dream," an illusion. The spirit and god are not so much seen as positive enemies in LaVeyan philosophy as they are illusions or unrealities that are *used* by the mass mind to console and protect itself through self-deceit.

The third statement targets this self-deceit, which is one of the Nine Satanic Sins. This opens the door to hypocrisy, which is one of the chief manifestations of the "herd mentality," against which LaVeyan Satanism seeks to fight. This is LaVey's version of the Delphic exhortation to "Know Thyself." Understanding of this and of the way the world is *really* put together represents the "undefiled wisdom" (see LaVey's translation of the nineteenth Enochian Key in *The Satanic Bible*).

The fourth statement, "Satan represents kindness to those who deserve it, instead of love wasted on ingrates!" relates to chapter V of the "Book of Lucifer" in *The Satanic Bible* ("Love and Hate"). In that chapter, LaVey argues that one cannot love without limitations: "If anything is used too freely it loses its meaning."[47] So LaVey teaches not to force one's self "to feel indiscriminate love," which he condemns as "unnatural." This very *unnaturalness* is what leads the Christian evangelist or inquisitor to be able to say "I love you," or "I'll pray for you," while harboring deep-seated hatred—or, worse yet, actually giving the thumbscrews one more turn. Love should be given to those one loves; hate should be given to one's enemies.

The fifth statement, which extols vengeance over "turning the other cheek," again relates to chapter V of the "Book of Lucifer" as well as to the most controversially titled chapter (IX), "On the Choice of a Human Sacrifice." LaVey gives the moral and ethical license to the true Satanist to take vengeance on his enemies—in a *magical* way. This is done either through "lesser magical" psychological methods or through a "greater magical" conjuration of destruction. It cannot be overemphasized that LaVey never advocates "human sacrifice" as conventionally understood. What is advocated is the inner freedom of Satanically aware individuals to "take justice into their own hands" and indulge themselves in a healthy, full-blown hatred for anyone or anything that has wronged them sufficiently to deserve it. This is a powerful sociopolitical statement, which speaks out for the sovereignty of the Satanic individual over and above the collectivist state "justice" system. It is almost as if LaVey could see the increasing and widespread breakdown in our criminal justice system from the still relatively pacific point in time in which he was writing in late-1960s.

Statement six, "Satan represents responsibility to the responsible, instead of concern for psychic vampires!" again has to do with the social relations of the Satanist and is further expounded in chapter VII of the "The Book of Lucifer" in *The Satanic Bible.* LaVey has always been most wary of people who attempt to ingratiate themselves with capable people and begin to take from them more than they give in return, regardless of the sort of human relationship in which this occurs. These people he calls "psychic vampires." Satanists will get whatever they need or want, either from their own resources or from others in a give-and-take relationship.

Statement seven is essential to understanding the basics of LaVey's anthropology, his theory of what constitutes mankind. He sees man as essentially "just another animal," as a natural creature and a "beast of the fields." But he must also account for man's special status. This he does by referring to man's "divine spiritual and intellectual development." Although he may not find the words agreeable, he must concede that there is *something* that separates humans from the "other animals."

LaVey views this factor as something man simply puts to natural use, and which increases his capacity for viciousness. This philosophical point on the true nature of mankind, and the relationship between the intellectual and bestial parts of man, remains problematic in LaVey's thought.

Statement eight, "Satan represents all of the so-called sins, as they all lead to physical, mental, or emotional gratification!" is a further expansion of statement one. It is a specific exhortation to indulge in those things that the collective or mass culture may call sins, because by virtue of their very rejection by the mass they can be exalted as worthy aspirations for the individualistic Satanist. The Satanist uses "public opinion" as a "reverse barometer" to analyze the social environment and to distinguish between the Satanic and non-Satanic.

The ninth statement is the ironic "punch line" to the series. It states that Satan historically has been an ally of the church, as he has kept the churches "in business all these years!" But this is not meant as flippantly as it might seem. The notion of "the other," the "opponent"—which is the essential meaning of the Hebraic term "Satan"—is always necessary to the maintenance of a right-hand-path institution or belief system, from the church to the marketplace. The right-hand path must always *have* an enemy, while the left-hand path somehow always seems to have to *be* that enemy.

THE NINE SATANIC SINS

(First published in 1987,
in issue 119 of *The Cloven Hoof*)

These "sins" provide an invaluable negative mirror of the LaVeyan philosophy. In the original presentation of the text, each of these key terms is provided with a short commentary.

1. The first sin is *stupidity* and is indeed the primary Satanic sin: "It depends on people going along with whatever they are told." LaVey views this as something the mass media actually *culti-*

vate in order to dupe the masses; the Satanist must learn to see through this.

2. The second sin is *pretentiousness,* which is seen as a corollary of stupidity, as it is one's proclivity toward pretentiousness that is appealed to through flattery ("Everyone's made to feel like a big shot") and thereby one is most easily manipulated.
3. The third sin is *solipsism,* which according to LaVey is very dangerous. This may also be because LaVeyan Satanism likes to think of itself as highly objectivistic, and as the word solipsism is generally defined it conveys the idea that *only the self exists*—a radical form of subjectivism. The world outside the self, and the relationship of the self (or ego) to that world is essential in defining the life and attainment of success for the Satanist. The outside world must be controlled in accordance with the will of the Satanist, which is reminiscent of the Epicurean attitude toward the external world.
4. The fourth sin is *self-deceit,* which was already cited as a highly undesirable trait in the third Satanic Statement. In a way, all of the other eight "sins" revolve around this key concept, which may be distilled as a lack of self-awareness or self-knowledge. Satanists must know themselves before they can indulge in those things that are truly an expression of their unique existences.
5. The fifth sin is *herd conformity,* which is especially heinous because not only would one be giving up personal control or sovereignty, one would be surrendering it to an impersonal collective mass. It is within the Satanic lifestyle to practice "dynamic submission," that is, giving over one's loyalty or freedom for another's use as long as it ultimately benefits (fulfills the true desires) of the one who so submits himself or herself. In this case, however, it is very personal and individual.
6. The sixth sin is a *lack of perspective,* which essentially means that the would-be Satanist is not keeping his or her actions in the "wider historical and social" context. If the larger patterns are

not perceived, focus is soon lost, and the will of the "wannabe" Satanist could be quickly led astray by the herd mentality.

7. The seventh sin, which LaVey calls a *forgetfulness of past orthodoxies,* is part of the lack of perspective; specifically, it is the lack of historical perspective. If one does not know the roots of something, it can easily be replaced by marketers as the "new" and hence (in the mass-mind) "improved" model. The Satanist generally realizes that there can really be nothing that is in its essence *new.*[48] The very ideology responsible for *orthodoxy,* the standardized imposition of a system of beliefs/values over a whole population, makes such forgetfulness possible (and profitable).[49]
8. The eighth sin is termed *counterproductive pride.* This acknowledges that one of the "Satanic virtues"—pride—can become a "sin" if it is out of balance with the pragmatic goals of the individual.
9. The ninth and final Satanic sin is a *lack of aesthetics,* which is interesting because LaVey's form of Satanism is one largely built up along aesthetic lines. Anton LaVey himself was very much an *artist*—a musician, a painter, a weaver of tales—and his "system" is largely a product of aesthetic constructs. Aesthetics comes from the Greek word for the "senses": it is what is pleasing or pleasurable as sense data. Aesthetics have a subjective and objective component, both of which should be observed and applied in Satanic activity. Ignoring this, or not cultivating it, is unthinkable in LaVey's world.

THE ELEVEN RULES OF THE EARTH

(Ca. 1967, first published in *The Cloven Hoof,* March 1970)

These Eleven Rules can be summarized as the *Lex Satanicus* (Law of the Satanist), which simply states: "Do unto others as they do unto you." Also implied in this is the *Lex Talionis* (the Law of the Talon, or

"Law of Tooth and Claw"), which supports the Darwinian view of the "survival of the fittest."

This body of laws may be taken as the essence of Satanic ethics as far as LaVey is concerned. Long after these rules were written, LaVey railed against those who would call themselves "ethical Satanists" because he felt this to be a redundant phrase.[50] However, he does feel it necessary to spell out exactly what the ethics of Satanism are in these Eleven Rules of the Earth, some of which simply consist of a codification of common courtesy.

The first three rules involve not overstepping the bounds of respect for other people. Don't give opinions or advice unless asked; don't tell your woes to others unless they want to hear about them; and when you are in someone else's home, show respect, or don't go. People should be given their space—psychologically, emotionally, and physically—and one should be able to expect the same respect in return. But the fourth rule tells one how to deal with a person who does not respect one's space: "treat him cruelly and without mercy."

The fifth rule, "Do not make sexual advances unless you are given the mating signal," harkens back to the message of the first three as the would-be Satanist is warned against making unwanted sexual advances. The devil is always a gentleman and never an overbearing oaf.

The sixth rule, which states that one should not take another's property *unless* it is a burden to the other person(!), is formulated according to a typically LaVeyan construct in which victimizers, or predators, only make victims, or prey, of those who appear *willing* to fulfill that role. The root of this construct or theme in LaVey's thought is found in his theories of sadomasochism, which will be discussed below.

The seventh rule shows LaVey's essential reverence and respect for the very *idea* of magic. He admonishes the Satanist to acknowledge magic if it has been successfully employed it to obtain some desire. LaVey maintains that if one denies magic after having successfully used it, one will then lose whatever had been gained. It is this technique of magic, rather than any symbol of it (such as Satan), which is singled out by him for this level of reverence.

With the eighth rule, LaVey returns to the two-edged construct of the victimizer/victim. He admonishes the Satanist not to complain about things to which it is unnecessary to be subject. Only this time, it is from the purely "masochistic" side: if one does not *need* to subject one's self to a situation, yet continues in it, then perhaps it is because one does *need* it after all. If so, there is no sense in complaining about it. Such behavior would be quite unseemly.

The ninth and tenth rules, "Do not harm little children!" and "Do not kill nonhuman animals unless attacked or for your food!" respectively, are of tremendous ethical importance. Long before the virulent and libelous "anti-Satanic" smear campaigns of the mid-1980s, in other words, before LaVey was really "defending" Satanism against any specific charges or accusations, he was repeatedly on record as standing against the harm of children and animals (or nonhuman animals to be more accurate). This topic is also addressed in some detail on pages 87–89 of *The Satanic Bible.*

The last Rule of the Earth comes back to the themes of the initial ones: "When walking in open territory, bother no one. If someone bothers you, ask him to stop. If he does not stop, destroy him." The Satanist should mind his own business when he is outside his own "lair." If someone violates the rules regarding him, he should inform the other of the violation. Now, if the other does not heed the warning, the violator must be *asking* to be destroyed—and the Satanist is within his natural rights to oblige.

Throughout the 1980s, LaVey made some interesting statements defining Satanism and the Satanist that provide further insight into his doctrines in more recent years.

In 1982, he wrote: "Satanism is more than a philosophy; it is a lone stand, a symbolic act of defiance against thought suppression."[51] In 1985, he provided a nine-point definition of the characteristics of a Higher Being—the deified Satanist—almost all of which LaVey himself regularly violated. Among them are "don't advertise"(!) and "Be creative . . . never rip off"(!), to name but two. Also among these characteristics is a bully-philosophy: "people will realize the benefits [of] contributing to your happiness, or the tough luck that can befall them by getting you sore."[52]

The next year, LaVey defined Satanism again and defended his use of the term by saying that his "brand of Satanism" is a conscious alternative to conventional and institutional thought. He identifies "Satanism" as a *stimulating* (or fun) *name* for the exercise of innovative thinking, which goes against the thoughtless conformity to mainstream thinking in any avenue of life. Here he perhaps foreshadows the "recreational religion" of contemporary society.[53]

THE SATANIC COSMOLOGY

Or The World According to the Abominable Dr. LaVey

Anton LaVey was not, nor did he intend to be, a systematic philosopher. He was more a weaver of images: a sorcerous philosopher and performance artist working in the social and imagistic media of the latter twentieth century. As such, it requires some work—and, I hope, some sympathetic understanding—to elicit from his written works the essence of his worldview. In many ways, LaVey poses some new questions for the would-be follower of the left-hand path. The role of society and of the interaction with other human beings (or the lack of same) become essential to his Satanic philosophy. But equipped with the analytical questions I have put to all the earlier schools of the left-hand path, the encounter with LaVey's Church of Satan yields a great harvest of new ideas about the nature and scope of the path of the left-hand. LaVey's Satanic cosmology will be seen to be materialistic, cyclical, dualistic, and limited. What remains, however, is the problem of the position of the will of the Satanic magician within this cosmos.

LaVey's system of thought is based on a uniquely *magical* form of materialism. For him, all things that exist do so in a material form. There is no such thing as "spirit," "god," or "heaven" as commonly believed in and taught by orthodox religions or held by popular superstition. This theoretical idea is the proverbial *forest* of LaVey's system, which the *trees* of individual manifestations of this concept sometimes obscure. It is easier to see the materialism in his understanding of mankind or the workings of magic than in the impersonal abstraction of cosmology. LaVey always begins and ends with concrete things that can be *sensed*. This approach rarely led him off into abstract speculation.

For LaVey, "God" (i.e., the ultimate power in the universe) is *Nature* and Satan is the embodiment of Nature.[54] This is not to reduce LaVey's philosophy to pure objectivistic positivism. There is indeed, and perhaps somewhat paradoxically, a definite *metaphysics* embedded in LaVey's materialism. The world may be a material reality only, but its functions can be so mysterious that vast amounts of its true character and structure remain hidden from normal mankind's view and understanding. For the most part, man brings this ignorance upon himself: for most people, it is simply more comfortable to be ignorant. This is why, as P. T. Barnum said, "There's a sucker born every minute."

LaVey's metaphysical materialism is not entirely original. He derived much of it from a number of sources that seem to include the Epicureans (whom he sometimes invoked),[55] Sade (ultimately La Mettrie), Marx, and Freud (whom he admired). More than anything else, it is this long-standing tradition of philosophical materialism that LaVey identifies as the *Satanic* philosophy or tradition. Here he is very much in keeping with the attitudes of the Slavs, both ancient and modern, who in their dualistic folk religion identified God with the spiritual world and the devil with the material one.

CYCLES OF FIRE AND ICE

The clearest statements made by LaVey concerning the abstract order of the cosmos are concerned with *cycles* or *rhythms*. In *The Satanic Rituals,* he wrote two pages (219–20) under the heading "The Unknown Known." Here he outlines a theory of the successive ages of the world, which cycle or oscillate between Ages of Ice, in which "God" rules and man (= Satan) is suppressed, and Ages of Fire, in which man rules and "God is beneath." These cycles are governed by the Law of Nine.

First, there is a nine-year period characterized by *action,* and then a subsequent nine-year period characterized by *reaction* to that original impetus. Taken together, the eighteen-year span of time is called a "Working." Nine Workings equal an Era (162 years), nine Eras add up to an Age (1,458 years), and nine Ages equal an Epoch (13,122 years).

The last Age of Ice came to an end in 1966. This pattern of oscillation between extremes is the clearest abstract model for another leitmotif in LaVey's thought: dualism. Dualism will be discussed at length in the next section, but another aspect of the cyclical pattern must not be overlooked: that of *rhythm.* Perhaps welling up from LaVey's obvious native musical nature and talent is an inherent sense of rhythm. He often writes of the importance of music to magic[56] and even concerning the primacy of rhythm over the actual meanings of words in magical incantations.[57]

The role of rhythms in ordering the world is more specifically addressed in a *Cloven Hoof* article in 1980 entitled "Megarhythm."[58] Here LaVey claims to be able to chart future public likes and dislikes "based on one simple rule: the attraction of opposites." In other words, if it's *in* today, it's destined by this megarhythmic law to be *out* tomorrow. The timing of these shifts is presumably somehow coordinated with the oscillation process within the eighteen-year period of a Working.

"Angles" form another abstract construct that gives shape to LaVey's cosmology. These "angles"—geometrical models with the power to create certain effects in the objective and subjective universes—are most precisely discussed in a *Cloven Hoof* article entitled "The Law of the Trapezoid." This law states that figures or spaces made up of obtuse or acute angles (those less or more than 90°) have an unsettling effect on the mind unless they are recognized as such, whereupon they can be empowering and energizing.[59]

Supposedly when LaVey was investigating haunted houses earlier in his career he discovered that it was not necessarily "departed spirits" that were causing the phenomena, but rather a by-product of the actual geometry of the building or room in which the "haunting" was taking place.

This aspect of LaVey's cosmology, or understanding of the world, can again be derived at least in part from one of his artistic interests—in this instance, from graphic arts and the influence of the theories of William Mortensen. Certain shapes, angles, and lines evoke first and foremost a visceral (even if unconscious) *fear,* and fear is the most basic and powerful emotion known to man because it is necessary to his physical survival. This remains so in today's "civilized" world, even if it is less obvious than in ages past. Knowledge of its power is therefore more useful than ever before.

LaVey made his most magically potent statement on the power of the angles in the ritual text of *Die elektrischen Vorspiele* (The Electrical Preludes), first published in *The Satanic Rituals.*[60] The German text printed there is a (poor) translation of the original English, not the other way around. There is no evidence for the validity of the German versions of any of LaVey's rituals. The original text, as performed on occasion by LaVey in his early Church rituals, is printed as Appendix 5 in Michael Aquino's *The Church of Satan.* In this text, LaVey speaks of a Barrier outside of which are predatory beasts ("Hounds") that can enter and exit this world through "angles" and according to certain "cycles." There is also a dichotomy between "angles" and "curved dimensions" (which are more of this world). The basic idea for this ritual came from the science-fiction story "The Hounds of Tindalos" by Frank Belknap Long (1901–1994), who was one of the circle of writers who knew H. P. Lovecraft. In a letter to Michael Aquino, Long recollects having pulled the word "Tindalos" in the title "out of thin air." He said it might have suggested itself to him through the word "tinder," as he was thinking of something fiery.[61] It is, however, more likely that this is an example of cryptomnesia and that somewhere Long had read about the Melanesian concept of *tindalo,* which is a "spirit" that can cause insanity when it possesses a person.

LAVEYAN DUALISM

There is a certain kind of "dualism" inherent in the very structure of the left-hand path because its practitioners always seek to separate or individuate themselves from the environment. There is always a "this" and "that," a "self" and "not-self." The right-hand-path practitioner seeks to destroy such distinctions and thus avoid this structural dualism, but can seldom avoid the moralistic dualism between "good" and "evil."

Anton LaVey's philosophy is founded on some basic dichotomies in the cosmological psycho-sensual and sociological realms and his thought is further peppered with dozens of other dichotomies.

The main dichotomy is the cosmological one between matter and "spirit." More accurately stated in LaVey's terms, this is the dichotomy between reality (actual, vital existence) and illusion (conditioned response). In a very real sense, LaVey turned Augustine on his head and claims "being" for matter and "lack of being" for the world of spirit. For LaVeyan Satanists, it comes down to seeing reality for what it is rather than allowing others to interpret and package a false reality for them. Invariably, when one allows someone else to create one's cosmology, the creator always *gains* something. Satanists will therefore not allow this to happen, preferring to base their cosmologies on the most objective facts known. Whether this objectivity is most accessible immanently in the world of the senses, or transcendentally in the world of the psyche, is the basic line of demarcation between the two modern branches of the left-hand path.

Within the realm of the senses, the principal LaVeyan dichotomy is between pleasure and pain. There is nothing more basic—and hence more powerful—in human existence and experience. LaVey's works are laden with overt references to sadomasochism. This is a complex topic in LaVey's thought, and one better discussed in detail below, in connection with his understanding of humanity. This dichotomy is so pervasive that it seems part of his dualistic cosmology and not just a subjective creation of the human psyche. The human mind simply perceives the universal dichotomy as pleasure/pain.

In two 1980 articles in *The Cloven Hoof,* LaVey explored the topic of "eustress," which is the opposite of distress. He theorized that in today's society distress is "so commonplace that it represents comfort, security, and—fun," and that distressful situations are transformed into *eu*stressful ones. According to LaVey, people feel insignificant in today's world: "There is overpopulation and underrecognition."[62] They feel that way for the most part because each individual truly *is* insignificant in the larger scheme of things. But the individual abhors this condition; it is really distressful. The whole marketplace of entertainment, glamour, and so on, is therefore geared to turn that distress into eustress (at a profit to the marketers). This is done by misdirecting the individual's attention to some vicarious existence: the lives and fortunes/misfortunes of movie stars, sports figures, or even fictional soap-opera characters. The person is made to *feel* significant—for a price of some kind.

In the sociological realm, LaVey's dualism is equally profound. The most essential element of this seems to be the dichotomy between the *individual,* the agent of nonconformity, and the *collective,* the agent of conformity. This element or theme in one way or another underlies more of his *Cloven Hoof* writings than any other. In his philosophy, the *summum bonum* is *indulgence* in the genuine desires of the individual carnal ego. In opposition to this stands *abstinence* from those desires governed by collective dictates or religion, politics, fashion, the media, *ad infinitum.*

The essence of LaVeyan Satanism is *indulgence* in individual desires according to the conscious will of that individual separate from, and contrary to, the dictates of forces outside the sovereign individuality. This is not as easy as the casual observer might assume. LaVey points out that most things people "indulge" in are actually things they are *supposed* to enjoy, according to their peer group, social stratum, or whatever. Most people just go along with the herd and "enjoy" the things they are supposed to enjoy—and then at the end of their lives wonder why they really had so little fun along the way. It is to this kind of life that the non-Satanist is condemned. This conformity to the herd mentality is the antithesis of structural Satanism. In the Middle Ages, the "white lighters" conformed to the dogmas of the church; today, those same conformists are more likely to kowtow to the dictates of political ideologies, trendy fashions, or media-generated consumerism. As LaVey put it, "The reason why an archetypical Satanist will eschew whatever is popular lies in his disdain for and avoidance of whatever has been programmed for others."[63]

So humanity itself is divided into two groups: the Satanic nonconformists (who indulge their genuinely individualized desires) and the "rubes" (who conform overtly or covertly to the herd mentalities of religion, science, politics, fashion, the media, and so forth). The self-aware Satanist is virtually always in a position to prey upon the rubes, the dupes of the mass mentality. The fact that LaVey points out this obvious fact makes his philosophy seem especially "politically incorrect" to many would-be critics. Few people like to be made to feel the distress of their present condition.

The division of mankind into two classes—those in the know as opposed to the "marks" or "rubes"—is, on the surface at least, an aspect of LaVey's philosophy illustratively drawn from his carnival experience. But if we strip away the hypocrisy in ourselves, we will see that those same "metagames" so obviously and crudely played in the carnival are reflected in most human endeavors—right up to the tops of our ivory towers and deep into our halls of state.

This division between Satanists and the conformist herd is essential to the first point in LaVey's later five-point program of "Pentagonal Revisionism": Stratification.[64] This will be discussed further in the "Vision" section later on. Stratification is the process of separating the "weak" from the "strong," or creating conditions that will facilitate that separation. LaVey always stood for such stratification and elitism based on merit and strength; this is apparently why he was drawn initially to the philosophy of Ragnar Redbeard. For LaVey, there is the "higher man" (= the Satanist, by whatever name) and the "lower man."[65] The "higher man" is aware of all the metagames in life and knows how to play them, while the "lower man" is merely a pawn in such games.

Besides these major dichotomies and dualities, LaVey often invoked the dichotomy between concepts such as the past and present, night and day (he detested the *sun*!), life and death, silver and gold, and dozens of others. At the same time, he is aware of the dangers of dichotomizing unproductively. He decries the "lower man's" thought process, and his language, as being "binaric."[66] This idea appears based on some of George Orwell's theories about language and thought.[67] "*Binaric* is based on the premise that only *one* of two choices can be readily processed by most (*including* human) computers. There are no shades of grey, so to speak. Either *on* or *off, understood* or *not understood.*"[68] He also rejects the labels of "white magic" and "black magic," and in so doing states: "There is no difference between 'White' and 'Black' magic, except in the smug hypocrisy, guilt-ridden righteousness, and self-deceit of the "White" magician himself."[69] LaVey based his rejection on the prejudiced definition of "white magic" as magic used for benevolent workings, whereas "black magic" is magic employed for malevolent ones. We have defined these terms differently for the purposes of this study. For LaVey, as for G. I. Gurdjieff, magic is conscious *doing.*

Before I leave the discussion of LaVey's dualism, I would like to note that he harbored two distinct types of dichotomies in his thought. One is truly oppositional—such as that between reality ("vital existence") and unreality ("pipe dreams"), or between the individual and the collective—while the other lies in a spectrum—such as that between pleasure and pain, distress and eustress. The first kind expresses the essence of the role of the Satanist as a categorical *opponent* or adversary to prevailing "norms" on a macrocosmic or microcosmic scale, while the second kind refers to the magician's ability to transform one quality into another as an act of will.

THE POWER OF LIMITED RESOURCES

LaVey always championed the cause of *limitation.* Sometimes this occurred as a reaction to current popular ideas about "unlimited" human potential, but first and foremost he saw limitation as being a cold, hard—if unpleasant—fact. He also understood it as a potential source of real power, as opposed to imagined unlimited resources.

I believe this attitude to be correlated to LaVey's basic materialism: in the "natural" world we see that resources are limited, and so in

LaVey's view there is no reason to assume that this is not likewise the case in matters of consciousness or human creativity.

In the chapter entitled "Love and Hate" in *The Satanic Bible,* LaVey posits that in reality the human capacity to love is limited.[70] We cannot love everyone. Love is a limited commodity. Those who claim to love universally always hypocritically harbor equally vast quantities of hate.

Like Gurdjieff before him, LaVey held that knowledge is also a limited commodity because the brain's ability to retain it is limited. Mr. G. openly stated that knowledge was a material substance. As LaVey put it, "I know damned well that a mind can only retain so much data . . . whatever new stuff that goes in, must boot some old stuff out."[71] LaVey cultivated a "trick" to ensure that his "knowledge bank" would retain its unique character. He called it the "augmentive principle." New data was only allowed entry if it directly related to a preexisting "favorite set of engrams." In this way, he believed himself able to arrest the process of meaningless mental change for the sake of change and retain "what seems to be the most valuable commodity in the world today: a strong, unique, personal, and lasting identity."[72] From a left-hand-path perspective, this speaks to the eventual necessity of crystallizing an essence, which is self-defined and delimited, and which becomes the subject of deification and eventual immortality. Despite LaVey's efforts at packaging his thoughts in a crude style (increasingly typical of his work after 1975), he here gave some left-hand-path technology that is profound and sophisticated, yet practical and "down to earth."

Not only are there natural limitations in place that affect human knowledge and creativity, but LaVey also saw the benefits of artificial restrictions on creative freedom. In a 1981 issue of *The Cloven Hoof,* he extolled the virtues of *censorship.* This demonstrates that the Black Pope was as able to "blaspheme" against the sacred cows of the "liberal establishment" just as well as he did against those of the "religious right." To him, they are all the same anyway: rubes and dupes. His defense of censorship (an artificial limitation of artistic or intellectual freedom) is based not on a desire to quell a certain viewpoint, but rather to encourage true creativity and vitality of imagination. A lack of limits promotes *sameness,* chiefly because artists are then free to practice excess, which in turn dulls the imaginative powers of the audience or readership. "Censorship is a means towards personal freedom, the most personal of freedoms: a mind that can still function as a creative and thinking tool, *not* by what it is 'free' to do in all its collective sameness, but what it is *motivated* to do because of certain limitations."[73]

LaVey's extolling of limitations is, or can be, a hallmark of the left-hand path insofar as it is a corollary of the necessity of *separation* of the self from the surrounding environment and transforming it according to innate patterns hidden within. Without such limits or boundaries, the self or individuality is quickly swallowed up by the mass—and even more quickly if the lack of limitations is promoted in the name of "individuality." LaVey always liked to point to the "hippies" of the late 1960s and early 1970s as examples of people who walked in lockstep (peer-group-approved clothes, drugs, opinions, verbal mechanisms, etc.), all in the name of "doing their own thing."

Of LaVey's many radical ideas, none seems as radical as his proposal that Satanists create and dwell in an artificial world and society of their own designs. Here he suggests a new view of cosmology, one that is at once material and a product of the human imagination. The fourth point of LaVey's five-point program of Pentagonal Revisionism is the design and manufacture of androids to act as artificial human companions or slaves. The fifth point of the program extends this idea to *total environments.* These are to be privately owned and operated communities or environments that totally conform to the aesthetic wishes of those living or visiting there. This is the basic idea behind LaVey's earlier talk about the establishment of "pleasure domes" in which the Satanist could indulge his particular tastes. In these total environments, the Satanist would be free from a kind of "aesthetic pollution" with which he is usually constantly bombarded, much to the detriment of his ability to indulge in his desires.

Androids and total environments are logical conclusions to LaVey's cosmology: they provide a material (real) option for the true Satanist to indulge his highly idiosyncratic tastes separate and free from the collective norms of society, which are an anathema to his view of "the good life."

THE SATANIC VIEW OF MANKIND

The human being is the central focus of LaVeyan Satanism. It is through our humanity we view the world—"Man is the measure of all things," said the Ancient Greek Sophist Protagoras—and it is in humanity we find the ultimate godhead. According to LaVey's philosophy, Satanism is the true religion of mankind, by mankind, and for mankind. At the core of his anthropology is a carnal understanding that places a high degree of importance on the erotic component in human life. This aspect is typical of philosophies having their origins in the twentieth century, from the psychoanalysis of Sigmund Freud to the sexual religion of Gerald Gardner.

MAN = BEAST = "GOD"

At least when talking about the Satanist himself, anthropology and theology are merged. But to the non-Satanist, the study of mankind is closer to demonology. This is because "white-light" religious systems equate "human nature," the natural desires of man, with manifestations of sin implanted by Satan. Indeed, the "Satan"—the "enemy" or "adversary" of the orthodox God—is humanity itself, of which the image of Satan is a symbol. This structure ensures that "Satan" will always be "tempting man to sin" and hence he will need the church to absolve that sin. This is how "Satan" has "kept the church in business all these years," as the ninth Satanic Statement proclaims.

The Satanist rejects this structure and embraces his own carnal individuality as the focus of any godhead. Man is seen entirely as a creature of Nature: a beast or animal with no "spiritual" component. LaVey writes, "[Man] no longer can view himself in two parts, the carnal and the spiritual, but sees them merge as one, and then to his abysmal horror, discovers that they are only the carnal—AND ALWAYS WERE!

Then he either hates himself to death, day by day—or rejoices that he is what he is!"[74] The former choice of self-hatred is that of orthodox religion; the latter choice of self-acceptance is that of Satanism.

Man is a natural beast, but self-aware in his bestiality. Since the true and only God (= Satan) is Nature, mankind is itself the physical embodiment of God as a self-aware entity. In this way, mankind is that part of Satan (= Nature/"God") that is aware of its own existence.

If man maintains a loving or respectful attitude toward himself, toward the true carnal and bestial "core self," then he will show love and respect for the most noble and pure embodiments of that self: children, animals, and other beautiful things. But if he is filled with self-hatred, he will wish to hurt and destroy any and all external symbols of himself and his true nature. This is why so many "white-light" religions have dying or suffering "gods" and why they are so ready to sacrifice themselves or other things. "The Satanist does *not* hate himself, nor the gods he might choose, and has no desire to destroy himself or anything for which he stands!"[75]

MAN AS A CARNAL EGO

The highest or most exalted element that defines the human being is the *carnal ego*. This "carnal ego" is at once material—it is a part of the fleshly vehicle—and a matrix for *awareness*. The ego, the "I," is aware of itself as the subject (= doer) of the actions it undertakes or wills. Man's awareness of this carnality provides the highest form of knowledge: the "undefiled wisdom."

This is a point LaVey spent very little time elucidating in his writings. It remains a vague yet vital and implicit part of his comprehensive worldview. The philosophical problem that remains is that as soon as I say, "man is just an animal, which is *aware* of its animalness," I have already myself made the essential distinction between man and animal: self-awareness. This problem is not unique with LaVey, of course; all philosophies that see humanity as an undifferentiated part of an all-encompassing Nature face this problem. Epicureans, Enlightenment rationalists, Romantic vitalists, Marxists, and anarchists all confront this quandary. Man—consciousness—seems to be so much outside Nature, working contrary to her "wishes," rebelling against her constraints, yet there is no truly objective and irrefutable evidence or data that proves the existence of some positive quality called "spirit" or "intelligence." The materialist simply posits that the laws by which matter is able to produce intelligence are so complex and mysterious that they have not yet been deduced. But in any event, the *idea* of an invisible "spiritual" reality in opposition to this material and vital existence has generally been used as a weapon against mankind since the beginning of history. LaVey's religious philosophy calls for an end to "spiritual pipe dreams" and extols the virtue of pure "vital existence."

SATANIC SOCIETY AND THE INVISIBLE WAR

Anton LaVey largely led a reclusive life. Especially after 1975, his writings increasingly demonstrated concern with social realities and problems from a Satanic perspective. This focus on social, interhuman realities is understandable from two angles. First, it is in keeping with the Satanic preoccupation with nonconformity against "herd mentality." Social norms help to define the limits of a possible Satanic society. Second, as society is a matter of here-and-now existence, it is of a higher concern to the materialistic Satanist than any metaphysical speculations.

LaVey saw society as an important reality, albeit an often distasteful one. It, more than anything else, is the matrix in which the LaVeyan Satanist lives. Society is LaVey's chief nemesis, as he has observed how the "white-light" value system has outgrown medieval religious forms such as Christianity and become ensconced in the new media-dominated consumer society of the late twentieth century.

As with most schools of the left-hand path, the Church of Satan proposes an elitist design for society. The Satanist is someone set apart from and above the mass of society.[76] What is more, the isolation from society that the Satanist cultivates, can, according to LaVey, be a great source of power. In a 1980 *Cloven Hoof* article entitled "Power through Alienation," he stated: "A Satanist is not a revolutionary, but an alien, who by his very alienation, is performing the ultimate revolt against the mindless drones who fear the very rejection on which a Satanist thrives."[77] By rejecting social norms and taking the role of Satanist (i.e., the alien), the individual is progressively freed from the constraints of society. At the same time, LaVey derided the illusory "miserable quest for 'individuality'" touted as the *norm* for present-day society. Everybody wants "to be like everybody else" and at the same time "think for themselves." Here the hopeless situation of the normal person comes into sharp relief.

For LaVey, society with its conformist norms acts as a great obstacle against which the Satanic will resists and asserts its nonconformity. This resistance of the Satanic will is painful but also gainful, for without the resistance, the Satanist would be awash in undifferentiated possibilities. Resistance leads to strength. This is not a benign relationship, either: the conformist world is seen as a great adversary bent on the destruction of the alien, the Satanist—and so there is now underway a great Invisible War.

The Invisible War was first mentioned by name in a 1986 issue of *The Cloven Hoof,* although it had really been an underlying theme from the beginning of the Church of Satan. In this first discussion of the subject, LaVey is somewhat vague in describing the parameters of the war, although he states that it is "highly sophisticated, breaking down normal mental and physiological functions until malaise, incompetence, or destruction befalls most individuals."[78]

The purpose of this war is the "containment and control" of individuals. Weapons used in this war (which is also called World War III) include weather control, viral and bacterial diseases, ultra- and subsonic technologies, television, chemicals in food and beverages, psychological smokescreens (diversions and misdirections from the true conflict), the extended weekend (time to consume and be further indoctrinated), and urban warfare (real violence induced mainly through drugs).[79]

It is an "invisible war" because the enemies are not obvious, perhaps even to themselves. Whenever confronted with one of the offensive weapons used in the "war," the fastest way to identify the enemies is to ask the question "Who gains?" This question usually renders some specific answers. But the true enemy lurks even deeper. The agents of the enemy—actual people undertaking actions to the benefit of the enemy's agents—keep the secret even from themselves. "They can't even be honest with themselves—so keeping *certain* secrets is easy. If it means losing money unless they keep their customers believing particular things, people will keep their mouths shut. If it means being hated and rejected for what the secret hides, then it's easy."[80]

People can keep "monstrous secrets" because they have been encouraged—by the opposing force in the invisible war—to *forget* who and what they truly are. LaVey writes, "*Forgetfulness,* relinquishing your past, is demanded by the State—anyone who chooses to disobey this rule is subject to substantial emotional and financial penalties."[81] This forgetfulness is equated with a mythic Greek "chair of forgetfulness," analogous to drinking the waters of the underworld spring Lethe, and identified as a punishment. It is interesting to compare LaVey's ideas on the virtues of remembering with those of G. I. Gurdjieff, or Plato for that matter. For LaVey, by remembering the past we preserve our individual selves and thus become aware of who we really are. In his typical fashion, however, LaVey takes this idea and reduces it to an insight that prevents us from being "sold a bill of goods."

Tempting as it might be for some to dismiss LaVey's notions about the Invisible War, many of his ideas seem valid and even obvious if one allows one's cynical or harshly realistic mind to rule rather than one's sentimental fantasies and wishful thinking. Also, his ideas are no less "paranoid" than a hundred special-interest groups scurrying about the contemporary scene—LaVey just puts them all together in a comprehensive vision.

"SATANIC SEX"

This is the title of the sixth chapter of the "Book of Lucifer" in *The Satanic Bible.* There can be no doubt that it was through sexual imagery that LaVey first brought great attention to the Church of Satan: his naked altars, "Topless Witches Review," photo layouts in "men's magazines," and so on.

In doing this, LaVey was practicing a magical talent for using the *timing* factor. The time—the late 1960s and early 1970s—was one in which such imagery could be effective, and it was. An early issue of *The Cloven Hoof* contains an indication that there were three main reasons people were joining the Church: sexual freedom, furtherance of a New Satanic Society, and the practice of magic. A new attitude toward sex and sexuality is part of the late-twentieth-century zeitgeist. Aidan Kelly has pointed out the intrinsic importance of new sexual doctrines, and again especially in the U.S., for the spread of modern witchcraft during the same period.[82] But "Satanic sex" is something quite different from any other religious sexual doctrine. LaVey declares sexuality to be both of primary importance in human behavior *and* an area of life in which absolute and free indulgence should be practiced. It consequently follows that this also includes the freedom to indulge in *abstinence.*

"Satanic sex" is utter sexual freedom. The only thing about sexual practice that a Satanist might feel "guilty" about would be, in the words of Sade's "Dying Man," "I repent: I only plucked an occasional flower when I might have gathered an ample harvest of fruit."[83] The essence of this philosophy is that of indulgence. One should find out what one's tastes and predilections *truly are* (apart from cultural and social pressures) and then freely indulge these tastes. This includes the right to indulge in asexuality.

Even in the midst of the "sexual revolution," LaVey was astute enough to see the fact that American culture remained (and would continue to remain, despite appearances) a sexually repressed society. This is basically good news to the Satanist because of the need for and existence of *limitations* that fuel the imagination of individuals. Many aspects of the "sexual revolution"—such as the idea of sexuality as therapy ("normal sex is *good* for you!"), unisex fashions and assertions ("there's *really* no difference between men and women"), and casual or "free" sex ("everybody's doing it!"), among other attitudes—lead to a *reduction* in the potential for real Satanic sex. This is because Satanic sex is based on "fetishistic" or highly idiosyncratic sexual tastes, the sexual polarity between male and female, and a significant emotional intensity.

GENDER POLITICS AND IMAGERY

Contrary to the general cultural drift toward unisex values and fashion trends of the last two decades, LaVey consistently promoted a strict aesthetic distinction between the sexes. He insists on the profound differences between men and women, which is consistent with his more general theory of *carnality*. If the flesh is different in form, it follows that the "soul" will be different in a corresponding degree.

LaVey's most extended treatise on this difference is his 1970 book *The Compleat Witch*. The essential problem it addresses is the same as that of feminist literature of the period: how can women achieve or obtain power? In both the works of LaVey and those of feminists (who would find LaVey's ideas abominable), it is generally conceded that the male gender either possesses the power sought, or that it embodies or behavioralizes that power. The feminist solution to the problem is for women to become more like men (in image and values) so that they will be able to wrest the power away from men themselves. LaVey's solution is for women to win a man and hold him with her particular feminine charms, thereby acquiring whatever power he has or will have. LaVey wrote, "[I]f a woman wants anything in life, she can obtain it easier through a man than another woman, despite woman liberationists' bellows to the contrary."[84] Such statements demonstrate his ability to be the adversary, the Satan, of contemporary cultural fashions and trends as much or more so than he is that of traditional orthodox "religion."

Although LaVey's stated preference is for men to be decidedly masculine and women to be decidedly feminine, there is a deeper reality revealed in a 1978 article in *The Cloven Hoof* entitled "Confessions of a Closet Misogynist."[85] Here he discusses himself as an example of a misogynist whose disdain for "soft, yielding, voluptuous woman" is based on *jealousy.* Such a woman creates "dualistic yearnings" in the strongly masculine man. "Essentially, a true misogynist is a straight man who, because he is a potential pushover for women and realizes it, resents the power a truly feminine woman wields, wishes he had a bit of it himself, secretly admires it, and seeks to capture it before it captures him."[86]

These ideas flow from LaVey's sophisticated conceptions about "epicurean sadism" and masochism, and his theory of the androgyny of the personality in which the majority self is made up of an apparent external personality, which is a reflection of a core personality very similar to it. The gender of this personality is the same as that of the body of the subject. However, LaVey theorizes that there is another, minority or demonic, personality that lies between the outer and core selves. This has the gender opposite that of the subject, and contrasts not only sexually but also in physical type. It is to this type of persona that the subject will be naturally attracted sexually.[87] These general principles are often applied by LaVey to a variety of studies in human behavior and society.

Another of LaVey's sexually conditioned theories revolves around the power of early erotic imprints on the consciousness of an individual. This phenomenon is called Erotic Crystallization Inertia (ECI) by LaVey. Later in life, the subject returns to the images imprinted in his or her ECIs for vital sustenance. ECIs are almost predicated on the idea that the subject has a strong sexual imagination so that images not overtly related to simple procreative functions of sexuality are endowed by the imagination with tremendous erotic power. Imagination—the power of the mind to creatively fill in or complete situations it encounters with emotional or intellectual meaning only vaguely suggested by the situation—is crucial to all of LaVey's thought. In many ways, his Satanism is a philosophy of the imagination.

"THE MARQUIS LAVEY"

In a discussion of the sexual connotations of LaVeyan Satanism, the topic of sadomasochism must be considered as a dominant theme.

Theoretically, it is in perfect accord with the entire body of LaVey's ideology. It is based on a carnal duality between pleasure and pain, between predator and prey. This again indicates the pervasive principle of there being polar extremes, positive and negative, active and passive, male and female, between which there is a law of the "attraction of opposites." Another principle of LaVeyan thought, that of *limitation* or restriction leading to creativity, also plays a role in his implicit doctrines surrounding sadomasochism.

The most comprehensive previously published view of this aspect of LaVeyan thought can be found in the chapter "Masochistic America" in Barton's book *The Secret Life of a Satanist.*[88]

Although primarily a sexual or erotic idea, sadomasochism is something LaVey sees as a factor prevalent throughout society, even in matters not considered overtly "sexual." In the relationship between the sexes, or between any two individual humans, LaVey always observes a dominant/submissive model. One will primarily dominate the other, one will be the master, the other will be the slave. But LaVey is quick to point out that there is also power to be gained in being the slave—it just depends on who the master is and what the slave gets in exchange for her (or his) slavery.

The already discussed idea of "eustress" in society has, according to LaVey, its erotic corollary in sadomasochism. Punishment, initially an unpleasant thing, evolves into a form of gratification—especially if it is handed out by a stimulating person.[89]

LaVey sees many "fitness" and "health" regimens of the recent past as eustress phenomena: thinly disguised (though properly sublimated and sanitized) forms of masochism. People burn themselves under the sun, exercise in ways designed to maximize discomfort ("no pain, no gain!"), and starve themselves in strict dietary disciplines.

In the wider socioeconomic context, inherent masochism is used as a marketing device to ensure consumer anxiety and dissatisfaction (= pain). This can then only be "alleviated" with products or consumer trends that are profitable, and which are usually in and of themselves painful (physically, emotionally, financially, etc.).

LaVey views some elements of mankind (and especially womankind) as needing a certain amount of misery, pain, and slavery. This inherent need *will* play itself out in life one way or another. If one is a "self-destructive masochist," this need will be played out in unhappy circumstances of life. Real defeat and misery are the result. But if one is a "self-affirming masochist," someone conscious of this element in the personality and who exercises it in a creative and self-aware manner, then the real defeat and misery will be exorcised in a pleasurable and fun way.[90] The latter expression of masochism is entirely positive and self-affirming. All inherently masochistic people *will* be slaves; self-consciously masochistic ones can choose their masters, while the zombie-slaves become the wretched cattle of "the company," "the cause," "the job," "the trend," or whatever impersonal "master" presents itself.

LaVey demonstrates his personal experience with masochistic women in his understanding of the phenomenon of "aggressively passive" or "demandingly masochistic" women to whom the obliging and enthusiastic sadist can soon become the slave.[91]

In keeping with his organic/materialistic cosmology, LaVey theorizes that women are especially masochistic because they are endowed with great amounts of "excess energy." This can apparently only be relieved through physical means, and so he has suggested the construction of "Auto-Erotic Agitation Tumblers" that vibrate and bounce the woman around until sufficient excess energy has been released—and orgasm is achieved.[92] The possible necessity for such devices also speaks to the general lack of men who can facilitate similar results.

LaVey's theories on sadism are also interesting and sophisticated. He realizes the role of the sadist or master as that of a facilitator of the self-aware masochist's experience. There is a true exchange of power in which both parties gain something they inherently need. He also recognizes the roots of the true sadistic impulse not in hatred or anger, but in jealousy or envy. He seems to see the masochist or slave as a projection of the sadist's or master's own "demonic self," which the sadist then proceeds to train, control, and—when necessary—punish.

The sadist is also the artist. Recall the profound definition of

Sadeanism given in chapter 6: "The pleasure felt from the observed modifications on the external world produced by the will of the observer."[93] This can also be true of the artist or magician. This "spur," which urges the subject to imagine something in the subjective universe and cause it to come about in the objective universe, is an essential component of LaVey's personal work. It recalls the myth of the misogynistic Pygmalion who created the sculpture of Galatea, his perfect woman. He then fell in love with her, but her stony form was unreceptive to his ardor. Aphrodite took pity on him and caused her to take on fleshly form so that she could be his wife. It is interesting to note that LaVey named his second daughter Zeena *Galatea.*

Another phenomenon that LaVey connects with sadomasochism is lycanthropy, or werewolfery. Some of his theories seem inspired by his favorite book on the subject, Robert Eisler's *Man into Wolf.* In a 1978 issue of *The Cloven Hoof,* LaVey first published his essay "How to Become a Werewolf: The Fundamentals of Lycanthropic Metamorphosis; The Principles and Their Application." (This was an excerpt from his then-unpublished collection of texts, *The Devil's Notebook.*)[94] The formula LaVey describes is one designed to transform the "civilized" man into an instinctive *sexual predator.*

LaVey invokes the Mortensen-esque emotional formula of sex, sentiment, and wonder as "triggering mechanisms" for the metamorphosis from man into beast. But he sees that in the person undergoing the transformation there is a basically bipolar personality: the perfect gentleman and the total beast.

The actual *place* where the metamorphosis occurs is one that has actually been "charged" with repeated acts of predation—this atmosphere then continues to attract both "hunters" *and* "hunted" alike. The hunted are attracted to the area because of the frightening thrills evoked by the *locus,* while predators are attracted by the presence of their prey.[95] The "preserve" can be a "lonely path through the trees," but it could just as easily be a singles bar or an S/M club.

In the game of predator/prey, LaVey suggests it is optimal if willing partners are involved. Lycanthropy is an indulgence by a "higher man" in his inherent bestial nature, which will never be apart from him as long as he is human. Again we see ritualized indulgence in behaviors otherwise considered destructive and certainly taboo.

The theme of sadomasochism is prevalent in the Church of Satan and not just a private obsession of LaVey himself. Another 1978 article in *The Cloven Hoof* by Priest Paul Pipkin (a real person, not a LaVey alter ego) is entitled "The Ritual Chamber at Roissy." This is an exploration of ritual and aesthetic themes drawn from Pauline Réage's *Story of O*.

The elements of limitation or restriction (bondage, slavery, humiliation, submission), dominance, predation (pain), gratification (pleasure), pride, and mastery—and, most of all, the realization of previously imaginary scenes—are all essential elements in both actual sadomasochism and in the philosophy of Anton LaVey. He demands that society come to a new understanding of terms such as slavery: to see them for the reality they present and to accept and indulge it. When such an arrangement is truly desired by the partners involved, he suggests that men and women enter into a "private pact" to center on the "master/slave component of a successful relationship."[96]

Even LaVey's later obsession with droids can be explained from the sadomasochistic perspective. If the master desires the absolute control or restriction of his slave, what could be more restricted or controlled than an inanimate object? LaVey's fascination with androids (gynecoids?) is rather like Pygmalion telling Aphrodite, "I liked Galatea better as a sculpture—turn her back to stone!"

It is no wonder that Sade's ideas on matters of sexuality are reflected in LaVey's philosophy, since the very underpinnings of Sade's understanding of the world and humanity's place in it are so remarkably paralleled in LaVey's own essentially materialistic ideology.

SATANIC ETHICS

The writings of Anton LaVey give expression to an internally consistent set of ethics, which he considers innate in the Satanic philosophy. In what some might consider a paradoxical and ironic way, the Black Pope is a man virtually obsessed with morality and ethics. Machiavellian though these ethics might be, they are nonetheless strong and vital. Just as the mythological, Miltonian figure of Satan is an expression of rebellion against the inherent cosmic injustice embodied in Jehovah, Anton LaVey is an expression of outrage against the institutionalized *hypocrisy* present in human society.

All of LaVey's doctrinal works—the Nine Satanic Statements, the Nine Satanic Sins, and the Eleven Rules of the Earth—are essentially documents concerning ethics. They provide the rationale for leading a Satanic life, a "counter-morality" meant to correct what is seen as an inherently corrupt and unnatural morality dominated by guilt, self-abasement, and self-deceit. LaVey does not propose doing "evil" instead of "good." Like Nietzsche, he urges the Satanist to go beyond these conventional categories imposed by illegitimate social "norms" and to return to a natural morality innate within the fiber of the carnal ego itself.

The ethical system that emerges from these writings is really a hyper-traditional one. It is one that harkens back to pre-Christian tribal ethics: you have the right and responsibility to live, thrive, and survive. Mind your own business as much as possible. If another challenges you or tries to thwart you in your legitimate efforts to live, thrive, and survive, you have the right to destroy him. We owe our allegiances and loyalties to those closest to us; we treat others according to their lesser status. Human relationships should be even give-and-take affairs; there is no such thing as "charity." Only enter into relationships where this is true.

These are apparently natural ethics, intended to be free of hypocrisy. Other ethical systems are thought to be flawed by the element of self-deceit or dishonesty inevitably built into them.

Some aspects of LaVey's ethical system seem to have an almost mystical component about them. These are encoded in the seventh, eighth, and ninth "Rules of the Earth." The seventh rule involves giving credit to *magic* when you have employed it successfully. For LaVey, this seems to go beyond just magic and directly to the symbol or reality of Satan himself. Magic is equated with the method of Satan; to deny magic or Satan seems an act of dishonor to the Black Pope. He often condemns those who "play the devil's game, but deny the devil's name." Honor and loyalty to magic, and to its master, Satan, is clearly an ethical principle with LaVey. The eighth and ninth "Rules of the Earth" express LaVey's almost mystical reverence for the life and well-being of children and (nonhuman) animals—he holds their *essence* in true reverence.

SATANIC IMMORTALITY

In left-hand-path systems, the quest for immortality has always been central. In LaVeyan Satanism, the focus is on "vital essence" in this world and in this life: the imperative to survive, to thrive, and to LIVE. But this does not mean that the idea of the survival of death itself is unimportant in the LaVeyan system. As with the use of magic, this is one of those instances in which LaVey radically departs from the materialistic Epicurean and Sadean foundations of his philosophy. Perhaps this is one of the reasons why the possibilities of immortality of the ego are relatively little discussed in LaVey's published works.

Anton LaVey himself obliquely claims to have found the key to immortality. He boldly claims that he won't die. His beliefs hinge on an idea of "eternal awareness" based on will. He also hints at belief in reincarnation when he says: "I will come back."[97]

In chapter X of the "Book of Lucifer" in *The Satanic Bible,* entitled "Life after Death through Fulfillment of the Ego," LaVey writes: "It is [the] lust for life which will allow the vital person to live on after the inevitable death of his fleshly shell." The implication of this and other statements is that there is some kind of substance or energy not entirely identical to the body itself—which is the "shell" that "houses" it—and that this substance *can,* if it is vital enough, maintain its existence after corporeal death. This pursuit appears to have been increasingly downplayed in the post-LaVey ideology of the Church of Satan as promulgated by High Priest Peter Gilmore.

What LaVey is primarily interested in is the continued existence of the self-aware individual ego. There are very few indications of *how* this might be achieved, but certain features are clear. *Vitality* of the ego is of the utmost importance. Anyone who would achieve immortality must *live this life* with a high level of intensity. Life is life—incarnate or discarnate. This ego- or self-awareness must be *unique* and readily identifiable. Perhaps it should not be overly complicated in image or content: a concentrated, vital and unique substance has a better chance of survival than a diffuse, weak, and ordinary one. The technique of ECI, of attaching one's vital ego-consciousness to certain scenes or objects, can be of tremendous aid in this process. Also important is the *fame* of the individual: this vital ego should be well known to a wide number of living persons. This can act as a support system for one's immortal status, but only when consciously combined with other factors.

In part of the Redbeard text, *Might Is Right,* selected by LaVey to serve as his "Book of Satan" section in *The Satanic Bible,* we find the exhortation:

> Make yourself a Terror to your adversary . . . Thus shall you make yourself respected in all walks of life, and your spirit—your immortal spirit—shall live, not in an intangible paradise, but in the brains and sinews of those whose respect you have gained.[98]

In ancient times, much of this was part of becoming a divine hero, or being deified in death. The Greeks, Romans, Germans, Slavs, and Celts all deified uniquely heroic individuals, and in many ways LaVey (actually, of course, Ragnar Redbeard) seems to carry on in their tradition.

SATANIC THEOLOGY

For the LaVeyan Satanist, no "theology" in the usual sense is possible. The theology and the anthropology are virtually identical, and so the question of theology becomes almost superfluous. God is Nature, but Nature is Satan—just as God is Satan: Hail Satan!

Behind these semantic shifts lies a coherent, if sometimes mysterious, view of the true nature of "god" or a "theology." The roots of this theological view can be seen in Epicurean philosophy over the past two millennia. Although he was an atomic materialist, the Epicurean Roman philosopher and poet Lucretius still spoke of the gods. He scorned their worship by the masses as destructive and hypocritical, but explained these unwholesome beliefs as ignorance of the true nature of the gods. The gods are simply extremely rarified structures existing in absolute tranquility beyond the limits of the world as men know it. They are there, but subject to Nature's laws and impotent to affect affairs on Earth. It is in the patterns and models of Nature herself that the Epicurean finds the true concept of "God."

For LaVey, "God" as conventionally understood (in a way more akin to the ancients' belief in the gods) is irrelevant to human experience. The complex patterns and models present in the whole of Nature, both in this world and beyond it, constitute the only thing the LaVeyan Satanist feels is worthy of the title "God." But because the masses of people who have founded (and been subject to) the religions of mankind have been incapable of knowing this, they have based their ideas about "God" on projections of their own fears, guilts, and other shortcomings.

The true "God" stands in *opposition* to this process and therefore bears the name "Satan." This is the coherent complex of patterns and models governing the universe, but not separate from it. Within the individual human being, the presence of this coherent complex of patterns is called the *carnal ego*. This is the representation, or the presence, of Satan in the individual. It is *carnal* because it cannot be separated from Nature; it is an *ego* because it can be aware of itself and its own actions. It is the *doer* of all that is done: the absolute subject. (The word *ego* is nothing other than the Latin word for the first-person singular pronoun "I.")

Does Satan then have an independent, or "personal," objective existence? In the earlier years, LaVey remained vague on this particular subject—obliquely referring to "the Man Downstairs," or to other quaint metaphors—but such a doctrine may have been a *secret* of the Church. In later years, however, LaVey insisted on Satan being only a symbol for Nature herself. It is clear that there is a model here for the objective independent existence of this complex of patterns (i.e., Nature), but there is little evidence for its visibility as a "personal deity." To make it ontologically *personal* would be tantamount to erecting a screen upon which to project those petty human emotions of fear, guilt, pity, and all the rest—thus turning the true *Other* (= Satan) into just another one of the *Same* (= God).

SATANIC MAGIC IN THEORY AND PRACTICE

For LaVey, magic is the Satanic method in and of itself. He defines magic generally as "the change in situations or events in accordance with one's will, which would, using normally accepted methods, be unchangeable."[99] This definition obviously owes something to Aleister Crowley's definition.

As noted earlier, LaVey does not like to distinguish between "black" and "white" magic. This is because he discusses the terms on a moral or ethical basis. All true magic involves "ego gratification and personal power as a goal," and so might be called "black" but for the hypocritical stance taken by those who would call themselves "white magicians" or "white witches." In the historical sense, LaVey is correct here. Since the Middle Ages, all *magic* has been considered de facto evil because it places (or can place) the will of the individual above that of "God." As the widely accepted definition of magic always places the *will* of the magician in the central position, this assumption of the validity of individual will over universal will continues to be essential. It is for this reason that all magic might be called "black magic" by those who decry any effort to strengthen and fulfill the ego as "evil."

SATANIC TECHNOLOGIES

The Practice of Greater and Lesser Magic

The use of magical technologies for personal transformation—what might be called "high magic" in some traditions—is little discussed in the Church of Satan system. This is not because it is unimportant but because it is seen as being such an *objective* matter that no amount of ritual or ritual technology could effect the actual transformation of an individual from a I° to a IV° or even a V°. Such transformation is only brought about through the coordination and correlation of every aspect of a person's whole life toward such magical goals.

Lesser Magic

In *The Satanic Bible,* lesser magic is defined as "non-ritual or manipulative magic" and is further characterized as "the wile and guile obtained through various devices and contrived situations, which when utilized, can create 'change, in accordance with one's will.'"[100] This type of magic has historically been called "fascination" or "glamour," but on a grander scale today it might be called "propaganda" or "advertising." Lesser magic works by means of psychological or psycho-biological laws that are known to the magician but which may be unknown to those upon whom the magic is being worked. This type of magic works, consciously or unconsciously, through the media of the five senses.

Some of LaVey's theoretical base for his practice of lesser magic stems from carnival-type experience. The tricks used by carny fortune tellers, stage hypnotists, and others are utilized here. Much of the content of *The Compleat Witch* is an outline of such techniques. Many of these tricks have more recently been "made legit" when couched in terms of "body language" and some of the techniques of "Neurolinguistic Programming" (NLP).

Another major source of his theories concerning lesser magic is *The Command to Look* by William Mortensen. Although this is not exactly clear in his discussion on pages 111–13 of *The Satanic Bible,* the magician must first command a subject to *look*—to pay attention to the source of the forthcoming magical message—and *then* the fascination can take place. The command to look is accomplished through a subtle message of fear or danger; the fascination can then be effected by one of three means: sex, sentiment, or wonder. These are the only three things people are enduringly interested in, so they are the most powerful channels through which they can be influenced.

In the practice of lesser magic, none of the five senses should be ignored. The art of fascination should make use of not only visual imagery, but also the voice (hearing), perfumes (smell), food (taste), and touch. Optimally, all of these should be combined in an effective manner.

LaVey himself was an obvious master of lesser magic over the years. He personally "charmed" most of those who came into contact with him and was able to cast his charismatic spell on the world around him. His striking physical appearance (he was the almost stereotypical image of Satan himself) commanded people to look. His stories of magic, curses, and other exploits at least *seemed* to deliver in the *wonder* category and thus riveted the observers' attention. In the early years of the Church, the *sex* category was also a greater factor with LaVey's nude altars, topless witches, and so on.

Lesser magic works through the five senses and appeals to primary human emotions in a direct way, making use of a wide variety of contemporary mythic symbols. Some might argue that lesser magic is "just applied psychology," which is certainly true. But then again, there is nothing really *scientific* about psychology as practiced on this level. The laws are mysterious and shift from person to person and from situation to situation, and so the discovery of methods that work in this field is as elusive as any Grail. Lesser magic constitutes a kind of meta-rhetoric by which magicians can persuade others to do their will, or to hold a certain opinion or feeling, for not entirely conscious "reasons."

Greater Magic

The other category of magic discussed by LaVey is ritual magic, which involves a formal ceremony that occurs in a special time and place. He notes that "Its main function is to isolate the otherwise dissipated adrenal and other emotionally induced energy, and convert it into dynamically transmittable force."[101]

In this definition, it is clear that LaVey sees greater magic as an entirely natural, materially based process. Its laws may be not fully known and its application is often mysterious and more an art than a science, but its mechanics are ultimately material.

An act of greater magic is, according to LaVey, to be driven by *emotional* and not intellectual concerns. Any intellectual work is done in preparing for the ritual. During the ritual, it is emotion, or chemistry, that is in charge.

LaVey isolates five factors that must be taken into account for a successful act of ritual magic:

1. Desire
2. Timing
3. Imagery
4. Direction
5. The Balance Factor

Desire is the first factor: "If you do not truly desire any end result, you should not attempt to perform a working."[102] A strong desire is necessary to success. *Timing* is a complex factor. The magician must be at a moment of peak efficiency during the working, while those whom he wishes to affect must be receptive to his "sendings." The sleep cycle may be important to this. LaVey suggests a window at approximately two hours before the object of the sending awakens. But timing is a matter of such factors as biological clocks and sleep cycles rather than mumbo-jumbo about the "hour of Venus" or whatever. *Imagery*—nonverbal signals—is used to focus the emotions of the magician on the object of his working. This could be done with drawings, paintings, sculptures, photographs, articles of clothing, scents, sounds, music, or whole scenarios incorporated into the ritual. Imagery is then manipulated according to the aim of the working and is "the very blueprint" that "becomes the formula, which leads to reality."[103] *Direction* involves the accumulation of emotional energy *within* the working and its *release* toward an effective result. Once the working is done, no further expenditure of *emotion* should occur. After this release, the magician is free to expend his energies in more productive activities.

Regarding the *Balance Factor,* LaVey explains: "One of the magician's greatest weapons is knowing himself; his talents, abilities, physical attractions and detractions, and when, where, and *with whom* to utilize them!"[104] Magic can most easily be used to change things by working for the most part in harmony with nature, making only slight alterations in the right place at the right time to "tip the balance" in one's favor.

As a rule for success, the Satanist would never use greater magic where the techniques of lesser magic could be more easily employed. Greater magic is reserved for those situations where it *must* be used.

In practice, LaVey is the greatest pioneer in the field of what might be called *pragmatic magic.* All the elements in his magical system are there to act as triggers for certain psychological effects. Nothing is there because "it's just traditional." The only rule seems to be: if it works, do it; if it doesn't work, leave it out or find something that does.

The Satanic Bible contains the formulas for three basic conjurations: lust (sex), compassion (sentiment), and destruction (wonder)—again the influence of Mortensen's theories are felt. These are the three main motivations for the performance of greater magic, according to LaVey. Lust is for gaining a lover, compassion for personal power, and destruction for the venting of anger or hate.

Similarly to other modern left-hand-path magical systems, there is no standard Satanic ritual that is repeated ad nauseam such as the Roman Catholic Mass. Each Satanist is encouraged to create his or her own rites suited to individual or group needs. But there are some pragmatic steps used (especially for group workings) that are designed to ease the ability of the will to trigger the most effective psychological responses.

LaVey outlined thirteen steps that are designed first to create an atmosphere isolated from outside influences and charged with emotionally stimulating sounds, symbols, and so on; then to direct all of the accumulated emotional energy toward the desired goal; and finally to reenter the atmosphere outside the chamber. All of the prescriptions of specific ritual elements are really in place as *suggestions* on how things might be done; in individual practice, things might be performed in a variety of different ways. There is usually a fairly standard opening sequence involving ringing a bell nine times, invoking the Powers of Darkness, drinking from a chalice (to link the celebrant with the powers invoked), invoking the cardinal points, and a benediction with a phallus. In the space following this sequence comes the *working* itself, which may be highly individualized. For the conclusion there is another brief closing sequence including the ringing of the bell nine times and the final words: "So it is done!"

SATANIC PSYCHODRAMATIC MAGIC

The elaborate rituals staged in the Black House until 1972 were for the most part psychodramatic workings of greater magic. That is to say, they were not meant to change the outside world so much as they were designed to alter the feelings and attitudes of those participating in the ritual—to free them of detrimental emotions (such as fear, guilt, etc.) or to give expression to forbidden desires, feelings, or thoughts.

The Satanic Rituals is a collection of this type of psychodramatic ceremonies. The "Black Mass" is the premier Satanic psychodrama, but its formula is usually misunderstood by non-Satanists. As LaVey writes in *The Satanic Bible,* "A black mass, today [1969], would consist of the blaspheming of such 'sacred' topics as Eastern mysticism, psychiatry, the psychedelic movement, ultra-liberalism, etc."[105] A "traditional" Black Mass, a direct parody of the Roman Catholic Mass, would only be used as a psychodramatic ritual to help ex-Catholics "deprogram" themselves. (This would be especially valuable for all those who were institutionally abused by the clergy in their younger years.)

LaVey points out that the whole idea of the Black Mass is most certainly first a propagandistic creation of the Church, which was then later embellished in literary works for pure shock effect. But this history does not lessen its potential effectiveness for ex-Catholics or others raised in rigid religions to break their psychological ties with their old faith. They are then free to move forward to discover their own religious values apart from those programmed into them by others. The Black Mass is simply a ritual formulation of the antinomian process inherent in the practice of the left-hand path generally.

"The Ceremony of the Stifling Air" is another form of the Black Mass with a pseudo-historical connection to the story of the suppression of the Knights Templar by the king of France, Philip the Fair, and the Pope in 1331. *Das Tierdrama* ("The Drama of the Beasts") is a celebration of the essence of the seventh Satanic Statement: "man is just another animal." It teaches humans to exult in their animal nature, to embrace and accept it. The "Homage to Tchort" is LaVey's celebration of the fleshly and libidinous appetites of his hero, G. Y. Rasputin.

These and other psychodramatic rituals practiced or suggested by the Church of Satan material are designed in some sense to make subjective changes in the celebrant(s) and/or to teach or illustrate some philosophical or historical idea within the Satanic tradition. That they are sometimes fictional creations—or even *based* on fictional creations (such as the Lovecraft rituals in *The Satanic Rituals*)[106]—makes them all the more *Satanic.* The true Satanist is free to create his own "religion" or to accept or reject elements of pre-existing systems according to his needs or will.

Psychodramatic rituals allow the Satanist to do more than just read about strange practices and beliefs. They allow the participants to experience these practices in an active, living way. Such rituals are another form of indulgence in which the participants enter into new and different worldviews, try them on for size, and take from them what they want or need *from experience.*

EROTIC CRYSTALLIZATION INERTIA

One of LaVey's most unique contributions to magical technology is the aforementioned theory and practice of ECI: Erotic Crystallization Inertia, also known as Emotional Crystallization Inertia. For a comprehensive understanding of LaVey's system, no other concept is more important than ECI.

According to LaVey, there are certain moments in life, usually in adolescence or young adulthood, in which we suddenly and vitally become self-aware. These moments are always emotional, and are usually erotic in nature. In the glossary of LaVeyan terms given in Blanche Barton's *Secret Life of a Satanist,* ECI is defined as the "point in time and experience in which a person's emotional/sexual fetishes are established."[107] These are usually *visual* stimuli and subsequent memories of them. An ECI moment gives pleasure and joy, and from that joy comes strength and vitality. For this reason, if a magician surrounds himself with things that stimulate his ECI moments or periods in life, he will be more vital and live longer in his vitalized state.

LaVey first wrote about ECI in a 1973 issue of *The Cloven Hoof,* in an article entitled "Erotic Crystallization Inertia (E.C.I.): Its Relationship to Longevity." There he wrote of how older people like to remain in (or move to) environments—small towns, old folks' homes—where the fashions and visual stimuli tend to remain the way they always were or actually revert to times past. This is in fact *stimulating* and invigorating to the old people—the trendy fashions of younger generations would actually be detrimental to their vitality.

In subsequent contributions on the topic of ECI, it becomes progressively clearer that LaVey is developing a new category of magical philosophy with ECI.[108] By consciously indulging in ECI-stimuli, the magician preserves and maintains his vitality and vigor, his memories are kept intact and thus his longevity is extended, perhaps beyond death. The ECI magician might build a room or seek out an environment similar to that in which his ECI moments were first generated; he might listen to music associated with them, smell odors, feel textures, taste foods and drink—but most of all he will re-view his ECI visions. All of these things are imprinted in the mind at moments of strong self-awareness and vital pleasure—this is why we *remember* them so vividly and are inexorably attracted to things that remind us of them. Consciously reconnecting with these stimuli (either physically or in our imaginations) virtually "feeds" our carnal egos with the vital sustenance it needs to thrive.

In a basement room of the Black House, LaVey built a replica of a seedy old hotel room (ca. 1945): "Outside the single window it is always night and always raining and the intermittent flash of a neon sign pulsates . . ."[109] This is an ECI ritual chamber for LaVey—perhaps a replica of the room where young Tony had his first sexual encounter? His magical interest in old songs, old cars, and "out-of-date" fashions all stem back to this technique of ECI. He "blasphemes" against such pieces of so-called conventional wisdom as "you've got to keep up with the times or life will pass you by," or "you can't live in the past." On the contrary, he says if *you* are to live in any vital way you must remain true to those things that make you vital, that stimulate you in reality—not those newfangled things advertisers want you to buy.

ECI stimuli, together with the progressive isolation and distillation of the unique individual ego of a person (perhaps coupled with the creation of a static controlled "society" in the form of androids), form elements in a comprehensive magical approach to longevity and even immortality.

TRAPEZOIDAL MAGIC

No area of LaVey's magical knowledge has remained more mysterious and perhaps "sinister" than that connected with the symbol of the trapezoid. We have already discussed his Law of the Trapezoid, but his use of this symbol goes well beyond that law. The magic connected with the trapezoid has a unique character, unlike any other school of magic. Little to nothing has been written about it outside the internal documents of the Church of Satan and the Temple of Set.

In theory, trapezoidal magic makes use of geometrical manipulations of the ritual environment (visual and spatial), the creation of certain electromagnetic fields in the chamber (ozonization, ionization, extremely low-frequency [ELF] waves in the atmosphere), and the manipulation of light and sound waves to establish ideal psychophysiological conditions for the focus, concentration, and projection of the will of the magician to any part of the universe. To practice this often technical form of magic, apparati such as Tesla coils, Jacob's ladders, Van de Graaf generators, strobe lights, ionizers, and so forth are used in a ritual context.

The only commercially available example of this kind of ritual from LaVey is published in *The Satanic Rituals* in the form of "Die elektrischen Vorspiele." The connections between this kind of magical technology and Nazi Germany, as suggested by LaVey in this section of the book, are indirect at best. This type of magic was, however, extensively explored by prewar occult groups in Germany. Most of what appears in the ritual in question is the product of LaVey's magical synthesis and imagination.

THE LAVEYAN VISION

Anton Szandor LaVey was a man with a hell of a vision. His written works are full of predictions for the future and magical declarations of how he and the Church of Satan have changed, or will change, the "Is-To-Be," as he calls the future. A review of his visions will, however, reveal a growing pessimism in his thought.

During the first ten years of the Church of Satan, LaVey had visions of the establishment of publicly institutionalized Satanic Churches—crosses were to be cast down from the steeples and tridents put in their stead. In 1972, LaVey was ready to relegate Christ to the category of a "well-known folk myth" by the year 2000 CE.[110] The Church was to establish "pleasure domes" for the purposes of the indulgences of its members. After 1975, these grandiose visions for the Church of Satan became much more modest—and with the expected "backlash" of the 1980s, such visions seemed far away indeed.

But according to LaVey's cosmological scheme of ages, this Satanic Age—or Age of Fire—is just underway and will not reach its zenith of power until the year 2695. In these first few Workings (nine-year periods), a number of setbacks (due to reactive forces) can be expected. In the later visions of what the Church of Satan would become, LaVey saw it more as an "underground" subcultural phenomenon or a *super*-cultural phenomenon (as it would be at the highest levels of the culture). Either way, it is something outside the normative mainstream.

LaVey's last major vision that he cast into the Is-To-Be was his five-point program of Pentagonal Revisionism:[111]

1. Stratification
2. Taxation of All Churches
3. Return to the Law of the Jungle
4. Development and Promotion of Humanoids
5. Development and Promotion of Total Environments

These are the things LaVey thinks Satanists should be working toward and focusing on in the near future. Notice that all are essentially *social* phenomena, not primarily personal magical ones.

Stratification is a process in society by which the elite, the "Satanic cream," will rise to the top. This is to be accomplished through selective breeding (eugenics), elitist stratification of the social order, reestablishment of polygamy based on eugenic criteria, and the eventual establishment of separate communities of Satanists based on these principles.

Churches should and must be taxed like any other corporation. If so taxed, many of them would soon go out of business. This attitude perhaps stems from the fact that LaVey never incorporated the Church of Satan as an actual legal *church* at all; it was run it as a sole proprietorship throughout the years of LaVey's High Priesthood.

The Law of the Jungle—or *Lex Talionis*—as outlined in LaVey's "Eleven Rules of the Earth" is the true Natural Law and in the Satanic Age there will be a return to this natural form of ethics and morality.

Humanoids—sexual robots—are important to LaVey's vision of the future because they will be able to satisfy the desires of men and women in the sexual marketplace without spreading disease or spawning genetically inferior offspring who are now taxing our cultural system to death. The subject of such robots became a dominant theme of LaVey's writings in the mid-1980s.

"Total Environments" can be construed, on the one hand, as commercial enterprises, like amusement parks, that create alternative worlds in which like-minded people can live together (for a fee). But, on the other hand, they could be seen as the Satanic communities of the future. Here we find the old "pleasure-dome" ideas at a fuller state of maturity.

LaVey's power of vision, similar to that of Karl Marx, is one part predication or interpretation of historical cycles and one part operative magic, as he nudges events in the predicted (= wished for) direction. Historically, LaVey stood for a eugenic solution to many of our social problems. As time went on, his conviction in this area seems to have become stronger. The breeding of a New (here: Satanic) Race is nothing new in the history of thought. Plato suggested it in *The Republic* and National Socialist Germany had had plans for such an undertaking, of course. LaVey's championing of this cause is very much in line with his general philosophy based on the paradoxical balance between *materialism* and *magic*. Eugenics is straightforwardly the magical principle of "causing changes to occur in conformity with will" as applied to the very *material* (DNA) of which the carnal ego is made. Here again, the Black Pope blasphemes against yet another of the "sacred cows" of the latter half of the twentieth century (though certainly *not* the first half): the idea that all individuals are somehow genetically equal, and if not, steps should be taken to ensure that they are made equal.

ANTON LAVEY AND THE LEFT-HAND PATH

Obviously, LaVey and his Church of Satan belong to the left-hand path as it has been defined in this book. He was perhaps the first, and certainly the most vocal, to claim allegiance with the left-hand path in Western culture since ancient times. LaVeyan Satanism virtually *defines* the immanent branch of the left-hand path as it is practiced in the Western world today. Still, whether we speak of the immanent or the transcendental branch, the same criteria of antinomianism and initiatorily magical deification of the individual self are valid.

LaVey's philosophy is a perfect example of external antinomianism. He enthusiastically embraces any and all symbols of "consensus evil," relishing his self-chosen role of the ultimate and absolute adversary or opponent: *Satan.* Furthermore, he extends this concept beyond traditional religious contexts into the secular or "real world." This is essential in a modern age in which the former Judeo-Christian symbolism has become increasingly anachronistic.

It is one of the main underlying principles of the Church of Satan doctrines that the individual carnal ego can realize its own "godhead," as LaVey puts it. It seems likely that LaVey's own personal ideas on this essential and implicit point of his overall philosophy were never fully expressed to anyone outside his closest circle. The general methods of such self-deification can be deduced as much from LaVey's own personal behavior and history as from what he wrote over the years.

Magic is the essential method employed in LaVey's system. His magic, as seen in *The Satanic Bible,* may seem simplistic when compared to the complex rigmarole found in systems such as that of the Golden Dawn, but this is deceptive. Actually, LaVey's system demands that Satanic magicians really *know* themselves and pragmatically apply the principles of the system in ways unique to themselves. In addition, many of the general principles are ones otherwise unknown in the magical traditions of the occult revival: ECI, the Law of the Trapezoid, command-to-look methodologies, and so forth. This makes LaVey's forms of magic in fact much more intricate than the recipe-book approach of most others. Magic, for LaVey, is a way for the individual carnal ego to demonstrate its freedom and potency in the world around it—in this life and perhaps beyond it.

The individual is supreme in LaVey's form of Satanism. This may be why it has proven so difficult to organize and maintain an organization of LaVeyan Satanists. In fact, such organization may be seen as an anathema to this form of Satanism. LaVey himself was far too absorbed in *his own world* to care very much about what is occurring in the outside world beneath the Sigil of Baphomet. If he had had a burning desire to put himself at the center of an adoring mass of followers whose lives he controlled à la A. Merritt's Satan, he could have done that and his life would have been very different. But true to the individualistic essence of his philosophy, he chose himself and his own world instead.

With regard to initiation, the idea that one gains mastery in gradual stages is an idea generally supported by LaVey's system. At one point in the history of the Church (1969–1975), this became formalized, but subsequent to that time it was less so. A formal system of initiation requires the "recognizing entity" to be intimately knowledgeable and involved with the person being recognized by the various levels of initiation. LaVey is essentially too ego- or self-centered to delegate such authority or to become so involved with the initiation of others at all. Again, this seems consistent with his general system of ideas. LaVey opted for an initiatory system in which his personal intuition and/or factors in the secular, objective world do the work of recognition.

Anton LaVey's principal contribution to the history of the left-hand path in the twentieth century is his unequivocal evocation of the very image of the Judeo-Christian Satan as an object of veneration and his own identification with not only that image but that name as well. While playing the devil's game, he took the devil's name as his own. He even went so far as to give his only begotten son, a child born to him and Blanche Barton on Halloween, 1993, the very name *Satan*.

Some may feel that this chapter goes too far in *systematizing* the LaVeyan philosophy. In essence, the philosophy seems to be an eternally youthful one: "Have fun. Read scary stories. Play music." The rest was perhaps created for effect only, or for the sake of image. However, even if it was by accident, the system LaVey created out of the dead leaves of half-forgotten books will continue to have a fascinating potential, and it is hoped that this study has done the justice to it that it deserves.

It must also not go unnoted that few other members of the fraternity making up the lords of the left-hand path can be said to have been so *ideologically passive.* It might be said that LaVey is in many ways a chameleon, one who took on the ideas of not only the books that surrounded him, but also from the members of his entourage. It is tempting to conclude with Lawrence Wright that the LaVey story is one of a "bookish musician" who has taken us all for a ride into not only his dark side, but into the dark side of modern American life.[112]

In as many ways as LaVey seemed to be a man born too late, whose true home was in the not-too-distant past, he seemed also to be a man born to soon—one whose home is in the Is-To-Be.

PHILOSOPHICAL DISTILLATIONS OF HIGH PRIEST PETER H. GILMORE

Peter H. Gilmore grew up in the Hudson Valley in New York. Gilmore holds a B.S. and an M.A. in musical composition from New York University. He has also been a devotee of the teachings of Anton LaVey since the age of thirteen. On Walpurgisnacht, 2001, he was named High Priest of the Church of Satan.

As it appears now, LaVey could have hoped for no better successor. Gilmore entered his tenure as High Priest as an exceedingly well-seasoned student of the Black Pope. He has not tried to change the LaVeyan teachings, but he has distilled and refined them in a mode that seems centered in the heart of the doctrines of the first High Priest. Gilmore has brought the many ambiguities and double-edged nuances inherent in LaVey's style into sharper philosophical focus. Gone are oblique references to "the Man Downstairs," or to the carnal body as a mere "shell," or to ideas of part of a person surviving death and gaining immortality. It is clear that LaVey himself was moving increasingly away from these notions toward the end of his life, during which time Gilmore was his personal student. Also, the more materialistic, epicurean approach was always at the epicenter of LaVeyan Satanism, so Gilmore's distillation of these elements is in no way a jarring departure. In many ways, current Church of Satan teachings can be described as atheism clothed in a dark aesthetic.

In the 1980s, Gilmore was editing a horror-fiction magazine

called *Grue* with his wife, Peggy Nadramia. LaVey met with Gilmore and Nadramia in 1986 in San Francisco. This marked the beginning of a collaboration that has culminated in Gilmore's rise to the High Priesthood and the degree of Magus, and Magistra Nadramia's appointment as High Priestess in 2002. In 1989, Gilmore undertook the editorship of *The Black Flame,* a sort of newsstand-style magazine for Satanists of various schools under the LaVeyan banner. There he wrote many essays, some of which were used in the compilation of his 2007 book entitled *The Satanic Scriptures.*

The Satanic Scriptures is the most important work of LaVeyan Satanism to be penned by someone other than LaVey himself. In these essays and rituals, Gilmore refines the epicurean essence of LaVey's teachings. Gilmore hammers home the importance of materialism, objectivism, aesthetics, and—most important of all—individualism. He does this in a style and manner very reminiscent of his mentor.

Many leaders of religious or philosophical movements throughout history would have to be disappointed by the turns their successors made in guiding the development of their schools after their departures. I do not think LaVey would be disappointed with the direction Gilmore has gone, as it appears to be a steady continuation of the Black Pope's views.

Yn'khe Rohz

10

Michael A. Aquino

The Temple of Set

I, Set, am come again to my friends among mankind
—Let my great nobles be brought to me.[1]

The Book of Coming Forth by Night

The Temple of Set is . . . an association of the Elect to honor Set, exalt his Gift to ourselves, and exercise it with the greatest possible wisdom. As Set is a metaphysical entity, apart from the objective universe, he may be described as a "god" as conventional society employs the term. In this sense the Temple of Set is a religion—not one which is

Figure 10.1. The Pentagram of Set

> *based on irrational faith, but one which derives its core principles from exercise of the evident Gift of its god.*[2]
>
> MICHAEL AQUINO

Rarely in this century has a man with such objectively exemplary qualities stepped into the occult theater as Michael Aquino. In a world usually filled with marginal personalities of little accomplishment outside their "occult" field, Aquino is a remarkable exception. The organization that he was instrumental in founding in 1975, the Temple of Set, has assumed some of these same qualities as well.

Aquino is an initiatory product of the Church of Satan and traces his magical roots to the teachings of Anton LaVey. In the end, however, as really from the beginning, Aquino showed unique qualities that distinguished his ideas from those of LaVey. The Temple of Set is a vital and viable organization with dozens of senior initiates around the world and scores of local groups, called Pylons, in North America, Europe, and Australia. It has been one of Aquino's most remarkable achievements that he has fashioned an organization that is not a "one-man operation," as such affairs usually are. Much more than with the Church of Satan, the shape of the Temple of Set has been influenced by a number of its initiates over the years. Early in the Temple's history, the leadership was assumed for a time by someone other than its founder. With regard to occult organizations, such a development was almost unprecedented. Subsequently, the High Priesthood has been held by three individuals other than Aquino.

Although Aquino is a highly qualified intellectual, holding a Ph.D. in Political Science from the University of California, and a man of numerous other accomplishments in the objective universe, he also brings various purely magical qualities to the pursuits of the transcendental branch of the left-hand path. Whereas Anton LaVey tended to gravitate mostly toward the practice of "lesser magic," Aquino's practical application of what he calls "greater black magic" returns the technology of magic to the intellectual levels it enjoyed millennia ago.

THE SAGA OF RA-EN-SET

The life of Michael Aquino is perhaps deceptively open and unmysterious. In sharp contrast to the shady background of his mentor LaVey, many of whose "shadows" have been artfully painted in as if they were part of a Caligari film set, Aquino's life has been very public and well documented. The mystery exists where mysteries thrive best: in the hidden interior of the psyche.

Influences

The short biography that follows will show the reader some of the many "institutional" influences on the shaping of Michael Aquino's comprehensive self. These have ranged from the Boy Scouts to the stock market, from the Green Berets to the Church of Satan, and from the University of California to the Academy of Magical Arts. From these and other institutions, he seems to have gleaned qualities that have found their way into the vision of the Temple of Set.

A list of thinkers and writers who helped shape Aquino's inner landscape, such as we have for Anton LaVey, would be interesting. No such synopsis has been published, but through a combination of analysis and conversation, a partial body of such influences can be put together.

At the top of such a list would appear the name of Anton LaVey, who was Aquino's magical mentor (or "magical father," one might say) from 1968 to 1975, and in many ways beyond that time. LaVey and the Church of Satan acted as a catalyst that put many divergent elements of the still young Michael Aquino's thoughts—existentialism, magic, political science—into a meaningful and practical form. The influence of LaVey on Aquino's ideas is usually quite obvious because Aquino himself is so much aware of it. His own mammoth written study entitled *The Church of Satan* is a testament to LaVey's philosophy.

Another important "mentor" would be Aleister Crowley, whom Aquino never met, of course, but who has had a direct and profound effect on his magical and philosophical development. Crowley's shortcomings, as seen from the Satanic and left-hand-path perspective, are not glossed over, but Crowley's contributions to the style, philosophy, and theory of magick have been digested and synthesized in Aquino's system in ways LaVey was uninterested in doing. Aquino sometimes sees himself in the magical legacy of the Beast, calling himself the Second Beast of Revelation (Revelation 13:11).

Aquino's third mentor died well over 2,000 years ago, but his shadow has been cast over Western thought for as many solstices: Plato. The core of Aquino's cosmology is solidly Platonic. In referring to the ancient Hellenic master's ideas he follows in the magical traditions of the Hermeticists and Renaissance magicians. Most would-be magicians since the Renaissance have, however, relied on "pre-digested" forms of Platonic thought, which has diluted their precision. Aquino returns to the source for a fresh synthesis and forges an alloy with the gold of Plato's sun.

Other influential shapers of his thought would include a number of writers. John Fowles's novel *The Magus* has helped shape Aquino's philosophy and ideas on initiatory development on many subtle levels. It is a book to which he often refers in his own writings. More romantically, Aquino cites Jules Verne's *20,000 Leagues under the Sea* as an early model for some of his ideas and predilections. Captain Nemo is the near-perfect artificial model for a lord of the left-hand path: he is isolated in a world of his own creation (the Nautilus), yet he is free to roam and interact in a seemingly omnipotent way with the worlds around him.

There are, of course, dozens of other thinkers and writers who have had some influence on Aquino's magical philosophy. He fully shares these with initiates of the Temple of Set by means of the Temple's extensive 24-category, nearly 300-title, annotated reading list, which is a part of a publication called *The Crystal Tablet*. Other well-represented writers on that list include P. D. Ouspensky, Friedrich Nietzsche, Eric Hoffer, H. P. Lovecraft, Thomas Szasz, R. A. Schwaller de Lubicz, and John Dee.

This reading list itself shows the breadth of Aquino's Setian interests. It contains topics on ancient Egypt, Satanism, historical and contemporary works on occultism, Aleister Crowley, the Enochian system of John Dee, Pythagoreans, sex in magic, fascism and magic, cybernetics, good and evil, life and death, magical geometry, parapsychology, space exploration, as well as vampirism and lycanthropy.

THE LIFE OF THE SECOND BEAST

And I beheld another beast
coming up out of the earth;
and he had two horns like a lamb,
and he spake as a dragon.
(REVELATION 13:11)

Michael A. Aquino was born on October 16, 1946. His father, Michael, was an Italian-born investment broker and his mother, Betty Ford, was an accomplished artist who had studied sculpture in the studio of Georg Kolbe in Germany during the 1930s.

Concerning his own birth, Aquino would write in a commentary to the magical text entitled *The Book of Coming Forth by Night:*

> Collectors of magical happenstance may take note of the following concerning the persona of Michael Aquino: He was born in 1946, precisely nine months after a Working by Crowley's California disciples to create a homunculus per a secret instruction of Crowley's to the IX degree of his Ordo Templi Orientis. He was also born dead, raising the question of the nature of the force inhabiting his subsequently revived body. On his chest he bears the same whorled swastika of hair born by Crowley and Buddha, and his eyebrows have always naturally curled upward into the horns described in the Biblical Book of Revelation (13:11). . . . He has taken the name of the Prince of Darkness as a part of himself: Ra-en-Set "He who Speaks as Set."[3]

Another and perhaps more sinister "magical happenstance" is that Aquino's day of birth is the same date upon which the principal defendants at the Nuremberg tribunal were hanged.

The young Aquino spent his early years in San Francisco, but went to high school in Santa Barbara. He was active in the Boy Scouts of America, and in 1965 was named National Commander of the Eagle Scouts.

After high school, Aquino took advantage of a number of scholarships to attend the University of California at Santa Barbara. Although he had a nomination to West Point, he decided the UCSB would afford him more freedom in the course of studies he wished to pursue.

In June of 1968, Aquino graduated from the university with a B.A. in political science. Shortly thereafter, he was to leave for a year's assignment at Fort Bragg, North Carolina. On a visit to San Francisco about a week after his UCSB graduation, Aquino happened upon the premiere of the film *Rosemary's Baby* where he just caught a glimpse of Anton LaVey as he left the theater.

Aquino spent his tour of duty at Fort Bragg with the 82nd Airborne Division as a cavalry officer and then a PSYOP/Special Forces officer with the JFK Special Warfare Center.

While on leave in San Francisco in March of 1969, he attended a lecture and Working at the Black House. Upon meeting LaVey, Aquino was struck with the man's charm, sincerity, and most of all, his engaging smile. The information he gathered on the Church was interesting enough for him to join soon thereafter.

Back at Fort Bragg, Aquino began performing his first Satanic rituals, sometimes with his fellow officers participating.

From the time of his joining to the time of his eventual resignation from the Church of Satan in 1975, Aquino was in almost constant contact with Anton and Diane LaVey, as well as with John Ferro, LaVey's chief lieutenant at the time.

In June of 1969, Aquino embarked on a tour of duty in Vietnam with the 6th PSYOP Battalion in III Corps Tactical Zone, South

Vietnam. In this capacity, among other things, he was engaged in experiments to disorient Vietcong and North Vietnamese soldiers by using amplified sounds—sometimes complete with "demonic screams"—blaring from helicopters flying over their heads. On return trips from the jungle, he would play rock music. This unintentionally led the troops to believe these operations were intended to disorient the enemy with the weird tones of the Jefferson Airplane.

In the fall of that year, Aquino began work on his first Satanic piece of writing, later published in installments in *The Cloven Hoof* as "The Satanic Ultimatum."[4] He was elevated to the level of Warlock II° upon the completion of his examinations in February of 1970.

Through his readings of Milton's *Paradise Lost,* Aquino felt inspired to write another work entitled *The Diabolicon.* This manuscript was created under the most difficult of combat circumstances; part of it was even destroyed at one point by enemy fire. For Aquino, there was something different about the way *The Diabolicon* was written: "As I wrote the sequential passages, I seemed to sense, rather than determine what they should say."[5] By the middle of March, the manuscript was finished and sent off to the High Priest. LaVey quickly responded: "I received *The Diabolicon* safely. It is indeed a work which will have a lasting impact. It is done in an ageless manner and with complete awareness. . . . [Y]ou may be assured it will assume a meaningful place in the Order." The High Priest used it at once in Workings held at the Black House.[6]

Upon his return from Vietnam, on the night of the summer solstice in June of 1970, Aquino was ordained to the Priesthood of Mendes in the Church of Satan by Anton LaVey in a ceremony held in the ritual chamber of the Central Grotto in San Francisco.

From shortly after his ordination until 1973, Aquino was stationed at Fort Knox in Kentucky. During that time he was deeply involved in the day-to-day administration of the Church of Satan "in the field." In those days, the Church was well populated with enthusiastic and sometimes "wild" characters.

In April of 1971, Aquino was asked by LaVey to write a new introduction to *The Satanic Bible,* which was about to go into its seventh printing with Avon, as well as being published in hardback by University Books. The resulting text appeared in the seventh to eleventh printings of the Bible.[7]

After the release of *Rosemary's Baby,* horror films about the devil and Satanists became the rage. A small company wanted to do a "devil worship" film in Louisville, and so made contact with Aquino, who was by then somewhat known in the area for his unusual religious beliefs. They wanted him to be a technical advisor. The result was that Aquino rewrote the concluding ritual sequence and lent some of his ritual equipment to give the scene some authenticity. The final product can be seen in *The Asylum of Satan*—a "grade-Z" horror flick with a grade-A ritual text.

In that same month, Aquino assumed the role of editor of *The Cloven Hoof,* which allowed LaVey to concentrate on other matters. Michael Aquino remained the editor of *The Cloven Hoof* until his resignation from the Church in 1975, and was responsible for the bulk of that journal's contents during the time between the end of 1971 and the middle of 1975. He was also chiefly responsible for getting the regional Conclaves together.

Anton LaVey recognized the special contribution Aquino was making to the Church and to Satanic philosophy in general when he named Aquino to the IV° (Magister Caverni) in a letter written in December of 1971. Along with the letter came a personally prepared certificate, which read in part: "By the authority of Satan, and We, His Exarch on the Terrestrial Plane . . ." This statement, among others, was clearly indicative to Aquino of LaVey's attitude at that time toward the character and essence of Satan.

As LaVey was preparing a volume to be entitled *The Satanic Rituals,* he asked Aquino to furnish material for a pair of "Lovecraftian" rituals and for a portion of the "Adult Baptism" to be included in the book. By early in 1972, Aquino was finished with the texts for the forthcoming book. For the Lovecraft-inspired rituals, he wrote the introductory sections as well as the rituals themselves, inventing the "Yuggothic language" in a totally artificial way after writing the English versions of the rites. He would later recount the story of the genesis of these rites in the May 1977 issue of the Lovecraftian fanzine *Nyctalops.*[8] It should be noted that Aquino composed the texts as a service to the Church and as a favor to his mentor, and received no royalties for his contribution.

By mid-1972, Aquino had finished his tour of duty in Kentucky and had moved back into civilian life in Santa Barbara where he began to pursue graduate degrees in political science and to work as an account executive at an investment firm. This also began a period in which he was the chief writer of lengthy articles appearing in *The Cloven Hoof,* which had been expanded from a newsletter to a bound digest format.

In the summer of 1973 Aquino was elevated by LaVey to Magister Templi level of IV°—the highest level within the Magistry and a level previously unattained by any other member of the Church of Satan.

For the next two years, Aquino continued in his role as the editor and chief contributor to *The Cloven Hoof,* and was certainly the Church official most responsible for dealing with the sometimes tumultuous membership "in the field."

In the summer of 1975, Aquino received copy from the LaVeys to be included in the upcoming issue of *The Cloven Hoof.* The text clearly stated that degrees in the Church of Satan could be awarded on the basis of financial or other types of contributions to the Church. This was immediately seen as a clear departure from LaVey's previous and exhaustive statements on the nature of the Satanic priesthood as he had envisioned it (see chapter 9). Aquino, assuming it to be some sort of mistake, wrote to the LaVeys, and received the curt command to print the text as they had written it. At that point, Aquino felt that the "Infernal Mandate" (as Aquino termed it) of Anton LaVey, as Exarch of Hell, had been broken. On June 10, 1975, Aquino sent a letter to LaVey announcing his resignation from the Church of Satan.[9]

In an atmosphere of crises, Michael Aquino, using his IV° prerogative of invoking the Prince of Darkness, called upon him on the night of the summer solstice (June 21–22)—and, according to Aquino, he came forth. The result of that Working of greater black magic was a text called *The Book of Coming Forth by Night.* In some ways, it might be seen as being similar to Crowley's *Book of the Law,* and reference to that book is made in *The Book of Coming Forth by Night.* But in fact the results of Aquino's Working are dissimilar in style and content to that of Crowley. The text has been the object of continual commentary by Aquino in the years since its reception.

In *The Book of Coming Forth by Night,* Michael Aquino is named to the V° as the Magus of the Word *Xeper* (pronounced "kheffer"). Xeper is an ancient Egyptian term. It literally means "to become; to be; to come into being." Aquino himself summarizes the magical meaning of the Word as the "transformation and evolution of the Will from a human to a divine state—by deliberate, conscious, individual force of mind."[10] At the same time, the contents of the book provide for the establishment of the Temple of Set and the transference of the "Infernal Mandate" from the Church of Satan to the Temple of Set.

After being informed of these magical developments, about a hundred members of the Church of Satan resigned that organization to become the founding body of the Temple of Set. By October of 1975, the Temple had been incorporated as a religious institution in the State of California.

As High Priest of the new organization, Aquino encouraged the widespread development of the organization and the maximal development of individual initiates within the Temple, even in ways independent of his own ideas. The Temple of Set grew steadily through its first five-year period as Aquino worked constantly on developing Setian philosophy and encouraging communication among Setian initiates. The Temple's journal, *The Scroll of Set,* was founded and continues today as the main forum for the exchange of Setian ideas.

During this same period between 1975 and 1980, Aquino continued a course of studies in graduate school at the University of California at Santa Barbara that culminated in his receiving of a Ph.D. in political science in 1980.

On the ides of March, 1979, Aquino took the oath of the

Ipsissimus, VI°. Synchronously with this event, a V° member of the Temple of Set, Ronald K. Barrett, known by the magical name Anubis, was nominated to become the High Priest of Set. This would in effect retire Aquino from the position of head of the organization he had founded in 1975. This step is almost unheard of in the history of "occult" organizations. Usually the leaders of such groups are leaders precisely because they wish to gain and hold on to some kind of power, real or imagined. With this move, Aquino objectively proved that he was different. He had founded an organization and had seen it develop to a point where he felt comfortable handing the reins over to another.

From the middle of 1979 to the middle of 1982, Barrett was the High Priest of the Temple of Set. During that time, many changes were made in the style and tenor of the Temple teachings, which is usually to be expected when a new titular head of such a group is installed, and especially one animated by a magical Word different from that of the founder. Most of these changes made the Temple more like other occult groups, with the same sort of foibles that similar groups would have. For example, Anubis instituted a policy by which all present Adepts would have to take a II° exam, similar to the type administered in the Church of Satan, in order to retain their degrees. Future Adepts would have to take the test as well.

The chief contribution made by Anubis to Temple lore is his magical Word *Xem,* "a state of Being," which was supposed to connote the "perfected man," the progressive target(s) or aim(s) of Xeper. Some in the Temple of Set today still study the ramifications of Xem, while others consider it apocryphal and largely irrelevant to present Temple directions.

In May of 1982, Anubis resigned from the Temple of Set. By the end of the turmoil surrounding this resignation, the membership of the Temple was down to a mere 30–35 initiates.

After Aquino had received his Ph.D. from the UCSB, his credentials allowed him to become a lecturer and eventually adjunct professor of political science at Golden Gate University in San Francisco from 1980 to 1986. The courses he taught there included Ancient Political Theory, Medieval and Modern Political Theory, United States Foreign Policy, Comparative Political Systems, and Dynamics of Western Culture. During this same period, he resumed active duty in the U.S. Army and was stationed at the Presidio. This is also the period in which he undertook his encyclopedic work on the history of the Church of Satan.

In the wake of the crises of 1982, Aquino was asked to resume his position as High Priest of the Temple of Set. He held this office continuously until 1996.

The early 1980s were spent in the slow rebuilding of the Temple. In 1982, while on a trip to Europe, Aquino visited Schloss Wewelsburg, an early seventeenth-century Westphalian castle that had been used as the ceremonial headquarters of Himmler's SS. On the night of October 19, he was able to gain private access to the "ritual chamber," the so-called Hall of the Slain, in the tower of the castle. There he performed the now famous—or infamous—Wewelsburg Working. As a result of events of that night, a new Order of the Trapezoid was instituted as a formal order within the Temple of Set, and Aquino became its Grand Master (Aquino referred to himself more specifically as the "second" Grand Master of the order, with Anton LaVey being acknowledged as the first).

From the middle of the next year, Aquino began to produce *Runes,* the journal of the Order of the Trapezoid. This contained much of his magical thought for the period he edited the journal (until 1986).

From the latter part of 1986 to the end of 1987, Aquino was stationed in Washington, DC, where he attended the National Defense University and George Washington University, receiving a Masters of Public Administration at the latter institution.

The Tree in the North

In May of 1986, the ABC television news program *20/20* aired a segment on "Satanic crime." This was the first highly visible sign of a growing tide of paranoia sweeping the country concerning "Satanic cults." In so many ways, this phenomenon was just the latest manifestation of a tradition going back to the paranoid fantasies of the Romans regarding the Christians, and eventually the Christians regarding everyone else, especially the Jews and other "heretics." The newly refurbished conservative/medieval values of the American religious right coalesced in an alliance with therapists and marginal police officials to form a new inquisition or witch-hunt.*

In all this the San Francisco Police Department seems to have been rather in the hot-seat since that city was the headquarters of the two major Satanic organizations in the country, yet the police "weren't doin' anythin' about it!" By October of 1986, the police had collected a false accusation from an army chaplain against Michael and Lilith Aquino that they had molested a child in San Francisco sometime during September or October of that year. Apparently they did not even check into the facts enough to discover that both Michael and Lilith Aquino were in Washington, D.C., at that time! But then again, when have witch-hunters worried about facts?

On the evening of August 14, 1987, a variety of police officials descended on the Aquinos' residence in San Francisco and "raided" it, confiscating various Temple documents, video tapes (mostly Disney productions!), and other equipment. It just so happened that the Aquinos were at home that evening, preparing for the upcoming Set VIII Conclave in Hollywood.

This was the beginning of protracted legal dealings with the police and courts. Aquino quickly nicknamed the whole episode "The Tree in the North," based on a passage in the Tenth Part of a text entitled *The Word of Set* (further discussed below), which reads: "The threat of your destruction grows as a tree in the north . . . it poisons the very air with its stench." The final outcome was that no actual charges were ever brought (because there was no evidence) and the police officials involved—at least one of whom had touted herself as an "expert on occult crime"—were eventually reprimanded for their "overzealousness."

*See the appendix, "The Urban Legend of Satanicism."

But that end did not come until years of harassment and thousands of dollars in lawyers' fees later.

But those who tended the "Tree in the North" for some time got what they wanted: a stench. The mere fact that Aquino had been "investigated" would be insinuatingly used in the media on countless occasions with no regard for the facts.

On another level, however, the police/therapy/church war on the Temple of Set backfired. The publicity generated by the accusations brought ever-increasing media attention to Dr. Aquino and the Temple of Set. Some of the media even allowed a bit of a balanced view to emerge. The ultimate result was that the Temple enjoyed a period of unprecedented growth in the late 1980s and early 1990s.

The Flourishing of the Temple

In spite of the "Tree in the North" problems, the Temple of Set flourished both domestically and abroad. Local Pylons were established in England, Germany, Finland, and Australia. Domestically, local Pylons grew from what had at one point been a single one functioning in Texas to thirty-five in every part of the country in 1996.

The various orders that exist within the Temple also began to function well during this most recent phase. In 1987, Aquino passed the Grand Mastery of the Order of the Trapezoid on to his associate Polaris. This allowed Aquino, as High Priest, to concentrate more exclusively on Temple-wide concerns for the next several years.

In 1990, Aquino retired from active duty as a Lieutenant Colonel in the U.S. Army and went on inactive duty in the Reserve. At the same time, he returned to his home in San Francisco to manage the family estate and to devote himself more intensively to the affairs of the Temple of Set.

One of the most important developments in the Temple of Set in the ensuing years was the proclamation of Working II in February, 1993. This working of greater black magic by the High Priest was designed to reorient the Temple of Set toward the future without the inherited negative baggage from the "Church of Satan days," and to reorganize the social bodies within the Temple to meet the Initiatory needs of the members more effectively. Additionally, Aquino has worked tirelessly to bring the Temple of Set into the age of the Internet and electronic communications.

On the Spring Equinox of 1996, Don Webb was Recognized to the Degree of Magus with the Word *Xeper,* further refined as "I have Come into Being." Later that same year, he was appointed High Priest of Set, and Michael Aquino retired from that office for the second time.

Michael Aquino has become a modern exemplary model for a lord of the transcendental branch of the left-hand path. He is in fact what so many "occult leaders" of the past have aspired to be—an academically trained intellectual who nevertheless is capable of inspired states of consciousness and direct communication with a preternatural entity. Aquino has proven himself to be a talented and capable organizer and director of Temple affairs, but what sets him apart from many would-be occult leaders of the latter half of the twentieth century is the unswerving dedication to the principles according to which he directs his will. Here it is not a matter of seeming to be more than one is, but rather indeed being even more than one seems. This is the most royal, and the most forgotten, of all arts and sciences.

HISTORY OF THE TEMPLE OF SET UNDER VARIOUS HIGH PRIESTHOODS

Don Webb served as High Priest of the Temple of Set from 1996 to 2002. Webb was already well known as a writer of fiction that ranged from the avant-garde to sci-fi and horror. In 1996, he began to venture out into the realm of the esoteric with a series of books: *The Seven Faces of Darkness* (1996), *Uncle Setnakt's Essential Guide to the Left Hand Path* (1999), and *Mysteries of the Temple of Set* (2004). These works brought Setian philosophy into the public eye as nothing else had before. With Webb's emphasis on the initiatory uses of scholarly explorations of the substance of the ancient Setian cult in Egypt, the Temple of Set became even more intellectually oriented. Under Webb, the Temple expanded its network and interactions between and among members worldwide.

A strange turn of fate came about in 2002 when Zeena, the daughter of Anton LaVey, was named High Priestess of the Temple of Set. Zeena had had a rather public falling-out with her father in the early 1990s and along with her partner, known as Nikolas Schreck, she had joined the Temple. They both rose through the degree system fairly rapidly, as might have been expected. Zeena would have embodied a sort of poetic "return to the source" on one level at least, and represent a reforging of the circle broken in 1975. But it was not to be. Within just a few weeks of her election, Zeena resigned from both the High Priesthood and the Temple altogether.

This necessitated Michael Aquino once more to take the High Priesthood and see the Temple through another set of growing pains. This interim was quickly over and in 2004 Magistra Patricia Hardy was elected as High Priestess.

The fact that in the more than thirty-five year history of the Temple of Set it has had seven different terms of the High Priesthood speaks perhaps to the character of its founder as one comfortable with political science as well as to an actualization of the idea that the initiatory system itself has a certain real vitality. Aquino has been able to watch these developments in his own lifetime and can take some satisfaction in the idea that the institution he nurtured will survive his passing. Nevertheless, such transitions are historically fraught with monstrous uncertainties.

SOURCES FOR THE STUDY OF THE TEMPLE OF SET

One of the main problems for those outside the Temple who wish to gain an understanding of what the Temple is all about, is the fact that none of its documents have (as yet) been published in a commercial way. All of its official documents, which would be considered as primary, are reserved for the use of its members. However, Dr. Aquino has always been forthcoming with legitimate investigators when asked about certain Temple teachings, and in such cases he has generally provided them with copies of the primary documents for research purposes. The main reason these documents are reserved for members only is to keep their contents flexible. Things can be added, deleted, and updated as needed. With such a policy, however, there might be a temptation to always treat such fluid documents in the manner of the Ministry of Truth in Orwell's *1984,* where the past is altered to fit present-day doctrines. Thus far, this temptation appears to have been avoided.

The Jeweled Tablets of Set

For each of the first four degrees within the Temple of Set structure, there is a volume of documents. These are collectively known as *The Jeweled Tablets of Set.* The document all I° Setians receive upon entry into the Temple is *The Crystal Tablet of Set.* It contains all of the most important texts of the Temple. Most of the contents of *The Crystal Tablet* are authored by Michael Aquino. The twin core of this document consists of sections entitled "Black Magic in Theory and Practice" and "The Book of Coming Forth by Night: Analysis and Commentary." The first is a sober and straightforward introduction to the whole idea of magic and its successful working. The second contains all the inspired texts penned by Aquino's hand. Another part of *The Crystal Tablet* contains the Temple's extensive annotated reading list.

Upon recognition to the II°, the initiate of the Temple may acquire a copy of *The Ruby Tablet,* which is a mammoth collection of documents (several hundred pages in length and growing) written by a wide variety of initiates within the Temple.

Available to the priesthood only is *The Onyx Tablet,* which contains some of Aquino's ideas and reflections on the true character of Set's priesthood, both ancient and modern.

The Magistry has its *Sapphire Tablet,* which is restricted to acquisition by members of the Temple of Set holding the IV°.

The rationale behind restricting access to the various *Tablets* is not so much about keeping "degree secrets" as it is about helping initiates remain as focused as possible on the Work of their particular degree. It is rather like not having freshmen physics students ponder the problems of quantum foam or chaos theory. Such exposure is simply thought to be "dangerous" to a student's rational development, as essential problems are taken out of sequence. This can end up just frustrating the student.

All members of the Temple receive a bimonthly journal called *The Scroll of Set.* This publication has been edited by perhaps a dozen people over its history and contains articles written by Setians of all degrees. It is actually a forum for all Setians to express themselves, rather than an organ for the leadership to communicate with the membership. In other words, it is not just a sounding board for the High Priest's latest ideas

The various orders within the Temple of Set (which are discussed below) also have their own journals or newsletters published at different intervals. These are often highly specialized for the work being done within that particular order and are not automatically made available to all members of the Temple. The most active of these journals are: *Trail of the Serpent,* published by the Order of Leviathan; *Nightwing* and *The Vampyre Papers,* produced by the Order of the Vampyre; and *Runes,* generated by the Order of the Trapezoid.

In more recent years, the published works of one-time High Priest Don Webb provide insights into the modalities of Setian thought from a source other than that of the first High Priest.

The Inspired Works of Michael Aquino

Besides this voluminous body of work by many authors within the Temple of Set, there are a number of texts that enjoy a special status in Temple teachings. These are the works by Aquino that have had a pronounced noetic component yet which seem to have been written with the aid of something other than the mundane mind of Michael Aquino.

The first of these texts is *The Diabolicon,* which was written over a three-month period in the war zones of South Vietnam during Aquino's early Church of Satan days. This text is in the form of prose-poetic statements from eight demonic entities: Satan, Beelzebub, Azazel, Abaddon, Asmodeus, Astaroth, Belial, and Leviathan. In this work, the Black Flame is first cited as a metaphor for the Gift of the Prince of Darkness: the Promethean fire of divine consciousness. *The Diabolicon* is, of course, written in the "Satanic idiom," yet in it the Platonic directions of Aquino's train of thought are already becoming clear. Aquino provided the text of *The Diabolicon* to Anton LaVey, but it was never released more widely in the context of the Church of Satan. It only found distribution within the Temple of Set in 1976.

Over a two-month period in the summer of 1974, while still active in the Church of Satan, Aquino undertook a Working similar to that of *The Diabolicon.* The result is what came to be called "The Ninth Solstice Message," which is addressed to Anton LaVey. On one level, it is a panegyric to LaVey, but on another level, it presages an upheaval in the order of the Church of Satan and contains apocalyptic undertones:

> My Age has begun, and I am come forth to uphold my bond with mankind. Yet I shall not illuminate all, nor even many—but a few. I seek the Elect, who in turn seek me. Man the god shall arise only from the ashes of man the beast—The blood is the life.
>
> Let the institutions of the Church of Satan be discarded. Their time has passed. Their time is past, and they have served my purposes honorably. Seek now the Elect, as the darkness draws near. No longer shall all who approach my Church find welcome—They shall grasp at empty air. Only the Elect shall find what they seek.

In retrospect, this text prefigures Aquino's departure from the Church of Satan and the establishment of the Temple of Set.

Another inspired text referred to directly in *The Book of Coming Forth by Night* is *The Word of Set.* This is the body of evocatory magical texts used by the Elizabethan magician Dr. John Dee. These texts are often referred to as the "Enochian Keys." After extensive magical work with the Enochian Keys, as used by LaVey and others, Aquino determined that it was impossible to treat the texts as being written in a cipher code or as an artificial language. Over a period of several years he magically worked on English "translations" of these texts. He finished this undertaking on April 13, 1981, an anniversary of Dee's initial Enochian Working.[11]

Finally, and most importantly, there is *The Book of Coming Forth by Night.* The book itself is only about 1,500 words in length. The chief functions of the book are to transfer the so-called Infernal Mandate, and to introduce the magical principle of Xeper, upon which the new Temple of Set was to be founded. In the text, written over a two-hour period on the night of June 21 to 22, 1975, an entity identifying itself as Set speaks directly to Michael A. Aquino. In the words of the text, many if not all of the basic cosmological and theological precepts of the Temple of Set are expressed.

The Book of Coming Forth by Night is not thought of as "holy writ" by Aquino himself—not as the Christian thinks of his Bible, or as the typical Thelemite thinks of *Liber AL.* His own assessment is that it is the result of a Working of greater black magic—the effectiveness of which can be judged by the results it demonstrates.

At this point, it should be noted that in general such Workings are the prerogative of initiates who have attained to the level of the Magistry as an objective fact, regardless of their organizational affiliation or lack of same. Such "revelations" through a mind less well-trained and disciplined are doubtful in the extreme.

Secondary Sources on the Temple

No systematic studies of the Temple of Set have been produced. Perhaps because of its relative secrecy and its rightly perceived intellectual seriousness, the Temple of Set has daunted most would-be investigators.

Gini Graham Scott's supposed sociological study, *The Magicians,* obscures the name of the Temple by calling it the "Church of Hu" and making up names for the various persons she encountered while working "undercover." This virtually negates its value as a historical document. It must be noted that the less-than-flattering picture she tries to paint of the Temple is one based on observations within the time Anubis was High Priest.

Scott's method is fatally flawed because she, as an admittedly unsympathetic observer, was actually hermeneutically incapable of understanding the real meaning of what was happening around her. She could only observe things from the outside and so any and all of her prejudices were neatly confirmed. This is why the Temple of Set has maintained the rule that no outsiders be allowed to view actual ceremonial Workings: the image of what seems to be happening and the reality of what is actually happening are often two different things. Those who see only images understand nothing.

A more common phenomenon has been unsystematic treatments of the Temple appearing in books that attempt to survey the "Satanic scene." Perhaps because the Temple of Set's ideology is not widely available, it appears that it has been left open to widespread and obviously consciously contrived misrepresentation. Two glaring examples of this misrepresentation are found in Jeffrey Burton Russell's *Mephistopheles* and Arthur Lyons's *Satan Wants You.*

Russell, who was a professor of religion at the University of California at Santa Barbara, and a self-confessed apologist for the Roman Catholic Church, had occasional contact with members of the Temple of Set for a period of time. Some had attended his lectures and even given guest presentations in his classes. He had ready access to Temple material, such as the General Information Letter. Yet even with a wealth of information at his disposal, he chose to write in his book:

> A distinction should be made among "Satanic" groups. Some are merely frivolous, like the so-called Temple of Set with its breathless hedonism in occult trappings . . .
>
> Anton Szandor LaVey founded his Church of Satan in 1966; in 1975 a schism produced the Temple of Set. Their *Satanic Bible* [sic] is a melange of hedonistic maxims and misinformed [!] occultism. Like most groups, LaVey's claims ancient origins; it pretends to arise from the cult of Set (Seth) in ancient Egypt. [sic] For modern Sethians, [sic] the Devil is no fallen angel but a hidden force in nature . . .[12]

I reproduce so much obvious misinformation here simply to show the lengths to which even an ivory-tower scholar is willing to go to create a false impression of the realities of the left-hand path. It is clear from the quoted passage that Russell is both confused on the facts as well as willful in his misrepresentation of the character of Temple teachings (Set as a "force in nature"!). Or maybe his misleading statements are simply the inept product of sheer laziness. In any event, it only casts doubt on the usefulness of all his other books. Faced with these facts, it makes me wonder: just who is the true representative of "radical evil" he is so fond of invoking? As we saw in chapter 7, it is neither Satan nor Wotan who is responsible for the horrors of the Nazi holocaust. If any "god" is to be held accountable, it must be that of the Roman Catholics and Lutherans—the only "god" with the motive, opportunity, and methods to commit the crime. Any other conclusion is simply criminologically untenable.

In the case of Arthur Lyons's book, *Satan Wants You,* disinformation about the Temple of Set seems to have been spread by Lyons acting as an agent for his friend and mentor Anton LaVey. His discussion is inaccurate on almost every count. No one can be that misinformed or confused—not even a journalist! The agenda here was simply to make it appear that the Temple was disintegrating, when in fact it was growing faster than it ever had before.

A more direct presentation of the Temple's philosophy is reflected in Larry Kahaner's *Cults that Kill* (1988). Although Mr. Kahaner had access to no more of the Temple material than any of the other would-be investigators, he made more objective and direct use of it. He allows the Temple documents to speak for themselves, and thus form a contrast with the nonsense being spouted by hysterical "experts" as well as with other would-be "Satanists."

Nevill Drury's *The Occult Experience* (1989), which is a book based on his research for the documentary film of the same name, contains a few well-balanced pages on the Temple of Set. At least Drury demonstrates that he understood the basic message of Aquino and the Temple of Set. He writes, "Their quest for self-hood and individual growth is undoubtedly a mature spiritual approach which takes man beyond mental crutches and the restrictions of dogma directly into the dark infinity of space."[13] He goes on to conclude: "Aquino himself is complex, intellectual and self-assured—convinced, in fact, that his particular type of magical exploration goes beyond the scope of orthodox mysticism and religion. In this respect, he may well be right."[14]

Such objective treatments were rare in the latter years of the twentieth century. The only plausible reason that the Temple of Set has been left open to so many attempts to misrepresent its true character is that it has not chosen to place before the public an official and generally available statement of that character. In such an environment, it seems, unprincipled "professors" and journalists feel freer to make up whatever they want to say about the subject.

THE ORGANIZATIONAL PRINCIPLES OF THE TEMPLE

The true magical authority for the establishment of the Temple of Set is considered to be derived from the mandate given by the Prince of Darkness in the *Book of Coming Forth by Night.* The Temple itself, the collective body of individual initiates (each thought to be a "microcosmic" Temple of Set in his or her own right), is a magical body, but to function effectively in this world the soul needs a body. That body is the corporation called "The Temple of Set, Inc."

In the weeks and months after the magical formation of the Temple of Set in 1975, the founders set about creating a fully functioning legal corporation under the laws of the State of California. It was felt that the "one-man rule" of Anton LaVey had been inappropriate for an association of true black magicians. The bylaws of the Temple of Set would, for example, provide for the expulsion of the High Priest by a vote of the Council of Nine should he betray the trust of the Temple.

As a fully operational nonprofit corporation, the Temple of Set is governed by the High Priest, the Chairman of the Council of Nine along with a voting body of nine councilors, and an Executive Director.

The Temple of Set is the only legally recognized Satanic "church" in the United States. It enjoys full IRS tax exemption as any other "church" would. No one is making any money from the activities of the Temple. In fact, its leaders often spend their own personal funds to finance publications of the Temple or its various orders.

As is made clear in its General Information letter, the Temple can only accept those over eighteen years of age as initiates. The main reason for this is that before that age most are unable to grasp the intellectual content of the Temple of Set philosophy. Temple members generally think that children before that age should be educated secularly and exposed to religion in a theoretical way only. The part of them that is active "religiously," the psyche, is not yet mature enough to be qualified to participate in Setian philosophy or Workings of greater black magic.

THE DEGREE SYSTEM OF THE TEMPLE OF SET

An initiatory grade system is seen as a tool in the philosophy of the Temple of Set. The criteria for recognition to the various levels or degrees are clearly defined on one level, yet remain flexible enough that each member of the priesthood or Magistry responsible for making these recognitions can develop his or her own personal criteria and philosophy about them. In the Temple of Set, initiates are not "initiated" by the Temple or by other members, nor are they "elevated" by means of the authority of those "above" them in the system. Rather it is a matter of potential initiates being given a map and some structural guidelines on how to travel with this map, which consists of the magical theories of the Temple and its initiatory system. Potential initiates then travel—Become—and communicate the results of their Becoming to members of the priesthood.

As a result of the observation of objective changes occurring in initiates in accordance with their wills, and in accordance with the roadmap provided by the theoretical degrees, a member of the priesthood or Magistry is able to recognize the transition from one initiatory state of being to another. It is then the purpose of the institution, which is the Temple, to certify this recognition—and make it a more objective fact. No ritual can make one become an Adept, Priest, or Master—this work must be undertaken on one's own and in one's own unique way. What the Temple does is *recognize* these transitions and states of being.

The Setian degree system is based directly on that of the Church of Satan, and indirectly on that of Crowley's A.'.A.'. and the G.'.D.'.. There are six degrees, each with its special purpose and character:

The Setian (I°) is somewhat of a probationer in the Temple. If one applies to the Temple and is accepted (and most are accepted unless their applications display gross misunderstandings of Setian philosophy or indicate the clear unsuitability of the individual to Temple work) there is a two-year period before the end of which the individual must have been Recognized to the II°. If this has not happened, the individual will be dropped form the Temple roster. The Setian will receive *The Crystal Tablet of Set* and will have access to other sources and resources within the Temple. There is no established Temple doctrine or ritual the Setian must learn in order to "advance."

The progress and the direction of that progress is entirely up to the individual. The Setian is distinguished by a silver Pentagram of Set on a white background.

The Adept (II°) is one who has been recognized by a member of the priesthood (III° and above) as having mastered some forms of magic, as being well versed in the principles of Setian philosophy, and as being a sane and reliable person who will be an asset to him- or herself, as well as to the Temple. Once the Adept has been recognized to the II°, he or she may remain as a permanent member of the Temple with no further official obligations to the Temple. The Adept is free to explore infinitely the depth and breadth of black magic. To aid the Adept magician in this, there is *The Ruby Tablet of Set,* which may now be obtained from the Temple. The Adept is distinguished by a silver Pentagram of Set on a red background.

The Priest/Priestess (III°) crosses a threshold of existence—it is a nonnatural event that an Adept Comes into Being as a Priest of Set. Such an occurrence can only be recognized by members of the Magistry of the Temple (IV° and above). Although different Masters of the Temple may observe different criteria for recognizing the III° status of an individual, what seems to hold them all together is the idea that the Black Flame—the direct and pure essence of the Prince of Darkness—has been made manifest in their beings, in their essences. This manifestation will, of necessity, lead to certain objective and tangible results in the behavior, life, and work of the nascent Priest or Priestess.

In the III°, there begins the transition from a human state to a divine one:

> Priesthood involves the opening of a very special kind of door: the merging of the consciousness, indeed the personality, with that of the Prince of Darkness himself. In this Working the Priest or Priestess in no sense loses personal identity or Self-awareness; rather one's consciousness is augmented, energized, and strengthened by that of Set. [T]he Priest or Priestess . . . is something more than human, something more than the individual whose human visage

> appears before onlookers. [H]e or she is not "possessed," but is rather become a veritable living Temple indwelled by the presence of Set.[15]

It only takes one Master to recognize a member of the III°, but this recognition must also be corroborated by two other members of the Magistry to make it official. The Priest or Priestess is distinguished by a silver Pentagram of Set on a black background.

Beyond the priesthood, it becomes difficult to speak in this format directly of the criteria for recognition. Aquino writes in *The Crystal Tablet:*

> As the Priesthood constitutes a merging of the individual soul with that of Set, so the Magistry constitutes an expansion of that merger to a full apprehension of the Aeon of Set. The Master knows not only the consciousness of Set, but the reach of that consciousness and the resultant view of creation and existence it embraces. All particular phenomena are evaluated, placed, and balanced within the continuum of the Aeon by the Master, and such adjustments in events as the Master makes are for Aeonic purposes . . . [T]he IV° is neither just an administrative promotion nor a reward for distinguished service; it is an initiatory state of being in itself.[16]

Aquino, operating from a left-hand-path perspective, rejects Crowley's hypothesis that upon attaining the grade of Magister Temple the initiate would undergo an "annihilation of the personality" and "absorption in the Universal consciousness."

In the Temple, a Master can only be recognized upon the nomination of the High Priest and confirmation by a majority vote by the Council of Nine. The Magister or Magistra is distinguished by a silver Pentagram of Set against a royal blue background.

The degree of Magus (V°) has only been attained by a handful of initiates in the Church of Satan/Temple of Set tradition. A Magus is a Master of the Temple who has stepped outside the totality of the Aeonic current to alter or modify it in an evolutionary way. This is done by means of a Working Formula, a Word. Theoretically, this could inaugurate a new Aeon, or improve or strengthen the existing one. In any case, the changes will be ones that are counter to preexisting values and will therefore be met with resistance. The implementation of the changes is spoken of as the "Task of the Magus," while the necessity that the Work must proceed against prevailing inertia is described as the "Curse of the Magus." (In this context, it might be noted that after 1975 the Temple of Set philosophy reinterpreted LaVey's use of the word "indulgence" in terms of an Aeonic Word, analogous to Crowley's *Thelema*. This dignity of the word was never formally claimed by LaVey, although he repeatedly summed up his Satanic philosophy in that word.)

In the Temple, a Magus can only be recognized upon the nomination of the High Priest and confirmation by a unanimous vote by the Council of Nine. The Magus is distinguished by a silver Pentagram of Set against a purple background.

The Ipsissimus (VI°) can be described as a "successful Magus": one whose Task has been completed.

> Inherent in such completion is a unique perception of the new Aeonic inertia which has resulted, placing the Ipsissimus at once within and without the Aeon itself. To function as a Ipsissimus he must work to perfect and harmonize not only the created or modified Aeon, but also its entire relationship with preexisting and potential Aeons.[17]

The Magus is best suited to determine for himself when he is ready to take the Oath of the Ipsissimus and be recognized to that grade. Initiates of that grade are distinguished by a silver Pentagram of Set against a gold background.

In practice, this system seems to have worked more or less effectively over the years. It would not seem to be entirely perfect, however. As with everything else truly conscious, it is evolving. What is perhaps most remarkable about it is the level of responsibility "delegated" to the

III° priesthood and to the Magistry for the recognition of Adepts and members of the priesthood respectively.

There are few "hangers-on" in the Temple. The two-year time limit on the I° is one that is enforced. Extensions have been known to be granted, but they must be warranted. As there is no set curriculum in the Temple, recognition must of necessity be based on individual work and initiative. In order to be aware of work of this kind, members of the priesthood must have the time and energy to interact with individual Setians. An unlimited number of I° members of the Temple would soon overburden the system.

One of the most effective tools of Setian initiation is the Pylon. Pylons are local groups of Setians, usually led by a member of the priesthood, who interact with one another both formally and informally and occasionally hold group Workings. The leader of the Pylon is called a Sentinel, who may also be a senior Adept sponsored by a member of the Magistry.

An inherent weakness in the system is that it is only possibly as good as the quality and integrity of the individuals at the higher levels allow it to be. The objective strength of the Church of Satan system, as it is practiced now, is that it focuses on external things, whereas the Temple of Set, true to its cosmology and theology, focuses on subjective matters. It is simply more difficult to work with subjective criteria than it is with objective criteria.

Ultimately, it is clear that the Temple of Set, with its system of degrees, is a tool for initiation. It is not an organization that tries to recruit and retain as many members on its rolls as possible.

ORDERS WITHIN THE TEMPLE OF SET

As a prerogative of the grade of Magister Templi, Crowley had earlier pointed out that those who attain it could form their own orders in harmony with the prevailing Aeonic current. In this spirit, Aquino urged the IV° initiates of the Temple to form their own orders. These were presented at the Set V International Conclave held in Santa Cruz, California, in 1984.

Space prevents me from discussing all of the orders within the Temple of Set, but as their functioning is an important part of the overall workings of the Temple as a whole, they must be discussed at least briefly.

The orders are, for the most part, expressions of the personal works of the Magister or Magistra Templi who is the order's Grand Master. The presence of the order system provides for a potentially infinite number of working environments for individual Initiates in the Temple. As a general policy, Setians may only join an order after they have been recognized to the degree of Adept. This would indicate that their general work in the Temple is at least nominally finished, and that they are ready to specialize in some area of magical study within the orders.

The Order of the Trapezoid officially enjoys no special status, yet has such by virtue of its heritage and destiny. As mentioned above, the order was "reconstituted" as a part of the Temple of Set by Michael Aquino during his now famous Wewelsburg Working in 1982. Prior to that time, it had been a designation for the Council of Nine both within the Church of Satan and the Temple of Set. But with the Wewelsburg Working, the order embarked on its own true mission: the Quest for the Grail of Life.

The Order of the Vampyre holds a special interest among romantic Setians. Fans of the Bram Stoker novel will remember that Count Dracula did not become a vampire in the "usual" way. It was as a result of his initiation into a Satanic sect, or, as Stoker put it, "dealings with the Evil One," and "learning his secrets in the Scholomance."[18]

The Order of Leviathan took as its original guiding principle the first part of the "Statement of Leviathan" in *The Diabolicon,* which reads: "Before God or Angel, Daimon or man, there was Leviathan alone, principle of continuity and ageless existence. By relation and time I have oft been sought, but Leviathan shall yield to none other than the final master of the Universe."[19]

The Order of Setne Khamuast is headed by Don Webb and focuses on the recovery of genuine and authentic magical and initiatory methods of working from ancient Egypt. It delves into the latest scholarly information produced by Egyptologists and attempts to make this information active and vital in an initiatory environment.

One of the most vibrant and unique orders in the Temple is that of Arkte, headed by Maga Lilith Aquino. It focuses on the protection and cultivation of nonhuman animal life. Historically, the Temple had been thought by outsiders to be a system that was somehow hostile to nature, simply because it focused on the fundamental idea that the Gift of Set—human self-awareness of its psyche—was *non*natural. Setians have always, in fact, been great friends of animals. The Order of Arkte has brought this idea into a more formal setting. In some ways, it seems to have its magical cradle in Aquino's Wewelsburg Working, wherein all of life itself was apprehended as a manifestation of the Gift of Set.

THE BLACK MAGICAL UNIVERSE—SETIAN COSMOLOGY

Individual Setian thought begins with logical suppositions and proceeds from them to more magical conclusions based on experience. Aquino states that the worldviews of other religions have perhaps been "aesthetically and/or emotionally attractive" to many in the past, but that "does not make any one of them true—merely popular." It is one of Aquino's essential operating principles that the Setian solution to fundamental problems of cosmology, theology, anthropology, and magic is the only correct one, "after having considered and dismissed the alternatives as untrue in whole or in part."[20] The Setian cosmology is posited as the best possible answer to fundamental philosophical and magical questions given the data available. It remains, however, open to evolution should any fallacy be identified or further data become known.

The application of Ockham's razor—"what can be explained by assuming fewer things should not be explained by assuming more"—is one of the great principles of Setian philosophy. Too often, students in magical schools of thought are off trying to scale "Jacob's Ladder" before they even know how to walk. The science of Setian initiation tries to avoid this situation.

The first assumption is that there exists a universe, which is defined as "the totality of existence, both known and unknown by humanity."[21] Within this internally consistent framework exists the objective universe, which is defined as "the vast expanses of space and the masses of animate and inanimate matter and energy occupying it."[22] This latter concept is what humans perceive as "the (natural) universe," and its laws are the "laws of nature." Beyond this, there exists the subjective universe, the psyche distinguished from the objective universe, which is "both apprehensive (reaching beyond the limits of the objective universe) and creative (enabling one to generate meaning, to initiate existence)."[23] More will be said on this component in the sections below. These are the three assumptions needed to act as building blocks for the black magical theory of the universe.

The discerning student of the history of ideas will see the influence of the cosmology of both Pythagoras and Plato on those of Aquino in many areas. It should be pointed out, too, that Aquino believes many of the ideas of Pythagoras and Plato have been derived, directly or indirectly, from those of Egypt.

The clearest, simplest, and yet most profound symbol of the Setian cosmology is provided by the Pentagram of Set. Aquino discusses this symbol in Appendix 1 of *The Crystal Tablet.* The perfect circle (which is a mathematical function of pi) around the pentagram represents the "mathematical order of the objective universe," while the pentagram itself can be seen as representing the consciousness and rationality inherent in the subjective universe. The fact that its points do not touch the circle signifies "that the Powers of Darkness are not derived from or dependent upon" the natural order. The pentagram is shown with two points upward "to imply change and movement in place of stasis and rest, and also to proclaim the evolutionary dialectic of thesis combined with antithesis to produce synthesis—instead of a foreordained and unavoidable absolute standard."[24]

It should also be noted that ancient Pythagorean depictions of the pentagram showed it most often in the so-called "inverse" position. This was because it was originally seen not as a "star" but as a geometrical figure resulting from the extension of the lines of a perfect pentagon.

In this Setian cosmology, it will be noted there is an inherent "dualism" between nature and "nonnature" that echoes the ancient Greek distinction between physis (nature) and psyche (intellect). This is not the hostile dualism of the Gnostics, but is rather more based on the fundamental existentialist distinction between not-self and self.

This distinction is also projected into the universe as a whole, positing that the objective universe and the subjective universe(s) exist in reality, although we, as human beings, may indeed be unable to perceive the objective universe directly without the medium of the subjective universe.

One thing that is striking about Setian philosophy, beginning with its cosmology, is that one does not have to resort immediately to an "arcane" vocabulary (of the Kabbalah, magick, alchemy, etc.) to understand its premises. The Setian can discuss his philosophy with secular philosophers if he so wishes and be perfectly comfortable. The more arcane concepts are reserved for when they are more rightly used—at the highest levels of magical Work. Basic Setian cosmology provides a theoretical framework sufficient for basic and essential black magical initiatory work; the further complications or elaborations are the work of individuals or orders with some specific need for them.

Also essential to the Setian view of cosmic order is the ancient theory of Aeons. Some of this is drawn from the work of Aleister Crowley on the subject, but other ideas have also gravitated toward the Setian philosophy of Aeons as well. *The Book of Coming Forth by Night* clearly establishes the idea that the year 1966 was the beginning of a New Aeon—one which supersedes the previous Aeon begun in 1904 at Crowley's Cairo Working that resulted in *The Book of the Law.* The Age of Satan lasted only ten years, as an inaugural period leading to the full establishment of the Aeon of Set. In purely Setian terms, the Age of Satan (1966–1975) was the time of Set-HarWer, when Set and his

"Opposite Self" could not be seen as fully articulated from one another. HarWer is Horus of the Crowleyan system. (See below.)

Thus, on one level, the Setian theory of Aeons is in basic accord with Crowley's linear model. But on another level, and based on more research on the tradition of Aeons as used in ancient Hellenistic philosophy, the Setian view becomes less linear, and more "synchronous." The Aeons exist beyond time as we know it, and so do not unfold in a linear fashion like a storybook. But that is the way we usually perceive them in the objective universe.

BEHOLD THE MAJESTY OF SET—SETIAN THEOLOGY

The topic of Setian theology is again a relatively streamlined one. Nothing is posited that is not necessary, but everything responsible for the phenomenon in question is accounted for. Theology is seen to coalesce with cosmology in the Setian system in that to apprehend in any accurate way the true character of the god Set, or any other supposed "god," one ultimately must be able to apprehend the impersonal first forms—or principles—upon which all such constructs are dependent. The Temple of Set is not a neo-Egyptian religion attempting to revive the cultic forms of the ancient worship of the Khemite deity called Set, although this form of the entity in question is undoubtedly the oldest such historical image (see chapter 3). As Set states in *The Book of Coming Forth by Night:* "In Khem I remain no longer, for I am forgotten there, and my house at PaMat-et is dust."[25]

The image of the god Set in ancient Egyptian iconography is that of an unknown (perhaps "imaginary") animal. In this he is unique. All other god-forms, if they have zoomorphic attributes, have those of well-known animals: the hawk, the hippopotamus, the ibis, the jackal, and so on. But the so-called Set-animal is otherwise unknown. This leads us to conclude that perhaps it is a creation of the very faculty that this god gives to mankind: the power to create forms and to apprehend that which lies beyond the natural universe.

In *The Book of Coming Forth by Night,* Set states:

> I am the ageless Intelligence of this Universe. I created HarWer [Horus] that I might define my Self. All other gods of all other times and nations have been created by men. This you know . . . from my manifest semblance, which alone is not of Earth.

Here it becomes clear that Set is Intelligence de-fined, made finite, and given shape by the objective universe (= HarWer), which it created to provide that shape and definition. Aquino himself comments on this passage:

> The Universe as a whole is mechanically consistent, but it does not possess a "God" personality that favors one of its components—such as mankind—above others. The Set-entity, however, is finite intelligence within the Universe and can draw such distinctions. Set is a being operating in disregard of the order of the Universe, not in enforced concert with it.[26]

The image of the principle (first form) of intelligence surrounded by a sea of darkness is the underlying esoteric rationale behind the title "Prince of Darkness." In a speculation that goes beyond standard etymologies, Aquino also holds that historically the name "Satan" was ultimately derived from a special honorific title of Set: Set-hen, which in Egyptian means "the Majesty of Set."[27]

An important and profound difference exists between Aquino's understanding of Set and LaVey's conception of Satan. In many ways, this difference underpins the distinction between the transcendental and immanent branches of the left-hand path. As Aquino pointed out in early Temple of Set writings,[28] in "conventional Satanism" (i.e., that of LaVey and others) there exists a "Satanic paradox," which arises from the conception of Satan as "a force of nature." Satan is somehow derived from or dependent upon God/Nature for his existence, and so remains ultimately subordinate to him/her. The Setian philosophy liberates the

Prince of Darkness from those particular constraints by observing that intelligence is something apart and separate from the mechanical and organic laws of the universe.

It will be recalled from chapter 3 that in the ancient Middle Eastern tradition reflected in the Book of Genesis, demonic forces were seen to have two aspects—one carnal (hence orthodoxy's abhorrence of the physical) and one intellectual (the forbidden fruit). In the esoteric tradition, this fruit is symbolized as a "Dark Fire in the West," derived from a reading of I Enoch, chapter 23.[29]

It must be said that within the Temple of Set, even at the senior levels of initiation, there is a variety of views on the character of the "Set-entity." Some do, in fact, seem to see him as the ancient Egyptian god-form who has survived and been remanifested in the Temple. Others may see him as a personal god-form, who takes some interest on a regular basis in the affairs of his Temple, while some see the image of Set as a convenient symbol for the self, useful in the formulation of magical Workings and for philosophical purposes. Ultimately, however, the view of Set as the first form of the self—the principle of isolate intelligence—seems the simplest and most direct apprehension of the entity. In this sense, Set is ontologically real. From a Setian-Platonic perspective, if we know we exist because we think (i.e., are self-aware), there must necessarily be a "first form" of intelligence from which each of our individual "intelligences" is derived. Set is the general principle; the individual psyche of a member of the Elect is the specific manifestation.

The left-hand path is the path of separation, of nonunion. The first model necessary for this formulation is that of a separate entity, which is distinguished from all that surrounds it. Without this, man lacks awareness—even of his "animal-ness," as Anton LaVey or others of the immanent branch of the path would have it.

In the passage of *The Book of Coming Forth by Night* cited above, HarWer is mentioned as the entity by which—or against which—the Set-entity defines itself as an act of its own will. Originally in Egyptian theology, the gods Horus and Set were one entity: the Hrwyfy, "the one with two faces." Here Set declares that the separation was a willful act of self-definition. The separate HarWer-entity is one that retains some of the self-awareness of the Set-entity, but which is equally a part of the objective universe. This conflicted nature makes HarWer—the Opposite Self of Set—"a strange and fitful presence," whose words are "tinged with . . . inconsistency and irrationality."[30]

The HarWer-entity is supposedly that which dictated *The Book of the Law* to Aleister Crowley in 1904. It is for this reason that Crowley's book is so full of apparent inconsistencies and emotionalism.

The "separation process" between Set and HarWer, described here as being internal to the Set-HarWer entity, is the theological or cosmological equivalent of the rebellion of the angels in heaven in the Judeo-Christian system. The implications are, however, quite different of course. In the Setian view, the "conflict" is implicit and a matter of essence, rather than explicit and a matter of "morality."

The same passage in *The Book of Coming Forth by Night* cited above states that "other gods" have been created by humanity, or actually by the principle of isolate intelligence incarnate in humanity. Aquino comments on this by saying:

> [O]ther gods, whether Egyptian or foreign, are derivative of Set or of the human mind. This does not imply they are "imaginary" in the vulgar sense. The mind is capable of substantive creation; it can give life to stereotypical, archetypical or unique gods or daemons.[31]

This has the net effect of elevating humans to the level of continuing co-creators with Set, which is consistent with the ancient view of humanity revived in the Renaissance.

Although the theology and cosmology of the Temple of Set are extremely important because they provide the road map for initiatory work, it is in the human psyche, in the individual or microcosmic manifestation of these macrocosmic and theological principles, where the real work begins and ends. Ultimately, the Temple of Set does not constitute a theocentric religion, but rather a psychecentric one. This is in the great tradition of the daimon-centered systems of ancient Greece or those of the eldritch north concerning the *fylgjur* (see chapter 3).

THE CHILDREN OF SET— SETIAN ANTHROPOLOGY

Setian philosophy is a psychecentric one, that is, it focuses the attention of the subject (actor) of any act of will back upon the subject or one doing the action. The structure of this subject is called, among other names, the psyche, intellect, soul, *ba* (in Egyptian), and so on. Aquino prefers not to split hairs on the analysis of this structure at this stage. It is sufficient for general purposes to realize the distinction between the part of man that partakes of the objective universe and is ultimately subject to its internally consistent mechanical and organic laws, and the part that constitutes a subjective universe not necessarily constrained by universal laws. This realization must come first. It must then be exercised in the form of acts of will or magic.

THE BLACK FLAME

The human being is seen as possessing a nonnatural component, the psyche, which is logically of nonnatural origin. Consciousness, it is logical to assume, did not arise from nonconsciousness. Aquino also objects to Darwinian theory that has the species evolve slowly over a period of several million years. His objection to this is largely on the grounds that it cannot reasonably account for the rapid development of consciousness in the species.[32] This nonnatural component is referred to as the "Gift of Set." Previously, in *The Diabolicon,* Aquino had identified it as the Gift of Satan/Lucifer. The pure essence of this Gift, and the means by which it was given to human beings, is called the Black Flame.

THE ELECT OF THE TEMPLE OF SET

In technical Setian terms, the "Elect" refers specifically to initiates in the Temple of Set of the II° and above.[33] However, in more general terms, this can refer to those who have realized their separateness from the universal order, and who have thus been selected out by the Prince of Darkness. It is as a tool or instrument for this process that the Temple of Set exists.

The concept of elitism in the Temple of Set was to some extent inherited from the Church of Satan. But Aquino's philosophy has refined the concept further and made it more objective. The very idea of elitism is an antinomian one in our current political climate, in the U.S. at least. Everyone is supposed to be created equal, which is a patently absurd notion.

In the Temple of Set, the initiate can learn to function in an environment that is, at least to some extent, an artificially elite one (in the sense that it is created by the subjective universe). Through this experience, the initiate can learn how to function more objectively in what Aquino calls the "World of Horrors," that is, the world of the noninitiated outside the Temple. True elitism can be recognized, and the lack of it seen clearly wherever it is apparent. Such recognitions are essential to objective work in the world.

The Temple of Set is not an ersatz society for misfits the way so many "occult societies," orders, covens, and so on, are for those who gravitate toward them. The degree system, often criticized by LaVey and others for rewarding behavior within the institution while ignoring "worldly accomplishments," is not an end in itself but rather a magical instrument or tool. The instrument is then to be used, as initiates will, in "worldly accomplishments," or any other accomplishments desired.

One of the most often heard metaphors for the Temple of Set's degree system is the university degree system. And indeed a Ph.D. does not make someone a great scholar in the objective sense; it is merely recognition by a group of qualified individuals that the person in question has the "equipment" to become a great scholar in the objective sense. This does not invalidate or negate the authority of universities to grant such degrees, but it does put that authority objectively into perspective.

It is not the purpose of this book to sink to the level of a "sociological study," but I will note the following from the perspective of one who knows: the senior initiates of the Temple of Set are, almost without exception, persons of significant "worldly accomplishments." This is not because there is a direct link between "advancement" in the degree system and such accomplishments, but rather because those who have worked with the instrument correctly have been able to use it according to their own wills to create the situations in life they desire.

THE GRAIL OF LIFE BEYOND DEATH

The question of the possibility for immortality is a central one in the magical Setian philosophy of Michael Aquino. His work in this area also goes back to his days in the old Church of Satan. In a 1973 issue of *The Cloven Hoof,* he wrote an article entitled "The Secrets of Life and Death," which used as a starting point Alan Harrington's book *The Immortalist.* There the trail ended with Harrington's technological answer involving cryonics.[34]

This article was followed up a decade later by another, entitled "The Secrets of Life and Death: Part II," which appeared in *Runes,* the journal of the Order of the Trapezoid. In this article, Aquino comments:

> The "scientific" argument for the authenticity of the *Book of Coming Forth by Night* hinges upon the notion that the consciousness is conceptually a violation of nature. The Wewelsburg Working goes one step further and asserts that life is conceptually contrary to nature. At first this assertion seems outrageous; after all there is quite a bit of life going on "in nature" as we see it on Earth. But have we found evidence of any life anywhere else? We have not; and the odds

> against life (as we understand it) evolving in any given part of the cosmos are billions and billions to one. Even on Earth, life is a delicate, temporary phenomenon which will cease altogether in another 500 million years.[35]

He further remarks that our own bodies have a rapid rate of cell-death, and that our physical vehicles are replaced many times over in our "natural" lifespans. This and other factors lead him to conclude that life, like consciousness, is not, in fact, dependent on the physical body. This liberates the rational black magician to seek immortality with accordingly nonnatural technologies.

This interest in the continuance of self-awareness after death is shared by all schools of the left-hand path. One entire reading list category in *The Crystal Tablet* is dedicated to this topic. However, within the Temple there is no dogmatic belief or conclusion about the means of attaining, or the character of, any postmortem state.

Besides the Order of the Trapezoid, several Orders within the Temple, including those of the Vampyre and Leviathan, have as central features the quest for the continuance of self-awareness, or immortality.

Aquino's philosophy is largely consistent on the question of immortality. The basic distinction between *soma* (body) and *psyche* (soul) is recognized as a logical and intuitive fact. Interestingly, this distinction has not led to the institutionalized practice of either asceticism or libertinage, such as we saw in Gnostic-derived schools emphasizing the body/soul dichotomy. Setian practice seems to reflect the older, more balanced and individualized attitudes of Hellenic synthesis, harmony, and moderation. A key to this is that the Setian attitude toward the dichotomy is not hostile or moralistic; it is merely realized as fact, as a starting point for further work. It is not an end in itself, nor is the eradication of one or the other a goal. Again, this seems to reflect the most ancient view—one untouched by the moralistic dualism of the Zoroastrians and Judeo-Christians.

SETIAN MAGICAL TECHNOLOGY

Black Magic in Theory and Practice

Those who tread the left-hand path do so using magical technology: the operations of their own wills. In the Setian tradition of Michael Aquino, magic, like everything else, is treated to a thorough analysis and noetic apprehension. Aquino's precise definitions and discussions of magical theory reject over-generalizations such as might be found in the works of Aleister Crowley, who defined magick as "the Science and Art of causing Change to occur in conformity with Will."[36] The real differences between what Aquino defines as white magic and black magic, and between lesser and greater aspects of these methods, make it necessary to keep each type distinct.

From a Setian point of view, the chief problem with Crowley's definition would seem to be the definition of "will." Oftentimes the will of an individual is more illusion, or the result of "mass hypnosis," than many would care to admit.

According to Aquino's analysis presented in his text "Black Magic in Theory and Practice," there are two approaches (natural and non-natural) to the two universes (objective and subjective).[37]

The natural approach to the objective universe is an effort to blend with that universe, to become one with Nature or God. Humans feel themselves to be apart from the natural order (which they are). They often respond to this situation by feeling "sinful" or "out of harmony," and proceed to attempt to integrate themselves into the perceived order. This is the essence of the highest purpose of white magic, whether performed by monotheists or "nature worshippers." This is what one might call conventional religion (the Latin word *religio* literally means "re-connection").

The natural approach to the subjective universe is that of the atheistic objectivists, materialists, or positivists. For them, the subjective universe has no reality except as a source for entertaining (and often profitable) products of the imagination. In this view, the subjective universe is in fact an illusion or unreality. The only value it serves is to provide emotional pleasure (entertainment) or to illustrate the "realities" of the objective universe. Epicureans, Sadeans, Marxists, and to some extent LaVeyans all fall into this category.

The nonnatural approach to the objective universe is that of those who have realized that they indeed stand apart from the objective universe and therefore any attempts to merge with it are pointless and illusory. At that juncture comes the understanding that the objective universe, and things in it, can be used as a tool of the subjective universe. This knowledge allows them to develop techniques for the control (or the powerful influencing) of entities and phenomena in the objective universe in accordance with their will. It is this type of magic at which LaVeyan Satanism excels. This is what Aquino calls lesser black magic. The wise application of these principles requires rigorous ethical training and standards.

The nonnatural approach to the subjective universe is the purview of greater black magic. It is the direct focusing of "the Will of the creative self to adjust features of the subjective universes (personal and others') to the desired state, which may or may not be 'real' in the objective universe."[38] By this method, it is possible to transform the content of the subjective universe and to influence patterns and events in the objective universe. Neither of these abilities is easy to master, however.

Essentially, then, white magic is the submission of the subjective universe to the inherent mechanical or organic patterns of the objective universe, while black magic is the exercise of the subjective universe's (the psyche's) "will to power," to borrow a Nietzschean term.

Aquino sums up the various approaches to the universes with the words:

> One is taught to become expert in natural approaches to the objective universe through conventional education in the social and physical sciences, and in natural approaches to the subjective universe through the arts. The Church of Satan taught the theory and practice of lesser black magic, and the Temple of Set adds to that the theory and practice of greater black magic.[39]

SETIAN WHITE MAGIC

Paradoxical as it might seem, true black magicians may freely use white magic—at least for pragmatic acts of sorcery, and as long as it is done with awareness and understanding. This is a practical form of white magic, not a philosophically consistent one. That is, it is not practiced as a part of a right-hand-path philosophy. Furthermore, it is the kind of magic practiced by most "conventional" magicians, whether they are Christians, Pagans, Thelemites, Chaos Magicians, or even LaVeyan Satanists.

> White Magic is a highly concentrated form of conventional religious ritual. The practitioner seeks to focus his awareness and powers of concentration via an extreme degree of autohypnosis. The technique may be used simply for meditation or entertainment through mental imagery ("astral travel"). Or it may be used to focus the will towards a desired end—a cure, curse, and so on. To accomplish this, the magician envisions a god or daemon with the power to achieve the objective, then concentrates his will into an appeal. The god or daemon then carries out the appeal, more or less effectively—depending on the strength of the magician's subconscious mind to sustain it as a functioning entity.[40]

In practice, this kind of white magic can be put to any use, and have virtually any configuration. Angels, gods, daemons, or spirits could be conjured by the psyche and used as a focus of the will for a variety of purposes. The difference between the committed white magician and the black magician who on occasion uses white magical techniques for practical ends is that the white magician has as his ultimate goal the fusion of his self-awareness with the mechanisms of the universe, whereas the black magician merely uses the techniques for temporary, critical, and pragmatic ends. White magic is simply easier and more flexible to use than black magic, and requires less training and a lower level of essential "being" to operate.

It was Anton LaVey's acceptance of the assumption that "black magic" was either "evil" magic, or magic using "demons" instead of angels, or the like, which led him to conclude that there is no difference between "black" and "white" magic.

At the highest level of Setian understanding of the will, all magic is black magic because the fully articulated and aware will (or psyche) will neither desire nor need techniques that aim to lead it, even temporarily, into a state of illusory "union" with the objective universe.

THE PRACTICE OF LESSER BLACK MAGIC

As a general rule of practice, the Setian, like the LaVeyan Satanist, will not use greater (black) magic when lesser means could be more rationally employed to gain the same ends. (Magic itself should in fact only be used when natural means are not sufficient.) Aquino defines lesser black magic as "the influencing of beings, processes, or objects in the objective universe by the application of obscure physical or behavioral laws."[41]

Perhaps the key to understanding the practice of lesser black magic is the fact that it works entirely through instruments in the objective universe, which must be perceived by any targeted subjective universes (the minds of others) through their five sense organs. Lesser black magic works largely in and through the world of five senses and three dimensions.

On one level, this is little more than the "trivial pursuits" of grammar, rhetoric, and logic as taught by the ancients: it is a way of effectively communicating your desires to others that they will wish to harmonize their wills with yours. It can be seen as the art and practice of "winning friends and influencing people." What keeps it a black magical category, then, is the level of consciousness or self-awareness the magician brings to the operation. Without the awareness of the dichotomy between the subjective universe of the operator and the objective universe in which the operator is working, the black magical perspective or focus can be lost.

Almost the entirety of the previous chapter on the Church of Satan and the philosophy of Anton LaVey is a treatise on the development and practice of a system of lesser black magic.

THE PRACTICE OF GREATER BLACK MAGIC

In Aquino's treatise on "Black Magic in Theory and Practice," greater black magic is defined as "the causing of change to occur in the subjective universe in accordance with Will. This change in the subjective universe will cause a similar and proportionate change in the objective universe."[42] According to Setian theory, in contrast to white magic, "Black Magic involves no autohypnosis or conditioning of the mind to make it receptive to subconscious imagery. Rather it is a deliberate and conscious effort to force the mind outward—to impact upon and alter the 'laws' of the mechanical Universe."[43]

Black magic is the function or technique for those philosophically aligned with the aims of the left-hand path. It might be said that black magic (as defined by Aquino) is synonymous with the practice of the left-hand path itself.

In *The Book of Coming Forth by Night,* it is written: "Now let the Setian shun all recitation, for the text of another is an affront to the Self."[44] This points up the enigmatic character of true black magic, when viewed from the outside. Such operations cannot be "seen," nor can they be reduced to recipes, formulas, and rituals. They are beyond the mechanical parameters implied by these categories. True black magic requires no props or symbols, no ritual or invocations—although certain things may be used to bring the subjective universe (= psyche) into a state of isolation in preparation for a true working of greater black magic.

The psyche is the god, or the closest thing to a god, to which most Setians have direct access. It is primarily for this reason that the Setian also shuns the use of drugs or narcotics of any kind. Such substances hinder and limit the capacity of the very thing the Setian is supposedly attempting to strengthen and develop. Drugs clearly hinder the capacity of the will, and so true Setian magic cannot be enhanced by their use.

As in LaVeyan Satanism, there is no established ritual in Setian magic, but there is a basic formula outlined in *The Crystal Tablet* that is used as a framework for workings of greater black magic. In many respects, this has been derived from the formula given in *The Satanic Bible* by LaVey. Important differences include the lighting of a fire (chemically treated to imbue the flame with a blue-black color) upon the altar. This is done to symbolize the Black Flame and to open a gateway of communication between the celebrant(s) and the Prince of Darkness.

Another factor is the wording of an Invocation to Set written by Aquino. In principle, this is used in most Setian group rituals. It is a verbal symbol that connects all Setians in those times/places where magical work is done.

Setian ritual symbolism is also sexually neutral; there are no nude altars, phalli, and so on. These are not forbidden, but merely thought to be inappropriate to most working aims and therefore unnecessary. The presence of animals—unless essential to the symbolism of the working—is discouraged.

Perhaps most importantly, the Temple expressly forbids the presence of nonmembers at workings. It does not allow tourists, "observers," and so on, who merely "want to see what's going on with those weird black magicians." Filming or photographing actual rituals is also strongly discouraged. Nonparticipants can never fully comprehend what actually occurs in such an environment. If Catholicism were not so well established and familiar, more people might think all that bell ringing, genuflecting, and censer swinging by guys in dresses wearing pointy caps was pretty strange, too. But the believing Catholic feels himself to participate in the Passion of his Savior through this formula. This unseen aspect is even stronger in Setian workings, which actually take place in a nonnatural realm.

One whole important category of the practice of Setian greater black magic involves the direct communication with the Set-entity. This is a difficult task to accomplish in reality, and one that is generally thought to require at least a level of initiation equal to that of the priesthood of Set (III°). First, the very act of consciously setting one's self apart from the laws of the Universe is a step in this direction, because in doing so the Setian commits "'the same crime against God (= the Universe) as did the Set-entity.'"[45] This would then be an act in imitation of the original rebellion of consciousness against the universal order, whether in the mythology of the Egyptians (= Set), or of the Greeks (= first Zeus, then Prometheus), or the Germanics (= Odin), and so on. The next step is the actual communication with the Set-entity as an independent being, which is an even more profound violation of the natural order. Reliable contact of this kind is only thought to be possible for Masters of the Temple.

XEPER—INITIATORY BLACK MAGIC

The central magical work of a Setian black magician is his or her own Xeper. This is the "Great Work" upon which the will must be focused. As outlined above, the Temple of Set initiatory degree system is a map or guiding instrument for the general parameters of that Xeper-process. Transformations that take place in the essence or being of the individual during this process are "objective" ones in the sense that they are real and permanent. The effects of magical work can, however, be undone through negligence and subsequent laziness.

In many respects, the initiatory system of the Temple is based on a framework similar to that employed by Plato when describing the levels of knowledge and being that students in his academy would undergo in their quests to become philosopher-kings (see chapter 3). This same structure underlies most Western "occult systems," although many try to obscure this fact. It is a system that has its objective criteria and is founded in reality, and hence it forms a useful instrument for personal initiation.

In this system, the initiate moves from a state of relative guesswork to one of objective certainty based upon knowledge (or understanding), which comes from direct apprehension of the first forms lying at the root of all phenomena in the objective and subjective universes. This comes only after sufficient "scientific" training in the observation of, and interaction with, the objective world has been successfully undertaken. This is one of the things that seems to distinguish between transcendental and immanent branches of the left-hand path. The transcendental branch assumes the transformations taking place in the subjective universe are real and require work, as does the transformation of any real thing. The immanent branch, as exemplified by the latter-day philosophy of LaVey, instead assumes that the subjective universe (such as it exists) is a relatively static thing—one must merely "realize one's innate godhood" rather than work to transmute the "substance" of the subjective universe into a divine state.

ULTIMA FUTURA—THE VISION OF THE TEMPLE OF SET

The Temple of Set is a notably forward-looking or "future-oriented" school of the left-hand path. One of its reading-list categories is called "The Future," and another is devoted to space exploration and scientific frontiers.

In the early years of the Temple, there was a strong apocalyptic, almost millenarian, aspect that was evident. This was perhaps first based on a passage in *The Book of Coming Forth by Night,* which says:

> I seek my Elect and none other, for mankind now hastens toward an annihilation which none but the Elect may hope to avoid. And alone I cannot preserve my Elect, but I would teach them and strengthen their Will against the coming peril, that their blood may endure. To do this I must give further of my own Essence to my Elect, and, should they fail, the Majesty of Set shall fade and be ended.[46]

In the late 1970s, there was for a while even somewhat of a survivalist mentality among some members of the Temple as these words in *The*

Book of Coming Forth by Night were taken more literally than they have been in more recent years. In his 1985 commentary on this passage in the text, Aquino wrote:

> During the first several years of the Aeon, I was inclined to interpret the warning of this passage in terms of the general ecological crisis confronting the human race as a whole during the next century. While factors presaging that crisis remain, it is increasingly obvious that the Temple of Set is far too selective in scope and interests to be a significant factor in confronting it. It seems more probable that Set's warning is meant to alert the Elect to the general fear which profane humans feel concerning Initiates of the Black Art, and in particular their tendency to search out scapegoats during times of stress, confusion, and crisis.[47]

More recently, the tenor of the Temple's orientation has been more toward the individual and more academic, in the Platonic sense. Initiates, engaged in the affairs of the world, but magically isolated at will from the "World of Horrors" (uninitiated society), seem to be most likely to survive any upheavals in that world. As this World of Horrors perhaps becomes progressively more stupid and brutish, ever more narrow-minded and simpleminded, the Temple of Set expects to have its resources for initiation called upon more and more as "refugees" from that uninitiated realm seek sustenance in a rational and rigorous system.

The Orders within the Temple of Set are projected to grow and give the Temple an increasingly multidimensional aspect. These will develop more and more sophisticated and specialized magical disciplines and techniques, each with its own contribution to what the future holds for the Temple as a whole.

As far as the World of Horrors is concerned, it seems clear that it will go on more or less as it has always been. The only way the Temple of Set will have an impact upon its quality is by facilitating the true initiation of individuals into the essence of the left-hand path. The influence of those individual black magicians will then make impact on the World of Horrors as it fulfills the unique wills of those individuals. And so is done the will of Set.

MICHAEL AQUINO AND THE LEFT-HAND PATH

It is clear that what Michael Aquino has done with the Temple of Set is quite different from what Anton LaVey did with his Church of Satan. They have differing philosophies but both are equally part of the left-hand path. In fact, each respectively exemplifies the essence of the transcendental and immanent branches of that path, as I have defined them.

LaVeyan Satanism accepts and revels in the role of the eternal adversary. Its theoretical mandate is to question every norm. Setian philosophy is based on an elitist and hierarchized theory, but is not necessarily adversarial. Set is seen as something opposed to a certain thing (Nature), but not systemically opposed to any and everything. This distinction is inherent in the mythic systems from which their respective philosophical ideas are drawn: Satanism from an anti-establishment mythology (Satan's rebellion against God); Setian religion from a previously established super- or extraordinary system (the ancient cult of Set). Satanism poses a head-to-head or lateral opposition, whereas Setian thought poses a vertical opposition.

In the greater historical perspective, LaVeyan Satanism accepts (or came to accept) the matter/spirit dichotomy of the ancient Gnostics, but declares its allegiance with the demiurge—the creator of matter and the flesh—as the "good god." In the ancient system, this would have been Yahweh/Iao! But even in LaVey's system, he must refer to something that separates man from "the other animals" (for better or worse), and to something else when addressing the issue of the possibility of immortality.

In the Setian philosophy of Michael Aquino, these contradictions are cleared away rationally by seeking and finding that which does separate man from the rest of the universe. This opposition then becomes the core of the philosophy. Humanity, and most especially the Elect, stand apart from the "laws of the universe" or "God."

This Setian equation between the Judeo-Christian God and Nature is one of the most troubling to modern would-be nature worshippers because they usually like to think of themselves as being somehow on the opposite side from old "Jehovah"—they see him as being somehow "supernatural" while they are "natural." But Setian philosophy is practiced on a level beyond these concerns, although they can be explained historically. Adherents of orthodox religions seeking a "God" who created "heaven and earth" simply have misinterpreted the more subtle laws of nature as "the laws of God." In fact, according to Setian ideas, these are both aspects of the static regularity or internal consistency of the objective universe. Ultimately, it is not a question of central importance to the Setian.

The Setian steps back and observes the picture from a new angle and sees the true distinction between Intelligence and nonintelligence in the universe. Intelligence "opposes" stasis and regularity. This opposition goes against "God" and "Nature," which are both marked by their static and inflexible laws.

The magical Setian philosophy of Michael Aquino is philosophically antinomian—violating cosmic law—and in times of social stress has shown itself ready and willing to become a symbol of conventional antinomianism as well. Curiously, when it was still relatively comfortable to call oneself a "Satanist," most Setians did not manifest a "Satanic" image, but as the social climate became more intolerant, the Setian philosophical antinomianism was activated and the "Satanic" imagery resurfaced—as an apparent act of cosmic and philosophical defiance against the ignorance and stupidity that drove the intolerance.

The ultimate aim of Setian philosophy is an active, aware, and potent state of relative immortality for the isolate, individual psyche. This is achieved through a system of magic that necessarily and to a great extent must be the unique invention of the psyche of the subject of the transformation or metamorphosis. It seems essential to the pro-

Figure 10.2. Xepera Xeper Xeperu

cess, however, that it be a matter of will, and that it be undertaken in grades or stages only as quickly as the conscious mind is able to absorb and understand the process it is undergoing.

The magical philosophy of Michael Aquino is certainly one of the most sophisticated theories of its kind to be expounded in modern times. This discussion can only provide the outlines of the system, of course. The future will hold more mysteries and more unfoldings of the Word of the Aeon.

AFTERWORD

Terminus Viae

The left-hand path is the way of the hero: the path of those who, having understood their own individual divinities, would dare to breach the gates of eternity and eat of the tree of life eternal. To stand against the inertia and ignorance of the whole of the universe, to strive against that which would thwart all intelligence and life, and to prevail against it—this is the aim of the sinister path.

The left-hand path is simply the *way of nonunion,* individuation, and independence. By contrast, the right-hand path is the way of union, collectivization, and dependence. The essence of the left-hand path has nothing to do with "evil." In fact, those who follow the left-hand path (by any name) today most closely approximate the ancient ideal of seeking the agathôn, "the Good." On the left-hand path, initiates seek to develop the self to the point of divinity; this heightened sense of self, once sufficiently developed, prevents any acts of true evil on the part of initiates because they have come to *know* and *understand* the Good.

The *via sinistra* is the path of sovereigns—those who would exercise sovereign power over themselves and their environments. Historical evidence for the presence of a true left-hand path is only obvious in cultures originally shaped by Indo-European ideology (Egypt being the only possible exception). The extremely ancient sovereign values of eternal life and unlimited power of the self are reflected in the philosophy of the left-hand path.

I have shown that there are two distinct approaches to the left-hand path: the transcendental branch and the immanent branch. The transcendental branch of the left-hand path makes use of an uncompromisingly subjective approach to the extant subjective universe—and thereby ultimately realizes the full reality and sovereignty of the self. The immanent branch of the left-hand path takes an indirect route. Those who go this way focus on their independent carnal existences and travel through images in the objective universe to arrive at a mysterious and often verbally indefinable state of being beyond the images. The branches terminate in a similar state, but their appearances are different.

The world needs to come to understand something of the left-hand path at this point in history as never before. This is because the world is now largely operating under a left-hand-path paradigm. It is clear that the motivations for most modern and postmodern individuals revolve around the extension of life, independence, freedom, knowledge, power, and pleasure. We live in a Faustian or Mephistophelean Age. The sooner the true character of this Faustian Age is recognized, the sooner those who live in it will be able to move about with some sense of confidence. This Faustian Age did not arrive easily, but if we look carefully at those times that preceded it, we also will see examples of those who have mastered the path: the lords and ladies of the left-hand path.

A lord or lady of the left-hand path is someone who has prevailed against the laws of the mechanical universe—the laws of stupidity, blind obedience to brute force, and eternal death of intelligence—and created from the substance of the self, by means of will, an immortal identity. In and of itself, this is the greatest stance of defiance against the universe. Such a sovereign individual stands alone amidst the storms and stresses all about—yet is not alone. For across the abysmal seas of the World of Horrors, this sovereign individual will see and come to know other dark stars hovering over the waters. By knowing them, the star of the singular self is made to burn with a brilliance of darkness unto the glory of desire.

Should there come a point in which all the individual intelligences, scattered about the vastness beyond the borders of time and space, are extinguished by force of necessity—it is their glory that will give the greatest brilliance to the whole, even if it only comes into being for a fleeting moment.

The only true enemy of the left-hand path is ignorance, that grinding human condition born of fear and expressed in vehement hatred. But this resistance, too, can be turned to strength by the power of the will, a force that belongs to the left-hand path to command. Where instances of such ignorance are found, the lords and ladies of the left-hand path will transform them into an illustration and illumination of the principles that distinguish their own brilliance and intelligence from the surrounding obscurity and gloom. The lords and ladies of the left-hand path can break the bounds of time and reach back to discover moments that give strength to their purpose of will and which form the resistance that gives shape and direction to their own power. In this way they defy the compulsions and coercions of the past—thwarting beyond time their eternal enemies who have embodied ignorance—and endow those moments with limitless possibilities for the future.

Reyn til Rúna!

APPENDIX

The Urban Legend of Satanicism

Much of the impetus for writing this book came from the need to demonstrate to an intelligent reading public the true character of the left-hand path. This was necessitated, I felt, by the monstrous emergence of rabid and irrational hatreds and fears manifesting themselves in Western culture especially during the late 1980s.

What the people fear and hate is not so much the left-hand path and Satanism as it actually is, and as it is actually practiced, but rather *their own* inner idea or notion of what it is or *must be.* This fantastic phenomenon, this mythic form of "Satanism," which seems to exist in no reality other than the subjective one of its creators, I choose to call by the neologism "Satanicism." This is done to keep the term Satanism uncontaminated by fictional creations of right-hand-path paranoia.

The best explanation of the "Satan scare" phenomena of the late 1980s is to be found in the complex world of urban legends or myths. This is not to dismiss the importance or danger of such mythologizing, or to reject the whole phenomenon as "pure fantasy." There is something *real* going on—it's just not what it *seems* to be.

An urban legend is most often encountered in the form of wild and usually weird stories that range from "Lady of the Lake" ghost tales to exploding poodle dogs in microwave ovens. Cases of urban legends have been collected and studied by University of Utah folklorist Jan Harold Brunvand in several volumes such as *The Vanishing Hitchhiker* (1981) and *The Choking Doberman* (1984). Urban legends almost always start with "A friend of a friend of mine said that . . ." They are always close enough or specific enough to be effective, yet far away enough to be beyond confirmation. It is essential to the effectiveness of an urban legend that it not be subjected to verification. All the urban legends that have been studied have been shown to be purely fictional creations.

These urban legends *do* have dramatic effects on society, however. Not one case of strangers putting poison, glass, or razorblades in kids' candy at Halloween has been confirmed. All such cases were either faked by attention-seeking kids or were the results of abuse inflicted on the children *by their own parents.* In spite of this, "trick-or-treat" customs have been disrupted and in many places hospitals have even offered free x-raying of Halloween candy!

Two popular urban legends that have affected major U.S. corporations are that McDonald's sent a portion of their profits to the Church of Satan and that the (old) Proctor and Gamble logo (an image of a man in the moon and some stars) was a "Satanic symbol." Both of these legends are, of course, fictitious. Nevertheless, Proctor and Gamble eventually changed their logo due to unrelenting public pressure.

Two investigators who have looked at the "Satan Scare" from the viewpoint of the urban legend or depth psychology are Arthur Lyons in his *Satan Wants You* and Chas Clifton in an article for *Gnosis* magazine.[1] Both have concluded that most, if not all, of the tales of "Satanic day-care centers," "breeder cults," and so on, ad nauseam, are the stuff of either urban legend or disturbed minds.

RECENT HISTORY

When we look at this most recent phenomenon, which reached its peak with the Geraldo Rivera television special on "Satanic crime" broadcast in October 1988, we discover a definite historical trend stretching back approximately thirty years.

Around the year 1975, reports of cattle mutilations began to sweep the western United States. These mutilations were all said to be the work of a well-organized Satanic cult. Official investigations showed them to be the work of animal predators. But in anxiety-ridden, post-Watergate America, Satanic cults seemed to be more the preferred "popular" answer.

In 1980, one of the first commercial exploitations of this new wave of cult anxiety appeared. This came in the form of a collaboration between a certain "Michelle Smith" and a psychiatrist, Dr. Lawrence Pazder. Together they produced a book called *Michelle Remembers* based on "memories" Michelle was able to produce while being treated by Dr. Pazder.[2] In this book, Michelle recounts the horrible cultic abuse she suffered at the hands of her family and strangers, complete with the depiction of the sacrifice and eating of infants. These accounts and others produced in the 1980s are remarkably similar to those produced by the Roman and Christian commentators many centuries ago (see chapter 5). No hard evidence was ever found to corroborate Michelle's story, but it continues to be accepted as true by those who need to believe. Dr. Pazder was so impressed he married Michelle.

When the anxiety and malaise of the mid- and late-1970s combined with the ideology of the religious right in the Reagan-dominated 1980s, the "Satan scare" was poised for development. Soon, bolstered by the pattern of Dr. Pazder and Michelle, there was a whole circuit of patients and their therapists traveling about like so many snake-oil salesmen hawking their wares of fear and dread to anyone who would listen—and pay their fees.

Another twist in the story arose in the early 1980s: the theme of the "Satanic day-care center." This reached its nauseating zenith in the famous McMartin day-care center case in California. A mentally disturbed, suicidal mother of one of the children accused the school of abusing her child. Therapists (inquisitors) were brought in to question the children. After being subjected to their "therapy" the children began to come up with stories of rituals, devils, bunny sacrifices, subterranean chambers with lions in cages, flights to faraway cities to attend unspeakable rites, and so on. The ensuing trial turned into the longest and most expensive in American history. Most of the charges were finally dropped, and in the end no one was convicted of anything. But many lives, both of the owners and staff of the school, as well as of the children and concerned parents, were destroyed or seriously damaged. The only ones to benefit were the therapists (they got paid and enhanced their reputations, at least temporarily), lawyers, and other legal professionals. The telling question of "Who gains?" can be applied here with enlightening effect.

The McMartin case was just the beginning of a massive wave of similar cases. Investigations were undertaken by law enforcement officials all over the country, some of whom began to "specialize" in "occult crime." Amateur and professional theologians and their possessed and abused "ex-cultists" produced books and went on talk shows. "The devil made me do it" became a legal defense for crimes great and small.

By the late 1980s, "Satanic crime" was the hottest-selling topic on the talk-show circuit. False accusations made against the High Priest of the Temple of Set, Michael Aquino, brought "philosophical Satanism" to center stage for the first time—and this was the beginning of the end of the "Satanic scare." This is because Aquino was able to fight back against the falsehoods about Satanism and eventually the truth began to emerge. But the "scare" would nevertheless continue for several years to come.

Perhaps the crest of the wave of public paranoia came with the aforementioned Geraldo television special. The electronic and print media were full of accounts of "Satanic" or ritual crime and abuse. Case after case was heard of people (mainly women—perhaps because they are the chief consumers of this material) ritually abused as children who "suddenly remember" it all under therapy, or in some cases due to religious conversions (shades of Diana Vaughan!*).

*See the discussion of the Taxil hoax in chapter 6.

HABEAS CORPUS!

Finally, the shocking—yet simple and rational—questions began to be *heard:* Who did this (name some names)? Where are the bodies? Were the police informed? Questions like this had been asked all along, but the public was not ready to hear the questions or the actual answers. By late 1989 and early 1990, however, the crushing answers had come in so often and so clearly that they could no longer be ignored.

In October of 1989, the National Center for the Analysis of Violent Crime at the FBI Academy in Quantico, Virginia, issued a paper by Kenneth V. Lanning. It is a detailed analysis of all the charges of "Satanic" or ritual crime brought in the U.S. over the previous decade. The paper concludes in part: "After the hype and hysteria is put aside, the realization sets in that most Satanic/occult activity involves the commission of NO crimes, and that which does usually involves the commission of relatively minor crimes."[3]

Later that same year, Shawn Carlson and Gerald Larue issued *Satanism in America: How the Devil Got Much More Than His Due* as a final report for the Committee for the Scientific Examination of Religion. This work systematically dismantles the scam perpetrated by some law enforcement officials in conjunction with modern-day, freelance witch-hunters. In their Abstract of the book, the authors summarize their findings:

> A great hoax is being perpetrated on the American public. A small group of religious fanatics, political extremists, bereaved parents, and the mentally ill, as well as a few well-intentioned individuals, are appearing on talk shows at police training seminars, at criminal trials, and in newspaper interviews as "expert" witnesses with an alarming message: Satanism is rampant in America; devil-worshippers are killing millions of children; Satanism is seducing teens into suicide pacts and driving our youth to violence. . . . These experts have gone virtually unchallenged . . . until now. As a result, lives have been destroyed, the practice of legitimate minority religions

> has been infringed and many millions of dollars have been wasted chasing the devil's tail.
>
> The allegations of large scale Satanic conspiracies are totally without foundation. In fact, the available evidence leaves only one reasonable conclusion: *they do not exist!*[4]

The authors go on to chronicle the real violence and sickness practiced by the latter-day witch-hunters themselves, and always in the name of God and Jesus. Some are seen to be mentally disturbed on one level or another, while others are following an extremist Christian political agenda.

In February of 1990, a rational voice was heard from a surprising yet welcome corner: the Christian media. Bob and Gretchen Passantino and Jon Trott published an article in the Christian magazine *Cornerstone.*[5] This was an exposé of a book entitled *Satan's Underground,* which was written by a "Lauren Stratford" (real name: Laurel Rose Wilson) with help and promotion from Johanna Michaelsen.[6] Apparently even the rational Christians had heard about all they could stand by this time. Closer investigation into the life of Wilson showed a pathetically disturbed hysteric whose accusations of abuse began when she was a teenager, and were for years first directed against family members and pastors of churches. It was not until 1985 that "Satanism" became a part of her stories and she joined up with the then-profitable business of the "Satan scare." In a truly bizarre twist, a decade after her exposure by the *Cornerstone* reporters, Wilson reinvented herself with a new identity in 1999. She now claimed to be "Laura Grabowski," a Jewish child-survivor of the Auschwitz-Birkenau concentration camp, and appeared on the talk-show circuit to relate her traumatic experiences with no less than Dr. Josef Mengele. Like the earlier Satanic abuse story, this entire tale was again exposed as a fraud.[7]

In 1991, the book *In Pursuit of Satan* by Robert D. Hicks finished blowing the lid off of the law-enforcement/psychotherapy/fundamentalism cabal.[8] From an objective point of view, Hicks showed how unscrupulous police, therapists, and activists of various stripes had *invented* the whole "Satan scare" to bolster their own particular positions and causes.

Both *Satanism in America* and *In Pursuit of Satan* approach the "Satan scare" from the perspective of an urban legend.

These beginnings of rationality have not quelled the hysteria completely, of course. More books and more tabloid-type media presentations would appear, but the rational law-enforcement officials as well as established religious leaders had begun to see the light. The "scare" moved more and more to the fringes. But there is no reason to conclude that ignorance and stupidity will remain down for long . . .

So what, if anything, is happening out there in America to make people believe that Satanic cults are abducting their children, breeding babies for sacrifice, and lurking behind every bush in suburbia? There is a phenomenon here, but it is not what it seems. The roots of the phenomenon are not in the groups and individuals this book is about—they are in the minds of those whose vague fears and narrow worldviews make them ripe for belief in monstrous conspiracies of evil forces all around them. These are the people who *need* to believe in these urban legends because of their nonspecific anxieties and fears, and who have the burning *desire* to believe in order to alleviate their grinding boredom and sense of insignificance. In many ways, the "Satan scare" of the 1980s was an attempt by bored individuals to make life interesting and exiting: it was more fun to believe that such evil conspiracies existed than to believe they did not exist. Most people believe what it gives them pleasure to believe, or what they need to believe because of their own inner fears.

America's first "witch scare" three hundred years ago in Salem, Massachusetts, and the "Satanic scare" of the 1980s have much in common. The Salem witch trials were carried out by Puritans with an extremely narrow worldview—one which allowed for little variation or personal freedom. Things that were different from the "norm" were looked upon with suspicion. At the same time, many of the parents of Salem had to work hard all day long just to be able to survive in the harsh new land. In 1692, taxes were high, war raged about them, and smallpox was in the land. They entrusted the care of their children to servants. One in particular was a West Indian woman named Tituba. When a group of pubescent girls for whom Tituba cared exhibited strange behavior and fits (probably first brought on by accidental ergot poisoning) the adults thought it must be witchcraft. The children were put to the question by the reverend folk and began at first to accuse social misfits: the slave Tituba, the beggar Sarah Good, and the cripple Sarah Osborne. Before the saga was over many people—including one of the reverends himself—were either hanged or pressed to death for witchcraft.

Our society today is under similar strains and stresses. In some cases these stresses are more subtle, and in some cases more profound. Society is in many ways breaking down completely: the cultural norms that brought us up from the Stone Age are disintegrating. In just two generations we have gone from multigenerational households (with children, parents, and often grandparents, great aunts and uncles, and so on) to nuclear families (with children and parents), to a time now when most children are either in single-parent households or in households where both parents must work to meet (at least perceived) economic needs. The upshot of this is that most kids are raised by a combination of television, other kids, and hired help (schoolteachers and day-care workers). There is a tremendous amount of profound, archetypal stress put on a culture when such transformations occur.

These sociological factors explain a good deal of the specifics with regard to "Satanistic" phenomena: children exhibit "strange" behaviors (strange to the parents because they hardly see the kids), the whole world seems to be falling apart, parents can't make enough money to acquire the things they want, preachers and therapists abound telling them that demons or organized cults of child molesters are invisibly lurking everywhere. It is always most effective to cast such paranoid suspicion on things that simply do not exist; that way, the lack of objective evidence will make the evil seem all the more sinister and simultaneously ensure that no positive, objective counter-evidence can be produced. It is not long before there is a general "scare." Of course, to the credit of the American people, such scares are not really taken *too* seriously, because on *some* level everybody knows it's show biz. But this is little consolation to the victims of the scare such as the McMartin workers or hundreds of others accused in this manner.

There is a deeper interpretation. What is responsible for the *need* to believe in these fearsome things, even when there is no evidence for them? The answer may be found in depth psychology. Another phenomenon that occurred at about the same time as the stories of "Satanicism" was the proliferation of tales of UFO abductees. These two phenomena have certain things in common: powerful, usually invisible conspirators together with sexual overtones or dominant sexual themes (probings of the body, "breeding experiments," etc.). In both phenomena, the victims typically "remember" such experiences after being subjected to "therapy." The "survivors" of UFOs and Satanic cults can explain their present unhappiness and maladjustments in terms of what some evil villain has done to them in the past. Perhaps this is some emerging and truly Satanic twist to the myth of "original sin": now it is not the human—the sinner—who is responsible, it is an external force. Man can now say, "Hey, it's not *my* fault!"

Those who suffer from deep-seated fears will inevitably project images of those fears into their environment. They will fear and detest what they imagine to see around them, which is at the same time a reflection of those things they fear and loathe within themselves. They fear and hate themselves, but instead of coming to terms with that, which is unacceptable, they project it onto convenient scapegoats. In extreme cases, Satanic cults or extraterrestrial invaders serve such roles.

Another factor that cannot go unmentioned when trying to explain the "Satanic scare" is its wider recreational dimension. It is fun to believe in for some people. In this regard it is also a commodity, like rock 'n' roll or the Freddy Krueger character from Wes Craven's *A Nightmare on Elm Street* films. Mr. Krueger is a good illustration of this phenomenon. The reason why there are so few "hellfire-and-brimstone" sermons in the churches anymore is because we have folks like Mr. Krueger or "Jason" from *Friday the 13th* taking up the slack. Those old sermons didn't *really* scare anybody but the most feeble-minded—they were sensationalistic entertainment. Now we have Clive Barker; we don't need the Reverend Billy Bob to do that any more. But some of the "reverends" have simply tried to make their "hellfire and brimstone" more believable by packaging it a bit differently. It's still entertainment, and it still sells. It's also great fun for the spinners and sellers of this material. They get to tell all the lurid details of their past experiences in the pornographic-orgiastic-homicidal-breeder cult, while testifying all the while to their born-again status today. A "wolf" could hardly ask for a better set of "sheep's clothing" than this! And just as it is with drugs, as long as there is a market for such stuff, there will be providers of it.

The modern-day witch-hunters have followed in the freelancing footsteps of Matthew Hopkins and others of the Protestant tradition who took the *Malleus Malificarum* as their handbook (today it comes in the form or an "occult crime seminar" or a "best-selling" book on the subject) and went to work hunting heretics and Satan-worshippers for fun and profit. Anyone who can create a "scare" has done his work—and then he appears with the antidote: more seminars, more books, more television exposés . . .

It seems clear that the vast majority of the horror stories of Satanic cults circulated over the past two decades should be relegated to the "urban-legend file." Does this mean the whole episode has been harmless, or that we can forget it? Not in the least. Because it will come back, as all such phenomena do. And it does do harm: millions, if not billions, of tax dollars are wasted on therapists, police investigations, and trials(!); the already epidemic anxiety is only exacerbated; fraud is committed by ex-cultists prying even more hard-earned money out of the hands of a fearful populace; and, worst of all, attention is deflected from the *real* problems of the breakdown of the family and child abuse (which is almost never the act of strangers in "Satanistic" cults and almost always the work of other members of the child's own family). This latter point is perhaps what has been the driving motivation behind much of this phenomenon: the family itself is morally sick and bankrupt and the "Satanistic cult" is the imaginary scapegoat.

All we can do is to call for rationality to be exercised not in a passive way, but actively. We must meet the problem where it actually exists: in the minds of the accusers and in their own families. Then we can ask the hard questions—Who? What? When? Where? How?—and, as the answers are found, act to bring light to the subject.

Glossary

antinomian: Derived from the Greek *anti-nomos,* "against the law (*nomos*)"; here meaning: against the laws of God, the mechanical/organic universe, and especially irrational psychological or social compulsion, convention, or habit.

black magic: A methodology for the exercise of independence from the universe and pursuit of self-oriented aims as defined by the left-hand path.

devil, the: From the Greek *diabolos,* "slanderer, enemy." See: *Prince of Darkness.*

duotheism: The idea that there are two objectively separate forms of divinity arranged along sexually polarized lines, for example, the God and the Goddess. Prevalent in both Indian tantrism (Shiva/Shakti) and modern Wicca or witchcraft.

evil: Term used to characterize unconscious acts of criminality and cruelty among humans. Conscious evil is impossible. Often used by right-hand-path fanatics to designate followers of the left-hand path. See: *good.*

good: Term used to characterize objects or acts that either demonstrate or promote consciousness and self-realization or knowledge. Often inconsistently used by right-hand-path fanatics to designate things for which they have a sentimental attachment. See: *evil.*

heretic: From Greek *hairetikos,* "one who is able to choose." Used to designate those who hold rebellious, unorthodox views or beliefs. A heretic practices heresy, which is often a punishable offence where right-hand-path fanatics control society. See: *heterodox.*

heterodox: From Greek *heterodoxos,* "differing in opinion." Used to designate a heretic, or one who has opinions different from those accepted by the norms of society. See: *heretic.*

immanent branch: The branch of the left-hand path in which the initiate seeks the left-hand-path goals of self-deification (through initiatory magic), immortality, and freedom from culturally and mechanically imposed norms, by means of an objective (carnal) approach to the universe through external symbols and behaviors. Exemplified by the philosophy of Anton LaVey and the Church of Satan.

initiation: A gradual, rationally designated evolution of the essence of a person from one state of being to another.

left-hand path: The path of nonunion with the objective universe, the way of isolating consciousness within the subjective universe and, in a state of self-imposed psychic solitude, refining the soul or psyche to increasingly perfect levels. The objective universe is then made to harmonize itself with the will of the individual psyche. Originally translated from Sanskrit *vamamarga,* "left-way."

lord (or lady) of the left-hand path: One who is capable of rejecting forms of conventional "good" and embracing those of conventional "evil," and practicing antinomianism, as part of an effort to gain a permanent, independent, enlightened and empowered level of being.

Lucifer: Latin name meaning literally "bearer of the light," also a name for the Morning Star. See: *Prince of Darkness.*

magic: The willed application of symbolic methods to cause or prevent changes in the universe by means of symbolic acts of communication with paranormal factors. These factors could be inside or outside the subjective universe of the operator. Magic is a way to cause things to happen that would not happen naturally.

objective universe: The part of existence that can be sensed and quantified. It is the mechanical/organic cosmic order characterized by its regularity and predictability, by the presence of *laws.*

orthodox: From Greek *orthodoxos,* "correct in opinion." The term can be used to designate any kind of thought that has a rigid standard of "correctness," especially ones that rely on arbitrary opinions or subjective criteria to establish such standards. Monotheistic religions (i.e., Judaism, Christianity, and Islam) are best known for this, but it can be secularized in forms of "political correctness."

Prince of Darkness: The first form or general principle of isolate intelligence from which all the particular manifestations of individual consciousness (or subjective universes) are derived: the ultimate deity of the left-hand path. An element of the nonnatural universe objectively within the universe itself, and therefore an independent sentient being in the objective sense because it is the very *principle* of that quality within the cosmos. Because of its categorical *separateness,* it is seen as rebellious and "evil" from the right-hand-path perspective. It is a more culturally neutral term for the same entity known in various left-hand-path schools as Satan, Lucifer, Set, and so on.

religion: From Latin *re-ligio,* "reconnection." Largely synonymous with the purposes of the right-hand path, to "re-connect," to unify the self (or soul) of the individual with some larger whole, such as God, Nature, the Absolute, the Tao, and so on.

right-hand path: The path of union with universal reality (God or Nature). When this union is completed, the individual self is annihilated and the individual will becomes one with the divine or natural order. Originally translated from Sanskrit *dakshinamarga,* "right-way."

Satan: From the Hebrew *śāṭān,* "opponent, adversary." Used as a historical and conventional label by modern Satanists as an expression of antinomian practice. The "Satan" is that which *opposes* the status quo in principle. See: *Prince of Darkness.*

Satanicism: A neologism meant to indicate not true Satanism but rather the ideas, patterns, and fantasies projected by the right-hand-path fears of superstitious and fearful noninitiates. These fantasies eventually surface as modern urban legends.

Satanism: The practice of the left-hand path as defined in terms of Judeo-Christian-based terminology. It does not denote the "worship" of Satan, but rather the practice of the left-hand path in some form.

subjective universe: The "world" of any sentient entity within the universe. There are as many subjective universes as there are sentient beings; each is the particularized manifestation of consciousness within the universe.

tantrism: A philosophical and religious tradition found in both Hinduism and Buddhism. Characterized by antinomian practice, the worship of the Goddess (a *contra*-sexual deity), and by sexual symbolism. Tantrism is a traditional methodology and can serve either right-hand-path or left-hand-path aims.

transcendental branch: The branch of the left-hand path by which the initiate seeks the left-hand-path goals of self-deification (through initiatory magic), immortality, and freedom from culturally and mechanically imposed norms by means of a subjective (intellectual) approach to the subjective universe. Exemplified by the modern Temple of Set.

Universe: The totality of existence, known and unknown.

white magic: A psychological methodology for the promotion of *union* with the universe and pursuing aims in harmony with the laws of the (objective) universe.

Notes

CHAPTER 1. THE LEFT-HAND PATH

1. A chief source for this discussion is Aquino, *Black Magic in Theory and Practice.*
2. Crowley, *Magick,* 131.

CHAPTER 2. THE EASTERN TRADITIONS

1. See Mallory, *In Search of the Indo-Europeans.*
2. For a critical study of Dumézil's works and ideas, see Littleton, *The New Comparative Mythology.*
3. Cornford, *The Republic of Plato,* 119–29.
4. See Nietzsche, *The Birth of Tragedy.*
5. For a convenient introduction to the Rig-Veda, see O'Flaherty, *The Rig-Veda.*
6. Evola, *The Yoga of Power,* 66.
7. For a discussion of tantric science, see Mookerjee and Khana, *The Tantric Way,* 93–125.
8. Farquhar, *An Outline of the Religious Literature of India,* 265–66.
9. Evola, *The Yoga of Power,* 30.
10. Godwin, *Arktos: The Polar Myth,* 33; see also Tilak, *The Arctic Home in the Vedas.*
11. Daniélou, *The Myths and Gods of India,* 382.
12. Eliade, *Yoga: Immortality and Freedom,* 142.
13. Sastri and Ayyangar, *Jivanmuktiviveka.*
14. Renou, *Hinduism,* 40.
15. Eliade, *Yoga,* 142.

16. Ibid., 128.
17. Evola, *The Yoga of Power,* 66.
18. One of the most coherent discussions of the process of personal transformation within tantrism is found in chapter 6 of Avalon (= John Woodroffe), *Shakti and Shakta,* 136–87.
19. Bhattacharyya, *History of the Tantric Religion,* 341.
20. Ibid., 341.
21. Ibid., 317.
22. Ibid., 318.
23. Evola, *The Yoga of Power,* 54–55.
24. Svoboda, *Aghora II: Kundalini,* 85.
25. Evola, *The Yoga of Power,* 55.
26. Ibid.
27. Avalon, *Shakti and Shakta,* 164; Evola, *The Yoga of Power,* 55.
28. Svoboda, *Aghora II,* 67–68.
29. Daniélou, *The Myths and Gods of India,* 258.
30. Bhattacharyya, *History,* 108.
31. Eliade, *Yoga,* 228–29.
32. Evola, *The Yoga of Power,* 68.
33. Ibid., 67, 66.
34. Ibid., 66.
35. Stutley, *Harper's Dictionary of Hinduism,* 67, 321.
36. King, *Tantra for Westerners,* 95.
37. Daniélou, *The Myths and Gods of India,* 383.
38. Ibid.
39. Svoboda, *Aghora II,* 27.
40. Ibid., 192.
41. Ibid., 198.
42. In the Vedantic school the only way to liberation is through *jnana.* Bondage is due to *avidya* (nonknowing) and involvement with the phenomenal universe is due to *avidya* alone. See Rao, *Jivanmukti in Advaita,* 31.
43. Renou, *Hinduism,* 35.
44. Mookerjee and Khana, *The Tantric Way,* 28–29.
45. Daniélou, *The Myths and Gods of India,* 382.
46. Evola, *The Yoga of Power,* 93–100.
47. LaVey, *The Satanic Bible,* 46–48.

48. Daniélou, *The Myths and Gods of India,* 382–83.
49. Ibid., 212.
50. Svoboda, *Aghora II,* 56.
51. Ibid.
52. Ibid., 21.
53. Ibid., 24.
54. Bhattacharyya, *History,* 109.
55. Ibid., 110.
56. Svoboda, *Aghora II,* 69.
57. Daniélou, *The Myths and Gods of India,* 212.
58. Walker, *Tantrism,* 49–76.
59. Ibid., 64–66.
60. Svoboda, *Aghora II,* 89–91.
61. Eliade, *Yoga,* 239.
62. Walker, *Tantrism,* 52.
63. Ibid., 50–52; King, *Tantra,* 92.
64. Walker, *Gnosticism: Its History and Influence,* 117.
65. King, *Tantra,* 92.
66. Svoboda, *Aghora II,* 85; 205–16.
67. Conze, *Buddhism,* 191–92.
68. Evans-Wentz, *Tibetan Yoga and Secret Doctrines,* 138.
69. King, *Tantra,* 92.
70. Cornford, *The Republic of Plato,* 227–35.
71. Walker, *Gnosticism,* 163–65.
72. Eliade, *A History of Religious Ideas,* vol. 2, 309–13.
73. Widengren, *Die Religionen Irans,* 23–26.
74. Eliade, *A History of Religious Ideas,* vol. 1, 309–15.
75. Boyce, *Zoroastrians: Their Religious Beliefs and Practices,* 54–56.
76. Eliade, *A History of Religious Ideas,* vol. 2, 309–13.
77. A basic study of Mithraism is offered by Cumont, *The Mysteries of Mithras.*
78. Eliade, *Patterns in Comparative Religion,* 290–91.
79. Eliade, *The Two and the One,* 50–55.
80. For a brief discussion of these parallels, see Hasenfratz, *Barbarian Rites,* 129–32.
81. Insightful studies of the Yezidis have recently been offered by Guest, *The Yezidis: A Study in Survival,* and Peter Lamborn Wilson, "Iblis, the Black Light," in his anthology *Sacred Drift,* 85–94.

CHAPTER 3. THE ROOTS OF THE WESTERN TRADITION

1. For a discussion of the original homeland of the Indo-Europeans, see Mallory, *In Search of the Indo-Europeans.*
2. Eliade, *A History of Religious Ideas,* vol. 1, 255.
3. Ibid., vol. 2, 257.
4. There were a number of Mystery Schools in ancient Greece; see Burkert, *Ancient Mystery Cults.*
5. Eliade, *A History of Religious Ideas,* vol. 1, 299–301.
6. Ibid., vol. 2, 187.
7. Ibid., 189–90.
8. Ibid., 190.
9. Cornford, *The Republic of Plato,* 351.
10. Eliade, *A History of Religious Ideas,* vol. 2, 190.
11. See Guthrie, *Orpheus and Greek Religion;* and Eliade, *History,* vol. 2, 190.
12. Eliade, *A History of Religious Ideas,* vol. 2, 191.
13. See the biographies of Pythagoras recorded by Guthrie, *The Pythagorean Sourcebook and Library,* 57–156.
14. See Waterfield, *The Theology of Arithmetic.*
15. T. S. Eliot, *Collected Poems,* 208.
16. For a study of the soul in Greek tradition, see Rhode, *Psyche: The Cult of Souls and Belief in Immortality Among the Greeks;* and for an introduction to the topic in northern Europe, see Flowers, "Toward an Archaic Germanic Psychology."
17. See Scholem, *Kabbalah.*
18. See Nicholson, *Studies in Islamic Mysticism.*
19. No real *school* of Neoplatonic Christian mysticism arose, but individual philosophers or theologians used Neoplatonic concepts. See Armstrong, *The Cambridge History of Later Greek and Early Medieval Philosophy.*
20. The most coherent presentation of Epicureanism is Lucretius, *On the Nature of the Universe.* Also see the general introduction provided by Saunders, *Greek and Roman Philosophy after Aristotle,* 13–57.
21. The classic text of later Stoicism is that of Aurelius, *Meditations*; see also the presentation by Saunders, *Greek and Roman Philosophy after Aristotle,* 59–150.
22. See Polomé, "Some Comments of *Völuspá* Stanzas 17–18," 268.

23. Concerning the runic initiation of Odin, see Turville-Petre, *Myth and Religion of the North,* 42–50.
24. Ibid., 63.
25. Concerning the spiritual gifts of the Germanic gods, see Polomé, "Some Comments."
26. Turville-Petre, *Myth and Religion,* 55–56.
27. For a comparison of the Celtic Lugh and the Germanic Odin, see Vries, *Keltische Religion,* 54; or Thorsson, *The Book of Ogham,* 36–40.
28. See Vries, *Altgermanische Religionsgeschichte,* vol. 2, 27.
29. Recorded by Grimm, *Teutonic Mythology,* vol. 4, 1709–36.
30. On the Erulians, see Flowers, *Runes and Magic,* 55, 137–38. On the esoteric interpretation of ancient rune-carving, see also Thorsson, *Runelore,* 12–22 (especially at 19), 76.
31. See Bennett's Introduction in Ouspensky, *Talks with a Devil,* 1.
32. Ibid., 1–2.
33. Dragomanov, *Notes on the Slavic Religio-Ethical Legends: The Dualistic Creation of the World,* 131.
34. Ibid., 10.
35. A review of the correlations between Zoroastrian and Hebrew traditions is provided by Forsyth, *The Old Enemy: Satan and the Combat Myth.*
36. On the existence of a pre-Yahwist Hebrew religion, see Hooke, *Middle Eastern Mythology,* 103–60.
37. For a general introduction to Sumerian civilization, see Kramer, *The Sumerians.*
38. As, for example, does J. B. Russell; see his *The Devil,* 84–86.
39. Eliade, *A History of Religious Ideas,* vol. 1, 58–59.
40. Internal evidence shows a close connection between the Sumerian world and that of the old Indus valley civilization, see ibid., 280–84.
41. Ibid., 42.
42. Ibid., 73.
43. Pritchard, *Ancient Near Eastern Texts Relating to the Old Testament,* 391–92.
44. For a convenient survey of Canaanite mythology, see Hooke, *Middle Eastern Mythology,* 79–94.
45. For a convenient introduction to this problem, see ibid., 103–64.
46. Forsyth, *The Old Enemy,* 44.

47. Ibid., 174.
48. Ibid., and Eliade, *Patterns,* 290–94.
49. On the relationship between Egypt and Mesopotamia, see Frankfort, *Kingship and the Gods.*
50. Budge, *Egyptian Language,* 15.
51. Jordan, *Egypt: The Black Land,* 78–83; Frankfort, *Kingship,* xxiv–xxv.
52. Helck and Otto, *Lexikon der Ägyptologie,* vol. 5, 13.
53. Ibid.
54. Ibid., 33–34
55. Ibid., 213.
56. Bonnet, *Reallexikon der ägyptischen Religionsgeschichte,* 714; Eliade, *A History of Religious Ideas,* vol. 1, 58–59.
57. Bonnet, *Reallexikon,* 714.
58. Romer, *Ancient Lives,* 67.
59. Ibid., 90, 92.
60. Doresse, *The Secret Books of the Egyptian Gnostics,* 249–309.
61. Eliade, *A History of Religious Ideas,* vol. 1, 178.

CHAPTER 4. THE FIRST MILLENNIUM

1. Tacitus, *The Histories,* 274.
2. Rudolf, *Gnosis: The Nature and History of Gnosticism,* 133–60.
3. See Jonas, *The Gnostic Religion,* 103–11; Rudolf, *Gnosis,* 294–98; and Walker, *Gnosticism,* 136–39.
4. See Robinson, *The Nag Hammadi Library,* 362–67.
5. Jonas, *Gnostic Religion,* 111.
6. Walker, *Gnosticism,* 138.
7. Ibid., 138–42; Rudolf, *Gnosis,* 298; 309–13.
8. Jonas, *Gnostic Religion,* 105.
9. Ibid., 110.
10. On the development of St. Augustine's thought, see Eliade, *A History of Religious Ideas,* vol. 3, 38–50.
11. On the concept of "binaric," see Anton LaVey, "Binaric, or Don't Try to Teach a Pig to Sing—It Wastes Your Time and Annoys the Pig."
12. Smith, *Jesus the Magician,* 45–67.
13. Ibid., 62.
14. The magical texts of the papyri have been translated by Betz, *The Greek*

Magical Papyri: Including the Demotic Spells: Texts; and the original Greek (with a German translation) is presented by Preisendanz, *Papyri Graecae Magicae: Die griechischen Zauberpapyri.*
15. Betz, *The Greek Magical Papyri,* 4–5.
16. Ibid., 41–42.
17. Smith, *Jesus,* 125–26.
18. Ibid., 9.
19. Eliade, *A History of Religious Ideas,* vol. 3, 116–51.
20. Wilson, *Sacred Drift,* 94.
21. Javad, *The Great Satan "Eblis,"* 67.
22. Wilson, *Sacred Drift,* 90.
23. Ibid., 91.
24. Ibid.
25. Arberry, *Sufism: An Account of the Mystics of Islam,* 70.
26. Walker, *Gnosticism,* 128.
27. Arberry, *Sufism,* 58.
28. Ibid., 60.
29. Wilson, *Scandal: Essays in Islamic Heresy,* 9.
30. Eliade, *A History of Religious Ideas,* vol. 3, 119–20.
31. Marco Polo, *The Travels,* 70–73.
32. Wilson, *Scandal,* 38.
33. Nietzsche, *On the Genealogy of Morals,* 150.
34. Wilson, *Scandal,* 38.
35. Ibid., 40.
36. Ibid., 45.
37. Eliade, *A History of Religious Ideas,* vol. 3, 120.
38. Burman, *The Assassins,* 61.
39. Eliade, *A History of Religious Ideas,* vol. 3, 120.
40. Burman, *The Assassins,* 174–85.
41. For example by Daraul, *A History of Secret Societies,* 141–55; and LaVey, *The Satanic Rituals,* 151–72.
42. Guest, *The Yezidis: A Study in Survival,* 31.
43. Wilson, *Sacred Drift,* 87.
44. See the *Black Book,* translated by Guest, *Yezidis,* 203.
45. Wilson, *Sacred Drift,* 92.
46. Guest, *Yezidis,* 40–41; and Wilson, *Sacred Drift,* 45.

47. Walker, *Gnosticism,* 74–75.
48. Guest, *Yezidis,* 201–2.

CHAPTER 5. THE PATH OF SATAN

1. Burns, *A History of the Ostrogoths,* 143–62.
2. Eliade, *A History of Religious Ideas,* vol. 2, 387–89.
3. See Lea, *A History of the Inquisition in the Middle Ages.*
4. Cohn, *Europe's Inner Demons.*
5. Ibid., 1.
6. Ibid., 19.
7. Eliade, *A History of Religious Ideas,* vol. 3, 184.
8. Ibid., 182.
9. Concerning these and other Free Spirit works of literature, see the appendix in Cohn, *The Pursuit of the Millennium,* 287–330.
10. Ibid., 172.
11. Ibid.
12. On Joachim of Fiore, see Cohn, *The Pursuit of the Millennium,* 108–10; and Eliade, *History of Religious Ideas,* vol. 3, 108–12.
13. Cohn, *The Pursuit of the Millennium,* 108.
14. Ibid., 154–55.
15. Ibid., 150.
16. Ibid., 183–85.
17. Ibid., 175.
18. Ibid., 177–78.
19. See Blakney, *Meister Eckhart: A New Translation*; and more generally Eliade, *A History of Religious Ideas,* vol. 3, 197–216.
20. LaVey, *The Satanic Bible,* 25.
21. Original Latin text in *Monumenta Germaniae Historica* (= MGH), *Capitularia Regum Francorum,* vol. 1, 223.
22. See Mackay, *The Hammer of Witches.*
23. Russell, *A History of Witchcraft,* 79.
24. Ibid., 103.
25. Goethe, *Faust,* xxii.
26. Jonas, *The Gnostic Religion,* 111.
27. Heffner, *Goethe's Faust,* 18.
28. Ibid., 19.

29. Passage, *Faust,* xiv–xv.
30. Ibid., xiv.
31. Heffner, *Goethe's Faust,* 20.
32. Ibid.
33. Ibid.
34. Ibid., 21.
35. Scheible, *Das Kloster*; Faust grimoires in vol. 2, 807–930; vol. 5, 1059–95.
36. Heffner, *Goethe's Faust,* 19.

CHAPTER 6. LUCIFER UNBOUND

1. On the revival of paganism in the Renaissance, see Seznec, *The Survival of the Pagan Gods.*
2. Fleming, *Arts and Ideas,* 221–23.
3. Printed in Cassirer, *The Renaissance Philosophy of Man,* 193–212.
4. Ibid., 223–54.
5. Ibid., 225.
6. Machiavelli, *The Prince,* 50.
7. Towers, *Dashwood,* 13–21, 231–46.
8. Blackett-Ord, *Hell-Fire Duke,* 46.
9. Ibid., 44–46.
10. Towers, *Dashwood,* 130–31.
11. Ibid., 148.
12. Ibid., 219–20.
13. Ibid., 160–70.
14. Ibid., 146.
15. Jefferson, *The Life and Morals of Jesus of Nazareth.* High-quality digital images of the entire book are now viewable online at the Smithsonian's Internet pages devoted to the artifact: *http://americanhistory.si.edu/jeffersonbible/.* In 2011, the Smithsonian also published a facsimile edition in book form.
16. Paine, *The Age of Reason.*
17. Ibid., 15.
18. See Jean Paulhan's introduction to Sade, *The Complete Justine,* 8–11.
19. Gorer, *The Life and Ideas of the Marquis de Sade,* 89–96.
20. Sade, *Philosophy in the Bedroom,* 211–12.
21. Sade, *Juliette,* 765–98.

22. For a discussion of this passage, see Gorer, *Life and Ideas of the Marquis de Sade,* 180.
23. Ibid., 171–85.
24. Ibid., 187.
25. Heffner, *Goethe's Faust,* 31.
26. Ibid., 30.
27. Ibid., 31.
28. Ibid.
29. See Jung, *The Grail Legend,* 150–51.
30. Rousseau, *The Confessions.*
31. Russell, *Mephistopheles,* 168–213.
32. Singer, *The Unholy Bible.*
33. Blake, *The Marriage of Heaven and Hell,* xvii.
34. For more on the "Process Church," see Wyllie and Parfrey, *Love, Sex, Fear, Death.* Facsimile reprints of the "Sex Issue," "Fear Issue," and "Death Issue" of the *Process* magazine, along with "The Gods on War" and other material are reproduced in *Propaganda and Holy Writ.*
35. Webb, *The Occult Underground,* 163.
36. Rhodes, *The Satanic Mass,* 156–62.
37. Ibid., 164.
38. Webb, *The Occult Underground,* 141–44.
39. Ibid., 156.
40. Ibid., 169.
41. Ibid., 173–74.
42. Rhodes, *The Satanic Mass,* 169.
43. Harrison et al., *Art in Theory 1815–1900,* 1057.
44. Webb, *The Occult Underground,* 144.
45. Rhodes, *The Satanic Mass,* 194–216.
46. Ibid., 212.
47. Ibid., 209–13.
48. Berlin, *Karl Marx,* 21–22.
49. Riemer, *Karl Marx and Prophetic Politics,* 64.
50. Ibid., 1–20.
51. Kolakowski, *Main Currents of Marxism: I: The Founders,* 409, 412, 414.
52. Berlin, *Karl Marx,* 229.
53. Riemer, *Karl Marx and Prophetic Politics,* 11–12.

54. Bakunin, *God and the State,* 10.
55. Ibid., 9.
56. Ibid., 10.
57. Carr, *Michael Bakunin,* 175.
58. Bakunin, *God and the State,* 12–13.
59. Kravchinsky, *The Russian Peasantry,* 57–71.
60. Fülöp-Miller, *The Mind and Face of Bolshevism,* 100–121.
61. These are reviewed by Fülöp-Miller, *The Mind and Face of Bolshevism,* in a chapter on secterianism. See also the lurid account by Lefebure, *The Blood Cults,* 100–105.
62. Walker, *Gnosticism,* 183–84.
63. See Wilson, *Rasputin.*
64. Fülöp-Miller, *Mind and Face of Bolshevism,* 29.
65. Ibid., 258–59.
66. Ibid., 265–66.
67. Kaufmann, *The Portable Nietzsche,* 565–656.
68. Kaufmann, *Nietzsche,* 307–33.

CHAPTER 7. AN INTERLUDE IN THE ABSOLUTE ELSEWHERE

1. Spence, *The Occult Causes of the Present War,* 20.
2. Goodrick-Clarke, *The Occult Roots of Nazism,* 217–25.
3. Flowers and Moynihan, *The Secret King,* 17–41.
4. Ibid., 33–65; Thorsson, *Rune Might,* 9–26.
5. Goodrick-Clarke, *The Occult Roots of Nazism,* 7–16; Rusten, *Was tut not?: Ein Führer durch die gesamte Literatur der Deutschbewegung,* 43–99; and Lother, *Neugermanische Religion und Christentum.*
6. Daim, *Der Mann, der Hitler die Ideen gab,* 176–77.
7. See Flowers and Moynihan, *The Secret King,* for a collection of these texts coupled with biographical and analytical material.
8. Rahn's works are collected in *Otto Rahn: Leben & Werk.* Two of the most important of these, *Lucifer's Court* and *Crusade Against the Grail,* have recently appeared in English translation.
9. See Rauschning, *The Voice of Destruction* [= *Gespräche mit Hitler*], 210. (It should be noted that the works of Rauschning are now largely dismissed as wartime propaganda, but in his assessment of Hitler's attitude

toward the manipulation of the masses, he may make a valid insider's judgment.)

CHAPTER 8. THE OCCULT REVIVAL

1. This is a major thesis of Webb's *The Occult Underground.*
2. Campbell, *Ancient Wisdom Revived,* 4–6.
3. Ibid., 33–34.
4. Ibid., 36–37.
5. Blavatsky, *Voice of the Silence,* vol. 1, 12, 20.
6. Ibid., vol. 1, 80.
7. Blavatsky, *The Secret Doctrine,* vol. 1, 193, 411–24; vol. 2, 60.
8. Ibid., vol. 2, 242–43.
9. Ibid., 475–83.
10. Ibid., 413.
11. Ibid., 416.
12. Ibid., 193.
13. Ibid., 60.
14. Ibid., 421.
15. Ibid., vol. 1, 198.
16. Ibid., vol. 2, 420.
17. Ibid., 421.
18. Ibid.
19. Ibid., 444–46.
20. Howe, *The Magicians of the Golden Dawn,* 54–55; and Colquhoun, *Sword of Wisdom,* 118–30.
21. The bibliography on the Golden Dawn is enormous. The best general history seems to be the one by Howe, *The Magicians of the Golden Dawn.*
22. Read in Crowley's typescript diary in the Humanities Research Center at the University of Texas, Austin.
23. Crowley, *The Magical Record of the Beast 666,* 14.
24. No extensive objective history of the O.T.O. exists; see King, *The Secret Rituals of the O.T.O.,* 9–35.
25. Bibliography on the modern occult revival of Kabbalah is voluminous. An interesting study of Kabbalah for *goyim* is provided by Davies, "The Kabbalah of the Nations: Anglicization of Jewish Kabbalah," 34–47.
26. Crowley, *Magick,* 341.

27. Crowley, *The Law Is for All,* 171–72.
28. See Bachofen, *Myth, Religion and Mother Right.*
29. Crowley, *The Book of the Law,* 21.
30. Crowley, *The Law Is for All,* 70.
31. Crowley, *The Book of the Law,* 22.
32. Crowley, *Magick,* 355–83, etc.; and see also *The Vision and the Voice.*
33. Crowley, *Eight Lectures on Yoga,* 7.
34. Ibid.
35. Ibid., 8.
36. Ibid., 9–10.
37. Ibid., 12–14.
38. Ibid., 20.
39. Printed in Hymenaeus Beta, ed., *The Equinox III, vol. 10,* 144.
40. Crowley, *Magick,* 238.
41. Ibid., 146.
42. Crowley, *Confessions,* 610.
43. Ibid., 394, 403–4, 452–53.
44. Crowley, *The Book of the Law,* 22.
45. Crowley, *Magick,* 296, 375.
46. Ibid., 172.
47. Crowley, *The Confessions,* 296.
48. Ibid., 347.
49. Ibid., 416.
50. Crowley, *Magick,* 418.
51. Ibid., 418–19.
52. Ibid., 343.
53. Ibid., 296.
54. Ibid., 172.
55. Crowley, *The Book of the Law,* 1:22.
56. Crowley, *Magick,* 131.
57. Ibid., 60.
58. Ibid., 294.
59. Ibid., 177.
60. Ibid., 299.
61. Ibid., 295.
62. Crowley, *The Magical Record of the Beast 666,* 47.

63. Crowley, *Magick,* 480.
64. Quotes on descriptions of grades from Crowley, *Magick,* 327–33.
65. Ibid., 295.
66. Ibid., 295–96.
67. Ibid., 296–97.
68. Ibid., 247–49.
69. Crowley, *The Law Is for All,* 192.
70. See Symonds, *The Great Beast,* 454.
71. Crowley, *Magick,* 331.
72. Aquino, *The Book of Coming Forth by Night,* 35.
73. Original edition: *Fire and Ice: Magical Teachings of Germany's Greatest Secret Occult Order.* Revised edition: *The* Fraternitas Saturni *or Brotherhood of Saturn: An Introduction to Its History, Philosophy and Rituals.*
74. See the bibliography provided in Flowers, *Fire and Ice,* 209–15.
75. Flowers, *Fire and Ice,* 1–4.
76. Ibid., 8.
77. See Randolph, *Sexual Magic.*
78. Flowers, *Fire and Ice,* 56.
79. Nietzsche, *Thus Spoke Zarathustra,* 200–202.
80. Gregorius, "Der Mensch in seiner höchsten Erkenntnisreife."
81. Ibid., 4.
82. Flowers, *Fire and Ice,* 61.
83. Ibid., 78–87.
84. Ibid., 41.
85. "Das weltliche Kloster," *Blätter für angewandte Lebenskunst.*
86. Grant, *Images and Oracles of Austin Osman Spare,* 7.
87. Ibid., 7, n. 1.
88. See Spare, *The Book of Pleasure (Self-Love).*
89. Speeth, *The Gurdjieff Work,* 149–65; and see Webb, *The Harmonious Circle.*
90. Gurdjieff, *The Herald of the Coming Good,* 3.
91. Louis Pauwels, *Gurdjieff,* 62–65; and Webb, *The Harmonious Circle,* 45.
92. Wilson, *The Occult,* 402–3.
93. The best objective biographies are provided by Webb, *The Harmonious Circle*; and Wilson, *G. I. Gurdjieff: The War against Sleep.*
94. Webb, *The Harmonious Circle,* 25–26.
95. Ibid., 35.

96. Ibid., 44–73.
97. Ibid., 187–88.
98. Ibid., 187.
99. Ibid., 314–15.
100. Peters, *Gurdjieff Remembered,* 92.
101. See Bennett's Introduction in Ouspensky, *Talks with a Devil,* 11.
102. Ibid., 10.
103. Ouspensky, *In Search of the Miraculous,* 59.
104. See Plato's "Myth of the Cave" in *The Republic* (Cornford, *The Republic,* 227–35, as well as specific references to the body as the "prison of the soul," e.g., in the *Phaedo*).
105. Ouspensky, *In Search of the Miraculous,* 47.
106. Plato, *Phaedrus,* 246, 253; Hamilton and Cairns, *Plato: The Collected Dialogues,* 493–95, 499–302; *Katha Upanishad,* 3; Hume, *The Thirteen Principal Upanishads,* 351–52.
107. Ouspensky, *In Search of the Miraculous,* 41–42.
108. Ibid., 40–41.
109. Note that this forms an interesting parallel to the attitude of the Marquis de Sade toward Nature.
110. Ouspensky, *In Search of the Miraculous,* 56.
111. Ibid., 57.
112. Ibid.
113. Ibid., 57–58.
114. Ibid., 58.
115. Ibid.
116. Ibid., 315.
117. Ibid., 71–73.
118. Webb, *The Harmonious Circle,* 520.
119. Speeth, *The Gurdjieff Work,* 119.
120. Ibid., 122.
121. Gurdjieff, *Views from the Real World,* 91.
122. Ouspensky *In Search of the Miraculous,* 158.
123. Ibid.
124. Ibid., 227.
125. Ibid., 226.

CHAPTER 9. ANTON SZANDOR LAVEY AND THE CHURCH OF SATAN

1. Wistrich, *Who's Who in Nazi Germany,* 126.
2. See Wilson, *Rasputin.*
3. Twain's two works most admired by LaVey, *No. 44, The Mysterious Stranger* and *Letters from the Earth,* were both severely "edited" (censored) in earlier editions because of the anti-Christian sentiments expressed in them.
4. Wolfe, *The Devil's Avenger,* 31–32.
5. See Aquino, *The Church of Satan,* appendix 19.
6. "The Hidden Source of the Satanic Philosophy," in ibid., appendix 11.
7. Wolfe, *The Devil's Avenger,* 27; Barton, *The Secret Life of a Satanist,* 23.
8. Wright, "Sympathy for the Devil," 66.
9. Wolfe, *The Devil's Avenger,* 33–40; Barton, *The Secret Life,* 29–37.
10. Wright, "Sympathy for the Devil," 67.
11. Barton, *The Secret Life,* 45–53.
12. *The Scroll of Set,* 17: 3, 8.
13. Wolfe, *The Devil's Avenger,* 50–58; Barton *Secret Life,* 59–60.
14. Wright, "Sympathy for the Devil," 68.
15. *The Scroll of Set,* 17:3, 7.
16. Barton, *The Secret Life,* 93–114.
17. *The Scroll of Set,* 17:3, 8.
18. Aquino, *The Church of Satan,* 17.
19. LaVey, *The Compleat Witch,* 100–101.
20. Aquino, "Lovecraftian Ritual," 13–15.
21. All of the early Church of Satan Conclaves are reported about in Aquino, *The Church of Satan.*
22. See Aquino, *The Church of Satan,* appendix 33; LaVey [= John M. Kincaid], "An Explanation of the Various Degrees in the Church of Satan," 7.
23. *The Cloven Hoof,* 8:3, 1.
24. Aquino, *The Church of Satan,* appendix 142.
25. Ibid., appendix 143.
26. Fritscher, *Popular Witchcraft,* 107–23.
27. See Barton, *The Secret Life,* 235–42.
28. Barton, *The Church of Satan,* 17.
29. Ibid., 355.

30. Alfred, "The Church of Satan."
31. Truzzi, "The Occult Revival as Popular Culture."
32. See Barton, *The Secret Life,* 235–42.
33. LaVey, "An Explanation of the Various Degrees," 8.
34. Alfred, "The Church of Satan," 191.
35. LaVey, "The Order of the Trapezoid," 3.
36. *The Scroll of Set,* 17:3, 7–8.
37. Alfred, "The Church of Satan," 184.
38. LaVey, "Untitled Editorial," *The Cloven Hoof,* 4:3, 12.
39. LaVey, "What is a Satanic Master," 1.
40. LaVey, "An Explanation of the Various Degrees," 8.
41. Ibid.
42. Barton, *The Church of Satan,* 122.
43. LaVey, "Hoofnotes," 2.
44. LaVey, "The Church of Satan, Cosmic Joy Buzzer," 3–4; and Barton, *Secret Life,* 248–52; and Barton, *The Church of Satan,* 122.
45. Barton, *The Church of Satan,* 122.
46. LaVey, "Working at Having Fun," 20.
47. LaVey, *The Satanic Bible,* 64.
48. LaVey, "What's New? Not Much," 3–4.
49. LaVey, "Don't Recycle Your Brain," 1.
50. LaVey, "For the Record," 4.
51. LaVey, "Untitled Editorial," *The Cloven Hoof,* 96, 1.
52. Abbreviated from LaVey, "Untitled Editorial," *The Cloven Hoof,* 113, 1.
53. LaVey, "Satanica," 1.
54. Wright, "Sympathy for the Devil," 105.
55. LaVey, "Misanthropia," 3; and "Confessions of a Closet Misogynist," 4.
56. LaVey, "Music for the Ritual Chamber," 27–30; "Illegal Music," 3; and "Music for the Chamber," 2–3.
57. LaVey, "Rhythm, Cadence, and Meter: The Foundation of Invocation," 1.
58. LaVey, "Megarhythm," 1–2.
59. LaVey, "The Law of the Trapezoid," 2.
60. LaVey, *The Satanic Rituals,* 106–30
61. Aquino, *The Church of Satan,* 208.
62. LaVey, "The Threat of Peace," 1.
63. LaVey, "Today's Madness is Tomorrow's Norm," 1.

64. LaVey, "Pentagonal Revisionism: A Five-Point Program," 1–2; and Barton, *The Secret Life,* 259.
65. LaVey, "Binaric, or Don't Try to Teach a Pig to Sing," 1.
66. Ibid.
67. Compare Orwell, "Politics and the English Language."
68. LaVey, "Binaric, or Don't Try to Teach a Pig to Sing," 1.
69. LaVey, *The Satanic Bible,* 110.
70. Ibid., 64–65.
71. LaVey, "Don't Recycle Your Brain," 1.
72. Ibid.
73. LaVey, "Untitled Editorial," *The Cloven Hoof,* 93, 1.
74. LaVey, *The Satanic Bible,* 44–45.
75. Ibid., 89.
76. LaVey, "Curses by the Dozen, or Wholesale Hexes," 2.
77. LaVey, "Power through Alienation," 2.
78. LaVey, "The Invisible War," 1.
79. LaVey, "Comparisons and Equivalents . . ." 2–4.
80. LaVey, "Give the Children a Chance," 2.
81. LaVey, "Farewell Trinity and Remember Los Alamos," 1.
82. Kelly, *Crafting the Art of Magic,* 3–4.
83. Sade, *The Complete Justine, Philosophy in the Bedroom, and Other Writings,* 166.
84. LaVey, *The Compleat Witch,* xii.
85. LaVey, "The Threat of Peace," 4.
86. LaVey, "Confessions of a Closet Misogynist," 4.
87. LaVey, *The Compleat Witch,* 21–26.
88. Barton, *The Secret Life,* 177–84.
89. LaVey, "The Threat of Peace," 1.
90. Barton, *The Secret Life,* 182.
91. LaVey, "Confessions of a Closet Misogynist," 4.
92. Barton, *The Secret Life,* 182.
93. Gorer, *The Life and Ideas of the Marquis de Sade,* 187.
94. LaVey, "How to Become a Werewolf." This is reprinted in Barton, *The Secret Life,* 253–58.
95. Ibid., 2.
96. Barton, *The Secret Life,* 183.

97. Wolfe, "The Church of Satan," 223.
98. LaVey, *The Satanic Bible,* 33. For the original source, compare the Conder edition of Redbeard, *Might Is Right,* 10.
99. LaVey, *The Satanic Bible,* 110.
100. Ibid., 111.
101. Ibid.
102. Ibid., 121.
103. Ibid., 125.
104. Ibid., 128.
105. Ibid., 101.
106. Aquino, *The Church of Satan,* 147, 150–51, 212–13; and appendices 69, 70, 71, and 72.
107. Barton, *The Secret Life,* 229.
108. The two most important articles by LaVey on the subject of E.C.I. are "Erotic Crystalization Inertia (E.C.I.): Its Relationship to Longevity" and "ECI Relative to Memory Retention: A Reevaluation of the Term *Occult.*"
109. LaVey, "Untitled Editorial," *The Cloven Hoof,* 103, 1.
110. LaVey, *The Satanic Rituals,* 53.
111. Barton, *The Secret Life,* 259–60; and *The Church of Satan,* 1–9.
112. Wright, "Sympathy for the Devil," 106.

CHAPTER 10. MICHAEL A. AQUINO: THE TEMPLE OF SET

1. Aquino, *The Book of Coming Forth by Night,* 20.
2. Aquino, *Black Magic in Theory and Practice,* 13.
3. Aquino, *The Book of Coming Forth by Night,* 20.
4. Aquino, *The Church of Satan,* appendix 9.
5. Ibid., 45.
6. Aquino, *The Church of Satan* (2009 edition), 71.
7. Aquino, *The Church of Satan,* appendix 10.
8. Ibid., appendix 72.
9. Ibid., 235–36 (also appendix 129 in the 2009 edition).
10. Aquino, *The Book of Coming Forth by Night,* 26.
11. Ibid., 9.
12. Russell, *Mephistopheles,* 253–55.
13. Drury, *The Occult Experience,* 114.

14. Ibid., 119–20.
15. Aquino, *Black Magic in Theory and Practice,* 59.
16. Ibid., 60.
17. Ibid., 61.
18. Stoker, *Dracula,* 246.
19. Aquino, *The Book of Coming Forth by Night,* appendix 2, 15.
20. Aquino, *Black Magic in Theory and Practice,* 3.
21. Ibid.
22. Ibid.
23. Ibid., 7.
24. Reprinted in Aquino, *The Temple of Set,* 254–55.
25. Aquino, *The Book of Coming Forth by Night,* 20.
26. Ibid., 10.
27. Ibid., 5.
28. Aquino, "Genesis III" (= Letter to the Priesthood of Set, September 29, [1975]).
29. Aquino, *The Book of Coming Forth by Night,* 7.
30. Ibid., 15, 17.
31. Ibid., 10.
32. Aquino, Genesis III.
33. Aquino, *The Book of Coming Forth by Night,* 22.
34. Aquino, "The Secrets of Life and Death," 1–10.
35. Aquino, "The Secrets of Life and Death II," 3.
36. Crowley, *Magick,* 131.
37. Aquino, *Black Magic in Theory and Practice,* 14–20.
38. Ibid., 19.
39. Ibid.
40. Aquino, *The Book of Coming Forth by Night,* 23.
41. Aquino, *Black Magic in Theory and Practice,* 21.
42. Ibid., 28.
43. Aquino, *The Book of Coming Forth by Night,* 23–24.
44. Ibid., 23.
45. Ibid., 24.
46. Aquino, *The Book of Coming Forth by Night.*
47. Ibid., 22.

APPENDIX. THE URBAN LEGEND OF SATANICISM

1. Clifton, "The Three Faces of Satanism."
2. Pazder and Smith, *Michelle Remembers.*
3. Lanning, *Satanic, Occult, Ritualistic Crime.*
4. Carlson and Larue, *Satanism in America,* v.
5. Passantino and Trott, "Satan's Sideshow."
6. Stratford, *Satan's Underground* (foreword by Johanna Michaelsen).
7. Passantino and Trott, "Lauren Stratford."
8. Hicks, *In Pursuit of Satan.*

Bibliography

Ach, Manfred, and Clemens Pentro. *Hitlers Religion.* Munich: Arbeitsgemeinschaft für Religions- und Weltanschauungsfragen, 1977.

Alfred, Randall H. "The Church of Satan." In *The New Religious Consciousness,* edited by Charles Y. Glock and Robert N. Bellah. Berkeley: University of California Press, 1976.

Angebert, Jean-Michel. *The Occult and the Third Reich.* New York: Macmillan, 1974.

Aquino, Michael A. *Black Magic in Theory and Practice.* San Francisco: The Temple of Set, 1987.

———. *The Book of Coming Forth by Night: Analysis and Commentary.* San Francisco: The Temple of Set, 1985. [Republished in Aquino, *The Temple of Set* (Draft edition). San Francisco: The Temple of Set, 2002–2010.

———. *The Church of Satan.* San Francisco: The Temple of Set, 1983, 1989, 1992, 2002, 2009. Citations in this book are from the 1992 edition, unless noted otherwise.

———. "Lovecraftian Ritual." *Nyctalops* 13 (May 1977): 13–15.

———. "Interview with the Founder of the Church of Satan" (= Black Pyramid, 1–3). *The Scroll of Set* XVII:3 (June 1991): 7–9.

———. "Official Degrees of the Church of Satan." *The Cloven Hoof* 4:3 (March 1972): 6–8.

———. "Revelation of the Beast: Aleister Crowley." *The Cloven Hoof* 2 (1970) (= *The Church of Satan,* appendix 19).

———. "The Secrets of Life and Death." *The Cloven Hoof* 5:1 (Jan./Feb. 1973): 1–10.

———. "The Secrets of Life and Death II." *Runes* 1:2 (Sept. 1983): 3.

———. "Sheep in Wolves' Clothing—Introducing the Process." *Cloven Hoof* 4:5 (1972): 15–16.

Arberry, Arthur John. *Sufism: An Account of the Mystics of Islam.* New York: Harper and Row, 1950.

Armstrong, Arthur Hilary. *The Cambridge History of Later Greek and Early Medieval Philosophy.* Cambridge: Cambridge University Press, 1967.

Aurelius, Marcus. *Meditations.* Translated by Maxwell Staniforth. Baltimore: Penguin, 1964.

Avalon, Arthur. *Shakti and Shakta.* New York: Dover, 1959.

Bachofen, Johann Jakob. *Myth, Religion and Mother Right.* Translated by R. Manheim. Princeton, N.J.: Princeton University Press, 1967.

Bacon, Francis. *Advancement of Learning and Novum Organum.* New York: Colonial, 1900.

Bainbridge, William S. *Satan's Power: A Deviant Psychotherapy Cult.* Berkeley: University of California Press, 1978.

Bakunin, Michael. *God and the State.* New York: Dover, 1970.

Barton, Blanche. *The Church of Satan.* New York: Hell's Kitchen Productions, 1990.

———. *The Secret Life of a Satanist: The Authorized Biography of Anton Szandor LaVey.* Los Angeles: Feral House, 1990.

Baudelaire, Charles. *Les Fleurs du Mal.* Translated by R. Howard. Boston: David R. Godine, 1982.

Berlin, Isaiah. *Karl Marx.* Oxford: Oxford University Press, 1963.

Betz, Hans Dieter, ed. *The Greek Magical Papyri in Translation: Including the Demotic Spells.* Chicago: University of Chicago Press, 1986.

Bhattacharyya, Narendra Nath. *History of the Tantric Religion.* New Dehli: Manohar, 1982.

Blackett-Ord, Mark. *Hell-Fire Duke: The Life of the Duke of Wharton.* Windsor Forest, UK: Kensal Press, 1982.

Blake, William. *The Marriage of Heaven and Hell.* Oxford: Oxford University Press, 1975.

Blavatsky, Helena. *Isis Unveiled.* 2 vols. Pasadena: Theosophical University Press, 1972.

———. *The Secret Doctrine.* 2 vols. Pasadena, Calif.: Theosophical University Press, 1974.

———. *Voice of the Silence*. Pasadena, Calif.: Theosophical University Press, 1971.

Blakney, Raymond B. *Meister Eckhart: A New Translation*. New York: Harper and Row, 1941.

Bonnet, Hans. *Reallexikon der ägyptischen Religionsgeschichte*. Berlin: De Gruyter, 1952.

Boyce, Mary. *Zoroastrians: Their Religious Beliefs and Practices*. London: Routledge and Kegan Paul, 1979.

Brennan, James Herbert. *The Occult Reich*. New York: Signet, 1974.

Brick, Hans. *The Nature of the Beast*. New York: Crown, 1960.

Brunvand, Jan Harold. *The Choking Doberman*. New York: Norton, 1984.

———. *The Vanishing Hitchhiker*. New York: Norton, 1981.

Budge, E. A. Wallis. *Egyptian Language*. London: Routledge and Kegan Paul, 1958.

Burkert, Walter. *Ancient Mystery Cults*. Cambridge, Mass.: Harvard University Press, 1987.

Burman, Edward. *The Assassins: Holy Killers of Islam*. Wellingborough, UK: Crucible, 1987.

Burns, Thomas S. *A History of the Ostrogoths*. Bloomington, Ind.: Indiana University Press, 1984.

Campbell, Bruce. *Ancient Wisdom Revived: A History of the Theosophical Movement*. Berkeley: University of California Press, 1980.

Carlson, Shawn, and Gerald Larue. *Satanism in America: How the Devil Got Much More Than His Due*. El Cerrito, Calif.: Gaia Press, 1989.

Carr, Edward Hallett. *Michael Bakunin*. New York: Vintage, 1961.

Cassirer, Ernst, et al., eds. *The Renaissance Philosophy of Man*. Chicago: University of Chicago Press, 1948.

Chamberlin, Eric Russell. *The Bad Popes*. New York: Dorset, 1969.

Clifton, Chas S. "The Three Faces of Satanism." *Gnosis* 12 (Summer 1989): 9–18.

Cohn, Norman. *Europe's Inner Demons*. New York: Basic Books, 1975.

———. *The Pursuit of the Millennium*. 2nd ed. Oxford: Oxford University Press, 1970.

Colquhoun, Ithell. *Sword of Wisdom*. New York: Putnam, 1975.

Conze, Edward. *Buddhism*. New York: Philosophical Library, 1961.

Cornford, Francis M, trans. and ed. *The Republic of Plato*. Oxford: Oxford University Press, 1941.

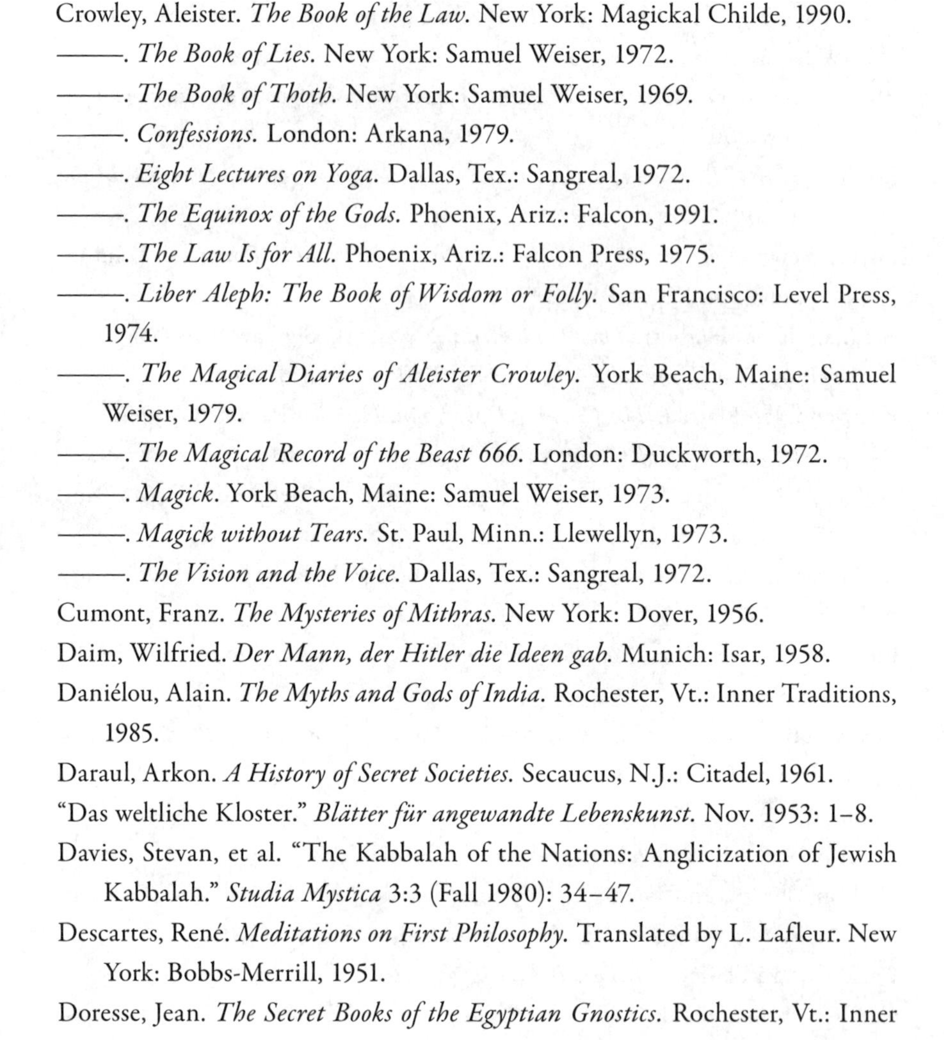

Crowley, Aleister. *The Book of the Law.* New York: Magickal Childe, 1990.
———. *The Book of Lies.* New York: Samuel Weiser, 1972.
———. *The Book of Thoth.* New York: Samuel Weiser, 1969.
———. *Confessions.* London: Arkana, 1979.
———. *Eight Lectures on Yoga.* Dallas, Tex.: Sangreal, 1972.
———. *The Equinox of the Gods.* Phoenix, Ariz.: Falcon, 1991.
———. *The Law Is for All.* Phoenix, Ariz.: Falcon Press, 1975.
———. *Liber Aleph: The Book of Wisdom or Folly.* San Francisco: Level Press, 1974.
———. *The Magical Diaries of Aleister Crowley.* York Beach, Maine: Samuel Weiser, 1979.
———. *The Magical Record of the Beast 666.* London: Duckworth, 1972.
———. *Magick.* York Beach, Maine: Samuel Weiser, 1973.
———. *Magick without Tears.* St. Paul, Minn.: Llewellyn, 1973.
———. *The Vision and the Voice.* Dallas, Tex.: Sangreal, 1972.
Cumont, Franz. *The Mysteries of Mithras.* New York: Dover, 1956.
Daim, Wilfried. *Der Mann, der Hitler die Ideen gab.* Munich: Isar, 1958.
Daniélou, Alain. *The Myths and Gods of India.* Rochester, Vt.: Inner Traditions, 1985.
Daraul, Arkon. *A History of Secret Societies.* Secaucus, N.J.: Citadel, 1961.
"Das weltliche Kloster." *Blätter für angewandte Lebenskunst.* Nov. 1953: 1–8.
Davies, Stevan, et al. "The Kabbalah of the Nations: Anglicization of Jewish Kabbalah." *Studia Mystica* 3:3 (Fall 1980): 34–47.
Descartes, René. *Meditations on First Philosophy.* Translated by L. Lafleur. New York: Bobbs-Merrill, 1951.
Doresse, Jean. *The Secret Books of the Egyptian Gnostics.* Rochester, Vt.: Inner Traditions, 1986.
Dragomanov, Mixailo Petrovic. *Notes on the Slavic Religio-Ethical Legends: The Dualistic Creation of the World.* Translated by Earl W. Count. Russian and East European Series 23. Bloomington: Indiana University Press, 1961.
Drury, Nevill. *The Occult Experience.* Garden City Park, N.Y.: Avery, 1989.
Eisler, Robert. *Man into Wolf.* London: Routledge & Kegan Paul, 1951.
Eliade, Mircea. *A History of Religious Ideas.* Translated by Willard Trask, Alf Hiltebeitel, and Diane Apastolos-Cappadona. 3 vols. Chicago: University of Chicago Press, 1978–1985.

———. *Patterns in Comparative Religion*. Translated by Rosemary Sheed. New York: Meridian, 1963.

———. *The Two and the One*. Translated by J. M. Cohen. New York: Harper and Row, 1965.

———. *Yoga: Immortality and Freedom*. Translated by Willard Trask. 2nd ed. Princeton, N.J.: Princeton University Press, 1969.

Eliot, T. S. *Collected Poems 1909–1962*. New York: Harcourt Brace Jovanovich, 1991.

Evans-Wentz, Walter Y., ed. *Tibetan Yoga and Secret Doctrines*. London: Oxford University Press, 1958.

Evola, Julius. *The Yoga of Power: Tantra, Shakti, and the Secret Way*. Translated by Guido Stucco. Rochester, Vt.: Inner Traditions, 1992.

Farquhar, John Nicol. *An Outline of the Religious Literature of India*. Delhi: Motilal Banarsidass, 1920.

Fleming, William. *Arts and Ideas*. 7th ed. New York: Holt, Rinehart and Winston, 1986.

Flowers, Stephen E. *Black Rûna*. Smithville, Tex.: Rûna-Raven, 1995.

———. *Fire and Ice: Magical Teachings of Germany's Greatest Secret Occult Order*. St. Paul, Minn.: Llewellyn, 1990. [Reprinted as *The Fraternitas Saturni*. Smithville, Tex.: Rûna-Raven, 1990.]

———. *Runes and Magic: Magical Formulaic Elements in the Older Runic Tradition*. 3rd revised ed. Smithville, Tex.: Runa-Raven, 2011.

———. "Toward an Archaic Germanic Psychology." *Journal of Indo-European Studies* 11:1–2 (1983): 117–38.

Flowers, Stephen E., and Michael Moynihan. *The Secret King: The Myth and Reality of Nazi Occultism*. Los Angeles and Waterbury Center, Vt.: Feral House/Dominion, 2007. [See also bibliographic entries for Thorsson, Edred]

Forsyth, F. Neil. *The Old Enemy: Satan and the Combat Myth*. Princeton, N.J.: University of Princeton Press, 1989.

Frankfort, Henri. *Kingship and the Gods*. Chicago: University of Chicago Press, 1948.

Frater U.·. D.·.. *Practical Sigil Magic*. St. Paul, Minn.: Llewellyn, 1990.

Fritscher, John. *Popular Witchcraft*. Bowling Green, Ohio: Bowling Green University Popular Press, 1972. Second, revised edition: Madison, Wisc.: University of Wisconsin Popular Press, 2004.

Fülöp-Miller, René. *The Mind and Face of Bolshevism: An Examination of Cultural Life in Soviet Russia.* London: G. Putnam's Sons, 1927.

Gardner, Gerald. *High Magic's Aid.* London: Michael Houghton, 1949.

———. *The Meaning of Witchcraft.* New York: Magical Childe, 1988.

———. *Witchcraft Today.* Secaucus, N.J.: Citadel, 1973.

Gilmore, Peter H. *The Satanic Scriptures.* Baltimore, Md.: Scapegoat, 2007.

Godwin, Joscelyn. *Arktos: The Polar Myth in Science, Symbolism and Nazi Survival.* Grand Rapids, Mich.: Phanes, 1993.

Godwin, Joscelyn, Christian Chanel, and John Deveney, eds. *The Hermetic Brotherhood of Luxor.* York Beach, Maine: Samuel Weiser, 1995.

Goethe, Johann Wolfgang von. *Faust.* Translated and edited by Charles Passage. Indianapolis, Ind.: Bobbs and Merrill, 1965.

———. *Faust: Eine Tragödie.* Edited by Erich Trunz. Munich: Beck, 1976.

Goodrick-Clarke, Nicholas. *The Occult Roots of Nazism.* Wellingborough, UK: Aquarian, 1985.

Gorer, Geoffrey. *The Life and Ideas of the Marquis de Sade.* London: Peter Owen, 1953.

Grant, Kenneth. *Images and Oracles of Austin Osman Spare.* London: Muller, 1975.

Gregorius, Gregor A. "Der Mensch in seiner höchsten Erkenntnisreife." *Blätter für angewandte okkulte Lebenskunst.* May, 1961: 1–9.

Grimm, Jacob. *Teutonic Mythology.* Translated by James Stallybrass. 4 vols. New York: Dover, 1966.

Guaita, Stanislas de. *Le Serpent de la Genèse.* 2 vols. Paris: Libraire du Marveilleux, 1891.

Guest, John S. *The Yezidis: A Study in Survival.* London: KPI, 1987.

Gurdjieff, George Ivanovich. *Beelzebub's Tales to His Grandson.* New York: E. P. Dutton, 1973.

———. *Herald of the Coming Good.* New York: Samuel Weiser, 1970.

———. *Life Is Only Real Then, When "I Am."* New York: E. P. Dutton, 1975.

———. *Meetings with Remarkable Men.* New York: E. P. Dutton, 1963.

———. *Views from the Real World.* New York: E. P. Dutton, 1973.

Guthrie, Kenneth S., ed. *The Pythagorean Sourcebook and Library.* Grand Rapids, Mich.: Phanes, 1987.

Guthrie, William K. C. *Orpheus and Greek Religion.* 2nd ed. New York: Norton, 1966.

Hamilton, Edith, and Huntington Cairns. *Plato: The Collected Dialogues.* Princeton, N.J.: Princeton University Press, 1963.

Harden, Grant. "Satanism's Gone Underground, but It's Alive and Flourishing." *San Jose Mercury-News.* Oct. 29, 1978. (= Aquino, *The Church of Satan,* appendix 142).

Harrison, Charles, et al. *Art in Theory 1815–1900: An Anthology of Changing Ideas.* Oxford: Blackwell, 1998.

Hasenfratz, Hans-Peter. *Barbarian Rites: The Spiritual World of the Vikings and the Germanic Tribes.* Translated by Michael Moynihan. Rochester, Vt.: Inner Traditions, 2011.

Heffner, Roe-Merrill Secrist, Helmut Rehder, and William Freeman Twaddell, eds. *Goethe's Faust.* Lexington, Mass.: Heath, 1954.

Helck, Wolfgang, and Eberhard Otto, eds. *Lexikon der Ägyptologie.* Wiesbaden: Harrassowitz, 1972.

Herodotus. *The Persian Wars.* Edited by George Rawlinson. New York: Random House, 1942.

Hesiod. *Theogony.* Translated by N. O. Brown. Indianapolis, Ind.: Bobbs-Merrill, 1953.

Heyden, Günter, Friedrich Engels, and Carl-Erich Vollgraf, eds. *Karl Marx, Friedrich Engels Gesamtausgabe.* 5 vols. Berlin: Dietz Verlag, 1975.

Hicks, Robert D. *In Pursuit of Satan: The Police and the Occult.* Buffalo, N.Y.: Prometheus, 1991.

Hooke, Samuel Henry. *Middle Eastern Mythology.* Harmondsworth, UK: Penguin, 1963.

Hornung, Erik. *Conceptions of God in Ancient Egypt: The One and the Many.* Translated by John Baines. Ithaca, N.Y.: Cornell University Press, 1982.

Howe, Ellic. *The Magicians of the Golden Dawn.* York Beach, Maine: Weiser, 1975.

Hugo, Victor. *The Hunchback of Notre-Dame.* Translated by Walter J. Cobb. New York: Signet, 1964.

Hume, Robert E. *The Thirteen Principal Upanishads.* 2nd ed. London: Oxford University Press, 1931.

Hunger, Ulrich. *Runenkunde im Dritten Reich.* Bern: Peter Lang, 1984.

Hutton, Ronald. *The Triumph of the Moon: A History of Modern Pagan Witchcraft.* Oxford: Oxford University Press, 1999.

Hymenaeus Beta, ed. *The Equinox,* Vol. III, No. 10. New York: Thelema, 1986.

Javad, Nurbakhsh. *The Great Satan "Eblis."* London: Khaniqahi-Nimatullahi Publications, 1986.

Jefferson, Thomas. *The Life and Morals of Jesus of Nazareth* [= *The Jefferson Bible*]. St. Louis, Mo.: N. D. Thompson, 1902.

Jonas, Hans. *The Gnostic Religion*. 2nd ed. Boston: Beacon, 1963.

Jordan, Paul. *Egypt: The Black Land*. Oxford: Phaidon, 1976.

Jung, Emma. *The Grail Legend*. Boston: Sigo, 1986.

Kater, Michael. *Das "Ahnenerbe" der SS: 1935–1945*. Stuttgart: Deutsche Verlagsanstalt, 1974.

Kaufman, Walter. *Nietzsche*. Princeton, N.J.: Princeton University Press, 1974.

———. *The Portable Nietzsche*. New York: Viking, 1954.

Kelly, Aidan. *Crafting the Art of Magic*. St. Paul, Minn.: Llewellyn, 1991.

King, Francis. *Satan and Swastika*. Frogmore, UK: Mayflower, 1976.

———, ed. *The Secret Rituals of the O.T.O.* New York: Weiser, 1973.

———. *Tantra for Westerners*. New York: Destiny, 1986.

Klapp, Orrin. *The Collective Search for Identity*. New York: Holt Rinehart & Winston, 1969.

———. *Heroes, Villains and Fools*. Englewood Cliffs, N.J.: Prentice Hall, 1962.

Kolakowski, Leszek. *Main Currents of Marxism: I: The Founders*. Oxford: Oxford University Press, 1981.

Kramer, Samuel N. *The Sumerians*. Chicago: University of Chicago Press, 1963.

Kravchinsky, Sergei M. *The Russian Peasantry: Their Agrarian Condition, Social Life, and Religion*. Westport, Conn.: Hyperion, 1977.

La Mettrie, Julien Offray de. *Man a Machine*. Translated by G. C. Bussey, et al. La Salle, Ill.: Open Court, 1912 [1748].

———. *The System of Epicurus*. [1764].

Lanning, Kenneth V. *Satanic, Occult, Ritualistic Crime: A Law Enforcement Perpective*. Quantico, Va.: National Center for the Analysis of Violent Crime, 1989.

Lautreamont, Comte de. *Maldoror and Poems*. Translated by Paul Knight. Harmondsworth, UK: Penguin, 1978.

LaVey, Anton Szandor. "Binaric, or Don't Try to Teach a Pig to Sing—It Wastes Your Time and Annoys the Pig." *The Cloven Hoof* 121 [XX:3] (1987): 1–2.

———. "Brains for Sale Cheap." *The Cloven Hoof* 65 [9:1] (Jan./Dec. 1977): 4.

———. "The Church of Satan, Cosmic Joy Buzzer." *The Cloven Hoof* 60 [8:2] (Mar./Apr. 1976): 3–4.

———. "Comparisons and Equivalents . . ." *The Cloven Hoof* 123 [XXII:1] (1988): 1–4.

———. *The Compleat Witch, or What to Do When Virtue Fails.* New York: Dodd and Mead, 1971.

———. "Confessions of a Closet Misogynist." *The Cloven Hoof* 75 (Sept./Oct. 1978): 4.

———. "Curses by the Dozen, or Wholesale Hexes." *The Cloven Hoof* 88 [XIII:1] (1981): 1–3.

———. *The Devil's Notebook.* Los Angeles: Feral House, 1992.

———. "Don't Recycle Your Brain." *The Cloven Hoof* 115 [XIX:1] (1986): 1.

———. "ECI Relative to Memory Retention: A Re-evaluation of the Term *Occult.*" *The Cloven Hoof* 88 [XIII:1] (1981): 3–4.

———. "Erotic Crystalization Inertia (E.C.I.): Its Relationship to Longevity." *The Cloven Hoof* 5:1 (1973): 31–38.

———. "Eustress, Vampires and Vicariousness Revisited." *The Cloven Hoof* 87 [XII:6] (1980): 1–2.

———. [writing as John M. Kincaid] "An Explanation of the Various Degrees in the Church of Satan." *The Cloven Hoof* 2:11 (November 1970): 7–8.

———. "Farewell Trinity and Remember Los Alamos." *The Cloven Hoof* 122 [XX:4] (1987): 1–2.

———. "For the Record." *The Cloven Hoof* 122 [XX:4] (1987): 4.

———. "Give the Children a Chance." *The Cloven Hoof* 122 [XX:4] (1987): 2–4.

———. "Hoofnotes." *The Cloven Hoof* 8:1 (Jan./Feb. 1976): 2–3.

———. "How to Become a Werewolf: The Fundamentals of Lycanthropic Metamorphosis; the Principles of Their Application." *The Cloven Hoof* 71 [10:1] (Jan./Feb. 1978): 1–4.

———. "How to be God (or the Devil)." *The Cloven Hoof* 113 [XVII:2] (1985): 1.

———. "Illegal Music." *The Cloven Hoof* 118 [XIX:4] (1986): 3.

———. "The Invisible War." *The Cloven Hoof* 116 [XIX:2] (1986): 1–3.

———. "The Law of the Trapezoid." *The Cloven Hoof* 64 [8:6] (Nov./Dec. 1976): 1–4.

———. *Letters from the Devil.* Edited by Kevin I. Slaughter. Baltimore, Md.: Underworld Amusements, 2010.

———. "Megarhythm." *The Cloven Hoof* 85 [XII:4] (1980): 1–2.

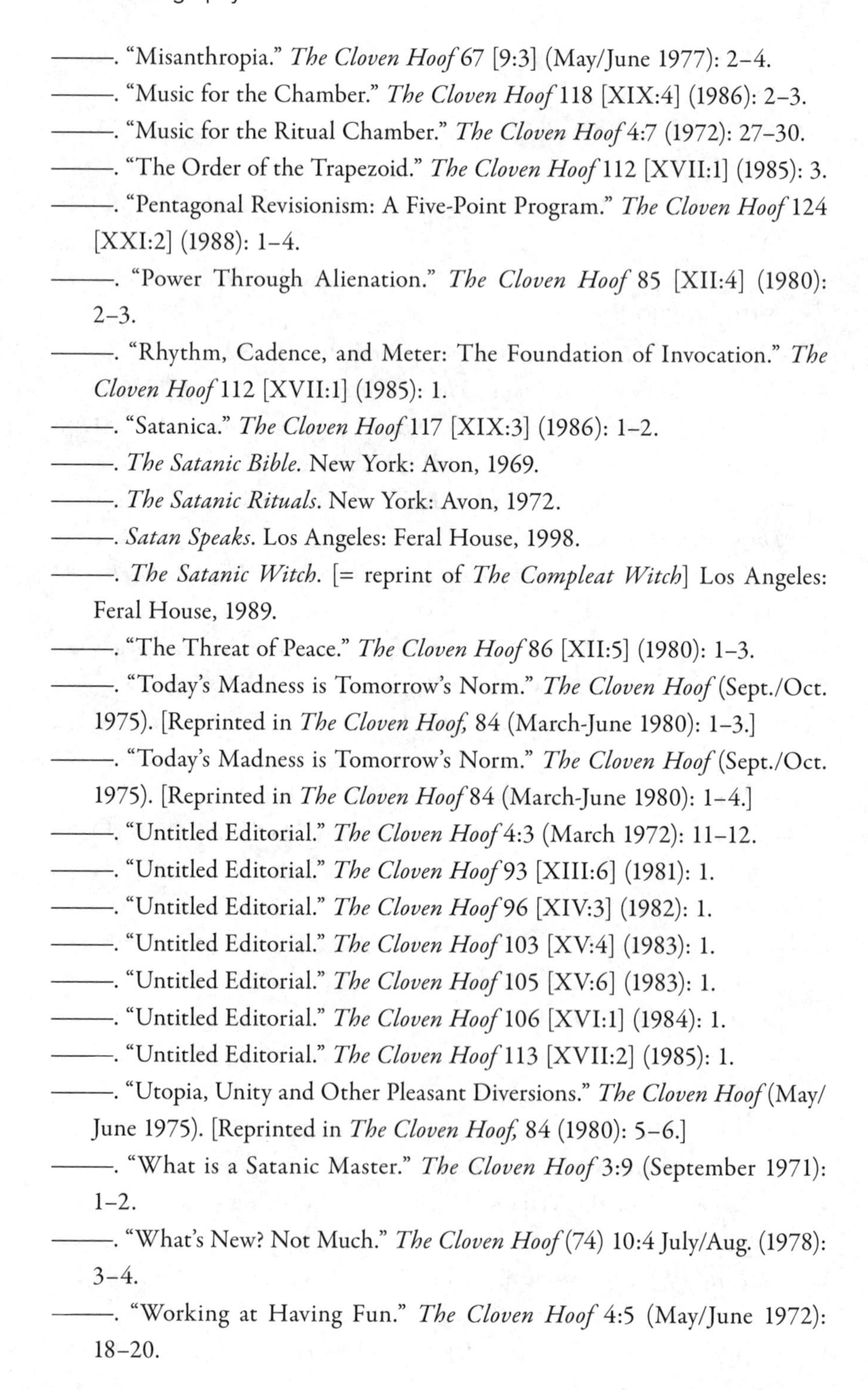

———. "Misanthropia." *The Cloven Hoof* 67 [9:3] (May/June 1977): 2–4.

———. "Music for the Chamber." *The Cloven Hoof* 118 [XIX:4] (1986): 2–3.

———. "Music for the Ritual Chamber." *The Cloven Hoof* 4:7 (1972): 27–30.

———. "The Order of the Trapezoid." *The Cloven Hoof* 112 [XVII:1] (1985): 3.

———. "Pentagonal Revisionism: A Five-Point Program." *The Cloven Hoof* 124 [XXI:2] (1988): 1–4.

———. "Power Through Alienation." *The Cloven Hoof* 85 [XII:4] (1980): 2–3.

———. "Rhythm, Cadence, and Meter: The Foundation of Invocation." *The Cloven Hoof* 112 [XVII:1] (1985): 1.

———. "Satanica." *The Cloven Hoof* 117 [XIX:3] (1986): 1–2.

———. *The Satanic Bible.* New York: Avon, 1969.

———. *The Satanic Rituals.* New York: Avon, 1972.

———. *Satan Speaks.* Los Angeles: Feral House, 1998.

———. *The Satanic Witch.* [= reprint of *The Compleat Witch*] Los Angeles: Feral House, 1989.

———. "The Threat of Peace." *The Cloven Hoof* 86 [XII:5] (1980): 1–3.

———. "Today's Madness is Tomorrow's Norm." *The Cloven Hoof* (Sept./Oct. 1975). [Reprinted in *The Cloven Hoof,* 84 (March-June 1980): 1–3.]

———. "Today's Madness is Tomorrow's Norm." *The Cloven Hoof* (Sept./Oct. 1975). [Reprinted in *The Cloven Hoof* 84 (March-June 1980): 1–4.]

———. "Untitled Editorial." *The Cloven Hoof* 4:3 (March 1972): 11–12.

———. "Untitled Editorial." *The Cloven Hoof* 93 [XIII:6] (1981): 1.

———. "Untitled Editorial." *The Cloven Hoof* 96 [XIV:3] (1982): 1.

———. "Untitled Editorial." *The Cloven Hoof* 103 [XV:4] (1983): 1.

———. "Untitled Editorial." *The Cloven Hoof* 105 [XV:6] (1983): 1.

———. "Untitled Editorial." *The Cloven Hoof* 106 [XVI:1] (1984): 1.

———. "Untitled Editorial." *The Cloven Hoof* 113 [XVII:2] (1985): 1.

———. "Utopia, Unity and Other Pleasant Diversions." *The Cloven Hoof* (May/June 1975). [Reprinted in *The Cloven Hoof,* 84 (1980): 5–6.]

———. "What is a Satanic Master." *The Cloven Hoof* 3:9 (September 1971): 1–2.

———. "What's New? Not Much." *The Cloven Hoof* (74) 10:4 July/Aug. (1978): 3–4.

———. "Working at Having Fun." *The Cloven Hoof* 4:5 (May/June 1972): 18–20.

Lea, Henry C. *A History of the Inquisition in the Middle Ages.* New York: Macmillan, 1888.

Lefebure, Charles. *The Blood Cults.* New York: Ace, 1969.

Lewin, Moshe. *The Making of the Soviet System.* New York: Putnam, 1985.

Liebenfels, Jörg Lanz von. *Theozoologie.* Vienna: Moderner Verlag, 1905.

Littleton, C. Scott. *The New Comparative Mythology.* Berkeley: University of California Press, 1973.

Lother, Helmut. *Neugermanische Religion und Christentum.* Gutersloh: Bertelsmann, 1934.

Lucretius. *On the Nature of the Universe.* Translated by R. Latham. Harmondsworth, UK: Penguin, 1951.

Lyons, Arthur. *Satan Wants You: The Cult of Devil Worship in America.* New York: Mysterious Press, 1988.

———. *The Second Coming: Satanism in America.* New York: Award, 1972.

Machen, Arthur. *The Great God Pan* and *The Inmost Light.* London: John Lane, 1894.

Machiavelli, Niccolo. *The Prince.* Translated by T. G. Bergin. Arlington Heights, Ill..: Harlan Davidson, 1947.

Mackay, Christopher S. *The Hammer of Witches: A Complete Translation of the* Malleus Maleficarum. Cambridge: Cambridge University Press, 2009.

Mallory, James. *In Search of the Indo-Europeans.* London: Thames and Hudson, 1989.

Merritt, Abraham. *Seven Footprints to Satan.* New York: Grosset and Dunlap, 1928.

Milton, John. *The Complete Poems.* London: Dent, 1980.

Monumenta Germaniae Historica (= MGH). *Capitularia Regum Francorum.* Edited by Alfredus Boretius. 2 vols. Hannover: Hahn, 1883–1897.

Moody, Edward J. "Magical Therapy: An Anthropological Investigation of Contemporary Satanism." In *Religious Movements in Contemporary America,* edited by Irving I. Zaretsky and Mark Leone. Princeton: Princeton University Press, 1974.

———. "Urban Witches." In *Conformity and Conflict: Readings in Cultural Anthropology,* edited by James Spradly and David W. McCurdy. New York: Little, Brown and Company, 1971.

Mookerjee, Ajit, and Madhu Khana. *The Tantric Way.* Boston: New York Graphic Society, 1977.

Mortensen, William. *The Command to Look.* San Francisco: Camera Craft, 1937.

Newton, Issac. *Mathematical Principles of Natural Philosophy.* Translated by A. Motte. London: Motte, 1729.

Nicholson, Reynold A. *Studies in Islamic Mysticism.* 2nd ed. Cambridge: Cambridge University Press, 1967.

Nietzsche, Friedrich. *The Birth of Tragedy.* Translated by Walter Kaufmann. New York: Vintage, 1967.

———. *On the Genealogy of Morals* and *Ecce Homo.* Translated by Walter Kaufmann and R. J. Hollingdale. New York: Vintage, 1967.

———. *Thus Spoke Zarathustra.* In *The Portable Nietzsche,* translated by Walter Kaufmann. New York. Viking, 1954.

North, Robert. *The New Flesh Palladium: Magia Erotica.* Smithville, Tex.: Rûna-Raven, 1996.

Nott, C. Stanley. *Teachings of Gurdjieff.* London: Routledge and Kegan Paul, 1961.

O'Flaherty, Wendy Donniger. *The Rig-Veda.* Harmondsworth, UK: Penguin, 1981.

Orwell, George. *1984.* New York: Harcourt and Brace 1949.

———. "Politics and the English Language." In *The George Orwell Reader,* edited by Richard H. Revere. New York: Harcourt Brace and Javonovitch, 1984.

Ouspensky, P. D. *The Fourth Way.* New York: Vintage, 1971.

———. *A New Model of the Universe.* New York: Vintage, 1971.

———. *The Psychology of Man's Possible Evolution.* New York: Bantam, 1968.

———. *In Search of the Miraculous.* New York: Harvest, 1949.

———. *Talks with a Devil.* London: Arkana, 1988.

Paine, Thomas. *The Age of Reason.* Buffalo, N.Y.: Prometheus, 1984.

Passantino, Bob and Gretchen, and Jon Trott. "Satan's Sideshow: The True Lauren Stratford Story." *Cornerstone,* vol. 18, issue 90 (1990): 23–28.

———. "Lauren Stratford: From Satanic Ritual Abuse to Jewish Holocaust Survivor." *Cornerstone,* vol. 28, issue 117 (1999): 12–16, 18.

Pausanias. *Description of Greece.* Translated by W. H. S. Jones. 4 vols. London: Heinemann, 1918–1935.

Pauwels, Louis. *Gurdjieff.* New York: Weiser, 1972.

Pauwels, Louis, and Jaques Bergier. *The Morning of the Magicians.* New York: Avon, 1968.

Pazder, Lawrence, M.D., and Michelle Smith. *Michelle Remembers.* New York: Pocket, 1980.

Péladan, Josephin. *La Vice suprême.* Paris: Dentu, 1892.

Pennick, Nigel. *Hitler's Secret Sciences.* Sudbury, UK: Neville Spearman, 1981.

Peters, Fritz. *Gurdjieff Remembered.* London: Gollancz, 1965.

Pipkin, Paul. "The Ritual Chamber at Roissy." *The Cloven Hoof* 73 [X:3] (1977): 1–3.

Polo, Marco. *The Travels.* London: Penguin, 1958.

Polomé, Edgar C. "Some Comments on *Völuspá* Stanzas 17–18." In *Old Norse Literature and Mythology: A Symposium,* edited by E. C. Polomé. Austin: University of Texas Press, 1969.

Pope, Alexander. *An Essay on Man and Other Poems.* London: John Sharpe, 1829.

Preisendanz, Karl, ed. *Papyri Graecae Magicae: Die griechischen Zauberpapyri.* Stuttgart: Teubner, 1973–1974.

Pritchard, James Bennett. *Ancient Near Eastern Texts Relating to the Old Testament.* 2nd ed. Princeton: Princeton University Press, 1955.

Propaganda and Holy Writ: The Process Church of the Final Judgment. Port Townsend, Wa.: Feral House, 2011.

Rahn, Otto. *Crusade Against the Grail: The Struggle between the Cathars, the Templars, and the Church of Rome.* Translated by Christopher Jones. Rochester, Vt.: Inner Traditions, 2006.

———. *Lucifer's Court: A Heretic's Journey in Search of the Light Bringers.* Translated by Christopher Jones. Rochester, Vt.: Inner Traditions, 2008.

———. *Otto Rahn: Leben & Werk.* Edited by Hans-Jürgen Lange. Engerda: Arun, 1995.

Rand, Ayn. *Atlas Shrugged.* New York: Signet, 1957.

Randolph, Paschal Beverly. *Sexual Magic.* Translated by Robert North. New York: Magickal Childe, 1988.

Rao, Ramachandra. *Jivanmukti in Advaita.* Gandhinagar, Bangalore: Prakashana, 1978.

Rauschning, Hermann. *The Voice of Destruction.* [= *Gespräche mit Hitler*]. New York: Putnam, 1940.

Ravenscroft, Trevor. *The Spear of Destiny.* New York: G. Putnam's Sons, 1973.

Redbeard, Ragnar. *Might Is Right.* Port Townsend, Wa.: Loompanics Unlimited, 1984 [1896].

———. *Might Is Right, or The Survival of the Fittest.* Edited by Darrell W. Conder. Springfield, Mo.: Dil Pickle Press, 2005.

Regardie, Israel. *The Eye in the Triangle.* St. Paul, Minn.: Llewellyn, 1970.

Renou, Louis, ed. *Hinduism.* New York: George Braziller, 1961.

Rhode, Erwin. *Psyche: The Cult of Souls and Belief in Immortality Among the Greeks.* Translated by W. B. Hillis. Freeport, N.Y.: Books for Libraries Press, 1972.

Rhodes, Henry T. F. *The Satanic Mass.* Secaucus, N.J.: Citadel, 1954.

Riemer, Neal. *Karl Marx and Prophetic Politics.* New York: Praeger, 1987.

Robinson, James M., ed. *The Nag Hammadi Library.* San Francisco: Harper and Row, 1981.

Romer, John. *Ancient Lives: Daily Life in Egypt of the Pharoahs.* New York: Henry Holt, 1984.

Rousseau, Jean-Jacques. *The Confessions.* Translated by W. C. Mallory. New York: Tudor, 1935.

Rudolf, Kurt. *Gnosis: The Nature and History of Gnosticism.* San Francisco: Harper and Row, 1987.

Russell, Dick. "Anton LaVey: The Satanist Who Wants to Rule the World." *Argosy.* June 1975.

Russell, Jeffrey Burton. *The Devil.* Ithaca, N.Y.: Cornell University Press, 1977.

———. *A History of Witchcraft.* London: Thames and Hudson, 1980.

———. *Mephistopheles.* Ithaca, N.Y.: Cornell University Press, 1986.

Rusten, Rudolf, ed. *Was tut not?: Ein Führer durch die gesamte Literatur der Deutschbewegung.* Leipzig: Hedler, 1914.

Sade, Marquis de. *The Complete Justine, Philosophy in the Bedroom and Other Writings.* Translated by R. Seaver and A. Wainhouse. New York: Grove, 1966.

———. *Juliette.* New York: Grove, 1968.

Sastri, S. Subrahmanya, and T. R. Srinivasa Ayyangar, eds. *Jivanmuktiviveka* (Liberation in Life) of Vidyaranya. Adyar: Adyar Library and Research Centre, 1978.

Saunders, Jason L. *Greek and Roman Philosophy after Aristotle.* New York: Free Press, 1966.

Scheible, J. *Das Kloster.* Stuttgart: N.p., 1846.

Scholem, Gershom. *Kabbalah.* New York: New American Library, 1978.

Sethe, Kurt. *Die ägyptischen Pyramidentexte.* 4 vols. Hildesheim: Olms, 1960.

Seznec, Jean. *The Survival of the Pagan Gods.* Translated by B. Sessions. New York: Harper and Row, 1953.

Singer, June. *The Unholy Bible.* New York: Putnam, 1970.

Smith, Morton. *Jesus the Magician.* San Francisco: Harper and Row, 1978.

Spare, Austin Osman. *The Book of Pleasure (Self-Love).* Toronto: 93 Publishing, 1975 [1913].

———. *Earth: Inferno.* London: The Author [1905].

———. *The Focus of Life.* Seattle, Wa.: Axil Press, 1984 [1921].

Speeth, Kathleen R. *The Gurdjieff Work.* New York: Pocket, 1976.

Spence, Lewis. *The Occult Causes of the Present War.* London: Rider, 1940.

Stoker, Bram. *Dracula.* New York: Signet, 1965.

Stratford, Lauren. *Satan's Underground: The Extraordinary Story of One Woman's Escape.* Eugene, Ore.: Harvest House, 1988.

Stutley, Margaret and James. *Harper's Dictionary of Hinduism.* New York: Harper and Row, 1977.

Svoboda, Robert E. *Aghora: At the Left Hand of God.* Albuquerque, N. Mex.: Brotherhood of Life, 1986.

———. *Aghora II: Kundalini.* Albuquerque, N. Mex.: Brotherhood of Life, 1993.

Symonds, John. *The Great Beast: The Life and Magick of Aleister Crowley.* Frogmore, UK: Mayflower, 1972.

Tacitus. *The Histories.* Translated by K. Wellesley. Harmondsworth, UK: Penguin, 1975.

Terry, Maury. *The Ultimate Evil.* New York: Doubleday, 1987.

Thorsson, Edred [= S. E. Flowers]. *The Book of Ogham.* St. Paul, Minn.: Llewellyn, 1992.

———. *The Mysteries of the Goths.* Smithville, Tex.: Rûna-Raven, 2007.

———. *Rune Might.* St. Paul: Llewellyn, 1989. [Reprint: Smithville, Tex.: Rûna-Raven, 2004].

———. *Runelore.* York Beach, Maine: Weiser, 1987.

Tilak, Bal Gangadhar. *The Arctic Home in the Vedas.* Poona: The Kesari, 1903.

Towers, Eric. *Dashwood: The Man and the Myth.* Wellingborough, UK: Crucible, 1986.

Truzzi, Marcello. "The Occult Revival as Popular Culture." *Sociological Quarterly* 13 (Winter 1972): 16–36.

Turville-Petre, E. O. G. *Myth and Religion of the North.* New York: Holt Rinehart and Winston, 1964.

Twain, Mark. *Letters from the Earth.* San Francisco: Harper and Row, 1962.

———. *No. 44, The Mysterious Stranger.* Berkeley: University of California Press, 1982.

Valiente, Doreen. *The Rebirth of Witchcraft.* Custer, Wa.: Phoenix, 1989.

Vondung, Klaus. *Magie und Manipulation: Ideologischer Kult und politische Religion des Nationalsozialismus.* Göttingen: Vandenhoeck & Ruprecht, 1971.

Vries, Jan de. *Altgermanische Religionsgeschichte.* 2 vols. Berlin: De Gruyter, 1956–1957.

———. *Keltische Religion.* Stuttgart: Kohlhammer, 1961.

Walker, Benjamin. *Gnosticism: Its History and Influence.* Wellingborough, UK: Aquarian Press, 1983.

———. *Tantrism.* Wellingborough, UK: Aquarian Press, 1982.

Waterfield, Robin, trans. *The Theology of Arithmetic* [attributed to Iamblicus]. Grand Rapids, Mich.: Phanes, 1988.

Webb, Don. *Mysteries of the Temple of Set.* Smithville, Tex.: Rûna-Raven, 2004.

———. *The Seven Faces of Darkness.* Smithville, Tex.: Rûna-Raven, 1996.

———. *Uncle Setnakt's Essential Guide to the Left Hand Path.* Smithville, Tex.: Rûna-Raven, 1999.

Webb, James. *The Harmonious Circle.* New York: Putnam, 1980.

———. *The Occult Underground.* La Salle, Ill.: Open Court, 1974.

Widengren, Geo. *Die Religionen Irans.* Stuttgart: Kohlhammer, 1965.

Wilson, Colin. *G. I. Gurdjieff: The War Against Sleep.* Wellingborough, UK: Aquarian, 1986.

———. *The Nature of the Beast.* Wellingborough, UK: Aquarian, 1987.

———. *The Occult.* New York: Random House, 1971.

———. *Rasputin.* Secaucus, N.J.: Citadel, 1964.

Wilson, Peter Lamborn. *Sacred Drift: Essays on the Margins of Islam.* San Francisco: City Lights, 1993.

———. *Scandal: Essays in Islamic Heresy.* New York: Autonomedia, 1988.

Wistrich, Robert. *Who's Who in Nazi Germany.* New York: Macmillan, 1982.

Wolfe, Burton. "The Church of Satan." In *Inside the Cults,* edited by Tracy Cabot. Los Angeles: Holloway House, 1970.

———. *The Devil's Avenger: A Biography of Anton Szandor LaVey.* New York: Pyramid, 1974.

Wright, Lawrence. *Saints and Sinners.* New York: Alfred A. Knopf, 1993.

———. "Sympathy for the Devil." *Rolling Stone* (Sept. 5, 1991): 62–68, 105–6.

Wyllie, Timothy, and Adam Parfrey, eds. *Love, Sex, Fear, Death: The Inside Story of the Process Church of the Final Judgment.* Port Townsend, Wa.: Feral House, 2009.

Periodicals

The Cloven Hoof. 1969–1988; 1995–1997; 2003; 2010–present.

The Equinox. Vol. I, nos. 1–10, 1909–1913.

The Scroll of Set. 1975–present.

Index

Page numbers in *italics* indicate illustrations.

BOOKS OF RELATED INTEREST